THE GREENHAVEN ENCYCLOPEDIA OF

ANCIENT GREECE

Other Books in the
Greenhaven Encyclopedia series

THE GREENHAVEN ENCYCLOPEDIA OF

ANCIENT GREECE

By Don Nardo

Robert B. Kebric, *Consulting Editor*

Christine Nasso, *Publisher*
Elizabeth Des Chenes, *Managing Editor*

GREENHAVEN PRESS
An imprint of Thomson Gale, a part of The Thomson Corporation

THOMSON
™
GALE

Detroit • New York • San Francisco • New Haven, Conn. • Waterville, Maine • London

LIBRARY OF CONGRESS CATALOGING-IN-PUBLICATION DATA

Nardo, Don, 1947–
  Ancient Greece / by Don Nardo.
    p. cm. -- (The Greenhaven encyclopedia of)
  Includes bibliographical references and index.
  ISBN-13: 978-0-7377-3388-4 (hard cover : alk. paper)
  ISBN-10: 0-7377-3388-8 (hard cover : alk. paper)
  1. Greece--History--To 146 B.C.--Juvenile literature. [1. Greece--History--To 146 B.C.] I. Title. II. Series.
  DF214.N37 2006
  938--dc22

                                                            2005033869

Printed in the United States of America
10 9 8 7 6 5 4 3 2 1

Contents

Contents

Contents

Contents

Contents

Contents

Preface

Students and others who have not yet had the good fortune to learn about the history of human civilization might ask: Why devote an entire encyclopedia solely to the ancient Greeks? Indeed, why bother to study ancient Greece at all? What do the thoughts and deeds of this long-vanished people have to do with people's lives and the workings of the world today? The answer to the last question can be concisely expressed in a single word: everything.

The vital connection between ancient Greece and modern Western society follows a nearly direct line. Almost four thousand years ago, the ancient Greeks created a culture and society that proved amazingly successful. Its durability was due in large part to the Greeks' unique combination of inventiveness, creative spirit, competitive drive, optimism, and sheer boldness. These vibrant qualities propelled them to the forefront of the march of Western civilization, a position they held for nearly two thousand years, until they were conquered by the Romans.

Fortunately, the Romans were impressed, even entranced, by numerous aspects of Greek culture. They absorbed a great deal of it and passed it on, first in the Romans' own expanding empire and ultimately to later European cultures that preserved it during the medieval era and rediscovered it during the Renaissance. The remarkable legacy of the ancient Greeks survived as, over time, many elements of Greek culture were incorporated into the fabric of European and European-based societies even when their Greek origins were not completely comprehended.

Thus it is no great exaggeration to say that Western civilization was largely founded by the Greeks and would not exist in its present form without the momentous cultural heritage they imparted. Greek architecture, sculpture, political ideas, social and military customs, literature, philosophical and scientific ideas, mathematical principles, and language helped to shape the cultures and ideas of all later Western lands and peoples. These Greek influences are everywhere, though the average person rarely connects their origins to the Greeks. When a young man or woman goes out for the track team or watches the Olympics on television, for example, he or she takes part in rituals that began with the establishment of the first Olympic Games in Greece in 776 B.C. The many modern banks and government buildings that feature rows of columns and triangular gables borrow and perpetuate the trademarks of classical Greek temple architecture. Similarly, when we listen to political speeches and debates and vote to elect leaders of government, we carry on a democratic tradition born in ancient Athens. The theater, plays, novels, history books, gymnasiums, political bills, lawsuits, trial by jury, civil liberties, the alphabet, and many other aspects of everyday modern life were also invented by the Greeks.

Thus, when someone asks why he or she should bother to learn about the long-dead ancient Greeks, the answer is both simple and profound. Their politics, customs, beliefs, and inventions laid the groundwork for all that came later. Indeed, in a very real sense the Greeks are still with us; their dynamic spirit lives on, having become a subtle but integral part of our own.

Academy

A school of higher learning—the first in the Western world—established by the Greek scholar-philosopher Plato on the site of a gymnasium and olive grove on the western rim of Athens in the early 380s B.C. It was destroyed when the Roman general Sulla sacked Athens in 86 B.C., but it was soon rebuilt and continued to be an important center of learning until the eastern Roman emperor Justinian perma-

The aging Plato converses with one of his students at the Academy in Athens. © <small>BETTMANN/CORBIS</small>

nently closed it down in A.D. 529.

SEE ALSO: Aristotle; Plato

Achaea

The northern region of the Peloponnesus, bordered by the territory of Elis in the west and the southern coast of the Gulf of Corinth in the north. Populated and then ruled by a Greek-speaking people in the fourteenth and thirteenth centuries B.C., hilly Achaea was one of the chief ancient divisions of the Greek peninsula.

SEE ALSO: Achaean League

Achaean League

An alliance of ten cities in the region of Achaea, established in 280 B.C. to provide mutual protection against the kingdom of Macedonia, which at the time controlled most of central and northern Greece. The league was a major political power of ancient Greece's Hellenistic Age (323–30 B.C.). In the Second Macedonian War (200–197 B.C.), the league sided with the Romans against Macedonia's King Philip V. In the years that followed, however, the Achaeans became increasingly uneasy about the growing Roman presence in Greece. The Romans recognized the potential threat posed by the league and in 167 B.C. deported about a thousand leading Achaeans (including the noted historian Polybius) as hostages to Italy. Fighting eventually broke out between Rome and the Achaean cities anyway. In the early 140s B.C., despite tough and at times heroic native resistance, the Romans defeated and dissolved the league and the Achaean cities were soon absorbed into a new Roman province.

SEE ALSO: Philip V; Polybius; Rome

Acharnians

A comic play by Aristophanes, first produced in Athens in 425 B.C. when the

Peloponnesian War (against Sparta) had been raging for six years. It is the earliest of his surviving works, and in spite of its strong antiwar message (or perhaps because of it), it won first prize in the annual Lenaea, (one of Athens's two drama competitions). The loose plot revolves around an Athenian farmer, Dikaiopolis, who longs for the old days of peace. With the aid of a minor god who has been sent from heaven to bring peace to Athens and Sparta, Dikaiopolis makes a separate peace for himself with Sparta. He ends up trying to defend his pacifism before the pro-war chorus, made up of Acharnians, residents of an Athenian village that has suffered particularly badly in the war. He manages to win them over to his antiwar views, however. Modern commentators see this play, clearly a daring plea for peace by the author, as evidence of the extraordinary degree of freedom of speech permitted in Athens's democracy, even in the midst of a devastating war.

SEE ALSO: Aristophanes, 1; theater and drama

Achilles

In Greek legend, one of the leading Greek warriors who besieged Troy and the central figure in Homer's epic poem, the *Iliad*. When he was an infant, his mother, the sea nymph Thetis, dipped him in the River Styx, which made his body invulnerable, except in the heel by which she held him. Later, to keep her son safe when the Greeks were assembling for the war against Troy, Thetis hid him on the Aegean island of Scyros. However, the hero Odysseus, king of Ithaca, found Achilles and persuaded him to go to Troy. There, Achilles led many successful forays against the Trojans. But after he and the commander of the Greek forces, Agamemnon, quarreled over a

woman, Achilles retired to his tent and refused to fight, which demoralized the Greeks. Later, however, Achilles' close friend Patroclus was slain by the Trojan prince Hector. Enraged, Achilles reentered the fray and slew Hector. Later still, Achilles himself met death when Hector's brother, Paris, fired an arrow into his vulnerable heel. Various ancient legends and writings mention Achilles' ghost; the most famous is Homer's *Odyssey*, in which, following Troy's fall, Odysseus encounters that ghost in the Underworld.

SEE ALSO: Hector; *Iliad*; Troy

acropolis

Literally, "the city's high place"; a hill, most often fortified, located in a central position in a number of ancient Greek city-states. The most famous one, in Athens, is generally capitalized (the Acropolis). The Athenian Acropolis, which is about 1,000 feet (305m) long and 165 feet (50m) high, may have featured a Mycenaean palace in the Bronze Age. Later it was used as a fortress, to which the city's inhabitants retreated when danger threatened. The hill also bore a series of religious temples and shrines, some of which were destroyed by the Persians when they occupied Athens in 480 B.C. Under the direction of the statesman Pericles, these were replaced later in that century by a magnificent complex of shrines that included the Parthenon, Erechtheum, and Temple of Athena Nike, all dedicated to the city's patron deity, Athena.

SEE ALSO: Athena; Athens; Erechtheum; Parthenon

Actium

A promontory on Greece's western coast, near which a historic sea battle took place in 31 B.C. between the Romans and the last major autonomous Greek ruler, Cleopatra VII.

SEE ALSO: Battle of Actium; Cleopatra VII

Admetus

In Greek mythology, a king of Thessaly (in central Greece) who became known for his kindness and justice. With the help of the god Apollo, who was impressed by the young man's good character, Admetus won the hand of Alcestis, daughter of King Pelias of Iolcos. Later Apollo arranged it so that Admetus could escape death by having another mortal die in his place. When no one else would do this for Admetus, the loving and loyal Alcestis volunteered. The moving story of Admetus and Alcestis was dramatized by Euripides in his great play *Alcestis*.

SEE ALSO: *Alcestis*

Adonis

In Greek mythology, a young man who became known for his phenomenal beauty and his love affair with Aphrodite, goddess of love. It was said that Adonis was born from the trunk of a tree (after the gods had turned his mother into a tree), after which Aphrodite fell madly in love with him. One day when the goddess and young man were out hunting, he was killed by a wild boar. In his honor, the distraught Aphrodite caused the blood he had shed to be transformed into the blood-red sea anemone. Adonis was worshipped as a minor god by some Greeks beginning in the fifth century B.C. His legend survives in modern-day references to an unusually handsome youth as an "Adonis."

SEE ALSO: Aphrodite

Aegae

An important early capital of Macedonia, situated several miles inland from the western shore of the Thermaic Gulf. Aegae (or Aigai) became the capital at an unknown date, replacing a town called Lebaea. Eventually King Archelaus (reigned 413–399 B.C.) moved the throne from Aegae to Pella, about 30 miles (48km) to the northeast. However, Aegae remained the burial site of the Macedonian kings. In Vergina, the modern town occupying Aegae's ancient site, archaeologists discovered a large necropolis (cemetery) filled with tombs, some of them large and splendidly decorated. In the 1970s one of these was identified as that of Philip II, conqueror of Greece in the fourth century B.C. and father of Alexander the Great. Inside the tomb the excavators found numerous finely made grave goods, including a ceremonial breastplate, a metal helmet, greaves (lower-leg protectors), and a stone coffin. Inside the coffin was a box bearing the king's ashes and decorated with a golden starburst, the symbol of Macedonian royalty. Recent scholarship has cast some doubt on the identity of the deceased, however; it may be that the tomb housed the remains of Alexander's half brother, Philip III Arrhidaeus. Whomever the tomb belongs to, archaeologists and architects kept it intact by constructing a magnificent underground and climate-controlled museum around it. Elsewhere in Aegae/Vergina people can visit the ruins of one of the Macedonian royal palaces; and near the palace lies the well-preserved theater in which Philip II was assassinated in 336 B.C.

SEE ALSO: Alexander III ("the Great"); Macedonia; Philip II

Aegean Sea

The inlet of the Mediterranean Sea that lies between the Greek mainland and western Asia Minor (called Ionia in ancient times). The Aegean was supposedly named for the mythical Athenian king, Aegeus, father of the hero Theseus. According to a popular legend, Aegeus threw himself into the sea and drowned when he mistakenly thought his son had been killed. Another ancient account said the Aegean was named after an Amazonian queen named Aegae. The sea stretches about 370 miles (600km) from the coast of Thrace in the north to the large island of Crete in the south, and on average some 250 miles (400km) from east to west. The Aegean is known for its many picturesque islands, many with historic or legendary associations, including the northernmost, Thasos; in the east Samos, Rhodes, Chios, and Lesbos; in the west Euboea, Scyros, and Aegina; and in the south, directly north of Crete, the rocky Cyclades group.

SEE ALSO: Aegeus; Lesbos; Rhodes; Theseus

Aegeus

In Greek mythology, the father of the noted Athenian hero Theseus and supposed namesake of the Aegean Sea. After becoming king of Athens, Aegeus slept with the daughter of Pittheus, king of Troezen (in the eastern Peloponnesus), a union that produced the baby Theseus. However, for many years Aegeus did not know about Theseus's existence. The boy was reared at Pittheus's court, and only when he journeyed to Athens as a young man and confronted his father did Aegeus find out. Aegeus then allowed his newfound son to sail to Crete to fight the Minotaur, a monster that had been eating Athenian hostages sent there annually at the demand of Minos, king of Knossos. Theseus fulfilled the mission, but on his return he forgot to raise a white sail (signaling success). Seeing a black sail, Aegeus assumed his son had been killed. In a fit of grief, he jumped into the sea and drowned.

SEE ALSO: Aegean Sea; Minotaur; Theseus

Aegina

An island polis, or city-state, that for many years was a rival of Athens and a leading naval and commercial power in Greece. At a mere 33 square miles (89 sq. km), Aegina was a relatively tiny island, but it was situated in a highly strategic position in the Saronic Gulf, roughly halfway between Athens and the Peloponnesus. The island was inhabited in Mycenaean times, but according to legend it was abandoned for a time before being colonized in the early Dark Age by Dorian Greeks. Partly because Aegina is mountainous and has little fertile land, its people then turned to the sea, and by the seventh century B.C. had developed large merchant fleets and begun accumulating wealth and influence. In about 550 B.C. the Aeginetans issued a silver coinage stamped with the image of a turtle that became one of the leading currencies in the Mediterranean sphere. Because of its growing rivalry with Athens, Aegina allied itself with Sparta and Thebes, states that sought to limit Athenian expansion. The Aeginetans did fight alongside the Athenians in the great naval victory over the Persians at Salamis in 480 B.C., but after the expulsion of the Persians from Greece, tensions renewed between Aegina and Athens. The Athenian statesman Pericles is famous for calling the island the "eyesore of the Piraeus," referring to the fact that it lay only 12 miles (19km) off the coast of Athens's port town. The result of the rivalry between the two states was a brief but important war fought in 459 B.C. Aegina was defeated and forced to join the Athenian-controlled Delian League. Not surprisingly, however, the Aeginetans later took Sparta's side in the Peloponnesian War (431–404 B.C.). In 322 B.C. Aegina fell under Macedonian control, in 210 B.C. it became part of the kingdom of Pergamum, and in 133 B.C. it was finally annexed by Rome.

SEE ALSO: Athens; seafaring; trade

aegis

In Greek mythology, a fabulous breastplate (or in some accounts a shield) belonging to Athena, goddess of war. Supposedly she painted the image of a Gorgon's face on the aegis to scare away her enemies. The great Athenian sculptor Phidias was careful to include the magical breastplate, Gorgon and all, on the towering statue of the goddess he erected inside the Parthenon.

SEE ALSO: Athena; Gorgons; Parthenon

Aeneas

In Greek mythology, a prince of Troy, which was sacked by the Greeks in the Age of Heroes (the late Bronze Age). Aeneas plays only a minor role in Homer's *Iliad*, in which the prince fights the mighty Greek warrior Achilles and lives thanks to some divine protection. Later the sea god Poseidon predicts that Aeneas will survive the fall of the city and rule later generations of Trojans. When the Romans, who were greatly influenced by Greek culture (especially Greek religion and mythology) heard this tale, they came to see Aeneas as the founder of their race. The first-century A.D. Roman poet Virgil wrote what became Rome's national epic, the *Aeneid*, which vividly recounts Aeneas's escape from Troy, his journey to Italy, and his marriage to the daughter of a local king.

SEE ALSO: *Iliad*; Rome; Troy

Aeolus

In Greek mythology, a powerful keeper of the winds. Aeolus was born a mortal, but Zeus, leader of the gods, admired him and made him king of the floating island of Aeolia. There, Aeolus watched over a cave that held the winds, which he unleashed when the gods told him to. A version of one of the principal myths about him appears in Homer's *Odyssey*. On encountering Odysseus, who is wandering in search of his homeland, the island kingdom of Ithaca, Aeolus gives the man a leather bag filled with strong winds that have the power to push Odysseus's ships to Ithaca. But the plan is upset when some of Odysseus's men open the bag too soon and the winds blow the vessels the wrong way. Aeolus was also credited with inventing the sail.

SEE ALSO: *Odyssey*

Aeschines
(ca. 390 B.C.–ca. 322 B.C.)

(ES-kineez) A leading Athenian orator who was noted for his bitter rivalry with Demosthenes, the greatest orator the Greeks ever produced. In 346 B.C. the Athenian government sent Aeschines and an associate, Eubulus, to negotiate peace terms with Philip II, king of Macedonia, who was threatening to overrun the city-states of southern Greece. Soon afterward Demosthenes, who had denounced Philip publicly, took Aeschines to court, claiming that he had taken bribes from Philip. Aeschines fought back, defending himself in his speeches *Against Timarchus* and *On the False Embassy*. Moved, the Athenians found him not guilty. Several years later, when Ctesiphon, a supporter of Demosthenes, suggested awarding Demosthenes a golden crown, Aeschines strongly objected and denounced the great orator in a speech titled *Against Ctesiphon*. This prompted Demosthenes to pen a stinging rebuttal, *On the Crown*, one of the finest surviving speeches of antiquity. Humiliated, Aeschines admitted defeat. As the Greek biographer Plutarch later told it, "Aeschines immediately left Athens and spent the rest of his life in Rhodes and Ionia as a teacher of rhetoric [public speaking]." (*Life of Demosthenes* 24)

SEE ALSO: Demosthenes; *On the Crown*; rhetoric

Aeschylus
(ca. 525 B.C.–456 B.C.)

An Athenian playwright who has come to be seen as the world's first great dramatist. Born at Eleusis (site of the goddess Demeter's temple and mystery cult), Aeschylus fought in the Battle of Marathon in 490 B.C., where his brother, Cynegirus, died. According to Herodotus, the young man "had his hand cut off with an ax as he was getting hold of a ship's stern, and so lost his life, together with many other well-known Athenians." (*Histories* 6.116)

Aeschylus also took part in the Greek naval victory over the Persians at Salamis (480 B.C.) and eight years later made that battle the centerpiece of his play the *Persians*, which fortunately has survived. (The play includes what appears to be an eyewitness account of some of the fighting.) Six other of his plays have survived as well, including *Seven Against Thebes* (produced in 467 B.C.), *The Suppliant Women* (ca. 463 B.C.), and *Prometheus Bound* (ca. 460 B.C.), the latter based on the myth in which Zeus punishes the Titan Prometheus by chaining him to a rock and having a giant eagle gnaw at his liver. The other three of

This is a bust of Aeschylus, the ancient Athenian playwright who is widely accepted as the world's first great dramatist. © ARALDO DE LUCA/CORBIS

Aeschylus's extant plays make up the *Oresteia* trilogy (458 B.C.)—*Agamemnon, The Libation Bearers*, and *Eumenides*.

In fact, it was Aeschylus who pioneered the trilogy form. He also introduced other theatrical conventions, including, as Aristotle reported in his *Poetics*, the use of a second actor, which increased the number of characters that could be seen on stage at the same time. Aeschylus's main talent lay in selecting primal core themes and emotions (usually drawn from popular myths) that all people could identify with and packaging them in formal but powerful language that gripped and moved his audiences. The great modern translator of his works, Paul Roche, says of him:

> The stamp of Aeschylus's soul was loyal, heroic, aristocratic, and uncom-

promising. There was a great deal of the inspired prophet about him—the seer, lofty and penetrating in thought, delving into the past and casting his look far into the future. What he saw he sent flooding out of him, crashing down in thunderous poetry. There was a kind of divine impetus in him that struck out great rending thoughts in magnificent language. . . . His vision of heaven and earth was grand and overwhelming. Aeschylus never minded if he shocked. . . . [He felt that] people must be made to see the truth, even if it shook them. (*The Orestes Plays of Aeschylus*, pp. xix–xx)

SEE ALSO: Battle of Marathon; Battle of Salamis; theater and drama; and individual names of Aeschylus's plays

Aesop
(early sixth century B.C. ?)

According to Greek tradition, the author of a number of charming fables, each having a simple but thought-provoking moral. Nothing certain is known about his life (assuming he was a real person, which remains unproven). But legends claim he was born a slave in Thrace and later dwelled on the Aegean island of Samos. Among his more familiar stories are "The Ants and the Grasshopper," "The Ass and the Wolf," "Belling the Cat," "The Cat and the Mice," "The Fox and the Grapes," "The Scorpion and the Frog," and perhaps the most famous of all, "The Hare and the Tortoise." In the latter Aesop describes a race between the title characters and has the tortoise win, showing that steadiness and perseverance can overcome overconfidence and haste.

SEE ALSO: Samos

Aetolia

The area of western Greece situated along the lower section of the Achelous River, north of western Locris and east of Acarnania. During the Archaic Age and first half of the Classical period, Aetolia consisted of scattered, largely unfortified tribal villages ruled by local chieftains and played little or no part in the Greek political and cultural mainstream. In about 370 B.C., however, the largest Aetolian towns formed a common alliance, the Aetolian League, which became a major player in Greek affairs in the early Hellenistic Age. In the Second Macedonian War (200–197 B.C.), the Aetolians backed Rome against Macedonia's King Philip V. But then, worried about Roman expansion into Greece, they began to oppose Rome. The Romans soon forced the Aetolians to sign a treaty that made Aetolia dependent on and subservient to Rome, and the region became part of the Roman province of Achaea in 27 B.C.

SEE ALSO: Aetolian League; Rome

Aetolian League

A confederacy of towns, the majority in Aetolia, the region lying directly east of Acarnania (in western Greece), established circa 370 B.C. The league had an elected president (who also commanded the common army) and a collective assembly that met twice a year in the centrally located town of Thermum (or Thermon). Slowly but steadily the league gained power and influence. In early Hellenistic times it also controlled the sacred sanctuary at Delphi, which it successfully defended against invading Celts in 279 B.C., as well as large parts of central Greece. With the coming of the Romans in the early second century

B.C., the league at first backed Rome against Aetolia's rival, Macedonia. But after the Romans had defeated Macedonia, the league members voted to switch their allegiance and called on the Seleucid king, Antiochus III, to oust the Romans from Greece. Militarily the Aetolians were no match for Rome, however, and by the 180s B.C. the league had lost nearly all of its former power. Meetings and elections continued for some time to come but amounted to little more than hollow ceremony.

SEE ALSO: Aetolia; Macedonia; Rome

afterlife

The Greeks believed in the existence of life after death, although conceptions of the world beyond earthly existence changed over time, varied in their details, and were sometimes contradictory.

SEE ALSO: burial customs; Underworld

Agamemnon

In Greek mythology, as well as in Homer's *Iliad*, the leader of the great Greek expedition to Troy and the king of Mycenae in the northeastern Peloponnesus. Agamemnon was also the brother of Menelaus, king of Sparta (both men belonged to the royal House of Atreus). So when the Trojan prince Paris abducted Menelaus's wife, Helen, the two brothers teamed up and, with the help of other Greek kings, mounted a siege of Troy. Homer describes how, during the siege, Agamemnon quarreled with the greatest of the Greek warriors, Achilles. Angry, Achilles stayed in his tent and refused to fight, embarrassing Agamemnon and demoralizing the other Greeks. After the fall of Troy, Agamemnon returned to Greece, where his wife, Clytemnestra, harbored a grudge against him for

killing their daughter, Iphigenia, in a sacrifice to gain favorable winds for the trip to Troy. She proceeded to murder Agamemnon, as depicted by the Athenian playwright Aeschylus in his play *Agamemnon*.

SEE ALSO: Clytemnestra; Iphigenia; Troy

Agamemnon (play)

A tragedy by Aeschylus, first performed in Athens in 458 B.C. The play was the initial installment of the author's great trilogy, the *Oresteia*, dealing with the troubles of several members of the royal House of Atreus. In the opening scene Clytemnestra, queen of Mycenae and Argos, awaits the imminent return of her husband, Agamemnon, who is on his way back from the Trojan War. She is accompanied by some local elders, who form the play's chorus. They recall the day ten years before when Agamemnon slew Clytemnestra's daughter, Iphigenia, in a sacrifice to the goddess Artemis. Still longing for vengeance, Clytemnestra now draws her plans to kill her husband. Soon he appears, bringing with him the Trojan princess Cassandra, who has the ability to see into the future. Cassandra realizes that the queen, aided by her lover, Aegisthus, will kill the king and Cassandra herself as well. After the murders have been committed, Clytemnestra tries to justify these crimes to the horrified elders. They express the hope that Agamemnon's son, Orestes, will come forth and avenge his kingly father.

SEE ALSO: Aeschylus; Agamemnon; Clytemnestra

Agathocles (late fourth–early third century B.C.)

A successful ruler of the Greek city of Syracuse in Sicily. In 317 B.C. he overthrew the city's oligarchic government and assumed dictatorial control. Then, circa 306, he went further by declaring himself king. Agathocles managed to conquer most of Sicily and parts of southern Italy before dying (perhaps by poisoning) in 289 B.C.

SEE ALSO: Syracuse

Agathon
(ca. 445 B.C.–ca. 400 B.C.)

An important Athenian playwright credited with being the first to compose a play (probably titled *The Flower*) with imaginary characters and story. Before him, dramatists had used stories taken directly from mythology or history (for example, Sophocles' tragedies about the mythical character Oedipus, and Aeschylus's play describing the defeat of the Persians at Salamis). Not much is known about Agathon's life, except that he departed Athens circa 407 B.C. and spent the rest of his days in Macedonia. Only a few lines of his plays have survived. His colleague, the comic playwright Aristophanes, made him a character with overt homosexual mannerisms in *Women Celebrating the Thesmophoria*, written in 411 B.C. There is also a brief exchange about Agathon in another of Aristophanes' works, *Frogs* (405): A person asks, "What of Agathon?" Someone answers, "Too bad, he's gone [i.e., has died]. A good poet [who is] sadly missed." The other responds, "Poor fellow." (*Frogs* 89–91) In addition, Agathon appears as a character in Plato's dialogue, the *Symposium*.

SEE ALSO: Aristophanes, 1; *Symposium* (dialogue); theater and drama

Age of Heroes

A term used by the classical Greeks to describe the era of their dim past when larger-than-life mortals supposedly performed great deeds and interacted with the gods. Modern scholars date the era to the last few centuries of the Bronze Age.

SEE ALSO: Greece, history of; Minoans; Mycenaeans

Agesilaus II
(ca. 444 B.C.–360 B.C.)

A renowned Spartan king who rose to power in the turbulent years following Sparta's defeat of Athens at the end of the Peloponnesian War (404 B.C.). Agesilaus, who reigned from 399 to 360, was a member of Sparta's Eurypontid royal house and ascended the throne following the death of his brother, King Agis II. In 396 Agesilaus led an army of about eight thousand Spartans and other Peloponnesian troops into Asia Minor to protect Sparta's allies there against Persian attacks. But he was forced to return to Greece in 394 to meet the challenge of an anti-Spartan coalition of Athenians, Boeotians, Corinthians, and others. He won a narrow victory over them that year at Coronea, then proceeded on to Sparta. It was partly Agesilaus's poor treatment of Thebes and its leaders, especially Epaminondas, that sparked a war between the two states in the late 370s. After Epaminondas defeated the Spartans (led by their other king, Cleombrotus) at Leuctra in 371, the hegemony, or dominance, of Greece passed from Sparta to Thebes. Later Agesilaus, now in his eighties, fought the Persians again, this time in Egypt. But he died on the homeward voyage. Most of what is known about the dynamic Agesilaus comes from a biography of him penned by his friend, the exiled Athenian historian Xenophon.

SEE ALSO: Battle of Coronea; Battle of Leuctra; Sparta; Xenophon

Agis IV
(262 B.C.–241 B.C.)

A controversial king of Sparta. He assumed the throne in 244 B.C. and proposed a number of reforms designed to revitalize Sparta, which in the previous century had undergone a serious decline in power and prestige. Among these reforms were abolition of debts and major land redistribution. Conservative Spartans opposed the proposals, however, and not long after he deposed his fellow king, Leonidas II, the latter retaliated. Agis was executed after having ruled for fewer than three years.

SEE ALSO: Sparta

agora

The marketplace and political meeting place of an ancient Greek town. The capitalized version of the word—Agora—usually denotes the one in Athens. Typical buildings in an agora included law courts, meeting halls, stoas, and shops.

SEE ALSO: money; stoa

Ajax

In Greek mythology, and in Homer's *Iliad*, one of the leading Greek warriors who fought in the Trojan War. Ajax (or Aias) was the son of Telamon, who ruled the island kingdom of Salamis (southwest of Athens). In legend and literature Ajax was depicted as a giant of a man possessing great strength and courage. In fact, Homer claimed that only Achilles (the central figure of the *Iliad*) was a better fighter among the Greeks. During the course of the war, Ajax and Achilles became friends, and Ajax carried Achilles' corpse back to the Greek camp after the Trojan warrior Paris had slain Achilles by shooting an arrow into his heel, the only vulnerable spot on his body. The principal myth about Ajax told how, when an argument erupted over who should gain possession of Achilles' armor, the other Greek leaders voted to award the armor to Odysseus (king of Ithaca). As depicted in Sophocles' play *Ajax*, the title character planned to slay his colleagues to get revenge. But then the goddess Athena rendered him temporarily insane and he killed some sheep instead. Sadly, after regaining his wits Ajax was so humiliated that he took his own life.

SEE ALSO: Achilles; *Ajax* (play); Troy

Ajax (play)

A tragic play by Sophocles, first produced in Athens in about 447 B.C. The story is set in the tenth year of the siege of Troy by the Greeks. Achilles, greatest of the Greek warriors, has been killed, and most of his comrades have decided to award his armor to the wily Odysseus, king of the island kingdom of Ithaca. This has enraged the huge and mighty Ajax, who badly wanted the armor for himself, and he has sworn to kill the other Greek leaders. As the play begins, the goddess Athena tells Odysseus how she made Ajax temporarily senseless, causing him to slaughter a herd of animals instead of his fellow Greeks. Meanwhile, Ajax, who has come to his senses and feels humiliated, contemplates and finally commits suicide by falling on his sword. Though some of the other Greek kings plan to leave his body unburied (a fate the ancient Greeks viewed as extreme and barbaric), Odysseus sees to it that Ajax receives a proper funeral.

SEE ALSO: Ajax; Odysseus; Sophocles

Ajax the Lesser

A noted mythical Greek warrior who came from Locris (in central Greece) and commanded soldiers from that region in the siege of Troy. This Ajax is usually referred to as "Ajax the Lesser" to differentiate him from his bigger and more famous colleague. The most famous mythical incident involving Ajax the Lesser occurred during the final sacking of Troy. He dragged away the Trojan princess Cassandra, who had been praying at the local altar of Athena. Outraged, the goddess caused Ajax's ship to capsize while he was sailing home; and though the man survived the wreck, he bragged that he had defied the gods, prompting Poseidon, god of the sea, to strike him dead.

SEE ALSO: Athena; Cassandra; Troy

Akroteri

A village on the southern coast of the Cycladic island of Thera, Akroteri (also Akrotiri) lies atop a large Bronze Age Minoan town that archaeologists have begun to excavate from a deep layer of ash. The ash, which buried the island to a depth of many feet, was laid down by Thera's volcano during the largest-known natural disaster of antiquity, which occurred sometime between 1620 and 1450 B.C. Ancient Akroteri (its Minoan name is unknown) has come to be called "the Pompeii of the Aegean," a reference to the Roman town buried in ash and beautifully preserved during a volcanic eruption in A.D. 79. Akroteri was discovered in the late 1960s by Spyridon Marinatos, then Greece's greatest archaeologist. He unearthed several streets filled with residences and shops, some of them two stories high. Inside some of the buildings were exquisite frescoes (wall paintings done on wet plaster), which have been removed to various Greek museums. Also found in the ruins were pottery and furniture items, storage containers, and other objects. Some

were made locally, but others originated in mainland Greece, Asia Minor, Cyprus, Syria, and Egypt, indicating that the town was involved in prosperous international trade. Evidence suggests that at least some of the town disappeared when the part of the island it occupied collapsed into the sea during the height of the great eruption. According to a theory popular among classical scholars, this disaster, combined with the eruption's devastating effects on Minoan Crete, may have given rise to the legend of Atlantis. Most of the surviving sections of the town are still buried. After Marinatos died in 1974, other archaeologists continued his work, but it will likely take decades, perhaps generations, to properly excavate and study the entire ancient city.

SEE ALSO: Atlantis; Crete; Minoans; Thera

Alcaeus
(early sixth century B.C.)

A famous lyric poet born in Mytilene on the island of Lesbos. He wrote love songs, drinking songs, hymns to the gods, and political statements, a few of which have survived nearly complete; numerous fragments of his other poems also have been found. His writing is concise, elegant, and often expresses personal feelings or observations of human activities (war, partying) and natural phenomena (storms, the seasons). Regarding the latter, he writes: "Zeus rumbles and a mammoth winter of snow pours from the sky. Agile rivers are ice. Damn the winter cold! Pile up the burning logs and water the great flagons of red wine [i.e., mix the wine with water]. Place feather pillows by your head and drink." ("Winter Evening") Alcaeus's poetry strongly influenced later ancient poets, including the Roman Horace.

SEE ALSO: poetry

Alcestis

In Greek mythology, the loyal and loving wife of the mortal Admetus, to whom Apollo gave the gift of eternal life. The catch was that the man would have to find someone else to die in his place. When no one else would do so, Alcestis gave up her own life, but later she was able to return from the depths of the Underworld. One ancient myth claimed that Persephone, queen of the Underworld, allowed Alcestis to leave her dark realm to reward her unusually deep love for her husband. Another account, used by the playwright Euripides in his play about Alcestis, said that the renowned hero Heracles gained Alcestis's release by fighting and beating Thanatos, god of death.

SEE ALSO: Admetus; *Alcestis* (play); Heracles

Alcestis (play)

A play by Euripides, first written and produced in Athens in 438 B.C. The characters and events of the play were taken from mythology (like those of most other dramatic works of Euripides' era). According to one of the most popular Greek myths, the god Apollo granted Admetus, king of Pherae (in Thessaly), the ability to evade death, providing he could find someone who would willingly die in his place. Admetus's wife, Alcestis, volunteered and soon Thanatos, god of death, arrived to take the young woman to the Underworld.

In the play's opening scene, Apollo asks Thanatos to have mercy and let Alcestis live; but the god of death says he is compelled to do his ghastly duty. Alcestis dies and Thanatos prepares to take her on her final journey. But then the famous strongman Heracles (whom the Romans called Hercules) shows up unexpectedly. When he learns about Alcestis's plight, he

This marble bust of Alcibiades, the notorious Athenian politician and traitor, captures his youthful energy. ALINARI/ART RESOURCE, NY

decides to do what no other human could—stop Thanatos from taking her to the Underworld. Heracles confronts the god of death, grabs hold of him, and the two engage in a fierce and desperate wrestling match. In the end, Heracles wins and Thanatos reluctantly withdraws, after which Alcestis wakes up from the sleep of death. Her rescuer takes her to Admetus, who is overwhelmed with joy.

SEE ALSO: Admetus; Alcestis; Euripides

Alcibiades
(ca. 450 B.C.–404 B.C.)

One of the more colorful political leaders of the Classical Age and the most famous traitor in Greek history. Alcibiades was born into a wealthy Athenian family of the controversial Alcmaeonid clan and was closely related to Pericles, the leading Greek statesman of the fifth century B.C. In fact, Pericles actually raised Alcibiades after the latter's father died. The young man impressed all who knew him with his good looks and sharp intelligence. But Alcibiades was also spoiled, self-indulgent, and, as he grew older, increasingly unscrupulous, negative traits that Pericles was unable to counter. According to the ancient Greek biographer Plutarch, Alcibiades "lived a life of prodigious luxury, drunkenness, debauchery [sexual excess], and insolence. He was effeminate [womanly] in his dress and would walk through the market-place trailing his long purple robes, and he spent extravagantly. . . . The leading men of Athens watched all this with disgust and indignation." (*Life of Alcibiades* 16) Despite the youth's excesses, however, many Athenians liked his brashness and quick wit and he won many friends, including the eccentric philosopher Socrates, who, not surprisingly, tried to get him to show his more positive qualities.

In 420 B.C. Alcibiades was elected *strategos* (general), and because he deeply hated the Spartans, he began urging his countrymen to renew the Peloponnesian War with Sparta. (At the time, a truce called the Peace of Nicias prevailed.) The Assembly listened to him, made an alliance with Sparta's enemies—Argos, Mantinea, and Elis—and the war promptly resumed. Three years later Alcibiades again won over the Assembly. This time he persuaded the Athenians to send a huge military expedition to Sicily and conquer Syracuse. The Assembly placed Alcibiades in joint command with Nicias, who had vehemently opposed the plan. On the way to Sicily, however, Alcibiades heard that he had been charged with defacing some religious statues back in Athens. Rather than face a trial, he suddenly abandoned his countrymen and fled to the last place anyone would have expected him to go—Sparta, which gave him refuge.

Under the poor leadership of Nicias, the Sicilian expedition then turned into a disaster in which Athens lost all of the ships and most of the men it had sent. Alcibiades felt no responsibility for these losses and instead continued his traitorous activities by trying to convince the Persians to enter the war against Athens. Yet incredibly, some Athenians were willing to forgive him for his past misdeeds if he would switch sides and help them fight the Spartans. He did so in 411 B.C., and the following year he defeated a Spartan fleet at Cyzicus, on the southern shore of the Propontis. In 407 Alcibiades returned in triumph to Athens. But soon he fell out of favor with the people once more and fled to a fortress on the shore of the Hellespont. In 404, the same year that Athens surrendered, ending the great war, Spartan and Persian leaders had Alcibiades murdered.

SEE ALSO: Nicias; Pericles; Syracuse

Alcmaeonids

A prominent Athenian clan whose members played important roles in Athens's social and political affairs from the seventh to fifth centuries B.C.. They all claimed descent from an ancient aristocrat named Alcmaeon. The most famous Alcmaeonids were Cleisthenes, who spearheaded Athenian democracy in 508 B.C.; Pericles, the leading Greek statesman of the fifth century B.C.; and Alcibiades, a leading politician in the era of the Peloponnesian War. The Alcmaeonids were frequently suspected of excessive ambitions and dirty

In this detail from the "Alexander Mosaic," unearthed in the Roman city of Pompeii, Alexander charges at his foe, the Persian king Darius III. LIBRARY OF CONGRESS

dealings, and honest politicians like Pericles had to work to overcome widespread distrust.

SEE ALSO: Alcibiades; Cleisthenes; Pericles

Alcman
(flourished ca. 630 B.C.)

A lyric poet whose birthplace is uncertain but who spent most of his life in Sparta. Alcman composed mostly choral works for religious festivals and feasts. Someone published his poems several centuries after his death, but only a few fragments and quotations in the works of other ancient writers survive. One fragment reads, "Narrow is our way of life,

and necessity is pitiless." (from "The Journey")

SEE ALSO: poetry

Alexander III ("the Great")
(356 B.C.–323 B.C.)

A Macedonian Greek king who at a young age conquered the Persian Empire in a mere decade, earning a reputation as one of the greatest generals of all time and ranking him, along with Aristotle, Plato, Cleopatra, Julius Caesar, and Jesus Christ, as one of the six most renowned figures of ancient times. Alexander was the son of Macedonia's King Philip II and Olympias, a princess of the small northern Greek kingdom of Epirus. The boy was an excellent student and at an early age displayed a driving ambition to achieve great deeds. Some of this ambition may have been imparted by Philip, who was an ambitious conqueror of the first order. Alexander was likely also influenced by his mother, who told him he was a god, and by Aristotle, who, at Philip's request, tutored the boy in science, ethics, and literature. The philosopher also gave Alexander a copy of Homer's *Iliad*, which the young man thereafter kept close at hand. Alexander developed a deep admiration for the *Iliad*'s central figure, Achilles, who consciously chose a brief life of fame and glory over a long one of obscurity. According to the Greek historian Arrian, whose history is the principal surviving source about Alexander, the latter asserted, "Those who endure hardship and danger are the ones who achieve glory, and the most gratifying thing is to live with courage and to die leaving behind eternal renown." (*Anabasis* 5.26)

With such a singular personal philosophy, it is hardly surprising that Alexander was eager to go along on his father's military campaigns. But Philip said no; not until Alexander was sixteen did his father finally give him a chance to prove himself. The young man received the title of regent, giving him the authority to run the country while Philip was away. Alexander proved himself in short order, crushing a local rebellion and establishing a new city. In an even more impressive display, in 338 B.C., at age eighteen, Alexander commanded a wing of Philip's cavalry in the decisive Macedonian victory over Athens and Thebes at Chaeronea. Alexander faced an even bigger test two years later, when Philip was assassinated and the young man found himself king of Macedonia and

captain-general of the new Greek confederacy Philip had recently forged. Alexander swiftly established himself as an able leader and ruthless adversary by destroying most of the city of Thebes, which made the mistake of rebelling against his authority.

Next Alexander applied himself to fulfilling his father's dream of invading Persia. In 334 B.C. Alexander crossed the Hellespont into Asia Minor at the head of a mixed army of Macedonians and other Greeks, numbering about thirty-two thousand infantry and five thousand cavalry. In large degree it was Philip's army, and many of the tactics it employed were those Philip had developed. Nevertheless, during the campaigns that followed Alexander innovated new tactics of his own and proved himself a general of the first order, which was particularly extraordinary considering his tender age. His first victory was at the Granicus River in northwestern Asia Minor, where he defeated some local Persian satraps (provincial governors). Alexander then made his way to Issus, in northern Syria, and crushed a much larger army led by Persia's king, Darius III, although Darius himself escaped.

Following this victory, the Greeks continued southward, besieged and captured the island-city of Tyre on the coast of Palestine, and proceeded into Egypt. There, Alexander was welcomed by the populace, who had suffered under Persian rule off and on for two centuries. One of Alexander's most important achievements in Egypt was the establishment of a new city—Alexandria—in the western Nile Delta. It was destined to become one of the leading commercial and cultural centers of the ancient world. Alexander never saw the city's rise to greatness, however; soon after approving his basic layout, he led his troops northeastward into the

Persian heartland (in what are now Iraq and Iran). There, in October 331 B.C., he clashed with Darius again, this time at Gaugamela, about 270 miles (435km) north of Babylon. Again the Persian monarch suffered a major defeat and fled the field. Alexander gave chase but once more was unable to catch his adversary. Later, however, some of the Persian king's own followers betrayed him and tried to trade him to Alexander in exchange for leniency for themselves. They ended up murdering Darius and were no doubt surprised when Alexander viewed this as a crime, hunted them down, and executed them.

After Darius's defeat, Alexander entered Babylon, which did not try to put up a fight. In the months and years that followed, the Greeks marched eastward into the arid regions of what are now eastern Iran and Afghanistan. Finally, late in 327 B.C. Alexander reached India. A local king, Porus, challenged him in a major battle fought near the Hydapses River in May 326, but the Greeks were victorious once more. Although Alexander wanted to continue eastward and conquer all of India, his troops, who were tired and homesick, told him they would go no farther; and reluctantly, he led them back to Babylon. There, on June 10, 323 B.C., he died unexpectedly, perhaps of alcohol poisoning, though the exact cause will likely never be known. He was only thirty-three. "He had a great personal beauty, invincible power of endurance, and a keen intellect," Arrian later wrote.

> He was brave and adventurous, strict in the observance of his religious duties, and hungry for fame. . . . He had an uncanny instinct for the right course in a difficult and complex situation. . . . In arming and equipping troops and in his military dispositions he was always masterly. Noble indeed

> was his power of inspiring his men, of filling them with confidence, and, in the moment of danger, of sweeping away their fear by the spectacle of his own fearlessness. (*Anabasis* 7.29)

Tempering these positive traits, however, were some decidedly negative ones. Alexander was also tremendously self-centered and stubborn, and he frequently employed unnecessarily brutal and inhumane tactics. His destruction of Thebes and sale of its surviving inhabitants into slavery was just one of many examples. After Alexander's death, his enormous new empire rapidly fell apart as his generals, the so-called Successors, fought over it, reshaping the Near East in the process.

SEE ALSO: Alexandria; Arrian; Battles of Chaeronea, Gaugamela, Granicus River, Hydapses River, and Issus; Darius III; Olympias; Persians; Philip II; weapons and warfare, land and siege

Alexandria

One of the greatest cities of the ancient world, Alexandria was established by Alexander the Great in 332 B.C. in the western sector of the Nile Delta. Alexander contributed several key layout and design ideas, then departed to continue his conquest of Persia, leaving the architect Deinocrates to actually build the city. Alexandria quickly grew large and prosperous under the leadership of King Ptolemy I Soter (formerly one of Alexander's generals) and his immediate successors. It was a highly cosmopolitan city, frequented by foreign merchants and travelers from far and wide and featuring a Jewish quarter as well as numerous Greek and Egyptian residents. However, Greek was the language of administration and business, and an upper crust of privileged Greeks controlled the government, the marketplace, and the army.

Alexandria became famous for its luxury products and magnificent buildings. The luxury products included fine examples of metalworking and glassmaking as well as textiles, perfumes, and books. To house the latter, the early Ptolemies erected the so-called Great Library, which became the largest library in the known world, in Alexandria. They also built the Museum (which adjoined the library), a research center for scientists and other scholars. Some of the greatest Greek scientists and mathematicians, including Euclid, Archimedes, Eratosthenes, Hipparchus, Herophilus, and Claudius Ptolemy, worked at one time or another at the Museum. Other imposing structures in the city included the Serapeum, a temple dedicated to the god Serapis, completed by Ptolemy III (reigned 246–221 B.C.); and the Pharos, a towering lighthouse that stood on a small offshore island of the same name. Dedicated in 279 B.C. by Ptolemy II, the Pharos was visible for miles in all directions and came to be listed among the Seven Wonders of the Ancient World.

Alexandria's architectural wonders took a backseat to political and military events in the first century B.C. when the last of the Ptolemies, Cleopatra VII, returned there after her defeat (by the Romans at Actium in Greece) in 31 B.C. She soon committed suicide, ending Greek rule of the city and of Egypt, which then fell under the control of Rome.

SEE ALSO: Ptolemy I Soter; Ptolemy II Philadelphus; Rome; science; Seven Wonders of the Ancient World

Alexandrian and other Hellenistic Greek literature

Much of the best literature produced during Greece's Hellenistic Age (323–30 B.C.) and the centuries that followed it was produced in Alexandria, Egypt, then ruled by the Greek Ptolemaic dynasty. Some Alexandrian literature was of a scientific nature, including Euclid's geometry text, the *Elements*, and a book by the Greek astronomer Aristarchus in which he correctly proposed that the Sun, not Earth, lies at the center of the cosmos. (This work did not survive, but another Alexandrian scholar, Archimedes, summarized the theory in one of his own books.) Hellenistic Greek literature also consisted of popular poetry and prose. Apollonius of Rhodes (third century B.C.) revived the genre of epic poetry with his *Argonautica*, about the mythical hero Jason and his quest for the fabulous Golden Fleece. And many thousands of shorter poems were composed by Meleager, Callimachus, and Theocritus. Meanwhile, a scholar named Zenodotus restored, edited, and published new editions of earlier classics, including Homer's epics.

The majority of books produced by Alexandrian and other Hellenistic Greek writers were at first aimed at a small number of well-educated, highbrow readers. Over time, however, educational opportunities expanded, which for the first time in history stimulated the growth of a fairly sizable general reading public. To meet the increasing demand for materials for readers of limited or average educational levels, second-rate writers multiplied and became successful. For the rest of Hellenistic times, and throughout much of Greece's Roman period (30 B.C.–A.D. 476), Alexandrian and other Greek literature consisted of both high-quality works that appealed to a limited audience and popular pulp for the masses.

Among the latter was an early form of a literary genre taken for granted today—

the novel. The first Greek novels appear to have been inspired by a mix of literary forms and writers, including the stories told in epic poems, comic plays by Menander and other Greek playwrights, and the pleasant pastoral poems of the Alexandrian writer Theocritus. Modern scholars usually call these early novels *romances*. They were fictional narratives that almost always dealt with two people in love. The lovers typically found themselves separated in various mishaps and adventures but were fortunately reunited in the end. Although most novels were of moderate literary quality at best, a few achieved higher standards. Perhaps the most notable example was *Daphnis and Chloe*, by Longus (third century A.D.), who hailed from the island of Lesbos. This excerpt describes the strange feelings that overtake Chloe as she falls madly in love with Daphnis:

> She did not know what was wrong with her, for she was only a young girl who had been brought up in the country and had never even heard the word "love" used by anyone else. But she felt sick at heart, and she could not control her eyes, and she was always talking about Daphnis. She took no interest in food, she could not sleep at night, [and] she paid no attention to her flock. One moment she would be laughing, the next she would be crying. (*Daphnis and Chloe*, Book 1)

SEE ALSO: Alexandria; Apollonius of Rhodes; Callimachus, 2; Euclid; poetry; Theocritus

alphabet

The Greeks derived their alphabet from the Phoenicians sometime in the eighth century B.C.

SEE ALSO: Greek language; Phoenicia

Amazons

A legendary race of warrior women depicted frequently in ancient Greek literature and art. Most ancient writers placed the homeland of the Amazons in the steppes lying west and north of the Black Sea, a region then little-known to the Greeks. The name *Amazon* came from the Greek *a-mazon*, meaning "without a breast." It referred to a custom attributed to these women—cutting off one breast to allow for more effective use of a bow, spear, and other weapons. Indeed, in most of the Greek myths about the Amazons, they engage in battle, often with Greek men. The Greeks called this type of warfare Amazonomachy. In one story, for example, the Athenian hero Theseus invades part of the Amazon homeland along the Black Sea coast and captures their queen, Hippolyta. The Amazons respond by landing an army near Athens and laying siege to the Acropolis, but they are eventually driven away by Theseus. The Greek strongman Heracles (whom the Romans called Hercules) also fought the Amazons in one of his famous twelve labors. Still another legendary battle between Amazons and Greeks took place in the famous Trojan War. The warrior women sided with the Trojans against the Greeks until the Greek hero Achilles slew the Amazon queen. (In a gruesome twist, afterward he fell in love with her corpse.) The most notable Greek artistic rendition of such episodes of Amazonomachy was a series of sculptures on the Parthenon, atop the Athenian Acropolis, completed in the 430s B.C.

SEE ALSO: Heracles; Parthenon; Theseus

ambrosia and nectar

In Greek mythology, food and drink that the gods consumed to maintain their immortality. Ambrosia was a sweet-smelling food and nectar a tasty liquid. According to legend, if a mortal ate ambrosia or drank nectar, he or she became immortal like the gods.

SEE ALSO: religion

Amphictyonic Council

Also known as the Delphic Amphictyony, a religious federation made up of representatives from city-states located mostly in central and northern Greece. Its original function was to manage the temple of Demeter near Thermopylae. Later the council performed the same function for the temple of Apollo at Delphi as well. The representatives (*bieromnemones*) attended council meetings twice a year to discuss and vote on policy and other matters pertaining to the temple precincts. Some of the member states of the Amphictyonic Council defended Delphi in various disputes, including the so-called Sacred Wars.

SEE ALSO: Delphi; Sacred Wars

Amphipolis

An Athenian colony located about 3 miles (4.8km) inland from the northern coast of the Aegean Sea. The first attempt to establish the colony, in 462 B.C., failed when natives from the local region (Thrace) killed the settlers. But the second attempt, in 437, was successful. The city became an important trading post that supplied Athens with gold, silver, timber, and slaves. In 357 B.C. Amphipolis was captured by Macedonia's King Philip II and thereafter remained a Macedonian city until Rome conquered Greece in the second century B.C.

SEE ALSO: Philip II

amphora

A tall pottery vessel with two handles used to transport liquids such as wine and olive oil (and sometimes solid foods such as olives, dates, and nuts). At least forty different kinds and styles of amphorae existed. But generally speaking, most were 3 to 4 feet (.9 to 1.2m) high, held from 6 to 20 gallons (23 to 76L), and had a wide body that narrowed to a small hole in the top. On the inside, an amphora was frequently coated with distilled pine tree resin or some other water-resistant substance. Typically the hole at the top of the vessel was sealed with a stopper made of cork or fired clay. Most amphorae, particularly in Hellenistic times, were stamped or painted with the names of the owners of the estates where they were made or the merchants who transported them. Weight and shipping information might also be inscribed. During transport on ships, amphorae were usually stacked in layers, and evidence from shipwrecks shows that a single merchant ship could carry several thousand of them at a time.

SEE ALSO: olives and olive oil; pottery; trade

Anabasis (by Arrian)

(most often translated as "The March Up-Country")

An important ancient chronicle of the campaigns of Alexander the Great written by the first-century A.D. Greek historian Arrian.

SEE ALSO: Alexander III ("the Great"); Arrian

Anabasis (by Xenophon)

A widely popular and influential prose narrative by Xenophon. It consists of the author's eyewitness account of the military

After a harrowing journey through enemy territory, Xenophon and his fellow Greeks reach the shores of the Black Sea. NORTH WIND PICTURE ARCHIVES

expedition launched in 401 B.C. by a Persian prince, Cyrus the Younger, against his older brother, King Artaxerxes II. To supplement his Persian troops, Cyrus hired ten thousand Greek mercenaries, including Xenophon. Cyrus marched his army from Sardis (in western Asia Minor) to Cunaxa, about 50 miles (80km) from Babylon (in what is now Iraq), where he was defeated and killed by Artaxerxes. Although the Greeks acquitted themselves well in the battle and suffered almost no losses, they now found themselves stranded in a foreign land and completely surrounded by hostile forces. Artaxerxes' officers invited the Greek commanders to peace talks, but then treacherously murdered

them. The Greek soldiers immediately chose new leaders, including Xenophon. Most agreed that there was nothing else to do but retreat and try to fight their way out of Persia. So the "Ten Thousand," as they came to be known, set out on an incredible overland trek of more than 1,000 miles (1,609km), in which they endured many dangers and hardships. In one passage, Xenophon recalls:

> A north wind blew in [our] faces, parching everything . . . and freezing the men. . . . The snow was [6 feet (1.8m)] deep, so that many animals . . . were lost, and soldiers, too, about thirty. . . . [We] kept the fire burning all night. . . . The whole of the next day [we] were marching through snow, and many men were faint with hunger. . . . [I] went round the baggage animals, and if [I] found food anywhere gave . . . some to the sufferers. As soon as they had had a bite, up they got and marched on. (*Anabasis* 4.5)

Eventually, Xenophon and his companions reached the shores of the Black Sea, where several Greek cities were located. A number of men sailed or hiked from there to their home cities. In the years that followed, the *Anabasis* inspired a number of Greek orators and military leaders to contemplate conquering Persia; Xenophon's book had shown that even a relative few Greek soldiers could successfully fight their way through the heart of that land.

SEE ALSO: Persians; Xenophon

Anatolia

A term meaning "the East," used by the ancient Greeks, in addition to the term *Asia Minor*, to describe the large peninsula now occupied by Turkey.

SEE ALSO: Asia Minor

Anaxagoras
(ca. 500 B.C.–428 B.C.)

One of the leading early Greek philosopher-scientists. Anaxagoras hailed from Clazomenae in Ionia, but he moved to Athens in about 480 B.C. and remained there for roughly thirty years. He was friend and mentor to the much younger Euripides, who would later become a prominent playwright, as well as to the noted statesman Pericles. And the latter's enemies, hoping to hurt him politically, charged Anaxagoras with impiety (insulting or denying the existence of the gods). The philosopher did not wait for the trial but instead fled to Lampsacus in northwestern Asia Minor. As a scientist, Anaxagoras held that Earth was a large disk floating in the cosmos, with the Sun, the Moon, and other heavenly bodies moving around it. He also envisioned that the tiny "seeds" of all physical elements exist in all things (an idea perhaps influenced by the atomists). He pointed out, for example, that when people eat food they grow flesh, bones, and hair; thus, the seeds of flesh, bones, and hair must lurk, unseen, within the food people eat. His single book is lost, but small sections survive in fragments, including the following: "Things contain many ingredients of the very greatest variety—the seeds of everything, having all kinds of characteristics, colors, and ways of affecting the [human] sensitivities. . . . In everything there is a portion of everything else, except of mind; and in some things there is mind also." (fragments 4 and 11)

SEE ALSO: Euripides; Pericles; science

Anaximander
(early sixth century B.C.)

An important pre-Socratic Greek philosopher-scientist. A student of the Ionian thinker Thales, Anaximander proposed that the underlying substance of nature (the *physis*) was an invisible, eternal substance called the *apeiron*, which translates roughly as the "boundless" or "indefinite." This material, he said, of which all things were made, was both indestructible and eternal; and earth, water, air, and fire came from it. Anaximander also envisioned Earth as a vast cylinder standing upright, with humans and their environs existing on the cylinder's flat upper surface. The later Greek biographer Diogenes Laertius credited Anaximander with producing the first map of the world as well as a map of the night sky, although these feats remain unconfirmed.

SEE ALSO: science; Thales

Anaximenes
(ca. 585 B.C.–ca. 525 B.C.)

The last important member of the Ionian school of Greek philosophical-scientific thought. Anaximenes, a pupil of Anaximander, did not accept his teacher's proposal that nature's underlying principle, the *physis*, was a mysterious substance called the "boundless." Rather, Anaximenes said, *aër*, or "air," is the *physis*. As he saw it, air is constantly moving and can take many forms. Thin air gives rise to fire, he postulated, while condensed, or thicker, air gives rise to water and earth. Earth (the planet), which is flat, floats on a cushion of air in the cosmos, Anaximenes stated, and even the gods were generated by a form of air. All of his works are lost, although a handful of fragments survive in the works of later ancient writers. One of these expressions of primitive science is poetic in its stunning simplicity and beauty: "As our souls, being air, hold us together, so breath and air embrace the entire universe." (fragment 2)

SEE ALSO: Anaximander; science

Andromache

In Greek mythology, as well as Homer's *Iliad*, the wife of the Trojan hero Hector. In a moving scene in the *Iliad*, she and her small son Astyanax say good-bye to Hector just before he leaves to fight the Greek warrior Achilles. After the Greeks sacked Troy, they threw Astyanax off the city's battlements, and Achilles' son, Neoptolemus, took Andromache as his mistress. (Her relationship with him is the subject of Euripides' play *Andromache*.) A few years later, however, he died and she married the Trojan prophet Helenus. In her old age, the legends claim, Andromache returned to Asia Minor and there founded the city of Pergamum (one of the leading cities and kingdoms of the Hellenistic Age).

SEE ALSO: *Andromache* (play); Hector; Helenus

Andromache (play)

A play by Euripides, first presented in Athens circa 426 B.C. As the play opens, Andromache, former wife of the Trojan hero Hector, is living in Thessaly (in central Greece) as mistress to the Greek warrior Neoptolemus, now king of Thessaly. Tired of Andromache, Neoptolemus plans to wed Hermione, daughter of Sparta's King Menelaus. Childless, Hermione blames Andromache for her condition, claiming the Trojan woman has used black magic on her. Fearing that Hermione will have her killed, Andromache takes refuge in the shrine of the sea goddess Thetis, until Neoptolemus's grandfather, Peleus, ensures Andromache's safety. Then Orestes (son of Agamemnon, leader of the Greek expedition to Troy) arrives and reveals that Neoptolemus is dead. All are surprised when Thetis appears before them. The goddess announces that Andromache and her son (by Neoptolemus), Molossus, will go to northwestern Greece and become the wife and son of the Trojan prophet Helenus.

SEE ALSO: Andromache; Helenus; Neoptolemus

Antigone

In Greek mythology, a Theban princess who became a central figure in the turmoil following the attack on Thebes by the so-called Seven Against Thebes. A daughter of King Oedipus, Antigone went with and cared for him in his exile (self-imposed after he learned that he had unwittingly killed his father and married his own mother). Later, following Oedipus's death, Antigone returned to Thebes, where her brother Eteocles was now the ruler. Her other brother, Polynices, and his comrades (who together made up the Seven) assaulted the city, and the two brothers slew each other. Hearing that the new king, Creon, would not allow Polynices a proper burial, Antigone buried him herself. For this insolence, she was sentenced to die. Sophocles dramatized these mythical characters and events in his *Oedipus at Colonus* and *Antigone*, as did Euripides in a play about Antigone that is now lost.

SEE ALSO: *Antigone* (play); *Oedipus at Colonus*; *Oedipus the King*; *Seven Against Thebes*

Antigone (play)

A tragedy by Sophocles, first presented in Athens circa 441 B.C. The work is one of the playwright's three plays based on myths about the Theban ruler Oedipus (the other two being *Oedipus the King* and

Oedipus at Colonus). After Oedipus left Thebes and went into exile (accompanied by Antigone), his sons, Polynices and Eteocles, agreed to share power; but Eteocles reneged on the deal. So Polynices and six other leading Greeks (together called the Seven Against Thebes) attacked the city. Eteocles and Polynices fought and killed each other, after which Creon (their uncle), who had taken power, refused to give Polynices' body a decent burial. Antigone saw this as ethically wrong. In one of the play's early scenes, she tries to get her sister, Ismene, to help her bury the corpse, but Ismene refuses, saying, "We are only women. We cannot fight with men, Antigone! The law is strong. We must give into the law in this thing. . . . I beg the dead to forgive me, but I am helpless. I must yield to those in authority. And I think it is dangerous business to be always meddling." Antigone answers, "If that is what you think, I should not want you [to help me], even if you asked to come. You have made your choice. . . . I will bury him. And if I must die, I say that this crime is holy. I shall lie down with him in death and I shall be as dear to him as he [is] to me. It is the dead, not the living, who make the longest demands. . . . I will bury the brother I love." (*Antigone* 70–95)

After Antigone buries Polynices, the irate Creon condemns her to death. Haemon, Creon's son and Antigone's fiancé, begs his father to rescind the order. But Creon holds firm. He has a change of heart, however, after speaking with the blind prophet Teiresias, who tells him that what he is doing is wrong in the eyes of the gods. Creon hurries to the cave in which Antigone is awaiting her execution, but he is too late. To his regret, he finds that Antigone has hung herself, and Haemon now makes matters worse by com-

mitting suicide in front of his horrified father. More misfortune soon plagues Creon as his wife, Eurydice, having heard the news of her son's death, also takes her own life.

Sophocles' *Antigone* remains a powerful, unforgettable portrayal of human love and loyalty and of an individual having the courage of his or her convictions even in the face of certain death. The playwright seems to call on all human governments to honor the worth and dignity of each individual, for communities are nothing more than groups of individuals and are doomed if they cannot uphold the basic human rights of their own people. In one of the greatest of the author's many great speeches, the play's chorus declares:

> Wonders are many, but none more wonderful than human beings. . . . Speech and wind-swift thought, and all the moods that create a community, they have taught themselves. . . . Cunning beyond the wildest of dreams is the skill that leads them, sometimes to evil, other times to good. As long as they honor the laws of the land and revere the justice of the gods, proudly their community will stand. (*Antigone* 368–406)

SEE ALSO: Antigone; Creon, mythological king of Thebes; *Seven Against Thebes*; Teiresias

Antigonus I
(ca. 382 B.C.–301 B.C.)

One of the oldest and strongest of the Successors of Alexander the Great. Very little is known about Antigonus's life before he was in his sixties, except that he was a contemporary of King Philip II and came from a prestigious old Macedonian family. While fighting for Philip as a young man, he lost an eye, earning him the nickname of Monophthalmos, meaning "the One-Eyed." According to the ancient Greek writer Plutarch, "It was his habit to make fun of himself about his one eye and once, when he received a petition written in big letters, he said 'This is clear even to a blind man.'" (*Moralia* 633 C) Evidently Antigonus found it less humorous when other people joked about his handicap, for he was said to have had someone executed for calling him a Cyclops.

Antigonus marched with Alexander into Asia Minor in 334 B.C. and commanded the non-Macedonian Greek troops in the battle fought at the Granicus River. The following year Alexander made him governor of Phrygia (in central Asia Minor). Many people likely thought this would mark the high point of Antigonus's career, but he proved them wrong. After Alexander's death in 323, he and his brash, ambitious son, Demetrius (later called Poliorcetes, "the Besieger"), set out to gain control of the vast realm that the dead conqueror had carved out in a mere decade. Antigonus fought numerous battles with the other Successors and proclaimed himself king in 306. A tall, burly man who became overweight in his last years, he remained impressive and formidable, not only physically but also in manner. As Plutarch puts it, "It was his custom to show a lofty and aggressive spirit before he went into any action. He would speak in a loud voice and use arrogant language . . . and reveal his own assurance and the contempt he felt for his opponent." (*Life of Demetrius* 28) Despite his confidence and daring, Antigonus was defeated and killed at age eighty by a coalition of the other Successors at Ipsus in 301.

SEE ALSO: Alexander III ("the Great"); Battle of Granicus River; Battle of Ipsus; Demetrius Poliorcetes

Antigonus II Gonatas (ca. 320 B.C.–239 B.C.)

The founder of the Hellenistic Macedonian kingdom. Antigonus II was the son of Demetrius Poliorcetes and grandson of Antigonus I. Following Demetrius's death in a Seleucid prison in 283 B.C., Antigonus proclaimed himself king of Macedonia, which had been contested by several of the Successors over the course of the previous generation. But though he held the title of king, Antigonus was unable to unify the country under his rule until he drove away a marauding army of Celts in 277. In that year he established the Antigonid dynasty, which ruled Macedonia until its defeat by the Romans about a century later.

SEE ALSO: Antigonus I; Demetrius Poliorcetes; Macedonia

Antioch

From the early Hellenistic Age to the fall of Rome, one of the greatest cities of the Mediterranean world. Antioch was established in 300 B.C. by Seleucus, a leading Successor of Alexander the Great, on the Orontes River in northern Syria. Seleucus named it for his son, Antiochus. At first it was the capital of the Seleucid Syrian province, but as it grew to rival Alexandria, Egypt, in prosperity and cultural pursuits, it became the capital of the entire Seleucid Empire. (Like Alexandria, Antioch came to have a highly cosmopolitan population, with merchants and craftspeople from across the known world and a large Jewish quarter.) The Romans took over the city in 63 B.C., and thereafter it retained its importance as a center of trade and culture until an army of Persians sacked it in A.D. 538.

SEE ALSO: Alexandria; Seleucid Empire; Seleucus

Antiochus III
(ca. 242 B.C.–187 B.C.)

One of the most prominent and capable but also tragic rulers of the Hellenistic Seleucid kingdom. Antiochus became king after his brother, King Seleucus III, died in 223 B.C. Early in his reign Antiochus distinguished himself for retaking some territories on the Iranian plateau, in the eastern part of the empire, that his predecessors had lost to the Persians. He also made significant headway in Palestine against the Ptolemaic rulers, who vied with him for the region (although he lost the Battle of Raphia to Ptolemy IV). When he invaded Greece in 192 B.C., however, the Romans, who had recently defeated the Macedonian kingdom, viewed him as a dangerous threat to their interests. First they defeated him at Thermopylae and drove him from Greece; then they beat him at Magnesia (in Asia Minor) in 189. In a sad and ignoble end for a once great ruler, Antiochus was caught and slain by the inhabitants of a Mesopotamian town whose temple he was trying to rob.

SEE ALSO: battles of Magnesia, Raphia, Thermopylae, 3

Antipater
(397 B.C.–319 B.C.)

A leading Macedonian general under King Philip II and later one of the principal Successors of Alexander the Great. While Alexander was campaigning in Asia, Antipater administered Macedonia and Greece with the title of regent. Two rebellions shook Greece during his regency—one led by Sparta's King Agis III in 331 B.C., the other by Athens and some other city-states directly after Alexander's death in 323. Antipater handily thwarted both uprisings. Although he was now in his seventies, he tried, with the aid of his friend Antigonus (who had also started out with Philip), to keep Alexander's vast new domain intact as other Successors began to jockey for positions of power. He died in 319, however, before he could secure any lasting unity for the empire. Immediately after his passing, his son, Cassander, seized Macedonia and Greece and the bloody wars of the Successors began.

SEE ALSO: Alexander III ("the Great"); Antigonus I; Successors

Antiphon
(ca. 480 B.C.–411 B.C.)

A prominent Athenian orator known for the speeches he wrote for court litigants and for instigating a right-wing coup that almost overthrew Athens's government. Three of Antiphon's speeches, all of which were composed for capital murder cases, have survived. His talent as a writer and orator are attested by the historian Thucydides, who knew him and remarked:

> Antiphon was one of the ablest Athenians of his times. He had a most powerful intellect and was well able to express his thoughts in words. He never came forward to speak in front of the Assembly unless he could help it ... since the people in general mistrusted him because of his reputation for cleverness. On the other hand, when other people were engaged in lawsuits ... he was the man to give the best and most helpful advice. (*The Peloponnesian War* 8.68)

In 411 B.C. Antiphon led the so-called Four Hundred in their failed attempt to take over the government. After most of his fellow conspirators fled, he was sentenced to death. At his trial he delivered a speech in his own defense that Thucydides called the best ever given in Athens up to that time.

The goddess Venus, depicted in this famous statue, was the Roman equivalent of Aphrodite, the Greek goddess of love and beauty. © LARRY LEE PHOTOGRAPHY/CORBIS

SEE ALSO: Four Hundred; laws and justice; rhetoric

Aphrodite

In Greek mythology, the goddess of love and beauty. Aphrodite's symbols, which sculptors and painters routinely surrounded her with, included doves, dolphins, rams, and roses. In his *Theogony*, the Boeotian poet Hesiod claims she rose from a mass of sea foam that had been created when the genitals of the god Uranus (cut off by his son Cronos) had fallen into the water. The first dry land she reached was in Cyprus, so many splendid shrines dedicated to her were erected on that island. She married Hephaestos, god of the forge, but dallied behind his back with Ares, god of war. Aphrodite also had

affairs with the gods Dionysus, Poseidon, and Hermes as well as with a few mortal men. This gave her an untrustworthy, irresponsible image among Greek men, who saw her as a poor female role model. In contrast, many Greek women admired her for her independence and gumption. Perhaps the most famous story about Aphrodite is the Judgment of Paris, in which she vied with the goddesses Hera and Athena for the title of "fairest of the goddesses." The official prize was a golden apple. The judge, the Trojan prince Paris, chose Aphrodite, after which she rewarded him by aiding him on several occasions during the Trojan War.

SEE ALSO: Ares; Hephaestos; Paris

Apollo

As told in Greek mythology, of all the Greek deities who dwelled atop Mt. Olympus, Apollo was the most well rounded. In addition to being the god of the prophecy, he oversaw poetry, music, shepherds, archery, colonization, and the healing arts. His principal symbol was the laurel tree. Apollo's mother, Leto, one of the first-race of gods known as Titans, mated with Zeus, leader of the Olympian gods, and soon afterward Apollo was born on the Aegean island of Delos. After growing to maturity, the young god searched for the right spot to establish an oracle (a place where a priestess, also called an oracle, would transmit his prophecies to humans). He found that spot at Delphi, in central Greece. As the legends say, not long after Apollo set up the Delphic Oracle, the Greeks began to stage musical contests and athletic games in his honor at Delphi (called the Pythian games after the Pythia, the title the god had given to priestesses of his temple there).

Many ancient myths featured Apollo

as either a major or minor character. In one, he and his sister Artemis, goddess of the hunt, killed the children of Niobe, a woman who had insulted Leto. Apollo also allowed a man named Admetus to escape death by finding someone else to die for him. (Admetus's wife, Alcestis, volunteered to die in her husband's place but was saved at the last moment by the hero Heracles.) In addition, Apollo built the walls of Troy with the aid of Poseidon, god of the seas; helped the Trojans in their famous war against the Greeks, including guiding the arrow that Troy's Prince Paris shot into the heel of the Greek hero Achilles; and defended the mortal Orestes, who had slain his own mother, Clytemnestra, in a trial overseen by the goddess Athena, a myth dramatized by Aeschylus in his play the *Eumenides*. It is unknown when worship of Apollo began in Greece. Some scholars think that the Dorian Greeks (who originated in the region north of Greece) introduced him in the early Dark Age. Others think he came from Asia Minor and entered the Greek lands by way of Ionia. In addition to the Delphic shrine, he had oracles in Ionia, on Delos, and elsewhere and was widely respected and prayed to throughout the Greek world (and eventually the Roman lands, too, after the Romans added him to their own pantheon of gods).

SEE ALSO: Artemis; Athena; Delos; Delphi; *Eumenides*; Paris; Troy

Apollodorus of Athens (flourished ca. 140 B.C.)

A Greek scholar known for composing several important historical and religious works. After studying at the Museum in Alexandria, where one of his teachers was the astronomer Aristarchus, Apollodorus moved to Athens. There he penned his best-known work, the *Chronicle*, which listed noteworthy events dating from the fall of Troy (which he thought happened in 1184 B.C.) to his own time. He also wrote *On the Gods*, a book explaining how the gods were worshipped. These works are lost, except for a few fragments. Apollodorus was also long credited with writing an encyclopedia of Greek mythology, called *The Library*, but evidence suggests that he was not the author.

SEE ALSO: Aristarchus of Samos; historical writing

Apollonius of Rhodes (ca. 295 B.C.–215 B.C.)

A famous Hellenistic Greek poet and scholar best known for his definitive written version of the mythical quest for the Golden Fleece. Apollonius (or Apollonius Rhodius) tutored Ptolemy III in Alexandria and also ran the Great Library there before moving permanently to the island of Rhodes. The best known of his works is his epic poem the *Argonautica* (*Voyage of the Argo*), which retells the famous story of Jason, the Argonauts, and their search for the Golden Fleece, which they find in the faraway land of Colchis. According to tradition, Apollonius got into a literary feud with one of his teachers (and an eventual colleague), the poet Callimachus, over the proper length of poetry. Supposedly Callimachus preferred short poems and criticized the younger man for aspiring to write epic poems having thousands of lines.

SEE ALSO: Alexandria; *Argonautica*; Callimachus, 2

Apology

One of Plato's most important works, more fully titled *Apologia Sokratous*, meaning *Speech in Defense of Socrates* because it purports to quote the speech made by Socrates to his jurors at his famous trial in Athens in 399 B.C. It remains uncertain how much of the work represents Socrates' own words and how much represents Plato's embellishments and additions; however, modern scholars believe it is a fairly reliable paraphrase of what the condemned philosopher actually said. In the *Apology*, Socrates questions his chief accuser, Meletus, and easily manipulates him, revealing the man's incompetence. Then Socrates confronts the charge that he worships gods other than those accepted by the state. He tricks Meletus into calling him an atheist. Then, in a brilliant display of logical reasoning, the philosopher shows that this and the charge against him cannot both be true at the same time. Next, Socrates strikes a defiant tone and tells the court that, no matter what its verdict, he will continue his mission of preaching virtue to his fellow Athenians. "Men of Athens," he says,

> I honor and love you; but I shall obey God rather than you, and while I have life and strength I shall never cease from the practice and teaching of philosophy, appealing to anyone whom I meet ... to interrogate and examine and cross-examine him, and if I think that he has no virtue in him, but only says that he has, I will reproach him. And I shall repeat the same words to every one whom I meet, young and old, citizen and alien, but especially to the citizens, since they are my brethren. For know that this is the command of God. ... For I do nothing but go around persuading you all ... to care most about improving your souls. I say that money does not bring virtue, but rather that from being virtuous one can attain money and many other good things. This is

the message that I teach, and if this is the philosophy that corrupts the youth, then I am a bad person. ... Either acquit me or not. But whichever you do, understand that I shall never alter my ways, not even if you kill me over and over again! (*Apology* 29–30)

Later in the speech Socrates suggests that the jurors should sentence him to pay a fine. But they view this as arrogant and sentence him to death. Seeing that his friends are distraught at hearing the sentence, he tries to comfort them, delivering one of the most insightful and beautiful passages of ancient literature:

> There is great reason to think that death is a good thing for one of two reasons. Either death is a state of nothingness and utter unconsciousness, or ... there is a change and migration of the soul from this world to another. Now, if you suppose that there is no consciousness, but a sleep ... death will be an unspeakable gain ... for eternity is then only a single night. But if death is the journey to another place, and there ... all the dead abide, what good ... can be greater than that? ... I shall then be able to continue my search into true and false knowledge. ... And I shall find out who is wise, and who pretends to be wise, and is not. ... In another world they do not put a man to death for asking questions. ... Be of good cheer about death, and know of a certainty that no evil can happen to a good man, either in life or after death. The hour of departure has arrived and we go our separate ways—I to die, and you to live. Which of these is better, only God knows. (*Apology* 40–42).

SEE ALSO: Plato; Socrates

aqueducts

Artificial channels that carried water from springs, rivers, or lakes to towns.

SEE ALSO: water supplies

Arcadia

The central region of the Peloponnesus, the large peninsula making up the southern third of the Greek mainland. Arcadia was highly rural and hilly and had few large towns outside of Mantinea, Tegea, and Megalopolis, the latter built in the fourth century B.C. after the Thebans, led by Epaminondas, liberated the Peloponnesus from Spartan domination. Because of its rugged, pastoral setting, the area became known for its supposedly rustic virtues and its shrines dedicated to woodland gods such as Pan. The people of Arcadia spoke a dialect of Greek that a number of modern scholars think is related to that of the Bronze Age Mycenaeans. Traditionally poor, hardworking farmers, the Arcadians of the Classical and Hellenistic ages had a reputation for being tough and resilient, and the region produced many top-notch mercenary soldiers.

SEE ALSO: Mantinea; Sparta; Tegea

Archaic Age

As determined by modern scholars, the period of ancient Greece lasting from about 800 to 500 B.C. For the major events and figures of the period,

SEE ALSO: Greece, history of

Archidamus II
(reigned ca. 470–ca. 427 B.C.)

A Spartan king who opposed his country's entry into the Peloponnesian War but who led its troops in that conflict once war

became a reality. Archidamus, who belonged to the Eurypontid royal house, was on the throne when Sparta was hit by a violent earthquake in 464 B.C. And he helped to put down the insurrection staged by the Spartan serfs (the helots) in the wake of that disaster. Later he correctly foresaw that a major war between Sparta and Athens would end up hurting both states, along with their respective allies, and urged his countrymen not to declare war. But when they did, he reluctantly but dutifully invaded Attica several times between 431 and 428 B.C. He was such a major player in the war's early years that historians often call that phase of the conflict "the Archidamian War."

SEE ALSO: helots; Peloponnesian War; Sparta

Archilochus
(mid-fifth century B.C.)

An important early Greek poet who hailed from the Aegean island of Paros. Little is known about Archilochus's life, except for what he revealed in his poems, including that he took part in the colonization of the northern Aegean island of Thasos. He fought in various battles, perhaps as a mercenary, in the northern Aegean. His most famous poem tells, with a touch of humor, how he once discarded his shield while retreating: "Well, what if some barbaric Thracian glories in the perfect shield I left under a bush? I was sorry to leave it—but I saved my skin. Does it matter? O hell, I'll buy a better one!" ("On His Shield") This and Archilochus's other works have survived only in fragments on bits of papyrus and in quotations by later ancient writers. His poems vary in tone from lighthearted, like the above example, to sad and pessimistic. In an example of

The Greek mathematician and inventor Archimedes oversees a demonstration of his famous screw, a device that raised water from one level to another. TIME LIFE PICTURES/ GETTY IMAGES

the latter, he laments, "I live here miserable and broken with desire, pierced through to the bones by the bitterness of the god-given painful love. O comrade, this passion makes my limbs limp and tramples over me." ("Love") Archilochus was sometimes so bold and frank in expressing his personal feelings that the Spartans banned his poetry in their territory because of what they viewed as offensive language.

SEE ALSO: Paros; poetry; Thasos

Archimedes
(ca. 287 B.C.–212 B.C.)

Widely viewed as the greatest mathematician and one of the leading inventors of

antiquity. Archimedes, who hailed from Syracuse (the chief Greek city on the island of Sicily), probably became interested in math and science because his father, Pheidias, was an astronomer who tried to measure the distances to the Sun and the Moon. As a young man Archimedes studied with other scientists in Alexandria, including Conon of Samos and Eratosthenes, before returning to his homeland permanently. The historian Plutarch said he was related somehow to Hiero II, who ruled Syracuse from about 265 to 216 B.C. Hiero recognized Archimedes' talents and urged him to use them for the benefit of the city and its people. In a well-known story about the two men, Hiero ordered a new crown to be made of pure gold; but when it was delivered he suspected that the contractor had cheated him by mixing some cheaper silver with the gold. In an effort to test the crown, Archimedes discovered what became known as Archimedes' principle. He dunked the crown in water, measured the volume of water displaced by the crown, made a piece of gold with the same volume, and found that the gold and crown did not weigh the same, only possible if the crown was not pure gold. In this way Archimedes showed that every object or substance has a specific density, and that the force that buoys up a body suspended in a fluid equals the weight of the fluid the body displaces. This law of buoyancy later proved vital to the sciences of shipbuilding and aeronautics.

Archimedes also experimented with levers and provided elegant mathematical proofs for how various weights placed at varying distances from the fulcrum of a lever will balance or not balance. According to tradition, these efforts led him to tell Hiero, "Give me a place to stand on and I can move the world," meaning that if he had a large enough lever he could lift the earth using only the power of his own muscles. Hiero demanded a practical demonstration. And as Plutarch tells it:

> Archimedes chose for his demonstration a three-masted merchantman [cargo ship] of the royal fleet, which had been hauled ashore . . . and he proceeded to have the ship loaded with her usual freight and embarked a large number of passengers. He then seated himself at some distance away and without using any noticeable force, but merely exerting traction with his hand through a complex system of pulleys, he drew the vessel towards him with as smooth and even a motion as if she were gliding through the water. (*Life of Marcellus* 14)

Archimedes designed other mechanical devices, including the first-known mechanical planetarium, with globes representing the Moon, Sun, and planets; the water screw (or "Archimedes' screw") a sort of pump that made it easier to raise water from one level to another; and some spectacular war machines. The latter were supposedly designed to defend Syracuse against an attack by the Romans in 213–212 B.C. According to Plutarch:

> Archimedes brought his engines [giant catapults] to bear and launched a tremendous barrage against the Roman army. . . . There was no protection against this artillery, and the soldiers were knocked down in swathes and their ranks thrown into confusion. At the same time huge beams were run out from the walls so as to project over the Roman ships. Some of them were . . . seized at the bows by iron claws or by beaks like those of cranes, hauled into the air by means of counterweights until they stood upright upon their sterns, and

> then allowed to plunge . . . [until they were] dashed against the steep cliffs and rocks which jutted out under the walls, with great loss of life to the crews. (*Life of Marcellus* 15)

Archimedes' antisiege devices were so effective that the Roman commander, Marcellus, ordered several retreats. He deeply respected the inventor and gave strict orders that Archimedes should not be harmed. However, when the Romans attacked again, one of them failed to recognize Archimedes and killed him. After the city fell, Marcellus gave the scientist a proper burial and made sure that the tomb bore the inscription the deceased himself had earlier chosen—an illustration of what Archimedes viewed as his greatest discovery, the ratio of the volume of a cylinder to that of a sphere.

SEE ALSO: Hiero II; science; Syracuse

architectural orders

Basic styles or motifs used by the Greeks and other ancient peoples in construction, most often in public buildings. Three principal orders developed in Greece in the period spanning the late Archaic and early Hellenistic ages—the Doric, Ionic, and Corinthian. The first two, which, respectively, were the oldest, were at first used exclusively for temples. But over time, other kinds of structures—such as treasuries, fountain houses, meeting halls, and large public altars—borrowed the architectural orders. Each order was essentially an artistic style expressed most overtly in the ornamental details of the columns that held up a building's roof. Before the sixth century B.C. these columns were made of wood, and the ornamental details were carved into the tops and/or bottoms of the columns. When temples and other public buildings switched to stone construction, tradition was maintained by copying these details in the stone versions.

The Doric order originated on the Greek mainland in cities that legend claimed had, in the dim past, been settled by the Dorians, such as Corinth. In this order, the capitals (tops) of the columns had simple, rectangular slabs and the bottoms had no decorative bases. In a Doric structure, the frieze (band of sculptures or paintings running above the colonnade) was broken up into separate rectangular panels called metopes.

The Ionic order first appeared in Ionian Greek cities such as Miletus and Ephesus and may have been influenced by Near Eastern decorative motifs. The columns had capitals decorated with volutes (curved scrolls or swirls) and featured decorative bases. Also, an Ionic frieze was a continuous, uninterrupted band. The most famous Ionic frieze is the one that originally graced the upper inside of the Parthenon's outer colonnade; however, the Parthenon also had a Doric frieze, as well as Doric columns, showing that architectural orders were sometimes mixed in a single structure.

The most ornate order, the Corinthian, developed in southern Greece, especially the Peloponnesus, in the fourth century B.C. as a more elegant variant of the Ionic. Corinthian column capitals were covered with curled masonry acanthus leaves. Impressed by the complexity and elegance of the Corinthian order, the Romans later adopted it for their own public buildings. And many centuries later, beginning in the Renaissance, European architects applied all three orders to the interiors and exteriors of all sorts of public and private structures. These orders remain in use today in banks, town halls, government buildings, and private mansions, to name

only a few examples.

SEE ALSO: building materials and methods; Parthenon; temples

archon

In Athens and a number of other Greek states, a government administrator who carried out the policies set by an assembly or ruling council.

SEE ALSO: government

Areopagus

A hill in Athens on which an important early legislative body of the same name met. Situated a few hundred feet west of the Acropolis, the Areopagus got its name (which means "Hill of Ares") from a mythical incident in which Ares, god of war, was tried there for slaying the son of Poseidon, god of the seas. The hill was supposedly also the site where the goddess Athena oversaw the trial of Orestes, who had murdered his mother, Clytemnestra. In real life the Areopagus was established perhaps during the late Dark Age as a combination of ruling council and law court. It became both aristocratic and highly conservative, which eventually put its members at odds with the democratic movement that grew in the city in late Archaic times. The reforms of Solon in the early sixth century B.C. weakened the Areopagus, and in the following century, the democratic reformers Ephialtes and Pericles stripped it of most of the rest of its powers. From the 450s B.C. on, it was mainly a special law court that heard murder cases.

SEE ALSO: Athens; government; Solon

Ares

The Greek god of war, often portrayed in art with one or more of his symbols—a burning torch, a spear, dogs, and vultures.

In Greek mythology, Ares was the son of Zeus, leader of the Olympian gods, and his wife, Hera. Ares never married, but he did take lovers, the most famous being Aphrodite, goddess of love. According to legend, their daughter, Harmonia, married Cadmus, founder of Thebes; they also had twin sons—Phobos ("Panic") and Deimos ("Fear")—who sometimes fought alongside their father in battle. Although he was acknowledged as a fearsome warrior, Ares was not as smart as most of the other gods, who easily outwitted him on a number of occasions. He also quarreled with some of his fellow Olympians. During the Trojan War, for example, Ares backed the Trojans while Athena, goddess of war, supported the Greeks. She insulted him repeatedly, goading him into hurling his spear at her, and when the weapon bounced off her breastplate, she knocked him down with a huge stone.

SEE ALSO: Aphrodite; Athena; Zeus

arete

No exact equivalent for this Greek word and important concept exists in English, but it is commonly translated as "personal excellence." In early Greek society, *arete* seems to have meant warlike valor. But over time it came to mean heroic strength, courage, and virtue as well, especially among aristocrats. In Homer's epics, as well as in the works of classical writers such as Aristotle, the term was also associated with feelings of personal pride and honor.

SEE ALSO: Homer

Argonautica

An epic poem by the Hellenistic Greek writer Apollonius of Rhodes about the mythical quest for the Golden Fleece, and the first ancient Greek literary work to explore the subject of romantic love from a woman's point of view. The *Argonautica* consists of four books. In the first, Jason, who sees himself as the rightful king of Iolcos in Thessaly, arranges for a ship. He finds the *Argo*, built by the master shipwright Argus. And Jason and the vessel's crew, thereafter called the Argonauts, ready themselves for the journey to the distant land of Colchis, said to harbor the fabulous fleece of a magical ram created by Zeus. Among the Argonauts are some of the strongest and noblest men of Greece, including the mighty hero Heracles (called Hercules by the Romans); the musician and singer Orpheus; the warrior Peleus (father of Achilles, the central character of Homer's *Iliad*); Zetes and Calais, the sons of Boreas, the North Wind; and Zeus's twin sons, Castor and Polydeuces (later called the Dioscuri). When all the preparations are made, the Argonauts confirm Jason as their leader and set sail from Iolcos in hopes of recovering the Golden Fleece.

The Journey to Colchis

In the second book of the *Argonautica*, Jason and his men have various adventures while on their way to Colchis. On the coast of Bithynia in Asia Minor, Heracles' oar breaks, and he and his faithful companion, Hylas, go ashore to find wood to carve a new one. But Hylas becomes lost and Heracles refuses to leave until he has found his friend. Thus, Jason is forced to continue the voyage without the famous strongman. Later the Argonauts encounter and help a starving old man named Phineus who is being harassed by the Harpies, who keep fouling his food, making it inedible. To thwart the disgusting creatures, Jason calls on the Argonauts Zetes and Calais, who have the ability to fly. The other Argonauts prepare a tasty feast for Phineus while Zetes and Calais take up positions on either side of the old man, ready to strike. "Phineus had scarcely lifted the first morsel [of food]," Apollonius writes, when "the Harpies dropped from the clouds proclaiming their desire for food with raucous cries. [Before the warriors could react], the Harpies had devoured the whole meal and were on the wing once more, far out to sea. All they left behind was an intolerable stench. . . . Raising their swords, the two sons of the North Wind flew off in pursuit." (*Argonautica* 2.271–278) Zetes and Calais manage to catch up to the Harpies and are about to slay them when Iris, goddess of the rainbow and sister of the creatures, appears. She says that if Zetes and Calais spare the Harpies, she will keep them away from old Phineus. Iris keeps her word, and Phineus is thereafter able to eat his meals without fear of the Harpies. Meanwhile, the Argonauts depart to continue their journey, which includes a moment of extreme danger as they pass through the Symplegades ("Clashing Rocks") at the north end of the Bosphorus Strait.

Jason and Medea

The third section of the *Argonautica* chronicles the events in Colchis after Jason's arrival there. He meets Medea, who is the daughter of the local king, Aeetes, and also a sorceress. Aeetes, who hates foreigners, does not want to surrender the Golden Fleece and comes up with a scheme that he hopes will cause Jason's death. Aeetes says that anyone who desires the fleece must first prove his courage by yoking two fire-breathing bulls and using them to plow dragon teeth into the earth. After the seeds have grown into an army of warriors, the person must fight and defeat them. Fortunately for Jason, Medea

has fallen in love with him, and she betrays her own father by helping the Argonauts. She gives Jason a vial containing a magic liquid. By rubbing this substance on his body and weapons, he is able to yoke the bulls, defeat the seed-warriors, and pass Aeetes' test.

In the fourth book of Apollonius's epic, Aeetes still resists giving up the fleece. But with more help from Medea, Jason makes it past the fearsome serpent that guards the fleece, grabs the golden prize, and he, Medea, and the Argonauts escape from Colchis. The travelers head for Greece, but on the way they must deal with more dangers. Among these is an encounter with the famous Sirens, treacherous female creatures that use lovely songs to lure sailors to their deaths. Jason manages to get past the deadly women by playing his lyre so loudly that his music drowns out the Sirens' voices. Then the Argonauts meet Talos, a bronze giant who guards the coastline of Crete. Talos hurls huge boulders at the Greeks until Medea casts a spell on the giant and removes a bronze nail from his heel, draining his lifeblood. Finally, the Argonauts make it back to their starting point in Iolcos.

One of the most remarkable qualities of Apollonius's epic at the time it was written was its portrayal of Medea. In contrast to Euripides' treatment of her (in his play *Medea*) as a scheming murderess, Apollonius presents her in a more sympathetic manner, emphasizing her love for Jason and her conflicting emotions as she must choose between him and her father. This vivid depiction of romantic love influenced later ancient writers, including the great Roman epic poet Virgil.

SEE ALSO: Apollonius of Rhodes; Jason, 1; Medea

Argonauts

The band of intrepid sailors and soldiers who accompany the hero Jason on his ship, the *Argo*, in the legendary quest for the Golden Fleece.

SEE ALSO: *Argonautica*; Jason, 1

Argos

A Greek town and city-state situated in the region of Argolis in the northeastern sector of the Peloponnesus. In the Bronze Age the area was a major Mycenaean stronghold dominated by the formidable stone citadels of Mycenae and Tiryns. In mythology, as well as in Homer's *Iliad*, the city of Argos was ruled by the Greek hero Diomedes, who owed allegiance to the king of Mycenae, Agamemnon. Also, the mythical House of Atreus, which came under a terrible, generations-long curse, was said to have been based either at Argos or Mycenae. In fact, Argos and Mycenae were frequently closely associated, or even used interchangeably, in myths. This suggests that after Mycenae declined in the final years of the Bronze Age, nearby Argos completely replaced it as the chief town in the region, absorbing much of its heritage in the process. Indeed, during the Dark Age (ca. 1100–ca. 800 B.C.), Argos became the strongest city in the Peloponnesus. Early in that period, the town was settled by Dorian Greeks who had entered the mainland from the north, and Argos became a major Dorian base of operations. The Argives (as its citizens were called) enjoyed great power and influence for at least four centuries. But in the sixth century B.C. Sparta and Corinth gained preeminence in the Peloponnesus and Argos declined in importance. In 494 B.C. the Spartans delivered the Argives a crushing defeat, further damaging their prestige. Probably because of its enmity for Sparta,

Argos took Athens's side in the fifth century B.C. and installed an Athenian-style democracy. In early Hellenistic times, Argos was often dominated by Macedonia. But in 229 B.C. the Argives joined the Achaean League and remained loyal members until Rome disbanded the league in 146 B.C.

SEE ALSO: Mycenae; Mycenaeans; Sparta

Aristagoras
(died 497 B.C.)

A ruler of the Ionian city of Miletus who played a major role in the events leading up to the Greco-Persian Wars. He was the chief instigator of the Ionian rebellion against the Persians in 499 B.C. and was able to convince the mainland cities of Athens and Eretria to help the Ionian cause. (For that help, the Persian king Darius I swore to get revenge on Athens and Eretria, which eventually led to the Battle of Marathon.) Aristagoras also tried to get the backing of Sparta but failed. As recalled by the historian Herodotus, Aristagoras showed the Spartan king, Cleomenes, a map of the world and begged him to help free the Ionian Greeks from Persian tyranny. Cleomenes at first seemed interested, but then

> he asked Aristagoras how far off [the Persian capital of] Susa was, and how many days it took to reach it from the Ionian coast. . . . In answering this question, Aristagoras made a bad mistake. If he wanted to induce the Spartans to invade Asia, he never ought to have told the truth. But he did and said it took three months. Cleomenes stopped Aristagoras from saying any more. . . . "Milesian," he cried, "you must leave Sparta before sunset. Your proposal to take Spartans [on] a three-months' journey from the

sea is a highly improper one." (*The Histories 5.52*)

After the Persians put down the Ionian rebellion, Aristagoras fled northward to Thrace, where he died soon afterward.

SEE ALSO: Darius I; Greco-Persian Wars; Ionia

Aristarchus of Samos (early third century B.C.)

A Greek astronomer best known for proposing that Earth revolves around the Sun. This thesis, proven in early modern times to be correct, was rejected by other ancient scholars in favor of the geocentric (Earth-centered) view because the Sun-centered view seemed to go against the "evidence" of direct observation. Most of Aristarchus's written works have not survived, and much of what is known about him and his ideas comes from the works of other ancient writers, notably Archimedes' *Sand-Reckoner*.

SEE ALSO: astronomy

Aristarchus of Samothrace (ca. 215 B.C.–ca. 143 B.C.)

A Hellenistic Greek often credited with being the first professional literary scholar. Little is known about his life, outside of the fact that he worked in Alexandria and briefly served as director of its famous library. His scholarly treatises included critical commentaries on Homer's epics as well as on the works of Hesiod, Pindar, and the leading Athenian playwrights.

SEE ALSO: Alexandrian and other Hellenistic Greek literature

Aristides (ca. 530 B.C.–ca. 467 B.C.)

During the turbulent years of the Greco-Persian Wars and their immediate after-math, a prominent Athenian general and statesman who was known as Aristides the Just for his honesty and fairness. Aristides was one of the ten generals who led Athens's troops against the invading Persians at Marathon in 490 B.C. In the wake of that battle he became a political rival of Themistocles, who may have been behind Aristides' ostracism in 482. Two years later the Athenians recalled Aristides from exile to help defend the city against the second Persian invasion of Greece. He also fought with distinction in the battles of Salamis and Plataea. Following the expulsion of the Persians, Aristides liberated Cyprus from Persian control and played a major role in the creation of the Delian League, a huge coalition of Greek states intended to protect Greece from further Persian attacks. The most famous story about Aristides recalls an incident that took place during his ostracism vote. He encountered a rural peasant who could not read or write and did not recognize him. The man asked him to write the name Aristides on his *ostrakon* (a pottery shard on which he recorded his vote). The general "asked the man what harm Aristides had ever done to him," Plutarch later wrote. "None whatever," the farmer replied. "I don't even know the fellow, but I am sick of hearing him called 'the Just' everywhere!" (*Life of Aristides* 7) Saying nothing, Aristides wrote his name on the *ostrakon*, handed it back to the man, and went on his way.

SEE ALSO: battles of Marathon, Plataea, and Salamis; Greco-Persian Wars; Themistocles

Aristophanes (ca. 445 B.C.–ca. 385 B.C.)

The greatest Greek comic playwright of the fifth century B.C. Very little is known about Aristophanes' personal life, other than that he was born in Athens. A remark in one of his plays hints that he was a landowner, and the plots and tone of most of his works suggest that, politically speaking, he was antiwar and at least suspicious of radical democracy since he often lampoons abuses of power by the Assembly and popular demagogues.

Aristophanes' eleven surviving plays (out of a total of about thirty he is said to have composed) are the only complete examples of the Athenian Old Comedy (the theatrical period roughly encompassing the second half of the fifth century B.C.) that now exist. They are: *Acharnians* (produced in 425 B.C.), *Knights* (424), *Clouds* (423), *Wasps* (422), *Peace* (421), *Birds* (414), *Lysistrata* (411), *Women Celebrating the Thesmophoria* (411), *Frogs* (405), *Women in the Assembly* (392), and *Plutus* (382). The settings and plots of these plays are for the most part fanciful, yet they satirize Athens, its people, and its leading figures in ways that were immediately obvious to ancient Athenian playgoers. Aristophanes was unafraid, uncompromising, and unrelenting in his witty, satiric, at times even vicious attacks on government institutions and prominent politicians and military leaders. In *Knights*, he harshly ridicules Cleon, a staunch supporter of the Peloponnesian War; in *Clouds*, he mocks the philosopher Socrates, portraying him as a corruptive influence on the people; and in *Lysistrata*, the playwright hammers home his antiwar message by depicting a sex strike staged by Athens's women to force their husbands to stop fighting.

SEE ALSO: theater and drama; titles of individual plays

Aristophanes
(flourished early second century B.C.)

A director of the Great Library at Alexandria, who is sometimes referred to as Aristophanes of Byzantium to differentiate him from the famous playwright of the same name. The later Aristophanes was noted for compiling new editions of classic works by Homer, Hesiod, Pindar, and other Greek literary masters. These versions contained critical commentary as well as corrections of errors that had crept into the texts over the centuries.

SEE ALSO: Alexandrian and other Hellenistic Greek literature

Aristotle
(384 B.C.–322 B.C.)

One of the greatest philosophers and scholars of the ancient world, whose ideas and written works exerted a lasting and profound influence on intellectual thought and endeavors in later ages. Aristotle was born at Stagira (on the Chalcidic Peninsula in the northern Aegean), so in spite of spending much of his life in Athens, he was never an Athenian citizen. He ended up in Athens because his father, Nicomachus, a physician to King Amyntas II of Macedonia, encouraged him to pursue higher learning, and the most prestigious school in the Greek sphere at the time was Plato's Academy in Athens. Aristotle spent twenty years there, at first as a student and later as an instructor, and became close to Plato. Following Plato's death in 347 B.C., the younger man traveled to northwestern Asia Minor and founded a school of his own there. Later he moved to the island of Lesbos and established another school. Aristotle also married a young woman named Pythias, who died prematurely only a few years later.

A nineteenth-century engraving shows Aristotle tutoring the young Macedonian prince Alexander III (later called "the Great"). NORTH WIND PICTURE ARCHIVES

During these years Aristotle became so well known as a scholar that in 343 B.C. Macedonia's King Philip II asked him to tutor the thirteen-year-old crown prince, Alexander III (later called "the Great"). Aristotle did so and wrote two treatises for the young man—*On Colonists* and *On Kingship*, now both lost. He also gave Alexander a personally edited version of Homer's *Iliad*, which the prince kept with him for the rest of his life.

In about 335 B.C. Aristotle returned to Athens and established his most important school, the Lyceum, a university-like institution that included both general and advanced classes. The school was supported by a huge monetary grant from Alexander and protected by Macedonian troops. This allowed Aristotle to vigorously lecture, write, conduct experiments, and explore the intricacies of politics, logic, law, physics, ethics, literary criticism, and other intellectual disciplines that fascinated him. His extraordinary scholarly endeavors were cut short, however, when Alexander died in 323 B.C. As a wave of anti-

Macedonian sentiment swept through Greece, Aristotle's association with the young conqueror now placed him in disrepute. He was forced to flee Athens to the island of Euboea, where the following year he died at the age of sixty-two.

During the busy twelve years he had spent at the Lyceum, Aristotle produced the bulk of his most influential written works. Almost all were published and a number of later ancient writers, including the Roman orator Cicero, praised them as stylish, witty, and very readable. Most of these works did not survive, however. The vast majority of those that did survive, sometimes called his "esoteric writings," are probably lecture notes compiled either by him or his students. Dry, formal, and difficult to read, they nevertheless provide a useful overview of his basic ideas. He upheld the view of earlier Greek scientists that all matter was composed of four basic elements—earth, water, air, and fire, but he added a fifth element—"ether," from which, he asserted, the heavenly bodies were made. Aristotle also agreed with those of his predecessors who had argued that Earth is a sphere floating at the center of the cosmos.

Aristotle's work in zoology and biology was much more revolutionary. He collected, dissected, and carefully studied thousands of specimens of animals, both alive and dead, and made numerous important observations in comparative anatomy, ethology (animal habits), embryology (pre-birth development), and ecology (the relation of animals to their environment), in the process virtually creating these scientific disciplines. Among other things, he established that whales and dolphins are mammals like people, described the four-chambered stomachs of cows, observed the stirrings of a baby chick in its egg, and invented a system of zoological classification that categorized the known animal species by type. His *History of Animals* and *Generation of Animals* are filled with observations and comparisons of the bodies of animals and humans, such as the following one on the eye:

> Of the eye, the white is pretty much the same in all creatures. But what is called the iris differs. In some it is black, in some distinctly blue, in some grayish-blue, in some greenish, and this last color is . . . well adapted for sharpness of vision. Man is the only, or nearly the only, creature that has eyes of diverse colors. The others have eyes of one color only . . . [although] some horses have blue eyes. (*History of Animals* 1.10)

For these efforts, later generations of scientists came to call Aristotle "the Father of Biology."

Aristotle's contributions in some other intellectual disciplines were no less far-reaching. In the field of logic (from a Greek term meaning "the art of reasoning"), as revealed in his *Prior Analytics*, he examines and explains the known forms of syllogism, a method of deduction. (A basic example would be: A. All dogs have four legs; B. Rover is a dog; C. Therefore, Rover has four legs.) In his *Metaphysics*, Aristotle examines the concept of divine intelligence and concludes that if God exists, he is an "unmoved mover," a universal intelligence having no interest in humans and earthly events. And in his *Nicomachean Ethics* (supposedly edited after his death by his son, Nicomachus), he attempts to define ethical concepts, including happiness and virtue. The attainment of happiness, he says, is the best of human endeavors. And "human good turns out to be an activity of soul in conformity with excellence, and if there is more than one form of excellence, in conformity with the best and most complete one." (*Nicomachean Ethics* 1.7)

Aristotle's impact on later generations of scientists, philosophers, churchmen, political leaders, and teachers alike, right up to the twentieth century, was nothing less than enormous. As noted modern classical scholar Michael Grant puts it, it was from Aristotle that

> philosophers and scientists of one generation after another have derived their . . . terminology which has entered into the inherited vocabulary of educated men and women, so that we employ these terms continually without any longer recalling their source. He has been seen throughout the ages as the supreme scholar pursuing the life of the intellect for its own sake, and his posthumous prestige has been more enduring than any other thinker's. (*The Classical Greeks*, p. 262)

SEE ALSO: Academy; Alexander III ("the Great"); Lyceum; Plato; science; and the names of individual works

Arrian
(born ca. A.D. 90)

A Greek historian who hailed from the Roman province of Bithynia in Asia Minor. Because his father was a Roman citizen, Arrian was, too, and his Roman name was Flavius Arrianus. As a young man, Arrian entered the Roman civil service and quickly rose through the ranks, eventually becoming a confidant of the emperor Hadrian and governor of a Roman province. Outside of politics, Arrian's passion was history, and he is most famous for his *Anabasis Alexandri* (*Alexander's March Up-Country*), the most complete and reliable surviving source describing the conquests of Alexander the Great. The work was based largely on now-lost histories by Alexander's general Ptolemy and one of Alexander's engineers. For this reason, modern scholars consider much of Arrian's well-written account to be reasonably accurate. Most of Arrian's other works, including *Events After Alexander*, are either lost or survive only in fragments.

SEE ALSO: Alexander III ("the Great"); historical writing

Arsinoë

The name of a number of Greek Ptolemaic queens and princesses during the Hellenistic Age. The most famous and resourceful was Arsinoë (ar-SIN-oh-eh) II, second wife and sister of Ptolemy II Philadelphus (reigned 283–246 B.C.). Very ambitious and shrewd, she frequently overshadowed her husband in courtly and cultural affairs. Thanks in large part to Arsinoë's advice and inspiration, the kingdom expanded its territory in the eastern Mediterranean and became richer and more prestigious than ever. Arsinoë's personal prestige and power is evidenced by the facts that her portrait appeared on coins alongside her husband's and that she was deified (proclaimed a goddess), as an incarnation of the Egyptian goddess Isis. One of Arsinoë's descendants of the same name was a sister of Cleopatra VII, last of the Ptolemies. This last Arsinoë was a schemer who opposed Cleopatra and was permanently silenced as a result.

SEE ALSO: Cleopatra VII; Ptolemy II Philadelphus

Artaxerxes

The name of four members of the Achaemenid dynasty, which ruled the Persian Empire from ca. 550 to 330 B.C. and frequently clashed or otherwise interacted with the Greek city-states. The first Artaxerxes (AR-ta-zerk-seez) reigned 464–424 B.C., the second 404–358, the third 358–338, and the fourth 338–336. All were largely self-absorbed, second-rate rulers who presided over an empire in rapid decline. The reign of the first Artaxerxes did witness the defeat of a large Athenian army in Egypt, an event that temporarily increased Persia's prestige; however, this success was the work of the capable Persian general Megabyzus rather than of the king himself.

SEE ALSO: Persians

Artemis

In Greek mythology, the goddess of the hunt, wild animals, nature, archery, and a protector of children, particularly young girls. She was also sometimes associated with the moon. Her chief symbols were deer, dogs, and cypress trees, and Greek artists typically depicted her roaming through the wilderness accompanied by deer, bears, and other wild animals. The daughter of Zeus and a female Titan, Leto, Artemis was said to have been born on the Aegean island of Delos, like her divine twin, Apollo. When the two gained maturity, she helped him slay the children of Niobe (a queen of Thebes) who had insulted Leto. Artemis also took part in the famous battle between the gods and giants, in which she killed a giant named Gration. Maintaining this image of a tough, no-nonsense woman, she turned a mortal, Actaeon, into a deer merely because he caught a glimpse of her bathing in the nude. And when Agamemnon, leader of the Greek expedition to Troy, angered her, she demanded that he sacrifice his daughter, Iphigenia, or else Artemis would refuse to provide the fair winds needed to launch the Greek fleet. Agamemnon complied, and Euripides dramatized it in his emotionally wrenching play *Iphigenia at Aulis*.

The Greeks saw Artemis as a virgin, so she had no children of her own. Still, it was thought she watched over pregnant women, and it was a common adage that women who died in childbirth had been slain by her arrows. Most modern scholars think she was a very ancient deity worshipped by the original non-Greek-speaking inhabitants of mainland Greece and that she is related to a goddess or series of nature goddesses worshipped in Minoan Crete. In this scenario, when the first Greek-speakers took over the mainland, they adopted Artemis into their pantheon of gods. From the Archaic Age on, a number of temples and shrines dedicated to her existed across the Greek world, the most famous being her enormous temple at Ephesus, called one of the Seven Wonders of the Ancient World.

SEE ALSO: Apollo; Ephesus; Seven Wonders of the Ancient World

Asclepius

According to Greek legend, the god of medicine. Asclepius was widely viewed as a son of Apollo, who was himself associated with the healing arts. The two sons of Asclepius, Machaon and Podalirius, whom he sired with a mortal woman, were also noted healers who supposedly helped wounded soldiers during the Trojan War. Another myth about Asclepius claims that Zeus killed him with a thunderbolt for conducting dubious experiments in the black art of bringing dead people back to life.

Actual worship of Asclepius as a divine healer came relatively late in Greek history—in the fifth and fourth centuries B.C. Thereafter, shrines honoring him were built far and wide. But his main temple was at Epidaurus in the eastern Peloponnesus, where, as in early modern times at Lourdes, France, sick, injured, and handicapped people came in hopes of miraculous cures. Usually such cures occurred through the process of incubation, in which an infirm person slept overnight in a building near the temple and Asclepius appeared to him or her in a dream. The temple priests then interpreted the dream and dispensed the appropriate medical advice. This shrine and others dedicated to the god also featured baths and gymnasiums designed to promote physical health. Asclepius's influence is still indirectly felt today because his symbols were the snake and staff, which survive in the familiar symbol of the modern medical profession.

SEE ALSO: Apollo; doctors and medicine; Epidaurus

Asia Minor

Today encompassing the nation of Turkey, the large peninsula bordered on the south by the Mediterranean Sea, on the north by the Black Sea, and on the west by the Aegean Sea. The Greeks called Asia Minor (also Anatolia) simply *Asia* until the term *lesser Asia*, or *Asia Minor*, came into use in the first century A.D. In the Bronze Age most of Asia Minor was controlled by the Hittites (an Indo-European people who called their kingdom there Hatti), although Mycenaean Greek trading posts seem to have existed along the Aegean coast. After the collapse of Hatti around 1200 B.C., an Asian people, the Phrygians, settled in Asia Minor. Phrygia, named for them, and located in the mountainous middle part of the peninsula, became only one of several regions into which the ancients divided Asia Minor in the centuries that followed. The principal ones included the Troad (where Troy was located) in the northwest; Ionia, the mostly Greek cultural area lying along the Aegean coast; Lydia, situated inland from Ionia and roughly encompassing the western third of Asia Minor; Caria and Cilicia, lying along the southern coast; and Pontus, on the northern coast bordering the Black Sea.

The Greeks who lived in mainland Greece and on the nearby Aegean islands had a vital connection to Asia Minor through Greek Ionia. In the Dark and Archaic ages, many Greeks migrated across the Aegean and established the Ionian cities, including the commercially prosperous Miletus, Ephesus, Samos, and others. Beginning in Ionia and moving eastward, Asia Minor was a strategic corridor leading from the Greek cultural sphere to the eastern Black Sea region, Mesopotamia (conquered, along with Asia Minor itself, by the Persians in the sixth century B.C.), Syria, and other Near Eastern regions. Trade, cultural ideas, and armies routinely moved back and forth through this corridor during Greece's Archaic, Classical, and Hellenistic periods. A major example consisted of the conquest of the Persian Empire by Alexander the Great in the fourth century B.C., which began in Asia Minor. After Alexander's death, his Successors, including Antigonus, who had governed Phrygia under Alexander, vied for control of Asia Minor. By about 280 B.C. most of the peninsula was part of the Seleucid kingdom (founded by one of the leading Successors, Seleucus). But soon a new kingdom, Pergamum, grew up in northwestern Asia Minor and became a rival of the Seleucid realm. Greek control of the region ended, however, when Rome took over most of Asia Minor in the second century B.C. and subsequently divided it into several Roman provinces.

SEE ALSO: Caria; Cilicia; Ephesus; Ionia; Lydia; Miletus; Phrygia; Seleucid Empire; Troy

Aspasia
(mid-fifth century B.C.)

The mistress and companion of Pericles, the leading Athenian statesman of the fifth century B.C. After Pericles divorced his wife in the 440s B.C., Aspasia, a courtesan (*hetaira*) from Miletus, in Ionia, moved in with him. They remained together until his death in 429, and it appears that they shared deep feelings of love, which was not the norm in a society in which most marriages were arranged. According to the Greek biographer Plutarch, Pericles "was attracted to Aspasia mainly because of her rare political wisdom . . . [and his] attachment to [her] seems to have been a . . . passionate affair. . . . Every day, when he went out to the marketplace and returned, he greeted her with a kiss." (*Life of Pericles* 24) Plutarch also reports that Aspasia and Pericles had a son together, whom they named Pericles. Because she was highly educated (as most *hetairai* were) and closely followed politics, the philosopher Socrates and some of his friends visited her from time to time, another unusual occurrence in ancient Athens, where most women lacked formal educations and could not competently engage in political discussions with men. Perhaps inevitably, Pericles' political enemies tried to discredit him by exploiting his relationship with her. They brought her to trial on a charge of impiety, but they were unable to obtain a conviction.

SEE ALSO: *hetairai*; Pericles; women

assemblies

In many Greek city-states, groups of citizens who met on a regular basis to discuss and debate local issues, vote on policy, and elect leaders. The capitalized version of the term (Assembly) generally refers to the one in Athens.

SEE ALSO: government

astronomy

Most of Greece's earliest philosopher-scientists (called the pre-Socratics because they predated the pivotal philosopher Socrates) spent at least some of their time contemplating the nature of and relationships among Earth, the Sun, the planets, and the stars. Thales, for example, postulated that Earth stays fixed in place because it floats on water. In contrast, Anaximander suggested that the stars are hoops of fire compressed by air. And the Pythagorean thinkers envisioned a universe made up of large, concentric, and invisible spheres. Earth, they claimed, is a sphere resting at the center of these nested spheres. Another pre-Socratic, Philolaus, correctly described Earth as a planet orbiting a central fire (although he incorrectly said that the Sun also moves around that central object). Such ideas about the workings of the universe constituted the beginnings of Greek astronomy, although none of these men, nor any of the later Greek thinkers, thought of himself exclusively as an astronomer. Astronomy did not become a separate scientific discipline until modern times.

The most important of the ancient Greek astronomical theories were those of post-Socratic thinkers, beginning with the fourth-century B.C. Athenian Plato. One of his dialogues, the *Timaeus*, contains a comprehensive description of his views on the origins, structure, and workings of the cosmos (universe). Most modern astronomers see this work as the founding document of the discipline of cosmology, the branch of astronomy that seeks to know how the universe came into being and evolved into its present form. In the work, Plato addresses the question of whether the universe has always existed or whether it had a definite beginning. He concludes that some sort of supernatural being, likely a god, had somehow constructed the cosmos. However, Plato cautions, it would be a waste of time for humans to try to describe this creator, who is beyond human perception and is unknowable. Plato also agrees with the Pythagoreans and most other pre-Socratic thinkers that all of the heavenly bodies, including Earth, are spheres.

Plato's student, Aristotle, envisioned a universe similar in a number of ways to that of Plato and the Pythagoreans. Like them, for instance, Aristotle believed that all substances on Earth were made up of four basic elements—earth, water, air, and fire. These, he said, were imperfect and changeable, while the heavens were perfect and incorruptible. Therefore, the heavens had to be made of a fifth and very special element, which he called ether. Aristotle also agreed that Earth was a sphere located at the center of the cosmos. He offered proof for this, saying that falling objects always move toward Earth's center:

> Its shape must necessarily be spherical. For every portion of Earth has weight until it reaches the center. . . . A thing which possesses weight is naturally endowed with a centripetal movement [motion toward the center]. . . . The motions of heavy bodies always make equal angles and are not parallel. This would be the natural form of movement towards what is naturally spherical. (*On the Heavens* 2.14)

In addition, Aristotle agreed with the Pythagorean concept of invisible, concentric spheres in the sky, as did his contemporary, Eudoxus. The difference was that Eudoxus postulated the existence of twenty-seven, rather than only three, spheres; and Aristotle upped that number to fifty-five. These men envisioned the celestial spheres as working together like a gigantic mechanical construction, a sort of "cosmic clockwork" that carried the planets, stars, and other heavenly bodies through the sky. In the centuries following Aristotle's death, several Greek astronomers modified his cosmic model slightly. Some introduced a system in which one cosmic object moved on an epicycle, or circular path, around another object, which moved along a deferent, a larger circle with Earth at its center. This system was perfected by the Alexandrian Greek scholar Claudius Ptolemy in the mid-second century A.D.

No matter how they described the cosmic motions, Aristotle, Ptolemy, and most other Greek thinkers were staunch supporters of the geocentric, or Earth-centered, model of the heavens. In this, as modern science has revealed, they were wrong. Only one ancient scholar got it right. This now largely forgotten pioneer was Aristarchus of Samos, who worked at the Museum in Alexandria in the early third century B.C. Influenced in part by the pre-Socratic thinker Philolaus, Aristarchus went much further and suggested that Earth rotates daily on its axis. Earth also moves in a circular orbit around the stationary Sun, Aristarchus said, along with the other planets. But though this conception of the heavens was correct, it failed to win over the rest of the ancient scholarly community. Some eighteen centuries would pass before another innovator, Polish astronomer Nicolaus Copernicus, would dare to reassert the heliocentric

A huge statue of the goddess Athena, designed by the sculptor Phidias, stood inside the Parthenon, on the Athenian Acropolis. NORTH WIND PICTURE ARCHIVES

view and thereby launch the modern science of astronomy. Copernicus readily admitted that he had been inspired by reading about Aristarchus's views; without ancient Greek astronomy, therefore, there would be no modern astronomy.

SEE ALSO: Aristarchus of Samos; Aristotle; Plato; Pythagoras; science

Athena

In Greek mythology, the goddess of war and wisdom, arts and crafts (notably spinning and weaving), and one of the most important of the major Olympian gods. Her symbols were the owl and the olive tree. Many Greek cities chose Athena (or Athene) as their patron deity (divine protector), the most familiar example being Athens, where the Athenians built several temples to honor her. Chief among these structures were the Parthenon and the Erechtheum, on the city's Acropolis. Inside the Parthenon stood the goddess's cult image, a giant statue fashioned by the master sculptor Phidias. The image of her captured in the statue, called Athena Parthenos, or "Athena the Virgin," was only one of her numerous manifestations. Others included Athena Promachos, meaning "Athena the Warrior Champion"; Athena Nike, or "Athena the Victor"; Athena Hygeia ("Athena, Goddess of Health"), and Athena Ergane ("Athena the Worker"). She was also frequently called Pallas Athena, a term of obscure origins. Some modern scholars think that Pallas may have been the name of a Bronze Age war goddess whose identity merged with Athena's in later times.

Athena also figured prominently in numerous Greek myths. In one of the more famous ones, she sprang, fully clad in her armor, from the head of her father, Zeus, the chief Olympian god. In another popular myth, Athena and Poseidon, god of the seas, engaged in a contest to decide which of them would become patron of Athens. Poseidon touched the Acropolis with his trident, producing a miraculous saltwater spring. Then Athena made an olive tree grow atop the hill, which prompted Zeus and the other divine judges to declare her the winner of the contest. Athena was also said to have hurled down an olive-wood statue of herself onto the Acropolis's northern edge, which thereafter became the site for a succession of temples, each called the Erechtheum (named for Erechtheus, a legendary Bronze Age Athenian king who came to be seen as a sort of partner to Athena or custodian of her

temples). Inside the Erechtheum rested the goddess's sacred statue, the Athena Polias ("Athena of the City"), which the Athenians draped with a new robe during each celebration of the Panathenaic festival.

Because she was a war goddess first and foremost, many of Athena's myths involved wars or other violent events. In the Trojan War, for example, she actively supported the Greeks against the Trojans, often in opposition to Ares, god of war, who backed the Trojans. Athena also helped a number of human heroes in their individual exploits, including Perseus, Bellerophon, Jason, Heracles, and Odysseus. Not surprisingly, therefore, the Athenian playwrights, who frequently dramatized these exploits, included Athena as a character in their plays. One of the more striking examples is in Aeschylus's *Eumenides*, the third play in his great trilogy, the *Oresteia*. In the play's climax, Athena intervenes in human affairs when Orestes, who is being hounded by the vengeful Furies for committing murder, flees to Athens. The goddess ensures that the young man receives a fair trial. After he is acquitted, also with her help, she miraculously transforms the Furies into the Eumenides ("the Kindly Ones"), in the process ending the terrible, generations-long curse of the House of Atreus.

SEE ALSO: Ares; Athens; Erechtheum; owl; Panathenaea; Parthenon; temples; Zeus

Athens

The leading city-state of Greece in the Classical Age and one of Greece's oldest, most famous, and most influential cities. Athens's urban center, which was surrounded by a stone defensive wall, was situated in the southern sector of the Attic peninsula, about 4 miles (6.4km) from the Saronic Gulf, a wide inlet of the Aegean

Sea; but Athenian territory came to include all of Attica. In the early years of the Bronze Age, perhaps as far back as 3000 B.C., a rudimentary version of the urban center grew up around the rocky outcrop that came to be known as the Acropolis. For a long time this habitation was only one, though the largest, of the many scattered towns and villages across Attica. Sometime in the late Bronze Age, according to legend, the Athenian king Theseus brought all these towns together into a single political unit. Legend also claims that a while later Athens was among the Greek kingdoms that assembled to attack Troy. In the catalog of combatants in his *Iliad*, Homer says the Athenians contributed fifty ships to the expedition. This may be based partly on fact, as evidence shows that Athens was a Mycenaean stronghold in this era; and it was probably a Mycenaean raid or war that inspired the legend of the Trojan conflict.

Following the collapse of Greece's Bronze Age civilization in the twelfth century B.C., Athens was one of the few Mycenaean towns that survived intact. However, its inhabitants steadily lost their heritage and came to think of themselves as Athenians rather than Mycenaeans. Not much is known about the city in the Dark Age. But it appears that in the subsequent Archaic Age (ca. 800–ca. 500 B.C.) it grew rapidly in size and its government underwent a series of reforms, each more progressive than the last. The ancient kingship (or whatever form of it existed in the Dark Age) was eliminated. For a while some kind of aristocratic council held power, but the common people increasingly came to resent the power of the nobles. And over the course of two or more centuries the Assembly (*Ekklesia*), whose exact origins are unknown, steadily gained authority. In the late seventh century B.C. a written law code was drafted by a man named Draco. But the people viewed these laws as too harsh, and it was not long before a civil war between the aristocrats and commoners became imminent. A bloody conflict was avoided by the intervention of Solon, a citizen known for his wisdom and fairness. He threw out Draco's laws (except for those dealing with murder), set up a new social ranking based on wealth rather than birth, and created the Council (*Boule*), a group of four hundred men chosen by lot from all classes. These moves provided a workable balance between the power of the aristocrats and that of the people. But that balance could not be maintained because Solon had—probably unintentionally—set in motion a slow but relentless democratic revolution. That progressive movement exploded in about 508 B.C., transforming Athens's government into a full-blown democracy, the world's first. Under a reformer named Cleisthenes, the Assembly gained far-reaching powers, including declaring war, making peace, and deciding foreign policy.

No sooner had the Athenians begun their historic experiment with democracy when they found themselves threatened with annihilation. In 490 B.C. Darius I, ruler of the Persian Empire, sent an army to capture Athens. The city appeared to be doomed; however, a small force of Athenian militiamen stunned the world by defeating the invaders on the plain of Marathon. The Persians invaded again ten years later. This time the Athenians led other Greeks in a major naval victory at Salamis, and after the war Athens emerged, along with Sparta, as one of Greece's two leading states. Athens spearheaded the formation of the Delian League to guard against further Persian incursions, but in the years that followed the Athenians transformed the organization into their own maritime empire. At its height, more than one hundred Greek cities came under Athens's economic and political influence. These states paid the Athenians tribute, and large amounts of this money was used to erect temples (including the magnificent Parthenon) and other public buildings, making Athens the marvel of Greece.

But during these same years Athens incurred the rivalry and wrath of the Spartans, who viewed Athenian ambitions as dangerous to the balance of power in Greece. Periodic disputes and small-scale fighting between the two states and their respective allies escalated and in 431 B.C. erupted into the ruinous Peloponnesian War. Athens surrendered in 404 B.C. and had to endure a Spartan hegemony (dominance) of Greek affairs for several years afterward. By the 370s B.C., however, the Athenians had recovered and were on the road to creating another maritime empire. What ultimately stopped them was the rise of Macedonia under King Philip II. He defeated a Greek coalition headed by Athens and Thebes at Chaeronea in 338. His son Alexander and other successors controlled Greek affairs, including those of Athens, for many years to come. In Hellenistic times Athens underwent steady economic and military decline and found itself occupied off and on by troops from the large Greek kingdoms that dominated that age. The city never regained its former power and glory, although it remained a popular tourist destination and important literary center for most of the rest of antiquity.

SEE ALSO: Athena; Cimon; Cleisthenes; Demosthenes; Greco-Persian Wars; Parthenon; Pericles; Solon; Themistocles; Theseus

athletics

The ancient Greeks were fascinated by, perhaps even obsessed with, athletic competitions, both as participants and as spectators. Their word for such competition was *agon*, which also meant a "contest" or a "struggle." In addition to many formal athletic competitions, a noteworthy physical culture (social institutions and customs surrounding physical fitness and athletic training) arose in the Greek lands in Archaic times. And by the advent of the Classical Age (ca. 500 B.C.), gymnasia, facilities in which men engaged in physical training and athletic events, had become common features of most Greek city-states. Indeed, for most Greeks athletics were not merely a leisurely pastime. They were also a serious matter, partly because the formal competitions were an integral facet of sacred religious festivals. The athletes who took part traditionally dedicated their creative or physical skills and prowess to a specific god.

Hundreds of local festivals of this kind were held across the Greek world in Archaic times and in later eras. But by the end of the sixth century B.C. four were viewed as the most prestigious, partly because they were international in character, attracting athletes and spectators from city-states far and wide. Most celebrated of all were the Olympic Games, honoring Zeus. They were staged at Olympia in the western Peloponnesus every four years beginning in 776 B.C. (at least according to tradition). The others included the Pythian Games, dedicated to Apollo, held at his shrine at Delphi in the third year after each Olympics; the Isthmian Games, honoring Poseidon, presented every two years on the Isthmus of Corinth; and the Nemean Games, dedicated to Zeus, held at two-year intervals at Nemea (just south of

Corinth). In addition to these "big four" festivals, the athletic games at Athens's Panathenaic festival, honoring Athena, were widely popular.

The athletes who competed in these contests were not, as scholars once thought, motivated mainly by a love of sport. The reality was that they were driven just as much, if not more so, by the desire to be first and reap the considerable material benefits garnered by the winners. Although crowns of vegetation were the sole prizes awarded at these games, many athletes had their training and expenses paid for by well-to-do patrons. And victorious athletes always received numerous financial and other awards when they returned to their home cities, including valuable bronze artifacts and jars of olive oil, which they could sell for a profit. In late fifth-century B.C. Athens, for example, a winning runner at the Panathenaea received a hundred jars of olive oil, worth as much as an average worker earned in four years.

Since winning was paramount to Greek athletes, they did not compete against the clock or measuring tape in an effort to set records, as is common today. Each competitor simply did his best to come in first in his event. The events varied somewhat from international to local games, although most competitions featured some basic events that were part of the program at Olympia. That program included horse and chariot races, which took place on a dirt track called a hippodrome; foot races; a running broad jump in which the jumpers held small hand weights as they leaped; the discus throw; the javelin throw; wrestling; boxing; and the *pankration*, a rough-and-tumble combination of wrestling and boxing moves.

Of these events, wrestling was one of the most—if not the most—popular. Most Greeks viewed wrestling training as the most crucial component of physical education, and Greek boys participated in informal wrestling bouts in the same manner that modern boys play backlot football. Evidence shows that the wrestlers at the major athletic games fought hard and often resorted to brutal tactics to ensure victory. Using strangleholds was not unusual, for example.

Local competitions featured not only wrestling and most other Olympic events but also some more-specialized contests, some of which only the citizens of the host city could take part in. In Athens, for instance, there was a sort of parade for two-horse chariots in which the teams were likely judged on their ability to march and drill in a precise manner. Another Athenian equestrian event featured galloping horses whose riders threw javelins at targets. Still another colorful contest, which only Athenians were allowed to enter, was the Pyrrhic dance, in which teams of men from different local tribes carried spears and shields while executing complex, precise moves in unison. Torch races, in which both individuals and teams participated, were also popular in Athens's Panathenaic games.

SEE ALSO: Elis; Olympia; Pindar

Athos, Mt.

The easternmost peak and promontory on the Chalcidic Peninsula located on the northern rim of the Aegean Sea. The peak of Mt. Athos (also called Mt. Acte) rises to just over 6,660 feet (2,030m), and the promontory is some 30 miles (48km) long. In 492 B.C. a Persian fleet sent to invade Greece was destroyed in a storm off the coast of Mt. Athos. Twelve years later, hoping to avoid a repeat of this disaster,

Persia's King Xerxes ordered construction of a canal across the narrowest section of the promontory. In medieval times the Athos promontory became a haven for Christian monks.

SEE ALSO: Greco-Persian Wars

Atlantis

A legendary kingdom, island, or small continent that supposedly sank into the sea in prehistoric times. The first ancient writer to describe Atlantis was Plato, whose dialogues *Timaeus* and *Critias* are the principal primary sources about the lost island. Plato claimed that his illustrious ancestor, the sixth-century B.C. lawgiver Solon, had visited Egypt and that while there some Egyptian priests had told him that long ago there had existed a powerful maritime empire called Atlantis, which had extended its power over all of Europe. They said that Athens had managed to defeat Atlantis and that not long afterward the island had sunk into the sea during an immense catastrophe. "There occurred violent earthquakes and floods," Plato writes, "and in a single day and night of misfortune all [the] warlike men in a body sank into the earth, and the island of Atlantis in like manner disappeared in the depths of the sea." (*Timaeus* 25) Solon told this story to his children, Plato said, who told their own offspring, and so on, until it reached Plato himself in the fourth century B.C. The Egyptian priests, Solon, and Plato all assumed that Atlantis was larger than Europe, so that it could not have fit inside the Mediterranean Sea. Therefore, they placed it in the then-uncharted Atlantic Ocean, lying beyond the Pillars of Heracles (the Strait of Gibraltar).

Many later ancient scholars accepted the existence of Atlantis without question. But their early modern counterparts came to view the tale as a parable that Plato had made up to support the literary points he was making in the two dialogues. It now appears, however, that the story was based on real events. The consensus of recent scholarship is that the Atlanteans were a garbled memory of the Minoans, whose fleets controlled the Aegean waters for several centuries in Greece's Bronze Age. Plato's description of a splendid palace in Atlantis's central city closely matches the sprawling, multilevel palace-centers of Minoan Crete, which he knew nothing about. And numerous other details Plato lists about Atlantis are eerily similar to Minoan towns and customs. The subsidence of Atlantis into the sea is likely another disjointed memory of a real event. Geologists have conclusively proven that a large portion of the island of Thera (north of Crete) collapsed into the sea during the great eruption of the Theran volcano that shook the Aegean in the middle of the second millennium B.C. Finally, Athens's triumph over the Atlanteans may be based on the Mycenaean Greek military takeover of Minoan Crete in the century or so following the catastrophe.

SEE ALSO: Crete; *Critias*; Minoans; Thera; *Timaeus*

Atlas

One of the Titans, the earliest race of Greek gods. One ancient legend holds that he guarded the pillars of heaven, which supported the sky. Other myths claim that he actually held up the sky or even the entire Earth. In one of the more famous stories about Atlas, the hero Perseus passed by one day holding the head of Medusa, the hideous monster he had recently killed. Atlas tried to drive Perseus away because he was afraid the young man would try to steal some golden apples that grew on a nearby magical tree. Perseus responded by showing him Medusa's face, which turned him to stone. Supposedly this was the origin of the Atlas Mountains in northwestern Africa.

SEE ALSO: Medusa; Perseus, 1; Titans

Atreus

In Greek mythology, the original head of the royal House of Atreus, which was smitten by a terrible generations-long curse. Atreus was said to have been a son of Pelops, the mythical character for whom the Peloponnesus was named. Eventually Atreus became ruler of Mycenae and sired two sons—Agamemnon and Menelaus. Meanwhile, Atreus and his brother, Thyestes, quarreled, and Atreus ended up killing most of his brother's children. In his anguish, Thyestes cursed Atreus, after which Thyestes' son Aegisthus avenged his father by murdering Atreus. These crimes ignited the curse, which was manifested later in the murders of Agamemnon and his queen, Clytemnestra, and other family misfortunes. Only when the goddess Athena intervened, as described in Aeschylus's play *Eumenides*, was the curse lifted.

SEE ALSO: Agamemnon; Clytemnestra; *Eumenides*; Orestes; Pelops

Attalids

A family line of seven rulers who governed the Hellenistic kingdom of Pergamum from 282 B.C. to 133 B.C. The Attalids were superb city planners, art patrons, and able administrators. They made Pergamum a center of Hellenistic culture.

SEE ALSO: Pergamum

Attica

The large peninsula of east-central Greece in which the urban center of Athens rests and which in ancient times was seen as the heartland of Athenian territory. Attica is roughly triangular in shape and covers an area of approximately 1,000 square miles (2,590 sq. km). In the Archaic and Classical ages, the urban center, then surrounded by defensive walls, was situated about 4 to 5 miles (6 to 8km) from Attica's western coast, along the Saronic Gulf (a wide inlet of the Aegean Sea). There, the Athenians originally had docks along the small bay of Phaleron, but in the early fifth century B.C. they built a new port farther north at Piraeus. Just northeast of Piraeus, across a narrow strait (where the Greeks defeated the Persians in a naval battle in 480 B.C.) was the island of Salamis, originally a possession of neighboring Megara; and northeast of Salamis, at Attica's western border with Megara, was Eleusis, home of the famous mystery cult of Demeter.

Moving northeastward from the urban center, one passed by Athmonum, Cephisia, and other villages until reaching Mt. Pentelikon (or Pentelikos) in the center of Attica, the site of the quarries that yielded the high-quality marble used in building the Parthenon and other famous public buildings. Beyond Mt. Pentelikon lay the plain of Marathon, where the Athenians defeated the Persians in 490 B.C. South of Mt. Pentelikon were villages, including Pallene, Oa, and Lamptrae; farther south was the rocky region of Laurium, where the Athenian silver mines were located. Cape Sunium marked the southernmost tip of the peninsula. Moving northward from Mt. Pentelikon, one passed through the district of Diacria, and turning northwestward from there, the region of Mt. Parnes and Mt. Cithaeron, with the small city-state of Plataea (long an Athenian ally) just beyond.

For the most part, Attica is dry and

rocky and possesses little fertile land. That is why the Athenians were forced to import so much grain from the Black Sea region and elsewhere during Classical times. Plato summed up the situation this way:

> There has never been any considerable accumulation of the soil coming down from the mountains, as in other places, but the earth [i.e., good soil] has fallen away all round and sunk out of sight. The consequence is, that . . . there are remaining only the bones of the wasted body, as they may be called . . . all the richer and softer parts of the soil having fallen away, and the mere skeleton of the land being left. (*Critias* 111)

But though Attica's soil was generally thin, in many places it supported cultivation of vines, olives, and figs. The most fertile region of the peninsula was a small plain near Eleusis.

SEE ALSO: Athens; Eleusis; Piraeus

aulos

A musical instrument with two pipes, each of which had either one reed (like a modern clarinet) or two (like an oboe). The *aulos* was and still is frequently mislabeled as a flute.

SEE ALSO: music and dance

Bacchae, The

A tragedy by Euripides, first produced in Athens circa 405 B.C., about a year after the author's death. The play deals with a famous mythical incident involving the fertility god Dionysus and some of his ecstatic, frenzied followers, known as the Bacchae. One day Dionysus, disguised as a mortal man, appears in Thebes. The god is shocked and dismayed to find that the local king, Pentheus, has forbidden his subjects to worship Dionysus. In a fit of rage Dionysus brings on an earthquake that wrecks Pentheus's palace. The god also makes the city's women go into a trance and roam the countryside as if they were wild animals. At the god's urging, Pentheus (who still does not realize he is talking to Dionysus) dresses up like a woman and goes out into the countryside to see for himself what is happening. But in their frenzied state, the women perceive Pentheus as a wild beast and proceed to tear him to pieces.

SEE ALSO: Dionysus; Euripides

Bacchylides
(ca. 520 B.C.–450 B.C.)

One of the leading lyric poets of the Classical Age. Bacchylides was born on the Aegean island of Ceos but spent much of his life elsewhere, including Macedonia, Sicily, and the Peloponnesus. About twenty of his poems have survived complete, including fifteen odes honoring victorious athletes. Thus, Bacchylides was a rival of Pindar, who was seen as the master of the victory ode. Bacchylides also wrote dithyrambs, hymns, patriotic songs, and other kinds of verses, often emphasizing the theme that life is short and can be cruel and unpredictable, and therefore people should do what they can to make the best of things and seek happiness whenever possible, including enjoying the company of good friends. One of his briefer lyrics states, "I cannot promise at my hearth great slabs of beef, and gold, and deep red carpet, but only the loving kindness of your host, and music, and clay crocks of local wine." ("Invitation")

SEE ALSO: dithyramb; Pindar; poetry

Bad-Tempered Man, The

A comedic play by Menander, it won the first prize in Athens's Lenaea festival in

A French engraving portrays the scene from Euripides' The Bacchae in which Pentheus is slain by frenzied women. SNARK/ART RESOURCE, NY

The Greenhaven Encyclopedia of Ancient Greece

317 B.C. The plot of *The Bad-Tempered Man*, or *Dyscolos*, follows the adventures of a wealthy young man named Sostratus. One day he sees a young woman praying to the god Pan and immediately falls in love with her. However, she lives with her father, Cnemon (the "bad-tempered man" of the play's title), an ornery old hermit. Sostratus tries to impress Cnemon by laboring long hours on the old man's farm, but to no avail. Eventually, Cnemon falls into a well and Sostratus helps rescue him, which causes Cnemon to have a change of heart. After more plot twists, Sostratus ends up marrying the hermit's daughter.

SEE ALSO: Menander; theater and drama

banking

Modern-style public banks did not exist in ancient Greece. There were, however, private bankers (*trapezitai*) who acted as money changers and, beginning in the fifth century B.C., performed other familiar banking services, such as making loans. These individuals often set up their tables (*trapezitai* translates literally as "table men") outside temples, street corners, or in marketplaces. When exchanging money or valuables (for example, exchanging Athenian drachmas for gold or foreign currency), they carefully weighed all items on a small balance scale (*stathmos*). The most common commission a banker charged for an exchange was 6 percent of the total amount of the exchange. The interest rate for loans was often 12 percent for ordinary customers and as high as 20 or 30 percent for those involved in shipping, which was a risky business subject to big losses through piracy and storms. Some Greeks, including Aristotle, disapproved of charging interest for the use of money, arguing that currency should be used strictly as a medium of exchange.

SEE ALSO: money; trade; weights and measures

baths and bathing

The frequency with which the Greeks bathed is uncertain. But they did wash on a fairly regular basis, even if it was just a "sponge bath" utilizing a bucket or basin of water. Private bathrooms had basins, which rested atop small tables; and by late Classical times most private bathrooms also had bathtubs, usually made of terracotta. These were generally filled by hand. There was public bathing as well, although before the early years of the Roman Empire it was not on the large scale known in Rome. Greek bathhouses (*balaneia*) were small rectangular or round structures that featured rows of bathtubs rather than large communal pools, as in the Roman versions. Greek bathhouses, as well as gymnasia, sometimes had showers, too. Surviving vase paintings show men standing beneath showerheads shaped like the faces of lions and boars. The water for both tubs and showers was sometimes brought in by hand by slaves, but some bathhouses featured clay pipes or troughs that carried water in from nearby fountain houses or aqueducts. Soap was largely unknown; most people rubbed their bodies with olive oil and then used a wooden scraper (strigil) to remove the oil and dirt.

SEE ALSO: grooming; houses; water supplies

Battle of Actium (31 B.C.)

The last battle of the Roman civil wars of the first century B.C. The Battle of Actium brought about the defeat of Cleopatra VII, last ruler of the Ptolemaic kingdom and the last major autonomous Greek ruler in antiquity. Cleopatra had joined forces with the Roman general Marcus Antonius (Mark Antony) against Antony's rival, Octavian (Julius Caesar's adopted son). Octavian and his skilled general Agrippa amassed roughly four hundred warships and troop transports and about eighty thousand land troops and cornered Antony and Cleopatra at Actium in western Greece. Antony had more than a hundred thousand land troops but decided to try to break out of the trap using his five hundred ships. These vessels were mostly large and heavy. In contrast, Octavian and Agrippa's ships were smaller and faster, so they employed the strategy of ramming the less maneuverable enemy vessels. Meanwhile, Antony's sailors and marines sprayed volleys of arrows, stones, and other missiles at the enemy ships. At the height of the battle, Cleopatra suddenly took the sixty ships that were under her command and slipped away. Antony soon followed her, abandoning most of his troops. These men fought on bravely but eventually suffered a decisive defeat. Antony and Cleopatra were unable to carry on the war and the following year took their own lives, marking the end of the Hellenistic Age and the beginning of Greece's long era of Roman domination.

SEE ALSO: Cleopatra VII; Rome

Battle of Aegospotami (405 B.C.)

A major naval engagement, it was the final, decisive battle of the Peloponnesian War. A Spartan fleet numbering about 150 ships, commanded by Lysander, moved into the Hellespont and captured the town of Lampsacus, an Athenian ally situated across from a stretch of coastline called Aegospotami. In response, a slightly larger Athenian fleet arrived. But at first Lysander refused to give battle. He waited until the Athenians had beached their ships and gone ashore to gather supplies, then launched a devastating surprise attack.

Some 170 Athenian ships were captured, along with thousands of their crewmen. This victory gave Sparta control of the Black Sea grain route that was essential to Athens's survival. The Athenians soon had no choice but to surrender.

SEE ALSO: Lysander; Peloponnesian War

Battle of Artemisium (480 B.C.)

A naval battle fought in the summer of that year. With the Persian army and navy bearing down on southern Greece, the Greeks attempted to halt the enemy advance partly on land in the pass of Thermopylae and partly at sea at Artemisium (on the northern coast of the large island of Euboea). The Greek fleet numbered about 380 ships, 180 of those from Athens. The Persian vessels numbered at least 450. The opposing formations of ships came close together and there was much boarding and hand-to-hand fighting. Although the Greeks acquitted themselves well, they decided to retreat when news came that the Persian army had broken through at Thermopylae (some 40 miles [64 km] to the west). Thus, the sea battle ended with a marginal Persian victory.

SEE ALSO: Battle of Thermopylae, 1; Greco-Persian Wars

Battle of Chaeronea (338 B.C.)

After Macedonia's King Philip II entered southern Greece and occupied Delphi, the Athenian orator Demosthenes organized a powerful anti-Macedonian alliance headed by Athens and Thebes. The opposing armies met in August 338 in the Cephisus Valley, near Chaeronea (west of Thebes). Philip placed a mass of skirmishers and light-armed troops on his right wing beyond the edge of his phalanx. Then he slanted his phalanx of pikemen back at an oblique angle. Leading the right wing himself, Philip pretended to be overcome with sudden fear of the enemy and began to retreat. Just as he had expected, this trick lured the Athenians into staging a forceful charge. In doing this, they steadily separated themselves from the Thebans and other allies and opened a fatal gap in the allied line. Philip's son Alexander (later called "the Great"), only eighteen at the time, led the Macedonian cavalry into the gap, thereby widening it. Seeing this, Philip suddenly halted his feigned retreat and ordered his phalanx to charge the oncoming Athenians. Many were impaled on the formation's mass of pikes, and the rest suddenly turned and ran, along with the other allied contingents. Only Thebes's small group of elite troops, the famous Sacred Band, stood its ground. Surrounded by the Macedonian phalanx, these truly brave men fought to the death. Their sacrifice was in vain, however, for Philip's victory over the city-states was complete and decisive.

SEE ALSO: Demosthenes; Philip II

Battle of Coronea (447 B.C.)

A small Athenian army commanded by Tolmides marched into Boeotia to deal with rebels who were defying Athens's authority in the region. As the Athenians were heading home, a large group of the rebels attacked them at Coronea in western Boeotia. In a clear-cut Athenian defeat, Tolmides was slain, along with many of his troops, and Athens was forced to sign a treaty heavily favoring the Boeotians.

SEE ALSO: Greece, history of

Battle of Coronea (394 B.C.)

During the so-called Corinthian War, Sparta faced off at Coronea against the al-lied forces of Athens, Corinth, Thebes, and Argos. The Spartans were led by one of their kings, Agesilaus II. When the two phalanxes clashed, the right wing of each defeated the opposing left wing. Casualties were heavy on both sides and the outcome was largely indecisive.

SEE ALSO: Agesilaus II

Battle of Cynoscephalae (197 B.C.)

The final battle of the Second Macedonian War, the outcome of which showed that the Greek military system had become outdated. The event also foreshadowed the eclipse of Greece by Rome. The Macedonian forces, commanded by King Philip V, and a Roman army led by Titus Quinctius Flamininus took up positions on opposite sides of Cynoscephalae ridge in central Greece. Each commander sent out a small group of soldiers to take control of the ridge. These troops encountered each other and initiated the battle, which grew in size and intensity over the course of a couple of hours. At the height of the fight, a Roman officer led a contingent of men against the rear of the Macedonian phalanx. Unable to swing their long pikes around in time, the Greeks were slaughtered in their ranks. Philip suffered some eight thousand killed and five thousand captured, while only seven hundred Romans died.

SEE ALSO: Philip V; Rome; weapons and warfare, land

Battle of Eurymedon (ca. 468–467 B.C.)

After the major Persian offensive against Greece ended with the Greek victory at Plataea in 479 B.C., the Greeks embarked on their own offensive, fighting Persian forces in Asia Minor when and where they could. One of the high points of these expeditions occurred when the Athenian general Cimon assaulted a joint Persian army and navy near the Eurymedon River in southern Asia Minor. First the Greeks attacked at sea, sinking some two hundred enemy ships. Then Cimon ordered his troops to go ashore and face the Persian army. Although the Greek soldiers were tired from the sea battle, they crushed their opponents and captured their camp. The Greek victory proved a major blow to the Persians' power base in Asia Minor.

SEE ALSO: Cimon; Persians

Battle of Gaugamela (331 B.C.)

One of the major battles of Alexander's invasion of Persia in the 330s and 320s B.C. In this huge military engagement, in which Alexander was opposed by King Darius III, the Greeks had roughly seven thousand cavalry and forty thousand infantry. The size of the Persian forces is unknown, but Darius's soldiers likely outnumbered the Greeks by three or four to one. The armies met near the village of Gaugamela, in what is now Iraq. After much maneuvering by units of both sides, a large gap appeared in the Persian line. Alexander led his main cavalry force, followed by a unit of infantry, into the gap and charged toward Darius's position. The Persian monarch fled, followed by some of his troops. Meanwhile, other Persian units managed to penetrate the Greek lines and assaulted Alexander's baggage train. A reserve unit of Macedonian infantry drove these intruders back, and eventually the rest of the Persian army took flight. Alexander pursued Darius to Arbela, some seventy miles (113km) distant, but was unable to catch him. The Greek victory was nothing less than enormous. Alexander lost only a few hundred men, while the Persian dead numbered at least forty thousand.

SEE ALSO: Alexander III ("the Great"); Darius III; Persians

Battle of Granicus River (334 B.C.)

Alexander the Great's first victory following his invasion of Persian-dominated Asia Minor. Ancient accounts of the event differ, but most modern historians accept that of Arrian, Alexander's chief ancient biographer. According to Arrian, the Persian cavalry outnumbered Alexander's five thousand horsemen by a factor of four to one. The Persian cavalry lined up along the bank of the Granicus River, waiting for Alexander to attempt to cross the river. He did so, leading the right wing of his own cavalry. At first the Persians were successful in keeping the Greeks from crossing, but more and more of Alexander's men made it across. Once across, Alexander led his horsemen from the far right into the Persian center and assaulted the Persian generals arrayed there. The Persian center soon broke and dispersed, after which the Greek infantry easily routed the Persian foot soldiers. Alexander lost fewer than two hundred men, compared to Persian losses of at least ten thousand.

SEE ALSO: Alexander III ("the Great"); Arrian; Persians

Battle of Himera (480 B.C.)

While Xerxes, king of Persia, was assaulting the Greek mainland, Carthage (in North Africa), with which he had made an agreement, attacked several Greek colonies in Sicily. Led by a general named Hamilcar, the Carthaginians moved on the northern coastal town of Himera. The ruler of Himera sent for aid from the nearby Greek city of Syracuse, whose ruler, Gelon, hurried to the scene with a large force. The Greeks burned many of the enemy ships and then decisively defeated the Carthaginian land forces.

SEE ALSO: Gelon of Gela; Greco-Persian Wars

Battle of Hydapses River (326 B.C.)

A major engagement fought between Alexander's forces and those of the Indian king Porus. The latter gathered roughly thirty thousand infantry, four thousand cavalry, and two hundred elephants along the river's eastern bank. From the opposite bank, Alexander led a picked force of cavalry across the river at a ford several miles upstream from his camp. As a contingent of Porus's army hurried to halt this advance, Alexander's general, Craterus, led the main body of the Greek army from the camp directly across the river. The Indian ruler tried to use his elephants, but the Greeks forced many of the beasts back into the Indian ranks, where they did a great deal of damage. Both wings of Porus's army were eventually disrupted and he retreated. Greek losses were about a thousand, compared to at least twelve times that number of Indians killed.

SEE ALSO: Alexander III ("the Great")

Battle of Ipsus (301 B.C.)

An enormous battle that pitted two of the Successors of Alexander the Great—Antigonus and his son Demetrius—against a coalition of other Successors led by Seleucus and Lysimachus. The site of the engagement was in Phrygia in central Asia Minor. Each side had perhaps seventy thousand infantry and ten thousand cavalry, but Seleucus had more elephants, which he managed to maneuver between Antigonus's and Demetrius's forces, separating them. Seleucus then outflanked

Antigonus's infantry. Antigonus was slain, but Demetrius escaped with some of his horsemen. The victors then proceeded to divide the loser's land holdings among themselves.

SEE ALSO: Antigonus I; Demetrius Poliorcetes; Seleucus

Battle of Issus (333 B.C.)

One of the major battles of Alexander's campaign against the Persian Empire. Alexander moved toward Issus, located on the northern fringe of Syria, where his opponent, King Darius III, was camped. Darius's forces may have numbered as many as two hundred thousand while Alexander had perhaps thirty-two thousand infantry and five thousand horsemen. Alexander deployed his infantry in the center of his line and placed his cavalry on the wings, commanding the right wing himself. As the two armies met, he led a forceful charge right into the Persian left wing, which quickly fell apart. Then Alexander moved straight at Darius, who was surrounded by Persian nobles and bodyguards. However, Alexander was forced to abandon this assault in order to reinforce his center, which was in difficulty. A some point Darius fled the field, after which most of his remaining forces followed suit. Persian losses exceeded one hundred thousand, but fewer than a thousand Greeks were killed.

SEE ALSO: Alexander III ("the Great"); Darius III; Persians

Battle of Leuctra (371 B.C.)

Threatened by a Spartan army commanded by King Cleombrotus, the Theban generals Epaminondas and Pelopidas marched out troops they had been specially training for just such an encounter. Epaminondas had experimented with a new way of organizing the phalanx. Instead of following tradition and placing his best troops in his right wing, he put his weakest troops on the right, his strongest on the left, and held the right wing back at an angle. He also made the left wing fifty rows deep (compared to the Spartan left wing's twelve rows) to give it more strength. Near Leuctra, a village 10 miles (16km) southwest of Thebes, this new approach to hoplite warfare proved its worth with devastating results. A thousand Spartans, including their king, were killed, while the Thebans lost only forty-seven men. Epaminondas's victory shattered the myth of Spartan invincibility and launched a Theban hegemony of Greece.

SEE ALSO: Epaminondas; Sparta; weapons and warfare, land

Battle of Magnesia (190 B.C.)

After the Seleucid king Antiochus III fled from mainland Greece in the wake of his defeat at Thermopylae in 191 B.C., the Romans pursued him into western Asia Minor. There, at Magnesia (or Magnesia-ad-Sipylum), Antiochus's larger forces of sixty thousand infantry and twelve thousand horsemen were crushed by thirty thousand troops under the Roman commander Lucius Cornelius Scipio. Antiochus fled, and, after discovering that his losses exceeded 50,000 (compared to a mere 350 Romans killed), immediately sued for peace.

SEE ALSO: Antiochus III; Battle of Thermopylae, 3; Rome

Battle of Mantinea (418 B.C.)

At the height of the Peloponnesian War, a number of Peloponnesian cities squabbled, leading to a major battle at Mantinea, north of Megalopolis in Arcadia. Sparta, Tegea, and their allies defeated Argos, Mantinea, and a small contingent from Athens.

SEE ALSO: Peloponnesian War

Battle of Mantinea (362 B.C.)

In the last of the police actions taken in the Peloponnesus by the Thebans, the Theban general Epaminondas reached Mantinea and faced off with a coalition of troops from Sparta, Athens, Elis, and various Arcadian cities. The battle involved more than fifty thousand combatants in all, an unusually large number for a fight among Greeks. Epaminondas utilized the same oblique (slanted) formation he had at Leuctra. But this time the maneuver was not as devastating and the encounter ended in a draw. According to Xenophon, "Both sides claimed the victory, but it cannot be said that with regard to the accession of new territory, or cities, or power either side was any better off after the battle than before it." (*Hellenica* 7.5.27) One definitely decisive aspect of the battle was that Epaminondas, Thebes's most capable leader, was killed.

SEE ALSO: Battle of Leuctra; Epaminondas

Battle of Marathon (490 B.C.)

The Persian king Darius I sent a force of at least twenty thousand troops and perhaps twice that number of sailors, all under the command of his generals Artaphernes and Datis, to sack Athens. That city's citizen militia, numbering perhaps nine thousand, hurried to the eastern end of the Marathon plain (northeast of Athens), near where the invaders had anchored their ships. About a thousand soldiers from the tiny neighboring city-state of Plataea soon arrived to reinforce

The Athenians and Plataeans drive the Persians to their ships in the climax of the epic fight at Marathon in 490 B.C. North Wind Picture Archives

the Athenians. Led by the Athenian general Miltiades, on or about September 12 the Greeks attacked, crashing into the Persian lines with tremendous force. At first the Persian center pushed the weaker Greek center back. But the Greek wings swiftly crushed the enemy wings and then turned inward on the Persian center, where a tremendous slaughter ensued. Some 6,400 Persians were slain, while Athenian losses numbered only 192. The victory gave the Athenians much prestige among other Greeks and inspired Darius to seek revenge on Athens.

SEE ALSO: Athens; Darius I; Greco-Persian Wars; Persians

Battle of Mycale (479 B.C.)

The last major battle of the Greco-Persian conflict initiated by King Xerxes I in the 480s B.C. A Greek fleet commanded by Leotychides moved against a large contingent of Persian ships anchored at Samos. The Persians retreated to Mycale, a promontory on the nearby mainland of Asia Minor, went ashore, and joined up with several thousand Persian and subject Greek Ionian foot soldiers. Leotychides' men beached their own ships and attacked, after which the Ionians switched sides and helped their fellow Greeks, ensuring a Greek victory. Large numbers of Persians were killed, many as they fled toward their provincial capital of Sardis.

SEE ALSO: Greco-Persian Wars

Battle of Plataea (479 B.C.)

The largest land battle of the Greco-Persian Wars, it was fought near the tiny polis of Plataea, north of Athens. King Xerxes had retired to Asia Minor following his defeat at Salamis the year before, leaving his general Mardonius with more than a hundred thousand troops and orders to subdue the Greeks. The Greek forces included five thousand Spartans, supported by many thousands of other Peloponnesians; some eight thousand Athenians; and smaller contingents from Tegea, Megara, and several other Greek states. The Spartan general Pausanias was the overall commander. The battle was long, complex, and involved two separate engagements. In the first, the Athenians and Megarians defeated a large contingent of Persian cavalry. In the second, the Spartans and Tegeans took on a full-scale attack by Mardonius's infantry and remaining cavalry. After Mardonius was slain, most of the Persians fled to the seashore or to their camp. The Spartans, Athenians, and other Greeks converged on the camp, penetrated its defenses, and slaughtered nearly all of those inside. Some Persians managed to make it out of Greece, but Xerxes' overall losses were huge, while the Greeks lost fewer than fourteen hundred men.

SEE ALSO: Greco-Persian Wars

Battle of Potidaea (432 B.C.)

A crucial battle that took place on the eve of and contributed to the outbreak of the Peloponnesian War. Potidaea, located on the Chalcidic Peninsula (in the northern Aegean), was a Corinthian colony that had become an Athenian subject. The Potidaeans rebelled against Athens, which reacted by sending some seventy ships and several thousand troops. The Corinthians and some other Spartan allies sent their own troops to help the Potidaeans. Each side both won and lost ground in a series of skirmishes until the Athenians forced their opponents to retreat behind Potidaea's walls. A siege ensued, and the city surrendered early in 429 B.C.

SEE ALSO: Peloponnesian War

Battle of Pydna (168 B.C.)

The climactic engagement of the Third Macedonian War, fought between the Macedonian king Perseus and a Roman army commanded by Lucius Aemilius Paullus at Pydna, near Greece's northeastern coast. Perseus's infantry at first managed to push the Romans back. But then the Macedonian phalanx began to falter, mainly because the ground it was on was not flat enough for it to maneuver well. Paullus seized the moment and sent contingents of his own troops into the gaps that were opening the enemy phalanx, which steadily fell to pieces. About twenty-five thousand Greeks were slain, compared to Roman losses of only about a hundred men.

SEE ALSO: Macedonia; Perseus, 2; Rome

Battle of Raphia (217 B.C.)

A struggle marking the climax of the Fourth Syrian War, the last of a quartet of conflicts in which the Hellenistic Seleucid and Ptolemaic kingdoms fought over possession of southern Syria. The Seleucid king, Antiochus III, marched an army of sixty-two thousand infantry, six thousand cavalry, and more than a hundred elephants to Raphia, on the border of Palestine and Egypt. There, he encountered Ptolemy IV, whose forces were roughly the same size. The opposing elephant brigades opened the battle. When Ptolemy's pachyderms fell back into his own lines, Antiochus led his cavalry against the enemy horsemen. In the center, however, Ptolemy's phalanx was victorious and the rest of Antiochus's army fled. Antiochus lost about ten thousand men, compared to twenty-two hundred killed on the other side.

SEE ALSO: Seleucid Empire

Battle of Salamis (480 B.C.)

The pivotal battle of the Greco-Persian Wars, it took place in the strait separating the island of Salamis from the Attic peninsula, a few miles southwest of Athens. King Xerxes sent his 600 warships into the strait while he watched from a throne set up on a nearby hill. Though the Greeks had fewer than 350 vessels (about a third of them Athenian), they won the day because the Persians found themselves hemmed in and unable to maneuver well in the narrow waterway. The Athenian playwright Aeschylus, who fought in the battle, gave this eyewitness account (from his play *The Persians*, in which a Persian messenger speaks to Xerxes' mother):

> At once ship into ship battered its brazen beak. A Greek ship charged first, and chopped off the whole stern of a Persian galley. Then charge followed charge on every side. . . . In that narrow space, our ships were jammed in hundreds; none could help another. . . . Meanwhile the enemy came round us in a ring and charged. Our vessels heeled over; the sea was hidden, carpeted with wrecks and dead men; all the shores and reefs were full of dead. . . . The Greeks seized fragments of wrecks and broken oars and hacked and stabbed at our men swimming in the sea. . . . The whole sea was one din of shrieks and dying groans, till night and darkness hid the scene. (*The Persians* 416–430)

SEE ALSO: Aeschylus; Greco-Persian Wars; *Persians, The*

Battle of Thermopylae (480 B.C.)

A famous battle of the Greco-Persian Wars, it was a tactical defeat but a symbolic victory for the Greeks. As King Xerxes' massive army moved southward through mainland Greece, the allied Greek plan was to send a small holding force to the narrow pass of Thermopylae (north of Boeotia) while the Greek states assembled larger forces. The Spartan king Leonidas commanded the holding force, which consisted of three hundred picked Spartan troops, about twenty-seven hundred men from Sparta's Peloponnesian neighbors, and a few thousand soldiers from Thebes, Thespiae, and other Greek states. The pass was extremely narrow, so only a few Persians could make it through at a time. These were repeatedly slaughtered by the Spartans and other Greeks. For three days the tiny band of defenders held the pass, inflicting enormous casualties on the enemy. Eventually, however, in exchange for gold, a local Greek, perhaps a sheep herder, agreed to show the Persians a little-known mountain path that led to the rear of the Greek position. On the morning of the fourth day, realizing he would soon be outflanked, Leonidas sent the bulk of the Greek troops away. He, his Spartans, and a few hundred Thespians and other volunteers, remained and fought to the death in a display of courage that became legendary.

SEE ALSO: Greco-Persian Wars; Leonidas; Xerxes

Battle of Thermopylae (279 B.C.)

An army of thirty thousand Greeks easily held the pass against a similar sized force of invading Celts from central Europe, led by Brennus. Eventually, however, Brennus used the same mountain path the Persians had two centuries before; rather than be outflanked and massacred, the Greeks withdrew.

SEE ALSO: Celts

Battle of Thermopylae (191 B.C.)

The Seleucid king Antiochus III, whose goal was to drive the Romans out of Greece, attempted to hold the pass against the enemy but was defeated with heavy losses.

SEE ALSO: Antiochus III; Rome

Bellerophon

One of the more swashbuckling heroes of Greek mythology. Bellerophon was said to be the son either of a Corinthian king or of Poseidon, god of the seas. In one of his chief adventures, the young hero went on a mission to slay the Chimaera, a horrifying monster that had been terrorizing the countryside. With the help of the magical winged horse Pegasus, which he had earlier tamed, Bellerophon confronted and killed the Chimaera. A king named Iobates sent the young man on many other dangerous missions, all of which he successfully completed. Later, however, Bellerophon allowed the constant praises he received for his great deeds go to his head and became arrogant. He rode Pegasus into the sky in an attempt to challenge the gods. This angered Zeus, leader of the Olympians, who caused the young man to fall off of Pegasus and suffer injuries that made him a poor cripple who could no longer accomplish heroic acts.

SEE ALSO: Chimaera; Pegasus

Berenice

The name of several women who held high positions in the royal courts of the large Hellenistic kingdoms. One of the most famous and important was Berenice I (b. ca. 340 B.C.), a granddaughter of Cassander, one of the Successors of Alexander the Great. From her first marriage, to a Macedonian nobleman, she had a son who later became king of Cyrene in North Africa. After her husband died, she went to Egypt and there became the lover of another of the Successors, Ptolemy (later King Ptolemy I Soter). The couple had two children—a boy who became Ptolemy's successor, Ptolemy II, and a girl, Arsinoë, who later became her brother's queen. A later Berenice was a sister of Cleopatra VII (b. 69 B.C.). This Berenice stole her father's throne while he was away, and when he regained it, he immediately ordered her execution.

SEE ALSO: Cleopatra VII; Ptolemy I Soter; Ptolemy II Philadelphus

biography

Among the many literary genres created by the ancient Greeks, biography was one of the last to develop. Thucydides paved the way in the late fifth century B.C. with the character sketches of leading generals and statesmen he incorporated into his groundbreaking *Peloponnesian War*. Soon afterward, in the early 300s B.C., Xenophon produced a few more formal biographical works, including the *Agesilaus*, about the famous Spartan king of that name, and the *Cyropaedia*, describing the Persian monarch Cyrus the Great. Also in the fourth century B.C. some of Aristotle's students experimented with biography, and they influenced a number of later Alexandrian biographers. Only fragments of the works of these writers have survived. But in their turn, they exerted a strong influence on perhaps the greatest biographer of antiquity—Plutarch (first century A.D.). His *Parallel Lives* consists of more than fifty detailed biographical sketches of leading Greek and Roman figures, most of which have survived. Another notable extant collection of ancient biographies is the *Lives of the Eminent Philosophers*, written by the third-century A.D. Greek Diogenes Laertius, although these are not nearly as long, accurate, and well written as Plutarch's.

SEE ALSO: Plutarch; Thucydides, 2; Xenophon

Birds

A comic play by Aristophanes, first performed in Athens in 414 B.C. As the play begins, two Athenians named Peisetairos and Euelpides agree that the hustle and bustle of city life is too much for them and depart Athens in search of novelty and adventure. Peisetairos eventually conceives the idea of building a city floating in the sky, called Cloud Cuckoo Land, where all birds would come to live. For food, he says, the birds can intercept the smoke from sacrifices (intended to float up to and nourish the gods). At first the birds are unsure about the scheme. But they eventually agree, after which Peisetairos and Euelpides grow wings and help them construct the city. However, it does not take long for the gods to notice what is going on. Negotiations between the birds and gods follow, and Peisetairos becomes engaged to Basileia, a daughter of Zeus.

SEE ALSO: Aristophanes, 1

Black Sea

The large waterway lying north of Asia Minor. The Greeks called it the Euxine ("Friendly") Sea and reached it by sailing first through the Hellespont (the modern Dardanelles strait) and then the Bosphorus strait (guarded by the prosperous city of Byzantium). During the great age of Greek colonization (the eighth through sixth centuries B.C.), numerous Greek cities were established along the Black Sea's coasts. The grain produced by some of these towns came to be imported by city-states in mainland Greece, particularly Athens, which became dependent on such grain shipments. In mythology, the Black Sea was most famous for the voyage of Jason and his Argonauts to Colchis (on the sea's eastern shore) in search of the Golden Fleece.

SEE ALSO: Byzantium; colonization; Hellespont

Boeotia

The region of mainland Greece lying north of Attica, east of the Gulf of Corinth, and south of Locris and Phocis. Boeotia (bee-OH-shya) featured two small fertile plains, where grain and olives grew and horses were bred. These plains were near Thebes and Orchomenus, the two largest towns in the region and the leading Mycenaean centers during the Bronze Age. A substantial number of myths of that period involved Boeotian events, towns, and characters, and twenty-nine of the region's towns were mentioned in the catalog of ships bound for Troy in Homer's *Iliad*. Later, in the Archaic and Classical periods, the major Boeotian towns numbered roughly a dozen, which formed the Boeotian League, an alliance headed by Thebes. The Thebans and other Boeotians had frequent disputes and battles with Athens and took Sparta's side in the Peloponnesian War (431–404 B.C.). However, they allied themselves temporarily with the Athenians in 338 B.C. in an attempt to stop the advance of the Macedonian king Philip II. Philip was victorious at Chaeronea in western Boeotia, after which Boeotia lost its independence and declined in prosperity and importance. In 197 B.C. the Boeotian hill of Cynoscephalae was the site of a major battle between the Romans and the Macedonians, and Chaeronea gained some minor notoriety beginning in the first century A.D. as the hometown of the great biographer Plutarch.

SEE ALSO: Greece, history of; Mycenaeans; Thebes

Boreas

In Greek mythology, the god of the North Wind. Writers usually described him as a vigorous, forceful wind, as opposed to the god Zephyrus, who personified the more gentle West Wind. Boreas was fond of horses, so artists often pictured him as a horse. His sons, Calais and Zetes, sailed with Jason in search of the Golden Fleece.

SEE ALSO: Jason, 1

Bosphorus

The narrow strait linking the Black Sea to the Propontis (Sea of Marmara). The city of Byzantium was strategically located on the Bosphorus.

SEE ALSO: Black Sea; Byzantium

boule

In ancient Greece, a governmental council, usually one working with and preparing the agenda for an assembly of citizens. The one created in Athens in the Archaic Age is generally capitalized (*Boule*).

SEE ALSO: government

Brasidas
(died 422 B.C.)

A Spartan general who served his country during the first phase of the bloody Peloponnesian War. He captured the Athenian colony of Amphipolis in the northern Aegean in 423 B.C. Brasidas was killed in the following year while defending the city against an Athenian attempt to retake it.

SEE ALSO: Amphipolis; Peloponnesian War

bronze

An alloy (mixture) of the metals copper and tin. Bronze was widely used for tools, weapons, utensils, coins, statues, and other items in the ancient world, including Greece.

SEE ALSO: industry; metalworking; mining; weapons and warfare, land

Bronze Age

As determined by modern scholars, the period of ancient Greece lasting from about 3000 to 1100 B.C. For the major peoples and events of the period, **see** Greece, history of.

SEE ALSO: Atlantis; Crete; Minoans; Mycenaeans; Thera; Theseus; Troy; Tiryns; weapons and warfare, land

building materials and methods

The building materials used in ancient Greece varied widely according to the types of structures in which they were used. From the Bronze Age to the Hellenistic period, houses, storage sheds, and other small buildings in rural settings (farms and villages) were generally made of highly perishable materials such as thatch, wood, and sun-dried clay bricks. Some walls utilized more durable fieldstones and/or rubble (irregular pieces of stone) from quarries, but these fell apart fairly quickly without constant repairs and

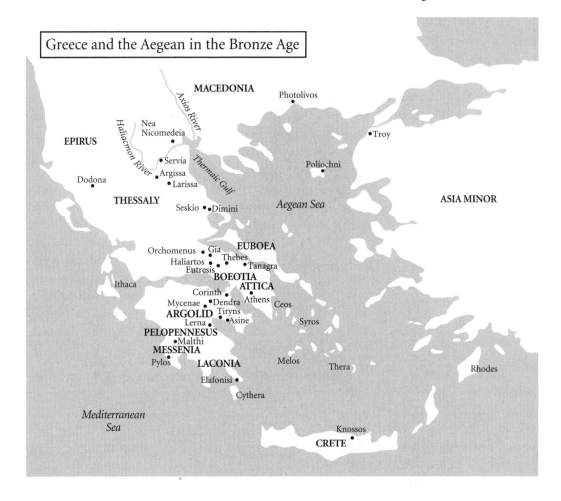

Greece and the Aegean in the Bronze Age

MACEDONIA

Photolivos

Axios River

Haliacmon River

Nea
Nicomedeia

EPIRUS

•Troy

Servia
Argissa

Thermaic Gulf

Poliochni

Dodona

Larissa

THESSALY

Seskio ••Dimini

Aegean Sea

ASIA MINOR

Orchomenus • Gia
Thebes
Haliartos •
Eutresis •Tanagra

EUBOEA

BOEOTIA
ATTICA

Ithaca

Corinth •Dendra Athens
Mycenae • Tiryns
ARGOLID •Asine
Lerna •
PELOPENNESUS
•Malthi
MESSENIA
Pylos •

Athens
Ceos

Syros

LACONIA

Melos

Thera

Rhodes

Elafonisi •

Cythera

Mediterranean
Sea

Knossos •
CRETE •

upkeep. The materials used inside these structures were also perishable and subject to rapid deterioration—hard-packed dirt, wooden planks, thin flagstones, straw mats, and so forth.

Larger houses, including country villas and townhouses in cities such as Athens and Olynthus, were only slightly sturdier and more durable. Clay bricks, sometimes reinforced with wooden timbers, were the norm, forcing homeowners to undertake frequent repairs. In homes of the more well-to-do some of the walls were coated with stucco (decorative plaster) and sometimes painted. Beginning in about 400 B.C., the better homes also featured floors made of mosaic tiles as opposed to the still-

common hard-packed earth covered by straw mats, although the floors of second-story rooms were most often made of wood because tiles would have been too heavy.

In contrast to the impermanent materials used in most private structures, many public buildings in Greece, especially temples, theaters, and palaces, employed more durable masonry (stone). These included huge blocks of granite and slabs of marble. After the blocks were quarried, they were transported to worksites on large wagons pulled by oxen, or, when the sites were more distant, by ship. Once the blocks had reached the worksite, stonemasons began dressing, or preparing, them so that they would fit into premeasured spaces in the walls. A mason's tools included flat-headed metal chisels and pointed instruments (called points), which he struck with a wooden mallet. With rare exceptions, no mortar was used and the blocks had to fit together precisely and tightly. When these were in place, workers joined one block to another with I-shaped iron clamps. The clamps in the top of one course of stone were hidden from view by the next course of stones placed above them.

Other masons dressed the stones for the building's columns (pillars). (Before stone construction became the norm across Greece in the 500s B.C., typical columns were made of thick wooden timbers, as in the case of those in Bronze Age palaces like the palace at Knossos.) Each of the rounded pieces of stone making up a column was called a drum. Tall columns, like those of the Parthenon and other major temples, featured up to eleven separate drums, topped by a capital (top piece) decorated in the Doric, Ionic, or Corinthian order (architectural style). Like wall blocks, two column drums were joined by metal fasteners that were later hidden by the drums stacked above them.

To lift the heavy drums and the blocks for the upper courses of a structure's walls, the builders used mechanical hoists. The most common kind was a derrick consisting of a wooden framework with ropes and pulleys attached. After the ropes had been attached to a stone block, teams of oxen or men pulled on the ropes, thereby lifting the stone, which was carefully guided into place. Workmen then used crowbars and raw muscle power to make an exact fit. Hoists were also used to lift loads of heavy roofing tiles. The most common type of tile used in public build-

ings from the Classical Age on was the Corinthian tile, which consisted of two flat pieces joined in the middle by an angular cover tile.

Greek public buildings usually featured elaborate decoration. Carved stone moldings of various sizes ran along the tops of crossbeams, under the roof eaves, and along the edges of pediments (the triangular spaces formed by the slanting roof eaves). Pediments frequently had sculpted figures, sometimes life-size or larger, in them. Also, most of the exteriors were painted in bright colors. Inside such structures, stucco walls featuring wall paintings were common, both in Minoan palaces in the Bronze Age and in temples and other large buildings in the Classical, Hellenistic, and Roman periods.

SEE ALSO: architectural orders; houses; Parthenon; temples

burial customs

Very little is known about burial customs in Bronze Age Greece. Inhumation (burial in tombs or in the ground) seems to have been the norm, and archaeologists have discovered a number of Mycenaean and Minoan tombs of diverse design. In Minoan Crete many tombs consisted of a few small adjoining rooms, like a miniature house, and each was probably used to inter succeeding generations of a family. People were also buried under *tumuli* (mounds of earth), in caves, and in shaft graves (narrow, vertical pits). *Tumuli* and shaft graves were also employed on the Mycenaean mainland. The most famous shaft graves are those found at Mycenae, the so-called Grave Circles, dating from circa 1600 to 1500 B.C. Mycenae also featured one of the best-preserved *tholoi*, or "beehive," tombs, which were used to house the remains of Mycenaean royalty across the Aegean region in the late Bronze Age. A *tholos* tomb consisted of a large chamber with conical stone walls.

In the Dark and Archaic ages, cremation (burning) replaced inhumation as the most common method of dealing with dead bodies. The ashes were placed in special pottery containers (*lekythoi*) and buried, along with grave goods (such as weapons, cups and vases, and jewelry) in pits or under small mounds. After about 600 B.C. these urns were also deposited in family tombs with small rooms similar to those used in the Bronze Age. Larger versions of family tombs (called *periboloi*) became popular in Athens in the Classical period. The beginning of that era also witnessed the revival of inhumation, although some cremation still took place.

Whether the body was buried or burned, a typical funeral in Classical Greece involved considerable ceremony, and some of the rituals involved may have dated back to the late Dark Age or even earlier. To prepare the corpse, family women washed it and rubbed it with olive oil. Then they dressed it in white garments and placed it on a bed with its feet pointing toward the bedchamber's door. The body lay in state that way for a day or two so that relatives, friends, and sometimes hired mourners could view it. Eventually the mourners carried the body to the grave site, almost always situated outside the city walls (because corpses, whose spirits had departed, it was believed, to dwell in the Underworld or afterlife, were thought to be "polluted," or religiously tainted, and must therefore be kept away from the living). Either before or after this funeral procession, the body was placed in a coffin (*larnax*). Poorer folk used wooden ones, while those who could afford it opted for stone versions, often ornately decorated.

(A number of magnificent examples from Macedonia and elsewhere in Hellenistic times have survived.) At the conclusion of the funeral, someone delivered a funeral speech (*epitaphios*), after which the body (or urn containing the deceased's ashes) was interred. The mourners shouted the deceased's name three times. Then they went home and underwent a ritual washing to purify themselves since their close contact with the body had rendered them polluted.

SEE ALSO: religion; *tholos*; Underworld

Byzantium

A Greek city occupying a strategic position on the European side of the Bosphorus strait, which leads into the Black Sea. Byzantium was established by colonists from Megara (situated west of Athens) in the seventh century B.C. and rapidly became prosperous thanks to trade passing between the Aegean and Black seas. In addition to the trade itself, Byzantine ships charged foreign vessels tolls for using the strait. Eventually the city fell under the control or influence of a succession of foreign powers, among them Persia (from ca. 513 to 478 B.C.); Athens (478–404), through Byzantium's membership in the Athenian-controlled Delian League; and Sparta (404–377). After that, Byzantium was independent until it became a part of the Roman realm in the first century B.C. In A.D. 330 the city and its environs became part of the new metropolis of Constantinople (named for its founder, the emperor Constantine I); it served as the Roman Empire's eastern capital until Rome's fall, after which the eastern Roman realm mutated into the Greek-speaking Byzantine Empire.

SEE ALSO: Black Sea; Rome

Cadmus

According to legend, the founder of Thebes, in Boeotia, who also taught the local people writing skills and other arts.

SEE ALSO: Thebes

calendars

All of the Greek city-states recognized a combination of civic and religious years containing twelve months. The religious elements were tightly interwoven with the civic ones, based on traditions dating back into the Dark Age or before. Each month began with a new moon and contained 29 or 30 days. The resulting lunar year added up to 354 days, eleven fewer than in a solar year (the kind used today). So local officials in each city-state periodically added extra days, weeks, or months to make the two systems match. In many cases individual city-states had their own distinct calendars, with their own local names for the months. It appears that these names most often derived from those of local religious festivals. In Athens, the months (with their approximate modern equivalents) were as follows: *Hekatombaion* (July), *Metageitnion* (August), *Boedromion* (September), *Pyanopsion* (October), *Maimakterion* (November), *Poseideon* (December), *Gamelion* (January), *Anthesterion* (February), *Elaphebolion* (March), *Mounichion* (April), *Thargelion* (May), and *Skirophorion* (June).

SEE ALSO: government; religion

Callimachus
(died 490 B.C.)

An Athenian general who fought in the Battle of Marathon in 490 B.C. At the time, he was Athens's *polemarch* (war archon), which by tradition allowed him to command the army's right wing. He broke a tie vote among the other generals, thereby authorizing an immediate attack on the Persians gathered on the Marathon plain. Callimachus perished in the ensuing struggle.

SEE ALSO: Battle of Marathon; *polemarch*

Callimachus
(ca. 310 B.C.–ca. 240 B.C.)

A noted Hellenistic poet and scholar who worked at the Great Library in Alexandria, where he cataloged a number of its volumes. Callimachus was famous for the large number of his own books, supposedly more than eight hundred in all. However, most were likely short, for he is said to have remarked, "A big book is a big evil." Tradition claims that this is why he did not write any epic poetry, which he saw as passé. That got him into a running argument with his Alexandrian colleague Apollonius, who favored epic poetry. The vast majority of Callimachus's poems have not survived. But his skills must have been great because he strongly influenced several later Roman poets.

SEE ALSO: Alexandria; Alexandrian and other Hellenistic Greek literature; Apollonius of Rhodes

Callisthenes
(ca. 370 B.C.–327 B.C.)

A Greek historian who was related to and studied with Aristotle. Callisthenes went along with Alexander the Great into Asia in 334 B.C. as the official historian of the expedition. In time, however, he got on Alexander's bad side, as the latter suspected the historian of taking part in a conspiracy against him. Callisthenes was executed seven years into the campaign. His partial account of the expedition and other writings did not survive.

SEE ALSO: Alexander III ("the Great"); historical writing

Calypso

In Greek mythology, a well-known nymph (minor Greek goddess). A daughter of the Titan Atlas, she ruled the far-off island of Ogygia, on which the Greek hero Odysseus landed after being shipwrecked. Calypso fell in love with him and managed to keep him on the island for seven years. Finally Zeus sent the god Hermes, who convinced her to let Odysseus go, and she helped the latter build a boat so he could make his way to his home (the island of Ithaca).

SEE ALSO: Odysseus; *Odyssey*

Cambyses
(reigned 530–522 B.C.)

The eldest son of Persia's Cyrus the Great and the second ruler of the Persian Empire. Before his death, Cyrus had been planning an invasion of Egypt, and Cambyses (cam-BEE-seez) completed this project. Early in 525 B.C. Cambyses led a large army into Egypt and defeated the Egyptian pharaoh Psammetichus III at Pelusium. Cambyses remained in Egypt for the next three years or so, then headed home. He had only just begun his long journey when he received news that a man claiming to be his dead brother (whom he himself had murdered) had usurped the throne. What happened next is unclear, for Cambyses soon died

under mysterious circumstances. Some accounts say the cause was the onset of gangrene after an accidental knife wound. Others claim that Cambyses was mentally unbalanced and, in a fit of despair over the news of the rebellion, committed suicide. Murder at the hands of rebel sympathizers also cannot be ruled out.

SEE ALSO: Cyrus II ("the Great"); Persians

Caria

A region of southwestern Asia Minor; Caria's fortunes were often tied to the Greek Ionian states to its north and to the Persian Empire, which held parts of Asia Minor off and on from the sixth to fourth centuries B.C. The Carians, who spoke their own Indo-European tongue, usually backed the Greeks against the Persians. In 499 B.C., for example, Caria joined in the Ionian rebellion against Persia, and in 467 the Carians aided the Athenian general Cimon against the Persians at the battle of Eurymedon. Caria grew in power and prominence in the fourth century B.C., but in the following century it came under the control of various Hellenistic states, including Ptolemaic Egypt and Rhodes. Finally, in about 133 B.C. the Romans incorporated Caria into their province of Asia.

SEE ALSO: Battle of Eurymedon

Carthage

A powerful and influential ancient city located on a peninsula projecting into the Mediterranean Sea at the tip of what is now Tunisia in North Africa. Established by traders from the Phoenician city of Tyre in the ninth century B.C., Carthage was for a while a trading post and a rest stop for Phoenicians traveling farther west. In the seventh century B.C., however, the city became independent of Tyre and rapidly began expanding its influence across the western Mediterranean region. The commercial and to some extent political empire it created included parts of southern France and the islands of Corsica and Sicily, all areas where local Greek cities resisted Carthaginian intrusion, and so war between the two peoples was inevitable. In about 600 B.C. a Greek fleet defeated a Carthaginian one near Massalia. Carthage countered by driving the Greeks out of Corsica circa 540 B.C. But the tables turned once more in 480 B.C., when Greeks from Syracuse and other Sicilian cities decisively defeated the Carthaginians at Himera. Carthage's interests in Sicily eventually brought it into conflict with Rome, leading to the three Punic Wars (spanning the period from 264 to 146 B.C.). Rome was victorious in all three conflicts and at the conclusion of the last one utterly destroyed Carthage. The city's survivors were sold into slavery.

SEE ALSO: Battle of Himera; Phoenicia; Rome; Syracuse

caryatid

An architectural column carved in the shape of a woman, traditionally said to represent women of Caryae, who were enslaved by the Greeks for siding with the Persians in their fifth-century B.C. invasion of Greece. The most famous examples in Greece were the six caryatids that held up the so-called Porch of the Maidens on the south side of the Erechtheum temple on Athens's Acropolis. (The versions seen there today are replicas; the originals are all in museums.)

SEE ALSO: Erechtheum

Cassander
(ca. 358 B.C.–297 B.C.)

The son of Antipater, one of the generals and leading successors of Alexander the Great. Following his father's death in 319 B.C., Cassander conquered Macedonia and much of mainland Greece. A few years later he had a direct role in the assassination of Alexander's mother (Olympias), son, and wife. Finally, in 305 B.C., Cassander assumed the title of king of Macedonia. There he established the town of Thessaloniki (named for his wife), which today is Greece's second-largest city. A few years after Cassander's death in 297 B.C., his kingdom fell to Antigonus Gonatas, grandson of another of the Successors, Antigonus I.

SEE ALSO: Alexander III ("the Great"); Antipater; Successors

Cassandra

In Greek mythology, a famous daughter of Priam and Hecuba, king and queen of Troy during the legendary Trojan War. In his *Iliad*, Homer depicted Cassandra (also called Alexandra) as the most beautiful of the Trojan princesses and also as a prophetess who could see into the future. Supposedly this gift was granted to her by Apollo, god of prophecy, who fell in love with her. However, she had the audacity to refuse his advances, and he punished her by seeing to it that she would always deliver truthful prophecies but that no one would believe her. Thus, Cassandra foresaw her brother Paris's abduction of the Spartan queen, Helen, and warned of the troubles that would occur as a result of it. Cassandra also cautioned the Trojans not to drag the wooden horse (which contained a hidden contingent of Greek soldiers) into the city. But none of the Trojans heeded her warnings, thinking her

The murder of Agamemnon by his queen, Clytemnestra, depicted here, was foreseen by the Trojan princess Cassandra. AKG-IMAGES

insane. When the Greeks captured Troy and began burning the city, Cassandra took refuge in the local temple of Athena. But the Greek warrior Ajax the Lesser entered, dragged the young woman away, and raped her. The angry Athena reacted by killing or scattering many of the Greeks on their homeward journeys. Meanwhile, the leader of the Greek forces, Agamemnon, made Cassandra his slave and took her back to Greece. There, she foresaw the murders of Agamemnon and herself at the hands of Agamemnon's wife, Clytemnestra, part of the terrible curse of the House of Atreus. As before, however, no one paid any attention to her warnings.

SEE ALSO: Agamemnon; Troy

Castor and Polydeuces

In legend, the brothers of Helen of Troy. The two young men were sometimes represented as sons of Zeus and after their deaths became immortal. For their story,

SEE ALSO: their collective name, Dioscuri

cavalry

The Greeks used cavalry, or mounted soldiers, sparingly in warfare until the fourth century B.C., when they began to be used in direct charges on foot soldiers.

SEE ALSO: weapons and warfare, land

Celts

A group of tribal peoples who spread across much of central Europe in the Bronze Age and the centuries that followed. Those Celts who occupied Gaul (now France) became known to the Greeks and Romans as Gauls; those who settled much later in central Asia Minor were called Galatians. Celtic culture featured rule by kings and chieftains, small walled towns rather than large cities, widespread illiteracy and an absence of written literature, considerable metalworking skills, and armies of warriors known for their bravery and ferocity but lack of discipline and military organization. The first significant Greek contact with the Celts occurred in the 600s B.C, when Greek merchants traded with Celts living in Gaul and Spain. In particular, the Greek city of Massalia (on Gaul's southern coast) developed a lively trade with the Gallic natives in the interior. Trouble erupted, however, when groups of Celts invaded northern Greece in the third century B.C. The intruders managed to capture the sacred sanctuary at Delphi and then crossed into Asia Minor, where the Seleucid king Antiochus I defeated them. Later, many Celts adopted Roman language and culture following Julius Caesar's conquest of Gaul in the 50s B.C.

SEE ALSO: Battle of Thermopylae, 2; Massalia; trade

centaurs

In Greek mythology, a race of creatures who were half man and half horse (their lower bodies being horselike). They were said to inhabit the region around Mt. Pelion in Thessaly (in central Greece). Most of the centaurs were slovenly, crude, inhospitable, and beastly characters, although one of their number, Chiron, was known for his kindness and wisdom. Legends claim that the centaurs fought a war with the Lapiths, an early group of Greeks who settled in Thessaly. The Lapith king, Pirithous, made the mistake of inviting his neighbors, the centaurs, to his wedding. There, the horse-men got drunk and tried to kidnap the Lapith women. The Lapith men gave chase, rescued the women, and slew numerous centaurs. The

Greeks called this legendary battle the Centauromachy, which became a common subject of sculpture and other art, an outstanding example being several sculptures on Athens's Parthenon temple depicting centaurs fighting Lapiths.

SEE ALSO: Chiron

Cerberus

In Greek mythology, a monstrous, many-headed dog that guarded the entrance to the Underworld.

SEE ALSO: Underworld

Chalcidice

A peninsula in northern Greece that extends southward into the Aegean Sea in three large promontories—from west to east, Cassandra, Sithonia, and Acte (or Athos). A number of Greek states began colonizing the area in the eighth century B.C. The most important of the new cities was Potidaea, established circa 600 B.C. Another important Chalcidic city, Olynthus, was destroyed by Macedonia's King Philip II in 348. Thereafter, Chalcidice remained more or less under Macedonian domination until Rome defeated Macedonia in the second century B.C.

SEE ALSO: Athos, Mt.; Olynthus; Potidaea

Chalcis

The main city on Euboea, the large island lying on the Greek mainland's eastern flank. Evidence suggests that Chalcis was one of the first towns in Greece to resume overseas trade following the collapse of Mycenaean culture at the close of the Bronze Age. Known for making fine metal artifacts, the Chalcidians sought metal ores in western Italy and established trading posts there in the 700s B.C. In about 700 Chalcis and another Euboean city, Eretria, fought a major war, the outcome of which is uncertain. Eventually Chalcis's commercial success was eclipsed by Corinthian shipping, and the Chalcidians were subsequently politically dominated in succession by the Athenians, the Macedonians, and finally the Romans.

SEE ALSO: Eretria

Chaos

In Greek mythology, the primordial void from which the first primitive deities emerged. Chaos gave rise to Gaia (Earth), Tartarus (the darkest part of the Underworld), Nyx (Night), and Erebus (Darkness).

SEE ALSO: Gaia; *Theogony*; Underworld

chariots

Archaeological evidence shows that chariots were used in Greek warfare in the last few centuries of the Bronze Age by the Mycenaeans (and maybe by the Minoans, too). But scholars are still not certain exactly how or how often they were used. In his *Iliad*, Homer describes chariots mainly as "prestige vehicles," in effect taxis that take prominent warriors to the battlefield, where they dismount and fight on foot. However, this is probably not the way the Mycenaeans employed their war chariots. First, the style of warfare Homer describes was likely that of the Dark Age rather than the Bronze Age. During the latter era, when the Mycenaean kingdoms were emerging on the Greek mainland, Near Eastern peoples, notably the Egyptians, Assyrians, and Hittites, developed battlefield tactics in which masses of chariots carrying archers charged at one another. Hundreds and sometimes thousands of chariots took part in the larger battles, in which specially trained foot soldiers supported the chariot warriors. The Mycenaeans were strongly influenced by the Near East in this period, so they likely used at least a modified form of such warfare. One difference was the size of the chariot battles in Greece. That land has few flat plains large enough to contain massed chariot charges, which means that most engagements between opposing chariot corps probably featured no more than a few hundred vehicles at most. Supporting this supposition is the evidence of inventories from the palace at Knossos in northern Crete, which list about 340 chariot frames and one thousand chariot wheels.

It appears, therefore, that the chariot, supporting an archer wielding a composite bow, was a major offensive weapon of late Bronze Age Greek land warfare. The arrows fired by these fighters, as well as by foot archers, must have created deadly rains of arrows, against which the chariot warriors required protection. And in fact, sculptures and paintings from ancient Egypt, Cyprus, and elsewhere from this era depict chariot fighters wearing suits of armor made of copper or bronze scales sown or glued to leather or linen jerkins. A surviving example of such armor was unearthed in 1960 at Dendra, located near Mycenae.

Although chariots may still have been used in Greece in the Dark Age, perhaps as described by Homer, the Greeks did not incorporate chariots into hoplite-style warfare, which they developed in the Archaic Age. This was because chariots were, by and large, no match for hoplites arrayed in a phalanx formation. This was proven during Alexander's invasion of Persia in the fourth century B.C. when he and his men faced attacks by old-fashioned Mesopotamian chariot corps. The Greek soldiers merely stepped aside, allowing the vehicles to pass by, then closed ranks, surrounded the chariots, and used spears and swords to slaughter the charioteers.

SEE ALSO: Mycenaeans; weapons and warfare, land

Charon

In Greek mythology, the grim boatman who ferried the souls of the dead across the River Styx into the Underworld.

SEE ALSO: Underworld

children

Ancient Greek society placed a strong emphasis on having children, partly to prevent family lines from dying out. Also, most Greek couples desired to produce at least one son because property and inheritance laws were designed largely to accommodate the needs of men and male-dominated families. It was also seen as essential to ensure that the community, made up of a group of local families, was perpetuated. Most Greek city-states were small and had only a few thousand inhabitants. If not enough children were produced, the polis might not have enough human resources to defend itself. Because of the emphasis placed on having boys, female babies were sometimes exposed (left outside to die). Male infants were occasionally exposed, too, but usually only if they were physically deformed in some way.

Deciding whether an infant should live or die constituted but one of many issues and customs surrounding children and childhood in ancient Greece. Certainly the very process of having babies was treated as a serious matter because the number of infants and mothers who died in childbirth was high. As many as 25 to 35 percent of children died in their first year of life (compared to less than 1 percent in the United States today). This means that many Greek women, perhaps a majority of them, lost at least one child in their lifetimes. The number of mothers who died in childbirth is unknown, but modern estimates run from 10 to 20 percent (compared to just .01 percent in the United States today). This high proportion was likely partly due to the fact that so many young mothers were teenagers, who even today run a higher risk of complications in pregnancy and birth. There was also widespread ignorance about proper hygiene in ancient times. In addition to these losses, numerous unborn children were lost to miscarriages and abortion. Ancient Greek beliefs about abortion are somewhat unclear. There were no laws against it, but it is possible that some religious sanctions discouraged abortions performed after the fetus had attained a certain level of development. Evidently an average abortion involved having the woman jump up and down and/or consume herbs known to induce premature delivery.

Ordinary deliveries typically took place in the home. Most often the woman's female relatives oversaw the birth, assisted by a midwife. Usually the woman gave birth seated upright on a birthing stool, although some women delivered while lying on their backs. Soon after the birth, the parents announced the event to the community by pinning an olive stem to the door if it was a boy or a piece of wool if it was a girl. The new mother also visited a shrine to thank the goddesses Artemis, who watched over expectant mothers, and Eileithyia, the goddess of childbirth. In

Athens, and presumably in many other Greek states, the child was formally accepted into the family and clan in two postbirth ceremonies. In one, the *amphidromia*, relatives made offerings to the gods and the father carried the child around the family hearth. Relatives and friends also sent gifts. In the other ceremony, the *decate*, relatives and neighbors socialized, danced, and ate cake.

It is unclear whether such ceremonies accompanied adoption in ancient Greece. Because of the importance placed on producing a legitimate male heir, some Greek parents resorted to adopting a boy. The child in question was usually a relative, most often a nephew or cousin. In cases where the parents could not adopt a son or the adoptee died in childhood, the law provided a loophole through which the family's blood line and property could pass on through a daughter. In Athens, such a young woman was called an *epikleros*, which meant "without property." On the death of her father, she had to marry a male relative so that the father's property would remain within the extended family.

The same childrearing methods were employed for both biological and adopted children. All children grew up in a culture that viewed corporal punishment, including beatings with wooden rods and leather straps, as perfectly acceptable. Also, there was little or no societal concern with making children happy or developing their self-esteem. Most adults believed that children lacked proper reasoning powers, courage, or even a moral capacity until they were at least in their teens. So it stood to reason that children must be carefully trained and harshly disciplined when necessary. Still, young children were allowed to have toys, including balls, tops, hoops, yo-yos, and dolls. They also played with miniature carts and chariots, some of which they made themselves from whatever materials were easily available. Children also kept pets, including dogs, ducks, weasels, and mice. But in addition to play, Greek children were expected to work. And by the age of eight or nine most children spent part of each day doing such tasks as tending sheep, cleaning houses or schoolrooms, running errands, doing laundry, or tending the family's animals.

SEE ALSO: education; family; women

Children of Heracles

A tragedy by Euripides, first performed in Athens circa 430 B.C. The main characters include Eurystheus, king of Argos and Tiryns, and the Heracleidae, the children of the renowned hero and strongman Heracles. In the play, Heracles has recently died, and Eurystheus (who had earlier imposed the Twelve Labors on Heracles) has been persecuting the children. As the play opens, the Heracleidae have tried to escape their pursuer by taking refuge in the sanctuary of Zeus in Athens. A messenger sent by Eurystheus demands that they surrender, but they refuse. And they receive the support of Demophon, king of Athens, who declares war on Eurystheus. In an unfortunate twist of fate, however, some local priests who have performed divination warn that the Heracleidae and Athenians will not be able to win the fight unless a high-born maiden is sacrificed to the gods. Hearing this, Macaria, one of Heracles' daughters, offers to give up her life, after which Eurystheus's army attacks the city. During the fighting, Iolaus, a friend of the Heracleidae, helps by capturing Eurystheus, who in the end faces execution.

SEE ALSO: Euripides; Heracles

Chimaera

In Greek mythology, a repulsive monster spawned by two other monsters—Typhon and Echidna. The Chimaera supposedly had the head of a lion, the body of a goat, and the tail of a snake. It wreaked havoc in the region of Lycia in southern Asia Minor until the Greek hero Bellerophon arrived on the scene and killed it.

SEE ALSO: Bellerophon

Chios

An island lying 5 miles (8km) off the coast of western Asia Minor, it was settled by Ionian Greeks during the early years of Greece's Dark Age (ca. 1100–800 B.C.). Its chief town, located in the eastern part of the island, was also called Chios. The Chians held that the great epic poet Homer was a native son, a claim that some Greeks accepted and others did not. Along with other Ionian cities, Chios fell under Persian control in the late 500s B.C., then tried but failed to break away in the rebellion of 499–494. After the Persians were defeated in 479, Chios joined the Delian League but later quit during the Peloponnesian War. The Chians supported Rome in its wars against Macedonia in the second century B.C., and during the early stages of the Roman Empire Chios was favored by Rome and enjoyed much prosperity.

SEE ALSO: Greece, history of; Homer; Ionia

Chiron

In Greek mythology, a centaur (a creature that was half man and half horse) known for being highly civilized and wise. Like the god Apollo, whom Chiron knew well, the friendly horse-man was well versed in the arts of healing, music, and archery. Because of Chiron's skills and purported wisdom, a number of gods and human rulers sent their offspring to him either to raise or to tutor. Among those who lived with or studied under him were Asclepius, god of healing; Asclepius's sons; Jason, who sought the fabulous Golden Fleece; and Achilles, the famous warrior who slew Hector at Troy. Though Chiron was immortal, he could feel pain. So when he was accidentally scratched by one of the poisoned arrows belonging to the renowned strongman Heracles, the centaur's agony was so great that he gave his immortality to someone else and allowed himself to die.

SEE ALSO: centaurs; Heracles

Cilicia

The coastal region of southeastern Asia Minor. Greeks first settled in Cilicia some time in the early Dark Age (ca. 1100–ca. 800 B.C.). The Assyrians ruled the area briefly in the eighth century B.C., after which native-born kings did so, including several who became vassals of the Persian Empire in the late sixth century B.C. Following Alexander's conquest of Persia, the Ptolemaic and Seleucid monarchs fought over possession of Cilicia, which was rich in timber, vines, olives, and dates. It also had numerous harbors and coves that made it an ideal haven for pirates. The Cilician pirates increasingly preyed on Mediterranean shipping until the Romans put a stop to them in the first century B.C.

SEE ALSO: Asia Minor

Cimon
(ca. 510 B.C.–ca. 450 B.C.)

A noted Athenian politician and military general who played an important role in making Athens a major international

The sorceress Circe greets Odysseus's men, whom she has transformed into pigs. HULTON ARCHIVE/GETTY IMAGES

power in the fifth century B.C. The son of Miltiades, victor of the Battle of Marathon, Cimon helped to organize the Delian League in 478 B.C., which was conceived at first to discourage any further Persian attacks on Greece. Over time, however, Athens began treating the other members of the league more as subject states than as allies. In the 470s and 460s B.C. Cimon was one of Athens's most influential leaders. He gained much fame for capturing the Aegean island of Scyros in 475 (in the process bringing back human bones said to be those of Athens's mythical national hero, Theseus). Even more glory came to Cimon for his major victory over the Persians at the Eurymedon River, near Asia Minor's southern coast, in about 466. Politically speaking, Cimon was conservative and pro-Spartan, which placed him in opposition to Themistocles, Ephialtes, and other radical democrats. And in 461 they were able to engineer his ostracism. Before his ten years of exile were up, however, the

government recalled him to broker a truce between Athens and Sparta.

SEE ALSO: Battle of Eurymedon; Delian League; Themistocles

Circe

In Greek mythology a witch or sorceress who dwelled on the uncharted island of Aeaea. The most famous story about her involves her dealings with the Greek hero Odysseus and his men during their wanderings in the wake of the Trojan War. After they reached the island, Circe changed several of them into pigs. It was said that the wolves, lions, and other beasts that roamed the woods near her house were also former men who had fallen under her spells.

SEE ALSO: *Odyssey*

citizenship

In ancient Greece citizenship was a social and political status of the utmost importance because in the polis (city-state) only citizens could vote in the assembly or hold public office. Also, in many city-states citizens were the only people who could own land. Because the poleis (plural of *polis*) were politically and legally separate nations, a citizen of one state was not a citizen of any others. Most of the surviving evidence about citizenship comes from Athens; and while its general approach to citizenship may have reflected the norm across most of Greece, it is likely that the details differed from state to state. In the Athenian territory of Attica, for example, only native males were eligible for complete citizenship rights, which could be exercised at age eighteen. These men were designated *politai*, or "citizens with political rights." The wives of male citizens were also citizens, but a special type—*astai*, or "citizens without political rights." Resident aliens, both non-Greeks and Greeks from other poleis who lived and worked in Attica, were called metics (*metoikoi*). Like women, they had no political rights, and neither did slaves or freedmen (freed slaves). However, male metics could serve in the army, whereas slaves could not (except in rare national emergencies). Whereas resident foreigners in Sparta, Thessaly, Elis, and a few other poleis were known as *perioikoi*, meaning "dwellers round about," referring to the fact that they were often segregated in their own villages, in Athens resident aliens were more integrated into society. Thus, full citizenship was seen as a precious right. And the loss of one's citizenship, known as *atimia* (literally "dishonor"), was viewed as a terrible fate. (People convicted of crimes were sometimes punished by stripping them of their citizenship.) In Athens, an *atimos* (someone who had forfeited his citizenship) was not allowed to speak in the Assembly or law courts, hold public office, or enter a temple or the marketplace. And the community as a whole strictly enforced these sanctions; any citizen who saw an *atimos* in a prohibited area was allowed to arrest him on the spot.

SEE ALSO: government; polis

city-state

In ancient Greece, a small nation usually consisting of a central town surrounded by dependent villages and farms.

SEE ALSO: polis

clan

In ancient Greek society, a pivotal kinship group consisting of a group of families that claimed descent from a common ancestor. Clan (or *genos*) leaders were usually more influential in family affairs than the heads of individual households. It was common, for example, for a clan leader to arrange marriages for his various sons, daughters, nephews, nieces, cousins, and grandchildren, who might come from many different families.

SEE ALSO: family; tribes

Classical Age

As determined by modern scholars, the period of ancient Greece lasting from about 500 B.C. to 323 B.C. (the year of the death of Alexander the Great). For the major events and figures of the period, **see** Greece, history of.

SEE ALSO: Athens; Peloponnesian War; Pericles; Sparta

Cleisthenes
(flourished late sixth century B.C.)

An Athenian statesman who played a leading role in the events that brought about the institution of full-fledged democracy in Athens at the dawn of the Classical Age. The tyrant Hippias (son of another tyrant, Pisistratus) had fled the city in 510 B.C. Soon afterward, a power struggle erupted among prominent aristocrats, Cleisthenes among their number. Many wanted to set up an oligarchy that would serve their own interests. To counter them, Cleisthenes shrewdly appealed for and got the support of the common people. Exactly why and how is unknown, but he and his followers managed to enact sweeping democratic reforms. They increased the authority of the Assembly and divided Attica into numerous small wardlike districts, the demes. Cleisthenes died circa 500 B.C. and received a public funeral in a cemetery just outside the city walls.

SEE ALSO: Athens; government; Hippias

Cleomenes
(ca. 520 B.C.–ca. 490 B.C.)

A Spartan king who supported Athens's aristocrats, led by Isagoras, against a leading member of the Alcmaeonid clan, Cleisthenes. The latter was forced to leave the city. But when Cleomenes tried to place Isagoras in power in Athens, a popular uprising drove Cleomenes away and allowed Cleisthenes to return and institute a democratic revolution.

SEE ALSO: Alcmaeonids; Cleisthenes

Cleomenes
(reigned 235–219 B.C.)

This Spartan king married the widow of his predecessor, Agis IV. Like Agis, Cleomenes tried to introduce social reforms to rehabilitate Sparta, which had recently declined in power. But Cleomenes was

defeated in battle and committed suicide before all of the reforms could be implemented.

SEE ALSO: Agis IV

Cleon
(died 422 B.C.)

One of Athens's leading politicians during the early years of the Peloponnesian War. Cleon started out as a staunch opponent of the radical democrat Pericles, and after the latter's death in 429 B.C., he argued that the war must go on until a clear victory over Sparta was obtained. In 425 B.C. Cleon and the Athenian general Demosthenes defeated the Spartans at Pylos in the southwestern Peloponnesus. Later, after the Spartan general Brasidas captured Athens's colony of Amphipolis in the northern Aegean, Cleon led an expedition to retake the city, but he died in the attempt. In his famous chronicle of the war, Thucydides portrays Cleon as an opportunist and a demagogue.

SEE ALSO: Peloponnesian War; Pericles

Cleopatra VII
(69 B.C.–30 B.C.)

The last of the Greek rulers of Egypt's Ptolemaic dynasty and one of the most famous, powerful, and controversial women of ancient times, indeed of all times. By the time of her birth in the Egyptian capital of Alexandria, the Ptolemaic realm had become a third-rate power, and its rulers were little more than pawns in the ongoing power struggles among the strongest Romans of the day. Cleopatra's father, Ptolemy XII Auletes, who died in 51 B.C., had been one of these pawns. He had wanted her and her ten-year-old brother, Ptolemy XIII, to rule Egypt together. However, a power struggle ensued in which Ptolemy XIII, manipulated by his adult advisers, drove Cleopatra from Alexandria. In 48 B.C., while she was in Palestine attempting to raise troops to fight her brother, the Roman general Julius Caesar defeated his chief rival, Gnaeus Pompeius (Pompey) in a much larger power struggle. Pompey fled to Egypt, was murdered there, and when Caesar pursued, Cleopatra shrewdly smuggled herself into the palace in Alexandria to meet him. The two became lovers, and he and his troops backed her against Ptolemy, who was deposed and killed. When Caesar left Egypt a few months later, Cleopatra was carrying his child. Not long afterward, Caesar invited Cleopatra and the new baby, a boy named Caesarion, to Rome. But when he was suddenly assassinated in March 44 B.C., she hastily returned to Egypt.

Back in her native land, Cleopatra went about the business of ruling it, a task that evidence suggests she performed with distinction. She managed the economy well and expanded Egypt's already large agricultural output. Because of that output, the leading Romans of the day relied on Egypt for food to feed their troops. So in 41 B.C. Caesar's former lieutenant Marcus Antonius, better known today as Mark Antony, summoned Cleopatra to his headquarters in Asia Minor to discuss his acquisition of Egyptian grain. It did not take long for the two to become lovers and form an alliance. That alliance was severely tested when Antony and Cleopatra faced off against his principal Roman rival, Octavian (Caesar's adopted son and heir). In what came down to a struggle for control of most of the known world, Octavian defeated Cleopatra and Antony at the Battle of Actium (in western Greece) in September 31 B.C.

The lovers fled back to Egypt and the following year committed suicide. Some ancient sources claim Cleopatra succumbed by allowing a poisonous snake to bite her. Both before and after her passing, Octavian and other Romans tried to discredit her by portraying her as a witch who had hypnotized Antony and as an evil schemer. But they could not erase the memory of her extraordinary personality and deeds. Nevertheless, with her death the last major autonomous Greek state of antiquity was absorbed by Rome, and Greece entered what modern scholars call its Roman period.

SEE ALSO: Alexandria; Battle of Actium; Ptolemy XII Auletes

clothing

Clothing materials and styles were similar from place to place across ancient Greece and did not change very much during the centuries of the Archaic, Classical, Hellenistic, and Roman periods. Most Greeks seem to have been clean people who preferred, when possible, to dress neatly. Most clothes were simple in shape and design but very comfortable and attractive. In general, clothing shapes and styles were dictated and limited by the shape of the looms, which produced the fabric for clothes. Because they were rectangular, looms produced rectangular pieces of cloth that people then draped and fastened around their bodies in a number of ways. This made the need for hand sewing minimal.

In the Archaic Age, it was common for women to wear a peplos. A large rectangular piece of cloth, a peplos was wrapped around the body and a corner of it was pulled over each shoulder, then the flaps were fastened with a pin. A belt or girdle secured the garment at the waist. Often shawls were worn over the peplos. Men in Archaic times, as well as both men and women in the Classical Age and later times, owned and frequently wore a tunic, or chiton, a rectangular piece of cloth sewn up the sides with holes cut for the head and arms. Men usually wore such a tunic, which hung like a skirt, knee-length. However, elderly men and all men on formal occasions wore their tunics ankle-length. While most Greek women wore them ankle-length, in Sparta knee-length was acceptable for women. (Some women still wore the peplos, often over the tunic.) It appears that most Greeks wore nothing under their tunics, although some men may have worn loincloths (*zoma* or *diazoma*); vase paintings sometimes show laborers and athletes wearing loincloths only.

Both genders also wore a himation, a very large rectangular piece of cloth that people wrapped around the body in various ways, usually over the tunic. A himation could be used as a protective cloak to keep a person warm and dry or as part of a formal outfit. By custom, one took a himation in the right hand and threw it over the left side of the body. This was called "dressing to the right," and those who did not dress to the right were viewed as country bumpkins.

To these basic garments, people added many accessories. For example, young men and soldiers often wore an outer cloak called a chlamys, which they fastened at one shoulder with a brooch or pin. And in formal situations, women wore colorful scarves and shawls over their himations. Another clothing basic, footwear, varied widely. Rural Greeks frequently went barefoot in the summer, but most urban dwellers wore leather sandals, and in

colder weather everyone donned leather shoes or boots. People also sometimes wore hats to protect themselves from the hot Mediterranean sun. A petasos, which had a wide brim, was widely popular.

SEE ALSO: baths and bathing; grooming; spinning and weaving

Clouds

A comedy by Aristophanes, the original version of which was produced in 423 B.C. The author later began revising it, and the partially altered version is the one that has survived. The play takes a satiric look at the supposed corruption of Athenian youth and culture by the eccentric philosopher Socrates. The main character, Strepsiades, is an elderly farmer who has gone bankrupt thanks to his spendthrift wife and son, Pheidippides. Strepsiades decides to enlist the aid of Socrates, who, by his cunning, will hopefully show the farmer how to elude his creditors. Both Strepsiades and Pheidippides attend Socrates' school (which Aristophanes calls a "think shop"), but only the son is smart enough to learn anything useful. The end result of these efforts is not what Strepsiades had wanted. Although he manages to foil his creditors, his son begins to beat him and, following the lessons of Socrates, offers arguments to justify the violence. In a fit of frustration, Strepsiades sets the think shop ablaze.

SEE ALSO: Aristophanes, 1; Socrates

Clytemnestra

In Greek mythology, as well as in several works by fifth-century B.C. Athenian playwrights, the sister of Helen of Troy and wife of Agamemnon, king of Mycenae, who led the Greek forces in the ten-year siege of Troy. Clytemnestra bore Agamemnon four children—Iphigenia, Chrysothemis, Electra, and Orestes. After Agamemnon sacrificed Iphigenia to the goddess Artemis to ensure favorable winds for his ships bound for Troy, Clytemnestra turned against him. Helped by her lover, Aegisthus, she murdered her husband soon after he returned to Greece from the war. This act enraged Orestes, who slew both his mother and Aegisthus. For more on these characters and events,

SEE ALSO: *Agamemnon*; Electra; Orestes

Cnidus

A city on the coast of Caria in southwestern Asia Minor. The Persians took control of Cnidus (or Knidos) in the mid-500s B.C., but the city gained its freedom when they were expelled from Ionia in 479. Soon afterward the Cnidians joined the Athenian-controlled Delian League. Following the death of Alexander the Great in 323 B.C., the city came under the control first of Ptolemaic Egypt, then of Rhodes. Cnidus was the birthplace of the noted Greek mathematician and astronomer Eudoxus.

SEE ALSO: Delian League; Eudoxus

Colchis

A region situated along the eastern shore of the Black Sea. In mythology it was renowned as the place where Jason found the fabulous Golden Fleece. The local king, Aeetes, wanted to keep the fleece, however, and tried to kill Jason. But aided by Aeetes' daughter, Medea, Jason managed to acquire the fleece and take it back to Greece. In real life Colchis was the site of several Greek colonies established by Miletus in the Archaic Age. These cities were known for their raw materials, especially iron and timber, and important trade routes leading

into Asia passed through the area.

SEE ALSO: Black Sea; Jason, 1; Medea

colonization

The largest single burst of Greek colonization began in the eighth century B.C. and continued for a bit longer than two centuries. The movement was motivated partly by the need to find new sources of metals and also by the desire to acquire land for citizens having trouble finding sufficient amounts of it in their home city-states. At first most of the colonies were located in southern Italy and other parts of the central and western Mediterranean. The Euboean cities of Chalcis and Eretria founded Pithecusae and Cumae in Italy and Naxus and Rhegium in Sicily. Other leading Greek colonies in Italy included Croton, Sybaris, and Taras (which the Romans called Tarentum). Phocaean colonists founded Massalia, in what is now southern France, and people from the Cycladic island of Thera (north of Crete) established Cyrene on the coast of North Africa. Some of the western Mediterranean colonies went on to establish colonies of their own. For example, Massalia founded Nicaea (modern Nice, also in southern France), and Taras established Heraclea in Italy.

In addition, Greeks colonized the northern Aegean and Black seas, areas in which the Ionian city of Miletus alone founded several dozen towns. Athens's neighbor, Megara, was also active in setting up colonies in these areas. Many of the Black Sea colonies went on to produce large quantities of grain and other foodstuffs, which cities in mainland Greece imported to feed their growing populations. By 500 B.C. these colonizing movements had expanded the Greek sphere of trade relations and cultural influence to

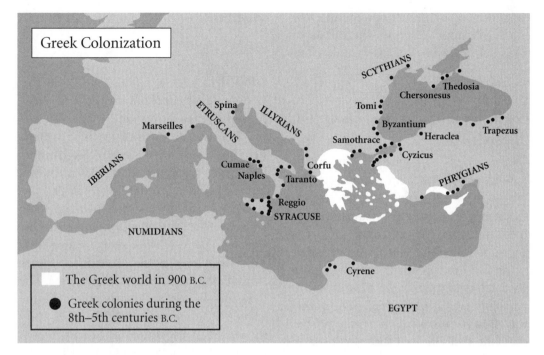

Greek Colonization

SCYTHIANS

Thedosia
Chersonesus
Tomi
Byzantium
Samothrace · Heraclea
Trapezus
Cyzicus

Spina
ETRUSCANS
ILLYRIANS
Marseilles

Corfu
Cumae
Naples · Taranto

PHRYGIANS

IBERIANS

Reggio
SYRACUSE

NUMIDIANS

Cyrene

☐ The Greek world in 900 B.C.

● Greek colonies during the 8th–5th centuries B.C.

EGYPT

STEVE ZMINA

cover an area stretching from the northern shores of the Black Sea in the east to the Strait of Gibraltar in the west.

SEE ALSO: Black Sea; explorers and exploration; Italy; Massalia

Conon
(ca. 444 B.C.–392 B.C.)

A prominent Athenian admiral during the final years of the devastating Peloponnesian War. In the wake of the Spartan naval victory over Athens at Aegospotami in 405 B.C., Conon was the only Athenian commander who was able to keep his ships from being captured. Eleven years later, when Athens and Sparta were again at odds, he won a decisive victory over the Spartans at Cnidus in southwestern Asia Minor. Afterward he returned to Athens and helped rebuild the Long Walls, which had been torn down at the conclusion of the Peloponnesian War.

SEE ALSO: Battle of Aegospotami; Long Walls; Peloponnesian War

Constitution of the Athenians (Aristotle)

A political tract by Aristotle, one of a set of 158 treatises, each consisting of a description and history of the constitution (here meaning "government") of a Greek city-state. Aristotle may have written several of these by himself; however, modern scholars believe that many were compiled by his students under his supervision. The one about Athens, written sometime between 328 and 325 B.C., is the only one that has survived. The work begins with the political division of Athens in the days of its legendary native son Theseus, then describes the law code of Draco and reforms of Solon. It then follows the tyranny of Pisistratus, the democratic revolution of Cleisthenes, the reforms of Ephialtes and Pericles, and the loss and restoration of democracy in the immediate aftermath of the Peloponnesian War. Finally, Aristotle describes the public officials and law courts of his own day.

SEE ALSO: Aristotle

Constitution of the Athenians (Old Oligarch)

An anonymous pamphlet or short treatise that criticizes Athenian democracy. Although the city's democratic government is efficient, the pamphlet says, it is too open and gives too much authority to common folk. The work was originally ascribed to Xenophon, but scholars eventually dated it to roughly the 420s B.C. (when Xenophon was a small child). The author, who remains unknown, is usually referred to as "the Old Oligarch" because he seems to favor oligarchy over democracy.

SEE ALSO: Athens; government

Corcyra

An island now called Corfu, located off the northwest coast of the Greek mainland. As early as the eighth century B.C., people from Eretria (on the island of Euboea) established a trading post on the eastern coast of Corcyra (or Korkyra). The Eretrians were soon ousted, however, by settlers from Corinth. Over time, relations between the Corcyraeans and Corinthians of the mother city became strained. In 435 B.C. a disagreement over a Corcyraean colony, Epidamnus (on the Balkan coast north of Corcyra), led to open warfare. The struggle soon drew in the Athenians and became one of the principal immediate causes of the Peloponnesian War. In that conflict, Corinth supported Sparta, and Corcyra backed Athens. In early Hellenistic times, various Balkan rulers, including Pyrrhus of Epirus, controlled Corcyra until the Romans intervened and turned it into a

naval base.

SEE ALSO: Corinth; Peloponnesian War

Corinth

Long one of Greece's oldest and most powerful, prosperous, and influential cities. The site of Corinth in the northern Peloponnesus, near the narrow isthmus bearing its name, was occupied in the late Stone Age. In the Bronze Age it appears to have been a Mycenaean town of little consequence. Later, however, in the Archaic Age, Corinth rose to become a major trading city whose pottery became popular throughout much of the Greek sphere. The Corinthians also vigorously colonized the islands of Corcyra (Corfu), Ithaca, and Sicily in the 700s and 600s B.C. The most important of these colonies grew into the Sicilian city of Syracuse, one of the major Greek powers in the Mediterranean sphere in the Classical Age (ca. 500–323 B.C.).

Corinth's period of greatest power and wealth was ca. 650–550 B.C., when the city, dominated by its lofty acropolis, the Acrocorinth, controlled trade, travel, and communications to and from central and southern Greece across the strategic isthmus. At the dawn of the Classical Age, however, Athens steadily gained commercial supremacy over Corinth, which resulted in frequent tensions between these states. In fact, it was a dispute and series of military skirmishes between them over Corcyra in the late 430s that proved to be one of the main causes of the Peloponnesian War (431–404 B.C.).

Later, after Macedonia's Philip II defeated the major southern city-states at Chaeronea in 338 B.C., he chose Corinth as the headquarters of his Panhellenic confederacy, the League of Corinth. Later still, in the Hellenistic Age, Corinth served as the capital of an alliance of Peloponnesian cities—the Achaean League. In 146 B.C., after the Achaeans attempted to resist the intrusion of the Romans into the area, a Roman general leveled Corinth.

SEE ALSO: colonization; Corcyra; Peloponnesian War; trade

Corinth, Isthmus of

The narrow and highly strategic land bridge connecting central Greece to the Peloponnesus.

SEE ALSO: Corinth; roads

Corinthian order

One of the three main architectural styles employed in ancient Greece, it featured columns whose capitals (tops) were ornately decorated with carved leaves and other details.

SEE ALSO: architectural orders

council

The governments of most ancient Greek states featured councils—groups of selected citizens—as ruling bodies, advisers to rulers, or legislatures.

SEE ALSO: *Boule,* government

Craterus
(ca. 370 B.C.–321 B.C.)

One of the leading Successors of Alexander the Great. Craterus made his reputation as a general in the battles of Granicus River (334 B.C.), Issus (333), Gaugamela (331), and Hydapses River (326), and he became one of Alexander's most trusted confidants. In 324 Alexander charged him with escorting many of the Macedonian veterans of the Persian campaigns back to Greece. Following Alexander's death in 323, Craterus

rushed to the aid of Antipater, another of the Successors, who was under siege by Greek rebels at Lamia. Craterus was killed two years later during a battle against two other Successors, Perdiccas and Eumenes.

SEE ALSO: Alexander III ("the Great"); Battle of Hydapses River; Successors

Cratinus
(flourished late fifth century B.C.)

An early Athenian comic playwright whose works had a considerable influence on a younger master of comedy, Aristophanes. None of Cratinus's twenty-seven plays has survived complete; however, more than four hundred fragments exist.

SEE ALSO: Aristophanes, 1; theater and drama

cremation

Burning the remains of the dead, which was widely practiced in the Greek lands in certain ages.

SEE ALSO: burial customs

Creon (ruler of Corinth)

In Greek mythology, as well as in Euripides' great play *Medea,* a ruler of the city of Corinth who provided refuge for Jason and Medea after their return to Greece with the Golden Fleece. Jason soon rejected Medea in favor of Creon's daughter, which motivated Medea to murder Creon, his daughter, and Medea's own children by Jason.

SEE ALSO: Jason; Medea; *Medea* (play)

Creon (ruler of Thebes)

In Greek legend and in Sophocles' trilogy of plays about the tragic character Oedipus, Creon was the brother of Oedipus's mother and wife, Jocasta. After Laius, king of Thebes, had been slain by an unknown person (who turned out to be Oedipus), Creon administered Thebes as regent. And when the Sphinx, a frightening monster, threatened the city, Creon offered the throne to any man who could drive away or kill the creature. The newly arrived Oedipus did so and became king. Later, after Oedipus's fall from power, Creon again became king of Thebes. Creon led the resistance against the attack of the so-called Seven Against Thebes, then condemned Oedipus's daughter, Antigone, to death for burying one of the slain leaders of the assault. Two mythological versions of Creon's death existed. In one, a usurper named Lycus killed him; in the other, the Athenian hero Theseus slew Creon.

SEE ALSO: Antigone; *Oedipus the King*; *Seven Against Thebes*; Thebes

Crete

The largest of the Greek islands, measuring about 150 miles (241km) long by between 7 and 34 miles (11 and 54km) wide. Crete is situated roughly 70 miles (113km) southeast of the southern Peloponnesus and directly south of the Cyclades isles. The island's central sector is mostly mountainous, the highest point being Mt. Ida at about 8,000 feet (3,048m); the highlands contain numerous limestone formations and caves, and the ancient inhabitants often conducted religious worship in the caves. A few flat or rolling plains exist, mostly near the coasts, where grain, olives, and grapes were raised.

Partly because of its strategic position between the cultural spheres of the Greek mainland, Asia Minor, Syria-Palestine, and Egypt, in the Bronze Age Crete became the homeland of a prosperous seafaring people—the Minoans, who traded with all

of these areas. Although the Minoans did not speak Greek, they created the first sophisticated civilization in Greece (and Europe) and exerted a powerful cultural influence on the Greek-speaking Mycenaeans who inhabited mainland Greece. A large proportion of the now famous ancient Greek myths arose from distorted memories of these two peoples and their interactions. In one of the more familiar examples, the Athenian hero Theseus traveled to Knossos in northern Crete, site of the palace of King Minos, and killed the Minotaur, a monster that lived in a maze (the Labyrinth). In another famous tale, the inventor Daedalus and his son Icarus escaped from Knossos by flying away on artificial wings.

Almost none of the real people and events of Bronze Age Crete are known with any certainty. Archaeologists have determined that the island was settled in the Stone Age, perhaps around 5000 B.C. More advanced settlers bearing bronze tools and weapons arrived in about 3000 B.C. and were likely the impetus for the rise of Minoan culture in the years that followed. Around 1600 B.C., Crete and the Minoans who lived there were badly battered by a massive eruption of the volcano on the nearby island of Thera, and soon afterward the Minoans succumbed to Mycenaean raids. The Mycenaeans, in turn, declined in the closing years of the Bronze Age.

In the Dark Age, Dorian Greeks (originally from the region south of the Danube River), reached Crete after some of their number had settled in Sparta, on the mainland. And for the rest of ancient times, Cretan social and political customs had a Dorian character and in some ways resembled those of Sparta. For example, Cretan aristocrats exploited a class of agricultural serfs, as the Spartans did the helots. The major city-states of Crete in the Archaic and Classical ages were Knossos, Gortyn, and Cydonia (now Khania). At first these cities were prosperous, but over time they became increasingly isolationist and declined in wealth and power. By the third century B.C. Crete was a cultural backwater dominated by pirate bands, a situation that prevailed until the Romans took over the island in the mid-first century B.C. In the Classical and Hellenistic periods, Crete was known for its fine archers, who worked as mercenaries in Greek armies far and wide.

SEE ALSO: Atlantis; Gortyn; Knossos; Minoans; Minos; Mycenaeans; Thera; Theseus

Critias
(ca. 460 B.C.–403 B.C.)

An Athenian nobleman best known for being a cousin of the philosopher Plato, a follower (when young) of Plato's mentor, Socrates, and the leader of the Thirty Tyrants, who seized control of Athens in 404 B.C. An opponent of democracy, Critias participated in the unsuccessful oligarchic revolution of 411 and was later banished. When Athens surrendered to Sparta in 404 at the close of the Peloponnesian War, however, Critias returned and helped institute a reign of terror. He was killed the following year during the rebellion that restored democracy. Despite Critias's dastardly deeds, Plato named one of his famous dialogues after him.

SEE ALSO: Peloponnesian War; Plato; Thirty Tyrants

Critias (dialogue)

A dialogue by Plato that forms a sort of sequel to another dialogue, the *Timaeus*. In the latter work, the discussion had briefly touched on the rise and fall of the legendary kingdom of Atlantis, a mighty nation that supposedly had been defeated by Athens and then had been destroyed by a natural catastrophe. In the *Critias*, the character Critias presents much more detail about Atlantis, including its cities, people, government, and religion. He asserts that nine thousand years have elapsed since the great war between Athens and Atlantis. Then he tells how the Atlantean kings long ruled justly and well, until they grew corrupt. The narrator is about to reveal how Zeus rained down destruction on Atlantis when the *Critias* abruptly ends. It is unknown why Plato did not finish it. Most classical scholars believe that he based his information about Atlantis on distorted memories of the devastation wrought on Crete and Thera by the eruption of the Theran volcano in the late Bronze Age.

SEE ALSO: Atlantis; Critias; Plato

Crito

A dialogue by Plato, its setting is the prison in which Socrates, who has been condemned to death by an Athenian jury, awaits his fate. The philosopher's friend Crito pays a visit and proposes that Socrates attempt to escape. But the condemned man argues that this course would be unjust and dishonorable. He points out that he has been sentenced through the process of Athenian law and asserts that adherence to his country's laws must come before personal considerations such as wife, children, and freedom. Crito finds himself unable to refute this argument.

SEE ALSO: Socrates

Croesus
(mid-sixth century B.C.)

The most famous king of Lydia, a non-

Greek kingdom in west-central Asia Minor. Although Croesus attacked and defeated the Ionian Greek cities, he was a devoted admirer of Greek culture and eagerly sought advice from Apollo's oracle at Delphi. Some of this advice caused his downfall, however. The Persians invaded Asia Minor and the oracle told Croesus that if he crossed the Halys River in central Asia Minor, he would destroy a powerful empire. Believing this empire was the Persian one, he crossed the river and attacked. But he was defeated, finding out too late that the realm the oracle had described was his own. His story appears in Herodotus's *Histories*.

SEE ALSO: Delphi; Lydia; Persians

Cronos

A son of the early deities Uranus and Gaia and the leader of the first race of Greek gods, the Titans. Cronos (or Cronus) gained his high position in heaven soon after Uranus imprisoned some of his and Gaia's other children, including the one-eyed Cyclopes. In retaliation, Cronos attacked Uranus, castrated him with a sickle, and seized his throne. After marrying his own sister, Rhea, Cronos sired the first Olympian gods—Zeus, Hestia, Hera, Poseidon, Hades, and Demeter. Worried that one of these offspring would overthrow him, just as he had overthrown Uranus, Cronos swallowed them one by one after they were born. But Rhea kept Zeus from suffering this fate by hiding him from her husband. Zeus eventually showed himself, forced Cronos to vomit up those he had swallowed, and led the Olympians in a war against him and the Titans.

SEE ALSO: Theogony; Titans; Zeus

Ctesibius
(early third century B.C.)

A Greek scientist and inventor who lived and worked in Alexandria in the early years of the Hellenistic Age. Ctesibius's (t'SIB-ee-us) most important invention was the simple cylinder and plunger, which became the basis of the piston, today common in car engines. In ancient times the device was used in pumps to raise water in mines and to aid in irrigation. Among Ctesibius's other inventions were a hydraulic pipe organ, the first accurate water clock, and a musical keyboard.

SEE ALSO: science

Cumae

A town established in about 750 B.C. by Euboean Greeks on the coast of Campania, located on the northern edge of the Gulf of Cumae (the present-day Bay of Naples) in southwestern Italy. The residents set up a thriving trade with the Etruscans and were instrumental in exposing these native Italian people to Greek culture, language, and ideas. Eventually, however, relations between Cumae and the Etruscans deteriorated and the two peoples fought. With the help of Greeks from Syracuse, the Cumaeans decisively defeated an Etruscan fleet in 474 B.C. A few decades later another native Italian people, the Samnites took control of Cumae, and not long afterward the town fell into Roman hands. No matter who ruled the city, it remained famous throughout the ancient world for its Sibyl, an oracle like the one at Delphi, who delivered prophecies.

SEE ALSO: colonization; Etruscans; Rome

Cybele

A goddess, often called "the Great Mother," who was not worshipped in Greece until the fifth century B.C. The center of Cybele's

Odysseus and his men put out the single eye of the Cyclops Polyphemus, who had trapped the Greeks in a dismal cave. © CORBIS

cult was in Phrygia in west-central Asia Minor, where she was associated mainly with fertility. People also believed that she could heal the sick, inflict disease as a punishment, and protect people in wartime. Her male consort, Attis, was later worshipped along with her. When the cult spread to Greece, it was confined mainly to parts of the Peloponnesus and to Piraeus and other port towns. People in these places associated Cybele with the ancient Greek fertility goddess Demeter and came to see the two deities as manifestations of the same goddess. Later the Romans carried Cybele's sacred black stone from Phrygia to Rome, where her worship became widespread.

SEE ALSO: Phrygia; religion

Cyclades

An important island group situated in the southern Aegean Sea immediately north of Crete. Among its principal members are Naxos, Paros, Delos, Melos, and Thera.

SEE ALSO: the names of the individual islands

Cyclopes

In Greek mythology, giants, each having a single eye. In his *Theogony*, Hesiod wrote that the original three Cyclopes (singular: Cyclops)—Arges ("Shiner"), Brontes ("Thunderer"), and Steropes ("Lightning-

Maker")—were the sons of Uranus and Gaia. Uranus feared them and so locked them up in Tartarus in the Underworld. Later, however, Zeus, who had recently defeated the Titans, freed the Cyclopes from Tartarus. They then worked for the gods, fashioning thunderbolts for Zeus and tridents for Poseidon. An alternate tradition about the Cyclopes came from Homer's *Odyssey*, which claimed that they were a race of uncivilized giants dwelling in caves on a remote island. The hero Odysseus and some of his men were trapped in the cave of a Cyclops named Polyphemus and had to blind him to facilitate their escape. Still another ancient legend about the Cyclopes said that some of these giants built the walls of a number of ancient citadels in mainland Greece. Among these were the walls of Tiryns and Mycenae in the eastern Peloponnesus, which are now known to have been erected by the Mycenaeans.

SEE ALSO: Mycenaeans; *Odyssey; Theogony*

Cynics

Members of a minor philosophical movement established in the early fourth century B.C. by Antisthenes, a student of Socrates.

SEE ALSO: Diogenes of Sinope, philosophy

Cyprus

A large island located directly south of Asia Minor, it long acted as a cultural bridge and trade conduit between the Greek lands to the west and Syria, Palestine, and Mesopotamia to the east. In succession, Syrians, Phoenicians, Assyrians, Egyptians, Greeks, and Persians all exerted their influence on the island between about 1000 and 500 B.C. During the Ionian rebellion of 499–494, the Greek towns of Cyprus backed

the Ionians, and the Phoenician towns supported the Persians. In contrast, all the Cypriote towns gave Alexander the Great allegiance in 333, and soon after Alexander's death ten years later, the island fell under the control of Alexander's general, Ptolemy. After the Roman power broker Octavian (the future emperor Augustus) defeated Cleopatra VII, the last of the Ptolemies, in 30 B.C., Cyprus became a Roman province.

SEE ALSO: Egypt; Phoenicia

Cyrene

A Greek city established in North Africa in the 630s B.C. by settlers from the Aegean island of Thera (north of Crete). Driven by famine on Thera, the colonists sailed to the area now occupied by Libya, but in ancient times called Cyrenaica. They built Cyrene on a well-watered plateau about 8 miles (13km) inland from the Mediterranean coast. In time the inhabitants skirmished with local Libyans as well as Egyptians. In about 525 B.C. Cyrene was absorbed by the Persians, who had conquered Egypt. A bit less than two centuries later, Alexander the Great brought the city and its surrounding territory into his short-lived empire, and following his death in 323 B.C., Ptolemaic Egypt controlled Cyrene off and on for the remainder of the Hellenistic Age. Among the famous Greeks born in Cyrene were the geographer Eratosthenes and the poet Callimachus.

SEE ALSO: Egypt; Thera

Cyrus II ("the Great") (ca. 599 B.C.–529 B.C.)

The first and greatest ruler of the Persian Empire. He traced his local Persian lineage back to Achaemenes, who in the dim past had supposedly founded a small nation in Fars, the region lying directly north of the Persian Gulf. When Cyrus was a boy, that nation was a mere vassal state dominated by the Medes, who controlled most of the Near East. As a young man Cyrus led a rebellion that rapidly overpowered the Median realm. During his reign (559–529 B.C.) he expanded the new Persian Empire both eastward and westward. In the westward thrust, his armies overran Asia Minor and subdued the Greek cities of Ionia on the Aegean coast, marking the first significant contact between Greeks and Persians. When Cyrus died and was succeeded by his son Cambyses, the Achaemenid dynasty lorded over the largest and strongest empire in the world.

SEE ALSO: Cambyses; Greco-Persian Wars; Persians

Cyrus the Younger (ca. 424 B.C.–401 B.C.)

A Persian prince who, in 401 B.C., led a force of Persians and Greek mercenaries, among them the historian Xenophon, against his brother, King Artaxerxes II.

SEE ALSO: *Anabasis*, 2.; Xenophon

Daedalus

In Greek mythology, a highly skilled Athenian inventor, craftsman, and sculptor who created statues so realistic that they appeared to be alive. The most important of his mythical adventures took place on the large island of Crete. There he built an underground maze, called the labyrinth, for King Minos. Inside the labyrinth Minos placed the monstrous Minotaur (a creature half man and half bull), which killed and ate young Athenian hostages. When the Athenian hero Theseus slew the Minotaur, Daedalus helped his countryman escape from the maze. In retaliation, Minos locked the inventor and his young son, Icarus, inside the labyrinth. But the clever Daedalus fashioned wings from wax and feathers, and with them he and Icarus flew out of the labyrinth. Daedalus warned the boy not to fly too close to the sun, but Icarus did not pay heed and died when the wax in his wings melted and he plunged into the sea. Daedalus eventually achieved revenge on Minos by tricking the king into climbing into a bathtub the inventor had specially rigged to flood with boiling water. Among the numerous other inventions attributed to Daedalus were masts and sails for ships, carpentry tools, glue, wooden puppets that could walk, and a reservoir in Sicily.

SEE ALSO: Crete; Minos; Theseus

daimons

In ancient Greek religious thought, supernatural spirits that were either vaguely defined or viewed in differing ways. In general, a daimon personified divine essence or power that was not identified with a specific god. The word could also refer to the guiding force of one's personal destiny, so that having a friendly daimon on one's side might bring good luck. In the fourth century B.C. Plato introduced the idea that daimons were beings existing spiritually halfway between humans and gods. Later still these spirits were sometimes viewed as evil.

SEE ALSO: religion

Danaus

In Greek mythology, one of the most important ancestors of the Greek race. Danaus was the son of the Egyptian king Belus and twin brother of Aegyptus. Aegyptus had fifty sons and proposed that they should marry Danaus's fifty daughters, called the Danaids. However, Danaus suspected that this offer was a ploy designed to allow Aegyptus to usurp most of Danaus's lands. To avoid trouble, Danaus took his daughters to Argos in Greece, and there the locals made him their king. Eventually Aegyptus's fifty sons, who felt they had been cheated of their promised brides, arrived in Argos and forced the young women to agree to marry them. Danaus then told each of his daughters to carry a dagger into her wedding bed and stab her new husband to death. All but one of the maidens did so. Later the god Hermes and goddess Athena forgave the Danaids for committing these murders, and the girls went on to find other husbands. The playwright Aeschylus retells much of this story in his play *The Suppliant Women*.

SEE ALSO: *Suppliant Women, The*

Darius I
(reigned 522–486 B.C.)

The third and one of the greatest kings of the Persian Empire, whose invasion of Greece in 490 B.C. marked the opening of the Greco-Persian Wars. After King Cambyses died under mysterious circumstances in 522, a usurper seized the throne. After a few months, however, a group of Persian nobles slew him and replaced him with Darius, an aristocrat who was distantly related to Cambyses. A large-scale rebellion soon broke out, but Darius showed that he was a strong leader by crushing it. He then reorganized the empire by dividing it into twenty satrapies (provinces). In addition, he wisely constructed several new roads to allow his couriers and armies to move more quickly. The most famous of the so-called royal roads stretched more than 1,500 miles (2,415km) from Susa in modern-day Iraq to Sardis in western Asia Minor. Next, circa 513 B.C., Darius crossed into Europe and invaded Scythia (west of the Black Sea) and Thrace (north of the Aegean Sea). The Scythian campaign was unsuccessful, but Darius forcefully quelled a revolt of the Greek Ionian cities that lasted from 499 to 494 B.C. He was enraged to hear that the Athenians had helped the Ionian rebels and vowed vengeance. According to Herodotus, Darius asked his advisers "who the Athenians were, and then, on being told, called for his bow. He took it, set an arrow on the string, shot it up into the air and cried: 'Grant, O God, that I may punish the Athenians.' Then he commanded one of his servants to repeat to him the words, 'Master, remember the Athenians,' three times, whenever he sat down to dinner." (*The Histories* 5.106) Darius sent an army to destroy Athens in 490 B.C., but it was repelled with heavy losses on the plain of Marathon northeast of Athens. The Persian king planned to retaliate by launching a larger invasion of Greece, but he died in 486 and that task fell to his son, Xerxes.

SEE ALSO: Battle of Marathon; Cambyses; Greco-Persian Wars

Darius III
(reigned 336–330 B.C.)

The last king of the Persian Empire. Two years after King Artaxerxes III (reigned 358–338 B.C.) was assassinated by a power-hungry royal adviser, the latter placed Darius on the throne hoping to make him a puppet ruler he could control. However, Darius shrewdly had the man killed. Although he seems to have been a mild-mannered, well-meaning ruler, Darius was unable to deal with the many problems the rapidly declining empire faced. Even worse, Alexander the Great invaded and rapidly brought the realm to its knees. The Macedonian king defeated Darius at Issus (in 333) and Gaugamela (331), after which the king fled. But then some of Darius's own followers held him for ransom and eventually murdered him.

SEE ALSO: Alexander III ("the Great"); Battle of Gaugamela; Battle of Issus; Persians

Dark Age

As determined by modern scholars, the period of ancient Greece following the collapse of the region's Bronze Age civilization and lasting from about 1100 to about 800 B.C.

SEE ALSO: government; Greece, history of

Delian League

An alliance of Greek city-states created in the wake of the Greco-Persian Wars. The Athenians spearheaded the effort to form the league, saying that it was needed to protect Greece from any further Persian incursions. To that end, in the winter of 478–477 B.C. Athens presided over a meeting of delegates from more than 150 Greek states from across the Greek sphere. Because the conference took place on the small Aegean island of Delos, the alliance became known as the Delian League. But its official name was "The Athenians and Their Allies." This reflected the reality that the league would be controlled by Athens, which possessed the largest navy in Greece. Indeed, over time the Athenians took advantage of their fellow league members by using that navy in heavy-handed ways. For example, in 469 B.C. the island state of Naxos opted to leave the league, which it had the right to do under the rules laid down at Delos. But Athens treated Naxos as a rebellious subject by assaulting the island and seizing its small fleet. More incidents of this kind occurred in the years that followed, turning Athens into an imperial power. The Athenians grew increasingly rich from the dues paid by the league members, and the Athenian statesman Pericles outraged Greeks far and wide when he transferred the league's treasury from Delos to Athens in 454 B.C. Nevertheless, most of the organization's member states supported Athens in the Peloponnesian War (431–404 B.C.), fought against Sparta and its Peloponnesian League.

SEE ALSO: Athens; Delos; Greco-Persian Wars

Delos

A tiny but important Greek island situated roughly in the center of the Aegean Sea. In mythology, Delos was the birthplace of the twin gods Apollo and Artemis, and throughout antiquity the island retained its close association with Apollo. This earned it the image of a sacred site, and a religious festival held annually there drew worshippers from across the Greek world. The island also hosted meetings of the Delian League, the alliance of city-states organized by Athens in 478 B.C., and guarded the league's treasury until the Athenians seized these funds in 454 B.C. In 387 B.C. Delos became headquarters of a new Athenian-controlled league, and in the early years of the Hellenistic Age a number of Macedonian kings constructed new buildings on the island. Delos came under Roman control in the second century B.C., and in the centuries that followed it housed the largest slave market in the eastern Mediterranean.

SEE ALSO: Apollo; Delian League

Delphi

The site of the renowned sanctuary of Apollo, which contained the most important oracle in Greece. The sanctuary, along with the town of Delphi, which grew up nearby, lay in a magnificent hillside setting in the state of Phocis, on the southern slope of Mt. Parnassus just north of the Gulf of Corinth. Beginning in the seventh century B.C., and perhaps earlier, religious pilgrims made their way to Delphi from all parts of Greece, from Greek cities abroad, and from foreign lands to seek answers to their questions about the future.

Apollo's temple also featured a hearth containing his "eternal fire." In addition, visitors could view the *omphalos* (navel), a stone widely thought to mark Earth's geographic center. Surrounding the temple were many other buildings, all richly decorated, including treasuries (which looked like miniature temples) erected by Athens and other city-states. There was also a stone theater that overlooked the temple, and higher up the hill a stadium

A nineteenth-century engraving depicts pilgrims consulting the Delphic Oracle, a priestess who supposedly communicated Apollo's words to humans. AKG-IMAGES

was located where the Pythian Games were held. Dedicated to Apollo, these games were among the "big four" athletic competitions of Greece.

The sanctuary of Delphi was administered and protected by the Amphictyonic Council (or Delphic Amphictyony), a religious organization made up of representatives from several neighboring states. In the period running from the late Archaic Age to the late Classical Age, both Delphi and the Amphictyony became involved in a series of disputes known as the Sacred Wars, in which various Greek states fought over possession of the sanctuary. But long after these struggles became a distant memory, indeed well into Roman times, the oracle continued to dispense wisdom and prophecy to eager visitors.

The last Delphic oracles were delivered in A.D. 391, the year the Romans closed the temple, along with all other pagan places of worship in the Greco-Roman world.

Today the ruins of the Delphic sanctuary are among the leading tourist destinations in the world. The stadium is almost completely intact, and the Greeks still hold athletic contests in it from time to time.

SEE ALSO: Apollo; Delphic oracle; Phocis; Sacred Wars

Delphic Oracle

The priestess of the temple of Apollo at Delphi in central Greece; or, in a more general sense, the sacred institution in which she supposedly relayed messages from Apollo to human pilgrims. The usual procedure was for a pilgrim to ask Apollo's priestess, known as the Pythia, questions about future events. It was thought that the Pythia, who sat behind a screen in the temple's innermost sanctuary (the *adyton*), was a medium who could convey Apollo's words. Thus, she answered the questions, but these answers (also called oracles) were usually mysterious, sometimes riddlelike, and frequently open to interpretation.

SEE ALSO: Delphi

deme

A village, parish, or city ward in ancient Attica, the territory controlled by Athens. The demes were introduced by Cleisthenes in the democratic revolution that began in 508 B.C. and replaced the ancient tribal groups that had formerly determined participation in government. Citizens registered in their local demes at age eighteen or nineteen. And state institutions, such as the Council (*Boule*), drew on the demes for their membership. Cleisthenes created ten new tribes, each with a membership divided into three groups. One group came from the demes in the urban center, another from the demes in Attica's coastal region, and the last from the demes in Attica's interior.

SEE ALSO: Athens; government

Demeter

In Greek mythology, one of the major Olympian deities and in historic times one of the most widely worshipped of these divinities. Demeter was essentially the goddess of grain crops, reflected in her chief symbol, a sheaf of wheat, as well as other plants, making her a potent fertility deity. Although she had shrines all across Greece in the Archaic, Classical, Hellenistic, and Roman eras, the principal one was at Eleusis, a few miles west of Athens. Here were held the famous Eleusinian Mysteries in her honor.

The most important myth about Demeter described how this shrine and its rituals came about. Persephone, Demeter's daughter, was out picking flowers one day when Hades, god of the Underworld, emerged from the ground, seized her, and carried her back to his dark realm. When Demeter found that Persephone was missing, she searched for her relentlessly. Eventually Demeter found out about the abduction, and in a fit of rage she unleashed famine and drought across Earth's surface. After that she abandoned Mt. Olympus, assumed human form, and began wandering from city to city. When she reached the town of Eleusis, near Athens, the locals treated her with great kindness. So she revealed herself to them and bade them construct a splendid temple for her, which, when finished, became her sole home. While Demeter brooded in her temple, Zeus, leader of the gods, worried that Demeter's famines, which were still ongoing, would wipe out humanity. So he sent various gods to try to reason with her. Eventually a deal was struck in which Hades would allow Persephone to spend part of the year on earth with her mother. The rest of the time she had to remain with Hades in the Underworld. Demeter reluctantly accepted the deal, ended the famines and droughts, and made sure that her shrine at Eleusis had a proper priesthood so it would thrive and attract many worshippers.

Whatever their very ancient origins, the Eleusinian Mysteries did indeed become widely popular. In Demeter's festival, which was held in September, one central ceremony reenacted the goddess's search for her missing daughter and their tearful reunion. New members of the cult (which welcomed men, women, and even slaves) had to complete a secret initiation, the details of which remain unknown. Keeping this and other aspects of the Eleusinian Mysteries secret was a priority throughout antiquity; in the fifth century B.C. the Athenian authorities investigated both the playwright Aeschylus and controversial politician Alcibiades on the suspicion that they had revealed some of the secrets. What is fairly certain is that the initiates purified themselves by bathing in the sea, then sacrificed a young pig. Next they marched in a solemn procession, carrying the cult's "sacred objects," whose nature is also uncertain. Once inside the sanctuary's initiation hall, a priest probably revealed the sacred objects to the congregation. Some scholars have speculated that one of the objects was a special sheaf of wheat that became part of a sort of thanksgiving ceremony honoring Demeter and Persephone. It appears that members of the cult accepted that these deities would watch over the souls of believers in the Underworld. Certainly the hope for a blissful afterlife to reward good behavior on earth was part of the appeal of this and later mystery religions, which in the first century B.C. strongly influenced early Christian beliefs about the afterlife. The sanctuary of Demeter thrived throughout the remainder of antiquity, until the Christian Roman emperor Theodosius I closed it down in A.D. 393.

SEE ALSO: Eleusis; Hades; Persephone

Demetrius of Phalerum
(ca. 350 B.C.–ca. 283 B.C.)

An Athenian politician who served as governor of Athens from 318 to 308 B.C. He was appointed by Cassander, one of Alexander's Successors, who then controlled much of mainland Greece. When Demetrius Poliorcetes (the son of another Successor, Antigonus) captured Athens in 207, Demetrius of Phalerum fled to the court of Ptolemy I in Egypt. There, the refugee became an adviser to Ptolemy, a noted intellectual and arts patron, and had a hand in planning the Great Library at Alexandria.

SEE ALSO: Alexandria; Demetrius Poliorcetes; libraries

Demetrius Poliorcetes
(336 B.C.–283 B.C.)

One of the more resourceful and colorful of the Successors of Alexander the Great. Demetrius was the son of Antigonus I, one of Alexander's leading generals. After Alexander's death, the father and son repeatedly tried to seize control of large parts of the huge empire Alexander had recently carved out. Demetrius took Athens from Cassander in 307 B.C. and about a year later defeated Ptolemy I in a large

naval battle near the island of Cyprus. Demetrius's most celebrated exploit was his large-scale siege of the island state of Rhodes, in which he brought to bear huge artillery pieces and siege towers. Although he was unable to take the city, he earned the nickname Poliorcetes, meaning "the Besieger," by which he was known ever after. In 301 B.C. Demetrius and his father were disastrously defeated at Ipsus by a coalition of other Successors. Amazingly, though, Demetrius rebounded and in 294 took control of most of Macedonia. His luck finally ran out in 285, however, when he was captured by his rival, Seleucus, and died in prison two years later.

SEE ALSO: Antigonus I; Battle of Ipsus; Cassander; Rhodes; Successors; weapons and warfare, siege

democracy

The world's first democracy, or government controlled by the people, was created in Athens at the dawn of the Classical Age. Numerous Greek states later adopted democratic systems.

SEE ALSO: Athens; citizenship; government

Democritus
(ca. 460 B.C.–ca. 357 B.C.)

A Greek philosopher-scientist best known for his advocacy of the first atomic theory of matter. Democritus was born at Abdera in Thrace. He traveled widely throughout the Greek world and penned many manuscripts covering such diverse topics as mathematics, grammar, ethics, and mechanics. These treatises have not survived, although small sections remain in the form of quotations in the works of later ancient writers. Democritus's chief accomplishment was to clarify and expand on the atomic theory proposed somewhat earlier by Leucippus. According to Democritus, all matter is composed of tiny particles called atoms, which are separated from one another by empty space. These particles, he said, can combine in various ways, producing the wide range of materials that make up the natural world.

SEE ALSO: Leucippus; science

demos

In ancient Greek city-states, a term denoting "the people" of a given state or community. It could mean the citizenry in general, but it also sometimes referred to the common people (as opposed to the aristocrats).

SEE ALSO: citizenship; government

Demosthenes
(flourished 426 B.C.–413 B.C.)

A leading Athenian general during the Peloponnesian War. Demosthenes became famous for his use of archers and javelin men (peltasts) to supplement his hoplites (heavy infantry) in battle. He died in 413 B.C. in the disastrous Athenian defeat at Syracuse in Sicily.

SEE ALSO: Peloponnesian War; weapons and warfare, land

Demosthenes
(384 B.C.–322 B.C.)

The finest of the Athenian orators and, along with the Roman senator Cicero, one of the two greatest orators of ancient times. Demosthenes, the son of a furniture maker, was early in life drawn to the art of public speaking, and, despite an initially weak voice and lisp, dedicated himself to becoming an effective orator. According to Plutarch, "He corrected his lisp and indis-

tinct articulation by holding pebbles in his mouth while he recited long speeches and he strengthened his voice by running or walking uphill, speaking as he went, and by reciting speeches or verses in a single breath. Besides this, he kept a large mirror in his house and would stand in front of it while he went through his exercises." (*Life of Demosthenes* 11)

The hard work paid off. Demosthenes began earning a living writing speeches for the litigants at trials and prosecuting public figures himself. He became most famous, however, for his opposition to the conquests of Macedonia's King Philip II. In 352 B.C. Demosthenes delivered the first of his great speeches denouncing Philip, which became known as the *Philippics*. Another set of speeches, the three *Olynthiacs*, called on the Athenians and other Greeks to keep Philip from seizing the city of Olynthus. When most of his warnings about Philip's aggressions were ignored, Demosthenes personally organized an anti-Philip coalition headed by Athens and Thebes. And the orator actually fought against Philip in the Battle of Chaeronea in 338 B.C.

After Philip won, some Athenians proposed giving Demosthenes a golden crown to reward him for his years of service to the state. But his longtime political rival, the orator Aeschines, objected, blaming Demosthenes for all of Athens's recent troubles. Countering Aeschines, in 330 B.C. Demosthenes delivered perhaps his greatest speech, *On the Crown*, which defended his anti-Macedonian crusade and denounced Aeschines. A few years later, in 323 B.C., Philip's son, Alexander (who had conquered Persia following Philip's death) died, and Demosthenes took part in a scheme to free Athens from Macedonian control. When the effort failed, the orator took his own life rather than be captured.

SEE ALSO: Aeschines; *On the Crown*; Philip II; *Philippics*

Description of Greece

A famous guidebook penned by the Greek geographer and traveler Pausanias in the mid-second century A.D. The work is divided into ten sections, each covering a selected region of Greece: 1. Attica and Megara; 2. Corinth and Argos; 3. Laconia, including Sparta; 4. Messenia; 5. and 6. Elis, including Olympia; 7. Achaea; 8. Arcadia; 9. Boeotia, including Thebes; 10. Phocis, including Delphi. Pausanias typically presents the history, religious beliefs, and myths of the main towns in each region. Often he pays particular attention to art and architecture, making his guidebook the principal surviving source for ancient Greek art.

SEE ALSO: Pausanias, 2

Deucalion

In Greek mythology, a character somewhat analogous to the biblical figure Noah. Deucalion, a son of Prometheus, creator of the human race, supposedly survived a great flood by building a big boat and afterward repopulated the world.

SEE ALSO: Prometheus

Dialogues

A group of twenty-five literary works by Plato, composed over the span of some fifty years. The exact order in which they were written is unknown. A typical dialogue consists of a conversation among several characters, often including Plato's old teacher and friend, the philosopher Socrates. Most of these works explore various philosophical and political themes. For example, *Protagoras* examines whether virtue can be taught; *Laches* explores the nature of courage; and *The Republic* discusses the kinds of institutions that might exist in a utopian state ruled by philosopher-kings. A few of the dialogues are somewhat atypical. The *Apology*, for instance, has only one character, Socrates, who speaks in his own defense at his famous trial in 399 B.C. And *Critias* and *Timaeus* describe the lost island-empire of Atlantis. Of the other dialogues, among the most widely read and studied are *Crito, Phaedo, Parmenides, Symposium*, and *Laws*. For details, see the entries for the individual dialogues.

SEE ALSO: Plato; Socrates

Diodorus Siculus (flourished ca. 60 B.C.–30 B.C.)

A noted Greek historian who hailed from Sicily, hence the name Siculus, meaning "of Sicily." Diodorus is best known for his huge *Library of History* (also called the *World History* or *Universal History*). It was made up of forty books, but only about fifteen of these have survived complete. Diodorus's historical prose was largely unoriginal and uncritical, and he often repeated and even contradicted himself. Still, modern scholars find his work valuable because it preserves a considerable amount of information from the lost histories he used as sources.

SEE ALSO: historical writing

Diogenes Laertius (early third century A.D. ?)

Nothing is known about the life of this Greek writer of *Lives of the Eminent Philosophers*. The work, consisting of ten books, presents mostly brief sketches of eighty-two notable Greek thinkers, orators, and other personalities. Among them are Solon, Anaximander, Socrates, Xenophon, Plato, Strato, Zeno, Pythagoras, and Democritus. Because Diogenes relied mainly on older biographies for his information, his work is usually only as reliable as his sources, which varied in accuracy.

SEE ALSO: biography

Diogenes of Sinope
(ca. 400 B.C.–325 B.C.)

A noted Cynic philosopher. Born at Sinope in northern Asia Minor, Diogenes at some point moved to Athens, where he adopted the austere lifestyle of Antisthenes (died ca. 360), founder of the minor philosophical movement known as the Cynics. Diogenes preached that a person could become happy only by dispensing with personal possessions, rejecting personal relationships, and living on the barest of essentials. Tradition holds that he carried a lantern around in the daytime in hopes of finding an honest man and regularly urinated in public, earning the nickname "the dog."

SEE ALSO: philosophy

Diomedes

In Greek mythology, one of the major Greek warriors who fought in the Trojan War. His father and grandfather died in a failed attempt to capture Thebes. So when Diomedes grew up, he instigated another attack on Thebes, which was successful, after which he became king of Argos. Later, when the Greeks sailed for Troy to retrieve Helen, queen of Sparta (who had been abducted by a Trojan prince), Diomedes led troops from Argos and Tiryns (located near Argos). In the great siege of Troy, Diomedes slew the Trojan prince Pandarus,

wounded another leading Trojan, Aeneas, and helped Odysseus, king of Ithaca, rescue the Greek warrior Philoctetes from the island of Lemnos. After Troy's fall, Diomedes returned to Greece and found that his throne was contested by several Argive noblemen. So he journeyed to Italy, settled there, and married a local princess.

SEE ALSO: Odysseus; *Seven Against Thebes*; Troy

Dionysia

Public festivals honoring the fertility god Dionysus. A number of Greek states had such celebrations, but the best known are the two in Attica, the territory controlled by Athens. The smaller of the two was the Rural Dionysia, held in December. The other—the Great (or City) Dionysia, held in March—was instituted (or significantly expanded) in 534 B.C. The highlight of the celebration consisted of the famous dramatic contests in which plays were presented in the Theater of Dionysus over the course of several days.

SEE ALSO: Dionysus; dithyramb; theater and drama

Dionysius I
(ca. 430 B.C.–367 B.C.)

A noted dictator of the Greek city of Syracuse on the island of Sicily. He was elected a Syracusan general in 406 B.C. Because of the increasing military aggressions of Carthage, Dionysius was soon able to convince his countrymen to grant him wide-ranging powers to thwart that threat. In the years that followed, he managed to defeat the Carthaginians and confine them to western Sicily. He also invaded and conquered parts of southern Italy (then the domain of various Greek cities). Dionysus appears to have been a curious mix

This detail from a vase painting dating from about 500 B.C. *shows the fertility god Dionysus (at left) and some of his followers.* TIME LIFE PICTURES/GETTY IMAGES

of ruthless warmonger and cultured artist. On the one hand, he became famous for his cruelty, as well as his innovations in siege artillery, including giant crossbows. On the other, he was an ardent admirer of the theater and entered a play (*Hector's Ransom*) in Athens's great drama festival.

SEE ALSO: Italy; Syracuse; weapons and warfare, siege

Dionysius of Halicarnassus (flourished late first century B.C.)

A noted Greek historian who moved to Rome in about 30 B.C. and became an admirer of Roman culture. He is best known for his *Roman Antiquities*, a huge historical tract of which a bit more than half survives. It covers Roman history from mythical times down to the beginning of the First Punic War (264 B.C.) and is seen by modern scholars as a valuable supplement to the works of

Livy and other Roman historians.

SEE ALSO: historical writing; Rome

Dionysus

In Greek mythology, the renowned god of the vine, wine, and fertility and the central focus of numerous important religious festivals across Greece and in other parts of the Mediterranean world (including Roman Italy, where he was called Bacchus). Dionysus started out as a fairly minor deity in the Dark and Archaic ages. But he grew increasingly popular, and by the opening of the Hellenistic period he was the most widely worshipped god in the Greek-speaking lands. In Athens he was honored as the patron of that city's great dramatic festivals. The plays and theater conventions that appeared in these festivals derived from the dithyramb, religious verses and rituals attending the cult of Dionysus. Central to his worship was the attainment of a state of joy or ecstasy, achieved through loud verbal expression, intoxication, and the temporary surrender of one's earthly identity, sometimes symbolized by wearing a mask.

Dionysus appeared in many famous Greek myths. Euripides used one of these for the plotline of his play *The Bacchae*, in which the god drove Thebes's women into a religious frenzy that made them wander and dance through the countryside. Other stories about Dionysus involved the daughters of various kings, who refused to join Dionysus's ecstatic female followers, the Maenads. For this affront, the god caused them to become insane and murder their own children. Dionysus was also said to have journeyed far beyond Greece. For example, legends claim that he went to Crete and on to Egypt, where he established an oracle.

SEE ALSO: *Bacchae, The*; religion; theater and drama

Dioscuri

In Greek mythology, the collective name of the characters Castor and Polydeuces. The term *Dioscuri* is derived from *Dios Kouroi*, meaning "Sons of Zeus" and refers to a myth in which Polydeuces is Zeus's immortal son. However, the epic poets Homer and Hesiod claimed that the Dioscuri were the sons of Tyndareos, king of Sparta, and the brothers of Helen of Troy. Whatever their ancestry, Castor and Polydeuces were said to have joined with the hero Jason in his quest for the Golden Fleece. At the end of the voyage, the brothers helped Jason destroy the city of Iolcos (or Jolcos), and in a later exploit they saved their sister Helen from the clutches of the Athenian king Theseus. In still another popular myth, following their deaths Zeus placed Castor and Polydeuces

in the sky, thereby creating the constellation of Gemini, the Twins. The Greeks came to see the twins as both protectors of sailors and patrons of athletes. And the Romans eventually expressed a strong interest in these heroes, worshipping them as the minor gods Castor and Pollux.

SEE ALSO: *Argonautica*; Jason, 1; Zeus

dithyramb

A special kind of choral song and ritual connected with worship of the fertility god Dionysus and influential in the early development of Athenian drama. Dithyrambic verses were usually divided between a chorus (originally a religious congregation) of worshippers and a single speaker (originally a priest), who interacted to tell about or comment on Dionysus's exploits or those of other gods or human heroes. A few examples of dithyramb have survived, including the following example by the fifth-century B.C. poet Bacchylides. Discovered on an Egyptian papyrus in 1896, it consists of an exchange between the mythical Athenian king Aegeus (here called "King") and a group of his leading subjects, who have heard that the hero Theseus (secretly Aegeus's son) is approaching the city.

> CHORUS : O King of holy Athens, lord of rich-living Ionians, why now does the bronze bell ring, the trumpet sound the song of war? Has someone evil overleapt the boundaries of our land, a general, a man? or bandits planning harm?. . .
>
> KING : Just now there came the windy way a messenger on foot, up the path from Corinth. [Great] deeds he tells of a mighty man [who] slew that arch-criminal Sinis . . . and that reckless man, [the bully and murderer] Sciron he slaughtered. . . .

CHORUS : Who is this man? From where? What does he say? What company does he keep? Is he with hostile forces, leading an army immense? or alone with his servants?. . . Or perhaps a god rouses him, to bring suit on unsuitable men?. . .

KING : About his gleaming shoulders hangs a sword . . . and in his hands two polished spears, a well-made dog-skin cap from Sparta on his head and tawny mane [of hair], a shirt of purple around his chest, and a woolen Thessalian jacket. His eyes reflect volcanic [Mt.] Etna [in Sicily], blood-red flame. He's said [to be] a boy of tender years. . . . He's said to seek the love of splendor, Athens! (*Theseus* 1–62)

SEE ALSO: Bacchylides; Dionysus; theater and drama

divination

The use of supernatural means, including religious rituals, to predict the future. The Greeks called this common practice *mantike*.

SEE ALSO: religion

doctors and medicine

Ancient Greek doctors developed a remarkably modern approach to healing, seeing disease not simply as a punishment inflicted by the gods but as a natural phenomenon that could be cured by human intervention. It is unknown when this great philosophical-scientific breakthrough occurred, but it seems likely that it took place gradually over the course of several centuries. By the fifth century B.C. several medical schools existed in the Greek sphere, frequently adjoining clinics associated with Asclepius, god of healing. The most renowned of these schools were in the Greek towns of Crotona in southern Italy, Cyrene in North Africa, the Aegean island of Rhodes, and Cnidus and Cos, towns lying northwest of Rhodes. The Crotona school produced the first important Greek doctor, Alcmaeon (b. ca. 500 B.C.), who correctly stated that the brain is the center of intelligence rather than the heart, as people had long thought.

Eventually the Crotona school and other medical centers came to be overshadowed by the facilities at Cnidus and Cos. They appear to have employed medical research, classroom lessons, and apprenticeships similar to (but obviously less sophisticated than) those of modern colleges and hospitals. The students took a solemn oath in which they swore to help the sick, to love humanity as dearly as their profession, and never to take the life of or sexually abuse a patient. This became the basis for the Hippocratic oath (named after the Greek doctor Hippocrates), to which modern doctors still swear.

Nothing substantial is known about Hippocrates, whom later ages came to call "the Father of Medicine." What seems fairly certain is that he was the director of the Cos school in the late fifth century B.C. That institution produced hundreds of medical writings on such topics as anatomy, treatment by diet and drugs, surgery, diseases of women and children, and medical ethics. Almost ninety of these works have survived and are collectively referred to as the Hippocratic Corpus. The chief achievement of the Cos and Cnidus schools was the concept that disease has natural, physical causes. The doctors at these institutions were sometimes wrong in their assessment of these causes; for instance, they thought that sickness resulted from an imbalance of the humors, the bodily fluids blood, phlegm, yellow bile, and black bile. Still, they made an honest attempt to explain health and illness in strictly physical terms. In addition, these physicians employed many practical treatments that work as well today as they did then. They prescribed warm baths and massages to reduce aches and pains, for instance, enemas to relieve constipation, and herbs and drugs to help the body fight illness. They also stressed the importance of proper diet and exercise as preventive measures.

Later, in the Hellenistic Age, further medical strides were made in the research facilities supported by the Ptolemaic rulers of Alexandria, Egypt. There, Herophilus of Chalcedon, who had studied at the Cos school, and his pupil, Erasistratus, made major advances in understanding the body's internal workings. Herophilus located the female's ovaries, described the spot where the veins meet on the back of the skull, and correctly divided the nerves into two categories, motor nerves (which initiate muscular activity) and sensory nerves (which carry messages to the brain). Erasistratus traced the paths of these nerves and tried to discover how they work. He also studied how animals and people metabolize food and excrete it as wastes, and he described the heart's pumping action. The Alexandrian school was notable for its emphasis on experimentation. But no Greek doctor performed experiments to better advantage than Galen, who, in the second century A.D., became the leading medical practitioner of the Roman Empire. His strides in anatomy and medical remedies surpassed the work of the Alexandrian doctors, as he learned much from dissecting dogs, pigs, apes, and other animals.

SEE ALSO: Alexandria; Asclepius; Galen; Hippocrates of Cos

Dodona

A city in Epirus, in northwestern Greece, famed for its sacred sanctuary of the god Zeus, which contained an important oracle. The oracle dated back to the late Bronze Age. In his epic the *Odyssey*, the eighth-century B.C. bard Homer tells how the legendary Bronze Age Greek hero Odysseus consulted the Dodona oracle. Later, in the fifth century B.C., the Greek historian Herodotus visited Dodona and afterward described its three priestesses, called "doves." Religious pilgrims wrote questions on thin sheets of lead and placed them inside jars. Then, in private, the priestesses (likely aided by male priests or officials) composed answers to the questions, supposedly inspired by Zeus. Dodona was sacked and devastated three times between 218 and 88 B.C. (the second time by the Romans), but it was rebuilt and survived for several more centuries.

SEE ALSO: Delphi; oracles; Zeus

Dorians

Modern scholars long theorized that this early, probably culturally backward Greek-speaking people, who hailed from the region just south of the Danube River, invaded Greece in the 1100s B.C., ending Greece's Bronze Age and initiating its Dark Age. But recent evidence has challenged this idea and laid the blame for the collapse of the Bronze Age cultures on other factors, including civil conflicts and economic problems. Thus, the Dorians were more likely opportunists who moved into mainland Greece after the fall of Mycenaean culture. They unsuccessfully assaulted Athens, then moved on, settling in the region of Sparta, on the island of

Crete, and elsewhere. In mythology, the Dorians were descendants of Dorus, son of Hellen, founder of the Greek race. They were said to have traveled with the sons of the heroic strongman Heracles (the Heracleidae) and helped them conquer the Peloponnesus.

SEE ALSO: Crete; Peloponnesus; Sparta

Doric order

The oldest of the three main architectural styles employed in ancient Greece, it featured columns whose capitals (tops) consisted of a plain square slab.

SEE ALSO: architectural orders; Parthenon

drachma

The basic unit of money in Athens and a number of other ancient Greek states.

SEE ALSO: banking; money

Draco
(seventh century B.C.)

A noted statesman (also known as Dracon) who was said to have introduced Athens's first written law code. These laws were seen as too harsh, however, so a later statesman, Solon, overhauled them, in the process setting Athens on the road to democracy.

SEE ALSO: government; laws and justice; Solon

education

Formal schools that taught reading and writing did not become common in ancient Greece until the fifth century B.C., and little is known about educational practices before that time. In Athens illiteracy was still widespread in the early 500s B.C., but by the end of the fifth century most adult Athenian men could read. Thus, Athenian society, and presumably Greek society in general, placed a markedly increased stress on education as that century progressed.

Most Greeks saw the education of boys as more important than that of girls, mainly because Greek society was highly male-dominated and it was seen as essential that young men be well prepared to run society and its institutions. Young Athenian boys began their educations in the home by listening to the stories and advice of their parents, grandparents, other relatives, and sometimes family slaves. The average age at which boys began attending school was seven or eight. In Athens most schools were privately run and paid for mostly by parents. Teachers known as *grammatistes* taught the boys to read and write. Then the students began absorbing the verses of popular poets, the most

Spartan youths train in the nude. Because of Sparta's renowned military system, the city-state strongly emphasized physical education. NORTH WIND PICTURE ARCHIVES

The Greenhaven Encyclopedia of Ancient Greece

important of which was Homer, whose epics, the *Iliad* and the *Odyssey*, were revered by all Greeks. Homer's works were seen as almost endless founts of religious, social, and political instruction as well as practical and moral lessons. Schoolboys also learned to sing and play the lyre (a small harp) from music teachers called *kitharistes*. And teachers known as *paidotribes* instructed them in athletic events and dancing.

Although the bulk of the surviving evidence comes from Athens, scholars believe that education in most other Greek city-states was similar to the kind practiced in that highly influential city. A major exception was education in Athens's archrival—Sparta. There, the *agoge*, a highly regimented system designed to turn out tough, fearsome soldiers, affected nearly all aspects of society, especially education. Spartan elders examined all male infants and ordered those they saw as too weak to be left outside to die. The surviving Spartan boys entered state-run schools at age seven. Most of the emphasis in these schools was on physical endurance and military training. As the famous first-century A.D. Greek writer Plutarch describes it:

> The boys learned to read and write no more than was necessary. Otherwise their whole education was aimed at developing smart obedience, perseverance under stress, and victory in battle. So as they grew older, they intensified their physical training, and got into the habit of cropping their hair, going barefoot, and exercising naked. ... They slept together ... on mattresses which they made for themselves from the tips of [river] reeds. (*Life of Lycurgus* 16)

Boys who could not measure up to these tough standards were called "tremblers"

and were treated with contempt and even cruelty.

As for young women, throughout most of Greece their schooling was less formal than that of boys and took place in the home. Mothers taught their daughters spinning, weaving, sewing, and fundamental math skills (for doing the family bills), although young women in the most progressive homes did learn basic reading and writing. Society did not see any compelling need for educating girls any further because, as a rule, women did not take part in politics and intellectual pursuits; also, it was widely accepted that women were intellectually inferior to men. Once again, the exception to the rule was Sparta, where the intellectual and athletic training of young women was encouraged. Spartan girls ran footraces and competed in trials of strength. And according to Plato, they were also trained in music and other arts and prided themselves on their mental development. This had to have included reading and writing because Sparta produced several female poets in the Classical Age, while Athens produced none.

SEE ALSO: children; family; science; sophists; Sparta

Egypt

Egypt and its ancient customs, ideas, gods, and exported foods and other commodities strongly influenced the Greek lands throughout antiquity. In the Bronze Age, both the Minoans, centered on the island of Crete, and the Mycenaeans, who inhabited mainland Greece, carried on regular trade with Egyptian ports. The Egyptians called these Aegean merchants Keftiu and left behind depictions of them in wall paintings. That trade seems to have ceased during Greece's Dark Age; but it began to revive in Archaic times, when the poet

Homer described the qualities of the island of Pharos, at the site on Egypt's northern coast where the city of Alexandria would later rise. In about 650 B.C. the Egyptians allowed some Greek traders to build a trading post at Naucratis in the Nile Delta. Through this outlet flowed a vigorous exchange of Greek silver and slaves for Egyptian grain and luxury items, including finely made crafts that influenced emerging Greek arts, including sculpture. Also, in the sixth century B.C. the Egyptians began hiring Greek mercenaries to help fight in local conflicts.

The Greeks got involved in Egyptian affairs more directly in the Classical Age, following the conquest of Egypt by the Persian Empire. In 460 B.C. a large military expedition (including as many as 120 ships) from the Athenian-controlled Delian League sailed to Egypt to help the natives in a rebellion against the Persians. Though successful at first, these forces were almost totally destroyed about five years later.

In the Hellenistic Age, Egypt actually became part of the Greek sphere, although more politically than culturally so. In 332 B.C. Alexander the Great liberated Egypt from Persia and established the new city of Alexandria there. And soon after his death one of his leading generals, Ptolemy, assumed control of the country, declared himself pharaoh (king), and set up his royal court in Alexandria. The Ptolemaic dynasty that he founded ruled Egypt as it had always been ruled—as an absolute monarchy. Ptolemaic Egypt continued to interact with other Greek kingdoms and city-states for the next few centuries, undergoing steady economic and military decline in the process. Meanwhile, cults of various Egyptian deities, including Isis and Osiris, became widely popular in the Greek

lands. After the last of the Ptolemies, Cleopatra VII, was defeated by Octavian (later to become Augustus, the first Roman emperor) in the Battle of Actium in 31 B.C., Rome directly annexed Egypt as a new province.

SEE ALSO: Alexander III ("the Great"); Alexandria; Cleopatra VII; Isis; Persians; Ptolemy I Soter; Ptolemy II Philadelphus; Seven Wonders of the Ancient World

ekklesia

In ancient Greece, an assembly of citizens (also spelled *ecclesia*) who met to discuss community issues and/or elect public officials.

SEE ALSO: government

Elea

A city on the southwestern coast of Italy, it was settled circa 535 B.C. by Greeks who had abandoned their homes in Phocaea, in Ionia (in western Asia Minor). It was not long before Elea (later called Velia) became renowned for its school of philosophy— the Eleatic school—established by Parmenides. Elea also became commercially prosperous thanks to vigorous trade relations with ports in the western Mediterranean. In time the Eleans allied themselves with the Romans, who went on to absorb all the Italian Greek cities, including Elea.

SEE ALSO: Eleatic school; Parmenides

Eleatic school

A philosophical school founded in the late sixth century B.C. by the Greek thinker Parmenides at Elea (a Greek colony in southern Italy). Members of the Eleatic school essentially taught that on its most basic level the matter making up the universe is continuous and indivisible because there is no such thing as "emptiness." This uninterrupted and supposedly unchangeable state of being they called a plenum. This view differs radically from that of the atomists, expounded by Democritus, that matter consists of individual pieces (atoms) with empty spaces around them.

SEE ALSO: Democritus; Parmenides; philosophy

Electra

In Greek mythology, the daughter of Agamemnon, king of Mycenae, and the sister of Orestes. Electra took part in Orestes' plot to kill their mother, Clytemnestra, a deed dramatized by both Sophocles and Euripides in their respective plays titled *Electra*. Electra also plays a major role in another of Euripides' plays, *Orestes*, as well as *The Libation Bearers* by Aeschylus.

SEE ALSO: Clytemnestra; *Electra* (play by Euripides); *Electra* (play by Sophocles); Orestes

Electra (play by Euripides)

A tragic play by Euripides, first presented in Athens sometime between 417 and 413 B.C. The plot is roughly similar to the one in Sophocles' play of the same name. One difference is that in Euripides' version Electra is forced by her mother's lover, Aegisthus, to marry a farmer to ensure that the young woman will not give birth to a noble son who might later attempt to gain the throne of Mycenae. Also, Euripides has Electra actually take part in the grisly murder of Clytemnestra. (In ancient Greek stage productions, this and other such violent acts happened offstage, and a messenger or other character entered and described what had occurred. Or some-

times stagehands wheeled in a platform, the "tableau machine," on which the characters involved in the violent act stood, frozen in place like statues, in the midst of performing the deed.) At the end of Euripides' *Electra*, the Dioscuri (the collective name of the brother-heroes Castor and Polydeuces) appear and deliver the judgment of the gods. For killing their mother, Electra and Orestes are to be banished from Mycenae. The Dioscuri also foretell that Orestes will be hounded by the Furies, the ghastly flying creatures who hunt down and punish murderers.

SEE ALSO: Dioscuri; Euripides; Furies; Orestes

Electra (play by Sophocles)

A tragedy by Sophocles, first produced in Athens circa 415 B.C. In the opening scenes, Orestes, prince of Mycenae, plots to kill his mother, Clytemnestra, in retribution for her recent murder of his father, Agamemnon. The young man tricks the queen and her lover, Aegisthus, into thinking he is dead; he then concocts a scheme with his sister, Electra, to arrange for Clytemnestra's demise. Orestes and a friend, Pylades, sneak into the queen's bedchamber and slay her and Aegisthus, after which the play's chorus, composed of Mycenaean women, expresses relief that Agamemnon has been avenged.

SEE ALSO: Agamemnon; Orestes; Sophocles

elegy

In ancient Greek and Latin literature, a poem that usually (though not always) expressed some form of lament and/or personal sentiment. Epitaphs and love poems were common examples.

SEE ALSO: poetry

Elements

A famous thirteen-book geometry text comprising definitions, axioms, theorems, and proofs, written by the Greek mathematician Euclid around 300 B.C. A fundamental work of mathematics, the *Elements* influenced the development of logic and scientific study and was an essential textbook in the ancient and modern ages.

SEE ALSO: Euclid; geometry

Eleusinian Mysteries

Important religious rituals connected with the goddess Demeter, they took place at her sacred sanctuary at Eleusis in western Attica.

SEE ALSO: Demeter; Eleusis

Eleusis

A town in extreme western Attica renowned as the site of the popular religious cult known as the Eleusinian Mysteries. According to Greek mythology, Persephone, reluctant queen of the Underworld, and her mother, the goddess Demeter, were reunited at Eleusis after Hades, lord of the Underworld, had abducted Persephone. Demeter then introduced the Mysteries to the local inhabitants to celebrate that reunion. The real origins of these rituals are uncertain, but they appear to date back to the late Bronze Age, when Eleusis was a small Mycenaean town. The remains of a Mycenaean shrine honoring an early version of Demeter have been found there. Much later, in late Archaic times, a major combination temple and meeting hall—the Telesterion—was erected in Eleusis to house the Mysteries. The building was destroyed by the invading Persians in 480 B.C., but the Athenians, led by Cimon and Pericles, soon rebuilt it. A temple dedicated

to Hades was also constructed near the town's Sacred Way, the path taken by the holy procession that marched to the Telesterion during Demeter's festival every September. A cave located near Hades' temple was traditionally held to be the entrance to the Underworld through which Persephone came and went in the dim past. Eleusis prospered until it was sacked twice by tribes from eastern Europe in A.D. 170 and 395. The town and its famous cult center were unable to recover from these assaults.

SEE ALSO: Demeter; Persephone; religion

Elgin marbles

A large collection of sculptures taken from the Parthenon and other structures atop Athens's Acropolis by a British statesman, Thomas Bruce, Seventh Earl of Elgin, better known as Lord Elgin. Like many other wealthy Europeans of the eighteenth and nineteenth centuries, he saw nothing wrong with removing pieces of ancient Greek and Roman structures to grace foreign museums and private collections. After getting permission from the Turkish authorities (because at the time the Turkish Ottoman Empire still controlled Greece), Elgin removed 247 feet (72m) of the total 534 feet (163m) of the Parthenon's magnificent Ionic frieze between 1801 and 1812. He also stripped away several of the large statues from the building's pediments and a number of sculpted panels on the metopes running along the sides above the colonnade. In addition, Elgin took pieces of the nearby Erechtheum temple and the Acropolis's monumental gateway, the Propylaea. Elgin sold these artifacts, which went on display in the British Museum a few years later. In 1939 they were transferred to the Duveen

Gallery, a new wing of the museum constructed especially for them.

Though many Europeans were thrilled to see these treasures, from the start a number of Western scholars and writers objected, viewing the removal of the so-called Elgin marbles as an outright theft and a desecration of Greece's greatest shrines. One of the most vocal critics was the English poet Lord (George Gordon) Byron, an ardent Grecophile (admirer of ancient Greece), who wrote in 1818, "Dull is the eye that will not weep to see thy walls defaced, thy moldering shrines removed by British hands, which it had best behooved to guard those relics never to be restored." (from *Childe Harold's Pilgrimage*). Since Byron's time, many concerned people, as well as officials of the Greek government, have requested that the British give back the Elgin marbles; but so far the position of the British government and British Museum is that the relics belong where they are. In the meantime, the new Acropolis Museum, completed in 2006, features a life-size arrangement of the surviving Parthenon sculptures. The plans are to leave the spaces where the Elgin marbles belong empty to remind visitors that these artifacts still languish in foreign lands.

SEE ALSO: Parthenon; sculpture

Elis

Originally a region of the northwestern Peloponnesus, Elis became a full-fledged city-state when the small towns of the area constructed a central city in the early fifth century B.C. A that time the old government, consisting of an oligarchic council made up of key members of the towns, was replaced by a democracy, probably at least partially modeled on that of Athens. Elis was famous for hosting the Panhellenic (all-Greek) religious festival and athletic games held every four years at Olympia, which lay in the nearby region of Pisa. The two regions hotly disputed ownership of Olympia in the Archaic Age until around 572 B.C., when Elis gained full control. Thereafter, heralds from Elis rode out every four years to all corners of the Greek world to announce the Olympic truce and summon athletes to the coming games. The trainers, officials, and referees at the games were also citizens of Elis. Although Rome subdued Greece in the second century B.C., out of respect for the Olympic festival the Romans allowed Elis an unusual degree of independence; thus, it came to be seen as a politically neutral international site. Between 1960 and 1981, archaeologists excavated parts of the ancient city, including the agora (marketplace), theater, and houses, dating from the Hellenistic and Roman periods. However, the ruins of the nearby sanctuary of Olympia routinely draw more tourists to the area.

SEE ALSO: athletics; Olympia

Elysium

In ancient Greek mythology and religion, a pleasant, idyllic section of the Underworld reserved for humans of heroic stature, also known as the Isles of the Blessed.

SEE ALSO: Underworld

Empedocles
(ca. 495 B.C.–ca. 435 B.C.)

One of the most brilliant and innovative of the pre-Socratics (Greek philosopher-scientists who predated the fifth-century B.C. Athenian philosopher Socrates). Hailing from Acragas, a Greek town in Sicily, Empedocles was said to have been an accomplished orator, and later Greek writers said that he invented the art of public speaking. He was also a doctor, and the later Greek physician Galen claimed that Empedocles founded Sicily's medical establishment. As a scientist, Empedocles held that nature's four fundamental elements—earth, water, air, and fire—are constantly affected by two powerful forces, Love and Strife. Love, he said, keeps these elements balanced and harmonious, whereas Strife makes them jumbled and chaotic. "When Strife had fallen to the lowest level of the vortex [the known universe]," he writes,

> and Love had reached its very center, then all things came together so as to be one single whole. This unity was attained not all at once, but according to the wishes of the things that were uniting, as some [came] from one direction, some from another. Yet along with the things that became mixed and unified, there were many things that remained unmixed . . . for Strife had not yet retreated entirely from them to the outermost limit of the circle [i.e., the vortex]. (fragment no. 35)

This fragment is one of approximately 450 that survive from Empedocles' large scientific works, the *Purifications* and *On Nature*, which were written in verse. Numerous later ancient writers were influenced by these works. Among them was the first-century B.C. Roman thinker and poet Lucretius, who wrote a scientific treatise in verse form in imitation of Empedocles' *On Nature*, even using the same title. Fortunately for posterity, in his long poem Lucretius preserves the kernel of one of Empedocles' most brilliant ideas—a theory of biological evolution similar in several ways to the one Charles Darwin introduced in the nineteenth century. Before humans appeared, numer-

ous and diverse species of living things had existed, Empedocles said (according to Lucretius). Some were not equipped to survive in the harsh conditions of their surroundings, so they died out, and stronger, more adaptable species took their place. As Lucretius summarizes the concept, which is similar to Darwin's theory of natural selection ("survival of the fittest"), "Monstrous and misshapen births were created, but all in vain. Nature debarred them from increase [reproduction and survival]. . . . Many species must have died out altogether and failed to reproduce their kind. Every species that you now see drawing the breath of life has been protected and preserved from the beginning of the world either by cunning or by prowess or by speed." (*On Nature* 5.873)

SEE ALSO: science

Epaminondas
(ca. 410 B.C.–ca. 362 B.C.)

A prominent Theban statesman and important military strategist whose tactical ideas influenced the Macedonian conqueror Philip, and, through Philip, Alexander the Great. Almost nothing is known about Epaminondas's life before he emerged as a Theban general in the late 370s B.C. What is certain is that in his youth Thebes was dominated by Sparta. The Spartans had occupied the Theban acropolis (the Cadmea) and dissolved the Theban-led Boeotian League (although the alliance had been restored by the time Epaminondas became general). Tension between the two states continued and finally, in 371 B.C., the Spartan king Cleombrotus marched on Thebes at the head of a large army. Epaminondas and his fellow general and patriot Pelopidas prepared the Theban troops, drilling them in new,

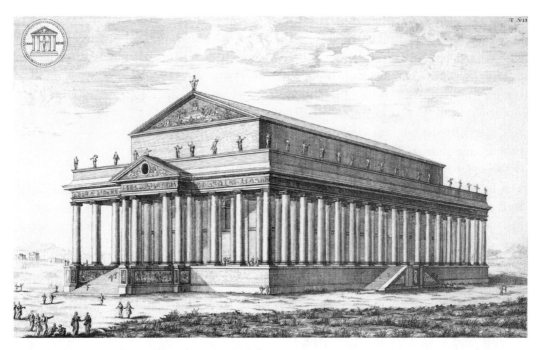

Some of the stylistic details of this eighteenth-century reconstruction of the temple of Artemis at Ephesus are thought to be inaccurate. © Historical Picture Archive/Corbis

innovative tactics Epaminondas had developed. In particular they placed extra troops on the army's left wing, greatly strengthening it, a move the Spartans had not anticipated. In July of that year the opposing armies clashed near Leuctra (10 miles [16km] southwest of Thebes), and the Thebans crushed the Spartan phalanx, forever destroying the myth of Spartan invincibility.

Under the guidance of Epaminondas, Thebes now embarked on a period of hegemony (political and military dominance) in Greece. The Thebans invaded the Peloponnesus and liberated the towns that had long followed Sparta out of fear. Epaminondas even camped his troops near Sparta in an effort to intimidate the Spartans, and he freed neighboring Messenia from Spartan control and helped the Messenians establish a new city—Messene. In 362 B.C. Epaminondas

entered the Peloponnesus again, this time to quell gathering hostilities among the local city-states, including Sparta. At Mantinea, the Thebans fought a strong coalition of troops from Sparta, Athens, Elis, and other cities. The huge battle proved indecisive, however, and Epaminondas was mortally wounded. His countrymen had no leaders of his stature to replace him, so in the years to come Thebes was unable to maintain its hegemony of Greece, paving the way for the intervention of Macedonia into Greek affairs in the decades that followed.

SEE ALSO: Battle of Leuctra; Battle of Mantinea; Boeotia; Pelopidas; Sparta; Thebes; weapons and warfare, land

Ephesus

One of the leading cities of Ionia, the Greek region along the western coast of Asia Minor in ancient times. Ephesus (or

Ephesos), which was situated slightly northeast of the island of Samos, was famous as the site of the gigantic Temple of Artemis, which was built in the sixth century B.C., destroyed by fire in 356 B.C., and then rebuilt. (It was later widely circulated that the temple's demise in 356 was a divine sign announcing the coming of Alexander the Great, who was born that year in Macedonia.) Inside the temple stood a large cult image (statue) of Artemis bearing twenty-four egg-shaped breasts, evidently meant to emphasize her powers of fertility. Later the temple was named one of the Seven Wonders of the Ancient World.

Ephesus was likely first settled by Greeks who migrated from mainland Greece to Asia Minor in the early Dark Age. In the sixth century B.C. the town came under the domination of Lydia (a kingdom encompassing much of western Asia Minor) and then of the Persians. The Ephesians were among the Ionians who rebelled against Persia in 499 B.C. and suffered defeat at Lade (south of Ephesus) in 494. After the Persians were driven from the region in 479, Ephesus at first supported Athens, but later, toward the end of the Peloponnesian War, switched allegiance to Sparta. The Ephesians were particularly prosperous in Hellenistic times, as evidenced by their large issues of valuable silver coins. The Romans eventually made the city the capital of their province of Asia; and it was in the early years of the Roman empire that the Christian leader Paul founded a church there and composed his Letter to the Ephesians. Ephesus continued to thrive in Roman times until it was sacked by barbarian invaders in the third century. Though damaged, Artemis's great temple survived, only to be vandalized by Christian zealots in the late fourth century. When modern archaeologists finally located the building, its battered remains were buried under thirty feet of sediment and rubble.

SEE ALSO: Artemis; Seven Wonders of the Ancient World

Ephialtes
(died 461 B.C.)

One of Athens's major early democratic reformers and the political mentor of Pericles, who became the leading statesman of Greece in the mid-fifth century B.C. In 462 Ephialtes convinced the Assembly to reduce the powers of Athens's ancient aristocratic council, the Areopagus, thereby dealing a blow to the local aristocratic faction. He also reformed the courts. Less than a year later, however, at the height of his influence, Ephialtes was assassinated by an unknown assailant (although it was widely assumed that the killer was either hired by the nobles or was one of their number). Pericles then wasted no time in carrying on his friend's policies.

SEE ALSO: Athens; government; Pericles

Ephialtes
(early fifth century B.C.)

A famous Greek traitor. Reportedly he showed Persia's King Xerxes a little-known path through the mountains, allowing the Persians to outflank and surround the Greek troops defending the pass of Thermopylae in 480 B.C.

SEE ALSO: Battle of Thermopylae, 1; Greco-Persian Wars; Leonidas

ephor

In ancient Sparta, one of five men chosen annually by the citizens to advise and watch over the conduct of the Spartan kings.

SEE ALSO: government; Sparta

Epic Cycle

An important and influential group of epic poems written by Greek bards in the seventh and sixth centuries B.C. In general, these epics covered the legendary gods, human characters, and major events of what the classical Greeks viewed as their dim past—the so-called Age of Heroes, which modern scholars know as the late Bronze Age. Some of the works in the Epic Cycle describe the mythical happenings that predated the Trojan War. The *Titanomachy*, for instance, which covered much of the same ground as Hesiod's *Theogony*, chronicles the rise of the first race of gods, the Titans, and the war in heaven between the Titans and the Olympian gods, led by Zeus. Three other early epics deal with the history and leaders of Thebes—the *Oedipodea* (*Story of Oedipus*), *Thebaïs*, and *Epigoni*. These works describe the rise and fall of Oedipus (who unwittingly married his own mother and killed his own father) and the failed attack on Thebes by the Seven Against Thebes. In the fifth century B.C. the Athenian playwrights drew a great deal of material from these epics; in particular, Sophocles' grand trilogy of Theban plays (*Oedipus the King, Oedipus at Colonus*, and *Antigone*) is based directly on them.

Among the other works in the Epic Cycle, six deal directly with the Trojan War, concentrating mostly on the events Homer had not addressed in his monumental epics, the *Iliad* and the *Odyssey*. The *Iliad* covers only part of the ninth year of the war, and the *Odyssey* tells only about Odysseus's homeward voyage, not the homecomings of the other Greek leaders. Thus, these six works were intended, in a sense, as supplements to Homer's works. The *Cypria* chronicles the events leading up to the opening of the *Iliad*; the *Aethiopis, Sack of Troy*, and *Little Iliad* tell what occurred in the war following the funerals of Patroclus and Hector (where the *Iliad* ends); the *Nostoi* (*Homecomings*) describes the return voyages of the Greek kings (except for Odysseus); and the *Telegony* covers the exploits of Telegonus, a son of Odysseus. The classical Greeks sometimes conveniently lumped these six works together with Homer's epics to form the Trojan Cycle. None of the poems of the Epic Cycle has survived complete; in fact, only 120 or so lines have survived, and their contents are known mainly from summaries in the works of later ancient writers.

SEE ALSO: Hesiod; Homer; *Iliad; Odyssey; Seven Against Thebes; Theogony*; Titans

epic poetry

Long, detailed poems, usually describing heroic or otherwise larger-than-life deeds and persons. The most famous Greek epic poems were the *Iliad* and the *Odyssey* of Homer.

SEE ALSO: Epic Cycle; Hesiod; Homer; poetry

Epictetus
(ca. 50 A.D.–ca. 120 A.D.)

A prominent Greek Stoic philosopher who was widely admired by many Greek and Roman writers, including the historian Arrian and philosopher-emperor Marcus Aurelius. Epictetus hailed from Phrygia in central Asia Minor but spent most of his youth in Rome. It appears that his master, a wealthy freedman named Epaphroditos, physically abused him, contributing to the ill health the philosopher endured as an adult. Eventually Epaphroditos freed him, and he studied with the renowned Stoic philosopher Musonius Rufus. Sometime in the early 90s Epictetus was exiled, along with other philosophers, by the emperor Domitian and settled in Greece. There, at Nicopolis, Epictetus founded a school, which the young Arrian attended. Arrian (who later gained fame for his *Anabasis*, chronicling the campaigns of Alexander the Great) did posterity a service by recording and eventually publishing many of his teacher's lectures. Arrian also published the *Manual*, a summary of Epictetus's philosophy. Following the widely accepted precepts of the Stoics, the philosopher held that all people are in a sense brothers; he also said that the human mind has the power to overcome most of life's problems and that by living a life of virtue one can achieve *eudaimonia*, a state of happiness. What made him different from most other Stoic philosophers was that he tailored his teachings to everyday people rather than the well-to-do.

SEE ALSO: philosophy

Epicureanism

A philosophical school founded by the Greek thinker Epicurus, it advocated, among other things, the atomist (or atomic) view of the universe's structure, including the idea that the soul is made up of atoms and can perish when they disperse.

SEE ALSO: Epicurus; philosophy

Epicurus
(341–270 B.C.)

A noted Greek thinker who established the Epicurean school of philosophy and championed the atomic theory. Epicurus was born in Ionia on the island of Samos, but in his thirties he moved to Athens, then recognized as the intellectual center of the Greek world. He founded a school widely known as the Garden and there lived in relative simplicity and seclusion with his students, who included women and slaves (at that time viewed as highly unusual, even suspicious, by most Greeks). Epicurus taught that wisdom and virtue could be gained in part by accepting the evidence of the senses as reality and rejecting superstition and divine intervention. He admitted that the gods might exist, but if so, he said, they had no interest in human beings. Following the ideas of Democritus and other earlier atomists, Epicurus said that tiny atoms are not only the building blocks of ordinary matter but also of the human soul. That meant that when people die the atoms making up the soul become separated, thereby extinguishing the soul. For this and other concepts deemed bold and revolutionary at the time, Epicurus later received what now seems overly extravagant praise from the first-century B.C. Roman thinker Lucretius:

> When human life lay groveling in all men's sight, crushed under the dead weight of superstition . . . a man from Greece was first to raise mortal eyes in defiance. . . . Fables and the gods did not crush him, nor the lightning flash and the growling menace of the sky. . . . The vital vigor of his mind prevailed. He ventured far out beyond the flaming ramparts of the world and voyaged in mind throughout infinity. Returning victorious, he proclaimed to us what can be and what cannot. . . . Superstition, in its turn, lies crushed beneath his feet, and we, by his triumph, are lifted level with the skies. (*On Nature* 1.93)

Despite Epicurus's conservative, moderate lifestyle and calls for people to limit their desires, over time his philosophy was distorted by those who did not understand it, which resulted in the now familiar and false definition of an Epicurean as someone who overindulges in food and physical pleasures.

SEE ALSO: Democritus; philosophy; science

Epidaurus

A small Greek city-state in the Argolis Peninsula in the northeastern Peloponnesus. It was best known for its religious sanctuary of the healer god, Asclepius, and for its theater, the best preserved in Greece, built circa 300 B.C. by the noted architect Polycleitus the Younger.

SEE ALSO: theater and drama

epigraphy

The study of inscriptions—written words or messages cut or scratched into stone or other durable materials. The earliest surviving Greek inscriptions date from the eighth century B.C. and consist mainly of names or short sentences etched on pottery items. One message on a cup made in the Greek town of Pithecusae, in Italy, circa 725 B.C., reads, "I am Nestor's cup. He who sips from me will be love struck by beautiful Aphrodite [goddess of love]." In the two centuries that followed, many inscriptions were longer and more sophisticated, and inscribed poems of various lengths became common. One of the longest Greek inscriptions still surviving is the law code of Gortyn, an important Cretan city.

SEE ALSO: Greek language; writing materials

Epirus

A small region and kingdom located in the extreme northwestern sector of the Greek mainland. During the Dark Age (ca. 1100–800 B.C.), tribal people speaking the Doric dialect of Greek inhabited Epirus. The tribes remained largely disunited until a local king, Alexander I, brought them together in the 340s B.C. In the early years of the next century, another Epirote monarch, Pyrrhus I, made the kingdom a major Hellenistic state, partly by invading Italy and Sicily and fighting several battles with the Romans. Within a generation, however, power struggles within Epirus itself caused its rapid decline, and by the late 200s B.C. the monarchy was defunct. One of the local tribes then backed the Macedonians against Rome, which proved disastrous. In 167 B.C. the Romans sacked Epirus and sold some 150,000 of its inhabitants into slavery.

SEE ALSO: Pyrrhus; Rome

Erasistratus
(early third century B.C.)

A Greek doctor and medical researcher who studied with the great anatomist Herophilus and worked alongside him at the Museum in Alexandria. Erasistratus later came to be called "the Father of Physiology" for his descriptions of several internal processes of the human body, including the heart's pumping action. For more about his work,

SEE ALSO: doctors and medicine; science

Eratosthenes
(ca. 285 B.C.–ca. 194 B.C.)

A leading Greek astronomer, geographer, and mathematician best known for his accurate measurement of Earth's circumference. He was also widely known in his own day as the longtime director of Alexandria's Great Library. All of his works are lost, although a few fragments have survived in quotations in the works of later ancient writers. The most important of these treatises were the *Geographica*, the *Chronographia*, and *On the Measurement of the Earth*. The writing of the *Geographica* marked the first attempt to create an atlas of the known world; the *Chronographia* was a chronology of Greek history beginning in 1184 B.C., supposedly the date of Troy's fall to the Greeks, and ending in 323 B.C., with the death of Alexander the Great in Babylon. More famous today is Eratosthenes' *On the Measurement of the Earth*, in which he used mathematics and brilliant logical deduction to accomplish the goal of the work's title. He was inspired by reading a book that claimed that in the Egyptian town of Syene (500 miles [805km] south of Alexandria) vertical sticks cast no shadows at noon on June 21, the summer solstice. On the next summer solstice, Eratosthenes planted a vertical stick in Alexandria and saw that it did cast a shadow. He realized that the fact that one stick cast a shadow and the other did not on the same day proved what Greek scientists already accepted—that the surface of Earth is curved. He also reasoned that the degree of that curvature was reflected in the different shadow lengths. His calculations suggested that the distance between Alexandria and Syene was equal to roughly seven degrees, or about a fiftieth, of Earth's total circumference. Now all he had to do was multiply the distance between the two cities by fifty. This produced a figure of 25,000 miles (40,234km), which is within 1 percent of the actual circumference as verified by modern measuring devices.

SEE ALSO: astronomy; science

Erechtheum

One of the two main religious temples (the other being the Parthenon) situated atop Athens's Acropolis and dedicated to the goddess Athena. According to a popular myth, long ago Athena sent an olive-wood statue of herself hurtling out of the sky, and the early Athenians built the first version of the Erechtheum (or Erechtheion) on the spot where the statue landed. Other versions of the temple rose there over the centuries until the most famous one was constructed during Pericles' grand building program in the late fifth century B.C. That structure had four porches, one each on its north, south, east, and west sides, all part of a clever, asymmetrical, split-level arrangement that was unusual for a Greek temple. The south-facing porch, which is the most famous, is called the Porch of the Maidens because its roof is supported by six caryatids, pillars shaped like maidens wearing flowing robes. (The caryatids standing there today are exact replicas, as the originals are safely housed in various museums.)

Today the inside of the ruined Erechtheum is largely empty, but in the structure's heyday the main chamber housed the sacred olive-wood statue of Athena that supposedly had landed there many centuries before. This image played a central role in Athens's most important religious festival, the Panathenaea. After marching through the city's streets, a solemn procession of citizens ascended the Acropolis and stopped in the open space between the Erechtheum and the Parthenon. A ceremony was then held involving Athena's sacred robe, the peplos. At the conclusion of the festival, worshippers draped this garment around the goddess's wooden statue in the Erechtheum, replac-

A reconstruction of the east face of the Erechtheum shows its sculpted frieze (the band located directly above the columns) and an outdoor altar. North Wind Picture Archives

ing the one from the previous festival.

SEE ALSO: Athena; Erechtheus; Panathenaea

Erechtheus

In Greek mythology, a legendary king of Athens and the great serpent that attended Athena, goddess of war and wisdom, as her consort. According to Homer, Erechtheus had no human parents but instead rose up in miraculous fashion from the ground. Finding him, Athena took charge of him and at some point brought him into her shrine on the Acropolis, which later became the temple known as the Erechtheum, named after him. In the Classical Age, Greek sculptors routinely pictured Erechtheus as a huge serpent coiled near the goddess's feet, the most famous version being the one the renowned sculptor

Phidias carved at the foot of the giant cult image of Athena inside the Parthenon.

SEE ALSO: Athena; Erechtheum; Parthenon

Eretria

A city situated on the western coast of the large Greek island of Euboea. In the early years of the Archaic Age (ca. 800–ca. 500 B.C.), Eretria was one of the leading cities of Greece, with considerable military power and political control of several nearby islands. The Eretrians were also vigorous colonizers who established towns or trading posts in western Italy, on the island of Corcyra (modern Corfu), and in the northern Aegean. Along with Athens, Eretria sent aid to the Ionians who rebelled against the Persians in 499 B.C. This brought down the wrath of King Darius I, whose troops burned Eretria in 490, shortly before engaging the Athenians at Marathon. After Eretria was rebuilt, it joined the Delian League and enjoyed prosperity for two more centuries. Finally, in 198 B.C., the city was destroyed again, this time by the Romans, and never fully recovered.

SEE ALSO: colonization; Euboea; Greco-Persian Wars

Eros

In Greek mythology, the god of love. Today he is better known in art and literature as Cupid, his Roman name. The Boeotian epic poet Hesiod claims in his *Theogony* that Eros was one of the first divine beings born out of Chaos at the beginning of time. Eros, whose name means "Love," was "the most beautiful of all the deathless gods," Hesiod writes. "He makes men weak, he overpowers the clever mind, and tames the spirit in the breasts of men and gods." (*Theogony* 120–123) Fulfilling his role as a promoter of sexual fertility, Eros encouraged the marriage between Gaia (Earth) and Uranus (Sky), whose children became the Titans, the first race of gods. A later, alternate myth claims that Eros was the son of Aphrodite, goddess of love, and Ares, god of war. Whatever his family background, as pictured in ancient Greek literature and art Eros was an astonishingly handsome and athletic young deity whose symbols were his bow and arrows and a torch. In Hellenistic times, when romantic love became a major theme of Greek literature and art, Eros/Cupid was frequently portrayed as a mischievous or mysterious deity intent on making people fall into or out of love (sometimes by shooting his arrows at their hearts). Some artists showed him as a winged child (or as a group of winged children). Under his

Roman name of Cupid, Eros was a leading character in one of antiquity's most popular stories about eternal love, Cupid and Psyche, which the Roman writer Apuleius tells in his Latin novel *The Golden Ass*.

SEE ALSO: Aphrodite; *Theogony*

Etruscans

An Italian people whose homeland encompassed the region lying north of the city of Rome. The area was called Etruria in ancient times and today is known as Tuscany, both terms deriving from the name of the people. The Greeks at first called them Tyrsenians and later Tyrrhenians. The fifth-century B.C. Greek historian Herodotus postulated that the Etruscans originated in central Asia Minor and migrated to Italy. Most other ancient scholars agreed. However, one dissenter, Dionysius of Halicarnassus, argued that the Etruscans were indigenous to Italy, and that conclusion has been accepted by most modern scholars.

Whatever the origins of the Etruscans, they were profoundly influenced by the Greeks. The establishment of a Greek colony at Pithecusae in western Italy in the mid-eighth century B.C. first brought the two peoples into proximity, and Greek pottery soon began to appear in Etruria. In the next century and a half, Greek traders brought goods from the Near East, as well as from the Greek lands, to Etruscan ports. At the same time, a number of Greeks immigrated to Etruscan cities, intermarried with local women, and established businesses. The Greeks also imparted their new alphabet (recently borrowed from the Phoenicians) to the Etruscans in this period, which allowed the latter to begin writing down their native tongue. In addition, sometime in the late seventh century B.C. the Greeks introduced their military system to the Etruscans. By the mid-500s B.C. the principal units of the armies of the Etruscan cities had adopted Greek-style hoplite armor and the phalanx formation. Finally, the Etruscans were influenced by Greek religion. Many Etruscan gods, who had been earlier viewed as formless spirits, took on human form in the style of the Greek deities.

Despite the many positive interactions and cultural exchanges between the Greeks and the Etruscans, in the 500s and 400s B.C., the two peoples clashed when Etruscan settlers penetrated Greek areas in southern Italy. In the following two centuries, however, both the Etruscans and the Italian Greeks fell under the control of the rapidly expanding Roman realm.

SEE ALSO: colonization; Italy; Rome

Euboea

The second largest of the Greek islands (after Crete), situated along the eastern shore of the Euripos, a narrow waterway separating the island from the important mainland regions of Attica and Boeotia. Euboea (or Evvia) is 106 miles (171km) long and 30 miles (48km) across at its widest point. In the Archaic and Classical eras its leading cities were Eretria and Chalcis, whose rivalry and domestic and foreign policies largely dominated the island's affairs.

SEE ALSO: Chalcis; Eretria

Euclid
(flourished ca. 300 B.C.)

One of the greatest mathematicians of antiquity and the author of the most widely used geometry text ever written. Nothing certain is known about Euclid's personal life. Some ancient sources say that he founded a school at Alexandria during the reign of King Ptolemy I. It was probably in the latter part of Ptolemy's reign that Euclid penned his great masterwork of geometry, *Elements*. A quaint story claims that Ptolemy was so taken aback by the book's complexity that he asked Euclid if there was some easier, shorter way to learn geometry. The mathematician supposedly replied, "There is no royal road to geometry." Still, throughout the text, Euclid guides the reader through the geometrical theorems and proofs in a clear, straightforward manner, each new idea building logically on those that precede it. Another value of the work is that it provides modern observers with a systematic overview of the Greek geometrical knowledge that had been accumulated before Euclid's day. After his death the book remained widely popular across the Mediterranean world until the fall of Rome. Then it was known only to Arab scholars until the early years of the Renaissance, when it was finally translated into Latin. Not until the 1500s was it translated into English and other modern European languages. Large sections of Euclid's text were later incorporated into geometry books that were still in wide use in the twentieth century.

SEE ALSO: science

Eudoxus
(ca. 400 B.C.–ca. 350 B.C.)

A noted Greek mathematician and astronomer whose ideas influenced Aristotle and other leading scholars. One of Plato's younger contemporaries at the Academy, Plato's school in Athens, Eudoxus made important contributions to the emerging field of solid geometry by showing how the volumes of pyramids, cones, and cylinders might be derived. In the field of astronomy, he promoted an idea first put forth by the Pythagoreans—that the heavenly bodies move along on vast, invisible concentric spheres. Eudoxus's younger contemporary, Aristotle, accepted this concept and later further developed it, mainly by increasing the number of proposed spheres. In particular, Eudoxus attempted to invoke the movements of these heavenly spheres to explain the periodically observed retrograde (backward) motion of some of the planets in the sky. His writings have not survived, but he is frequently quoted in the extant works of Aristotle and other ancient writers.

SEE ALSO: Aristotle; astronomy; science

Eumenes
(ca. 362 B.C.–ca. 316 B.C.)

One of the leading generals and governors under Alexander the Great, the ambitious men who came to be called the Successors. Born in Thrace, Eumenes had the distinction of being one of only a handful of non-Macedonian Greeks who rose to high positions in the Macedonian army. He started out as personal secretary to both Philip II and Alexander, but Alexander eventually recognized Eumenes' military abilities and promoted him to general. After Alexander died in 323 B.C., Eumenes became governor of Cappadocia in central Asia Minor, where another Successor, Antigonus I, besieged him. Later, in another struggle against Antigonus, Eumenes was betrayed by his own troops and executed.

SEE ALSO: Alexander III ("the Great"); Antigonus I; Successors

Eumenides

A tragedy by Aeschylus with a positive, hopeful ending, first performed in Athens in 458 B.C. The *Eumenides* was the third play in the *Oresteia*, the author's mighty trilogy dealing with the last years of the mythic curse of the House of Atreus (a centuries-long curse affecting the royal dynasty of the kingdoms of Mycenae and Argos). In the trilogy's second play, *The Libation Bearers*, Orestes, son of King Agamemnon (who led the Greek expedition to Troy), slays his mother, Clytemnestra, to avenge her assassination of Agamemnon. In the conclusion of that play, Orestes is forced to flee from the Furies, hideous creatures who chase down and annihilate murderers.

In the opening scenes of the *Eumenides*, the god Apollo, who has offered his protection to the young man, suggests that he escape the Furies by going to Athens, where the local patron goddess, Athena, will surely find a way to help him. After Orestes departs, his mother's shade (ghost) appears and urges the Furies to pursue the youth. (In a brilliant stroke by Aeschylus, these creatures also make up the play's chorus.) Orestes makes it to Athens and there asks Athena for aid. Soon the Furies arrive and give their side of the story, insisting that Orestes must die for his crime. The goddess decides that the young man should undergo a trial on the nearby Areopagus hill, where a jury of Athenian citizens will judge him and decide his fate. At the conclusion of the trial the jury is evenly split; and, following the custom of real-life Athenian courts (which Aeschylus injects into the mythical setting), Athena points out that when there is an equal vote the defendant must be acquitted. The Furies are angry over this verdict. But in a series of moving speeches Athena convinces them to stop their vengeful pursuits and end the curse of the House of Atreus and other destructive cycles of hatred and violence. She then performs a miracle by transforming them into the Eumenides, "the Kindly Ones." "Now, as I gaze on these formidable faces," she tells them, "great is the gain I foresee. . . . Blessed by the blessed and worshiped always, while steering the city and its people to do right and good things, you shall receive high honors forever." (*Eumenides* 987–995)

SEE ALSO: Aeschylus; Athena; Clytemnestra

Euphorion
(mid-fifth century B.C.)

The son of the great playwright Aeschylus. After the latter's death in 456 B.C., Euphorion entered some of his father's unproduced plays in Athens's drama festivals.

SEE ALSO: Aeschylus; theater and drama

Euphorion
(third century B.C.)

A renowned epic poet who hailed from Chalcis on the island of Euboea. Early in life, Euphorion moved to Antioch in Syria, where he worked as a librarian. Only fragments of his works have survived, but several ancient writers attested to his talent, and his influence on later Roman poets was considerable.

SEE ALSO: poetry

Euripides
(ca. 485 B.C.–406 B.C.)

One of the leading Athenian playwrights of the fifth-century B.C. and today seen as one of the greatest writers of tragedy in theatrical history. Euripides was not as popular in his own time as his older contemporaries, Aeschylus and Sophocles. This was due in part to the fact that the latter were more traditional, whereas Euripides tended to question traditional religious and social values. Also, Euripides' characters were less archetypal (stereotypical heroes, kings, and so on) and more like real people. He often gave a powerful voice to socially insignificant characters, such as women and slaves, or showed kings and heroes wounded or wearing torn clothes in situations that called for it. Many Athenians and other Greeks saw such informal and unconventional approaches to drama as undignified. But today he is widely viewed as the first playwright to deal with human problems in a modern way.

Of the eighty-eight plays credited to Euripides, nineteen have survived complete. They are *Alcestis* (438 B.C.), *Medea* (431), *Children of Heracles* (ca. 430), *Hippolytus* (428), *Andromache* (ca. 426), *Hecuba* (ca. 424), *The Suppliant Women* (ca. 422), *Madness of Heracles* (ca. 420 to 417), *Electra* (ca. 417 to 413), *The Trojan Women* (415), *Iphigenia in Taurus* (ca. 414), *The Phoenician Women* (ca. 412 to 408), *Helen* (412), *Ion* (ca. 412), *Orestes* (408), *The Bacchae* (405), *Iphigenia at Aulis* (ca. 405), *The Cyclops* (date unknown), and *Rhesus* (date unknown). Eleven of these works end with the sudden appearance of a god or goddess who helps the characters out of their dilemmas, a theatrical device called deus ex machina. As a result, a number of later critics held that Euripides too often resorted to the easy way of resolving the plot. This amounts to a relatively minor criticism of a dramatic artist whose works, despite the passage of more than twenty-five centuries, are still widely loved and performed.

SEE ALSO: Aeschylus; theater and drama; and the individual names of Euripides' plays

Europa

In Greek mythology, the mother of Minos, king of Crete, and the namesake of the continent of Europe. Seeing Europa for the first time in Phoenicia, her homeland, the god Zeus transformed himself into a bull. When the young woman tried to ride him, he jumped into the sea and carried her to Crete. There, he revealed his true identity—the leader of the gods—after which the two made love and she gave birth to three sons—Minos, Rhadamanthys, and Sarpedon. Minos later became ruler of Crete and built the famous labyrinth (underground maze), where the frightening Minotaur roamed. In the meantime, Europa's father sent his son Cadmus to Greece in search of Europa, and there the young man founded the city of Thebes.

SEE ALSO: Minos; Minotaur; Zeus

explorers and exploration

The Greeks and other ancients generally referred to the lands surrounding the Mediterranean Sea, including southern Europe, North Africa, and the Near East, as the "known world." They were aware that other lands lay beyond this familiar region. For example, they spoke of the "tin lands" (or "tin islands"), said to be located somewhere beyond the Pillars of Heracles (the Strait of Gibraltar). A number of Greek explorers actually attempted to reach such distant lands. Like Columbus and later European explorers, they were usually experienced ship captains who daringly sought to open up new trade routes and possible areas to colonize. The first of these explorers whose name was recorded was Colaeus. In about 630 B.C. he reached Gibraltar, became the first Greek to sail into the Atlantic Ocean, and established trade relations with the town of Tartessos

in southern Spain. A few decades later a Greek named Scylax was hired by Persia's King Darius I to establish a practical sea route connecting the Near East and southern India. To this end, Scylax sailed down the Indus River, then headed westward around Arabia and reached Egypt. The Indian Ocean was also explored by two later Greeks, Nearchos (fourth century B.C.) and Hippalus (first century B.C.).

Meanwhile, a younger contemporary of Nearchos, Pytheas, made a remarkable journey into the North Atlantic region. Lured by the prospect of opening a seagoing tin route, Pytheas set out from the Greek city of Massalia in southern Gaul (France) and crossed southern Gaul by foot and riverboat. Reaching the Atlantic coast, he bought or chartered a larger, seagoing craft, sailed north, and crossed what is now the English Channel to Cornwall in southwestern Britain. From there he sailed northward between Britain and Ireland, rounded Scotland, and explored the Orkney and Shetland islands, lying north of the British isles. The remainder of Pytheas's journey is less certain. But many modern scholars accept that he reached Iceland (then called Thule). He may even have ventured farther north and crossed the Arctic Circle. What is certain is that after he made it safely back to Massalia, Pytheas described his incredible journey in a book, *On the Ocean*, published in about 320 B.C., now lost. A number of later ancient Greek geographers used information from Pytheas's book in their own works.

SEE ALSO: colonization; science

exposure

The practice of leaving an unwanted infant outside to die, which was widely practiced across the ancient world.

SEE ALSO: children

family

The family, or *oikos* (EE-kos), was the central unit of Greek society, as each community was made up of a number of local families roughly collected into larger kinship groups, including clans, phratries, and tribes. Many Greek families were extended, so the father, mother, and their children often shared the house with grandparents, married siblings, in-laws, and cousins. Household slaves also lived in the house and sometimes were treated as family members; thus, an owner who had grown close to a slave and trusted and valued him or her might refrain from selling the slave to someone else. Greek families were male dominated (patriarchal) because in Greek society only men had legal and political rights, including the rights to vote in the Assembly, hold public office, sue someone in court, and sit on a jury. The father or husband (or grown son, uncle, or other male relative, if the father or husband was deceased) was therefore the natural head of the household. He made the rules, enforced them when necessary, hired servants or bought slaves, and arranged for his children's education. His wife, mother, children, other live-in relatives, and slaves were expected to do as he said and perform their respective household duties.

Still, many Greek men did not actually

The women of a well-to-do ancient Athenian household engage in spinning and embroidery while a female slave sees to the laundry. NORTH WIND PICTURE ARCHIVES

run their households on a day-to-day basis. This was because a majority of men did little more than eat and sleep in their homes and busied themselves in such outside activities as working in the fields, vineyards, or marketplace; serving as jurors or in public office; working out or relaxing at a gymnasium; serving in the army; and so on. (This was especially true in Sparta, where men spent years away from their homes and families training for and fighting in wars.) A man's wife or mother (or daughter, if the wife and mother were deceased or absent) more often ran the household. And within the home, women's roles and responsibilities were as important to the household's success as their husbands' and fathers' were to the success of the larger community. It is not surprising, therefore, that women's duties, roles, and struggles to maintain domestic order were the predominant themes of Greek family life. For more on family members and their duties and experiences,

SEE ALSO: children; clothing; education; grooming; houses; women

farming

In ancient Greece, as in other parts of the ancient world, agriculture was the main occupation and principal basis of the local economy as well as the most widely respected profession. Xenophon summarizes its importance well:

> The land bears not only the means for people to live, but also . . . provides all the things people use to decorate their altars. . . . The land provides the greatest abundance of good things, but doesn't allow them to be taken without effort. It trains people to endure the cold of winter and the heat of summer. It exercises and strengthens small landowners who work it with their hands. . . . Agriculture also

contributes to training people in cooperation. . . . Whoever it was who said that agriculture is the mother and nurse of all other arts was right, because when agriculture is faring well, all the other arts are strengthened, too. (*Oeconomicus* 5.3–7)

Xenophon wrote these words in the Classical Age, and it is unknown if such sentiments about farming prevailed in the first era of Greek agriculture, the Bronze Age (ca. 3000–ca. 1100 B.C.). What is known about farming in those early centuries is that the Mycenaean Greeks practiced a collective form of agriculture in which rich palace-centers and aristocratic estates employed serflike farmers. Evidently the palaces and estates collected the harvested crops and redistributed them to various members of society, including the serfs. Plows seem to have been made of wood, tipped with bronze. Livestock were widely raised, both on the mainland and in Crete, especially cattle, as evidenced by the frequent depiction of these animals in art. Also, the place names Boeotia and Euboea, lands that at the time made up a hefty portion of the Mycenaean heartland, both contain the root *boes*, meaning "cattle."

After the fall of Greece's Bronze Age civilization, agriculture became more localized. Most farms were small and privately run by subsistence farmers who became the backbone of the economies and armies of the city-states that rose in the Archaic Age. The first written description of the Greek farming methods of the Archaic Age and the eras that followed appeared in Hesiod's long poem the *Works and Days*, likely penned in the early seventh century B.C. This work, along with other evidence, shows that farmers planted grain crops, of which barley and wheat were the main ones, in October. Planting in the fall ensured that the crops would get plenty of water because the rainy season was in the winter. To sow these crops, farmers employed wooden plows, now tipped with iron instead of bronze, drawn by oxen or mules. A man directed the animals and plow, while helpers followed along tossing the seeds and, when necessary, covering them with dirt. Harvest time was in April or May. After collecting the grain in bushels or bundles, the farmer and his helpers threshed it (separated it from the stalks and husks) by placing it under the hooves of mules made to walk in circles on a stone floor. The other staple crops in Greece were grapes and olives. The planting and harvesting calendars for these crops were different from the ones for grain, as grapes, for example, were picked in September. Workers crushed the grapes by foot (a method still widely used today) to make wine. Olives, on the other hand, were harvested between October and January, either by handpicking or by using sticks to knock them out of the trees. They were then pressed for oil.

Raising livestock was also common in ancient Greece, and the principal farm animals included goats, sheep, and pigs. From goats and sheep people got milk, cheese, and meat, and sheep provided an extra bonus—wool to make clothes. (The fibers for linen came from the flax plant.) Other common farm animals included cattle, oxen, chickens, donkeys, mules, and horses. Breeding the latter, which were used both for racing and in warfare, was expensive, and horses were raised mostly by well-to-do people. The chief horse-breeding region in Greece was Thessaly, which boasted the largest fertile plain on the mainland. Horses and some other animals ate millet, a grain grown for fodder rather than human consumption (although people did eat it when supplies of barley and wheat were lacking). Domesticated animals were raised not only for food, pulling plows, shearing, riding, racing, and so forth, but many, especially cattle, goats, and pigs, were routinely used in sacrifices.

SEE ALSO: food and drink; olives and olive oil; spinning and weaving

Fates

Three minor goddesses thought to have the ability to guide people's destinies. Their names were Klotho ("the Spinner"), Lachesis ("the Drawing of Lots"), and Atropos ("the Inevitable"), frequently collectively referred to as the Moirai. Artists and writers usually depicted them as old women spinning or weaving. One belief was that their spinning led up to and stopped at the moment when a person was born, whereas another held that the goddesses' spinning continued throughout life until the thread ran out. The Fates played only minor roles in a few myths. In one, the god Apollo got the Fates drunk to trick them into allowing a mortal man, Admetus, to live longer than normal.

SEE ALSO: religion

Five Thousand, the

A special assembly of citizens that ruled Athens briefly from late 411 to early 410 B.C.

SEE ALSO: Four Hundred, the

food and drink

The ancient Greek diet consisted of a healthy mix of meats, vegetables, fruits, and grains. Beef was eaten in banquets following public sacrifices of cattle, but outside of religious festivals, it was only rarely consumed. Similarly, with the exception of members of the wealthier classes, who could afford richer diets, people only occasionally ate lamb, fowl, pork, and other meats at their main meals. However, fish was widely popular among and eaten often by members of all classes.

Still, even fish was not usually the mainstay of the average Greek diet. Most people dined primarily on grains, fruits, and vegetables, which, with few exceptions, they took in moderate quantities, which made obesity extremely rare. The chief grains were barley and wheat. Wheat was the more expensive of the two because it did not grow well in most parts of mainland Greece. Thus, large city-states like Athens imported most of their wheat from foreign ports, especially those on the shores of the Black Sea. Among the staple fruits were pears, figs, apples, pomegranates, plums, sour cherries, watermelons, grapes, and olives. Common vegetables included lentils, beets, cabbage, lettuce, basil, garlic, onions, mushrooms, mustard greens, radishes, and cucumbers. Also widely popular were almonds, walnuts, hazelnuts, and other nuts. In addition, the Greeks ate goat cheese and eggs. Their main sweetener was honey, and their chief cooking medium was olive oil.

Preserving these foodstuffs was difficult and sometimes impossible because refrigeration, taken for granted today, was unknown. Thus, meat and fish had to be dried, salted, or smoked to make them keep for longer than a few days. Grapes, figs, plums, and some other fruits were preserved by drying, and people pickled a number of fruits and vegetables as well as some varieties of fish.

As for drinks, wine was the most popular across the Greek lands. It was almost always diluted with water—in a ratio of roughly two parts water to one part wine—by mixing in a special bowl-like container called a krater. Most Greeks liked their wine chilled, so they either stored it underground to keep it cool or, if they could afford it, had slaves haul in ice from the nearest mountains. A few poorer Greeks drank goat's or sheep's milk, but in general this was viewed as a barbaric practice.

The regular meals in which the Greeks consumed wine, fruits, vegetables, and other foodstuffs varied in number and size over the centuries. During the Archaic Age and probably well before, most Greeks had a light breakfast soon after sunrise. Then they ate a large afternoon meal, the biggest of the day, and a lighter supper after dark. In the Classical Age that followed, people most often skipped breakfast and ate a light lunch, called *ariston*, then had a main meal, *deipnon*, in the evening. The main foods consumed at lunch were bread, cheese, and fruit. The main meal consisted of bread, vegetables, porridge (made from barley or wheat), lentil soup, sometimes fish, and occasionally meat, followed by cake, nuts, and/or fruit for dessert. Toward the end of Classical times, however, breakfast (*akratisma*) became more common again and remained so for several centuries to come. It was still a light meal, featuring a little bread (sometimes soaked in wine) and maybe a bit of cheese or fruit. Family members, both male and female, usually ate together, except when the head of the household entertained his guests in the *andron*, in which case the women and small children dined separately.

See Also: houses; olives and olive oil

Four Hundred, the

An oligarchic council that briefly ruled Athens during the last phase of the

Peloponnesian War. In the spring of 411 B.C., hoping to convince the Persian king to back Athens in the war, a group of citizens led by the politician Pisander and the orator Antiphon staged a coup. They deposed the democratic Council of Five Hundred (*Boule*) and replaced it with the Four Hundred. Later that year, however, Athenian democrats overthrew the oligarchs and replaced them with a special assembly of five thousand citizens (the so-called Five Thousand). The following year, the Five Thousand was disbanded and the city's traditional democracy was restored.

SEE ALSO: Peloponnesian War

freedmen

Freed slaves. (The term *freedmen* refers to both male and female former slaves.) For details on the status, rights, and professions of freedmen,

SEE ALSO: slaves and slavery

fresco

A painting done on wet plaster.

SEE ALSO: Akroteri; painting

frieze

A decorative band of sculptures or paintings adorning the interior or exterior of a structure. In ancient Greece friezes were most often seen on temples and large public altars. The most famous Greek example was the Parthenon temple's Ionic frieze.

SEE ALSO: Parthenon; sculpture

Frogs

A comic play by Aristophanes first performed in Athens in 405 B.C. At this time the Athenians were exhausted by the Peloponnesian War and sorely missed the great tragic playwrights Aeschylus, Sophocles, and Euripides, all of whom were now dead (Sophocles and Euripedes had died only the year before). In the opening of the play, the fertility god Dionysus (here portrayed as a boob) expresses his desire to go to the Underworld and bring back Euripides. The god claims that Euripides possesses the wisdom to show the Athenians how to bring the present devastating conflict to a swift conclusion. So Dionysus dresses up like the famous mythical hero Heracles and descends into the Underworld. There, as he rows across the River Styx, a chorus of frogs provides a steady beat by croaking: "Brekekekex ko-ax ko-ax, Brekekekex ko-ax ko-ax." After a series of encounters with other colorful characters, Dionysus finds the shades (spirits) of Euripides and Aeschylus. They are presently competing (as they did in life) to determine who is the better poet. Dionysus judges the contest and to everyone's surprise chooses Aeschylus the winner. Shocked, Euripides initiates the following exchange:

> EURIPIDES : What have you done, you foulest of all men?
>
> DIONYSUS : Me? I've picked Aeschylus to win. Why not?
>
> EURIPIDES : Do you dare to look me in the face after you've done the dirtiest of deeds?
>
> DIONYSUS : What's dirty if this audience approves?
>
> EURIPIDES : You're heartless. Will you never think of me now that I'm dead?
>
> DIONYSUS : What if living isn't really dying, or breathing dining, or sleep a

pillow slip? (*Frogs* 1472–1477)

Thus, as the play ends, Aeschylus prepares to leave with Dionysus to save Athens.

See Also: Aristophanes, 1; Dionysus; Euripides

Furies

In Greco-Roman mythology, a group of hideous, scary female creatures who hunted down and punished murderers, particularly those who slew a father, mother, brother, or other relative. The Greeks called them the Erinyes, but they came to be more commonly known by their Latin name, Furiae, which translates into English as "Furies." According to legend, they were the daughters of the ancient spirit-force Nyx (Night). In Greek art and literature, the Furies were frequently depicted as flying beings who carried torches and whips with which to torture their victims. Perhaps the most famous myth about the Furies was the one in which they chased after Orestes, who had slain his mother to avenge her murder of his father, Agamemnon. Aeschylus dramatized this story in his play the *Eumenides*, in the climax of which the goddess Athena transforms the Furies into more benign beings, the Eumenides.

See Also: *Eumenides*

Gaia

A goddess dating from at least as early as the Dark Age and probably earlier, she was viewed as the first of the original group of spirits who emerged from the primeval Chaos. According to the Archaic Age poet Hesiod in his *Theogony*, Gaia (or Gaea), who personified Earth, gave rise to Uranus, who personified the sky or heavens. The two then mated, and their children became the first race of Greek gods—the Titans. Gaia and Uranus were also said to have given rise to three one-eyed giants and three one-hundred-handed giants. The Greeks believed that Gaia had the power of prophecy and therefore linked her to the famous oracle at Delphi. Some ancient sources say that she was the first deity to have a shrine there, which was guarded by a big serpent, Python. The legend claims that when the god Apollo slew Python and seized the shrine, he compensated Gaia by establishing the Pythian Games, consisting of poetry and, later, athletic contests.

SEE ALSO: Cronos; Titans; Uranus

Galatea

In Greek mythology, a nymph who was pursued by the Cyclops (one-eyed giant) Polyphemus. Galatea thought him ugly and uncouth and rejected his advances, however. When Polyphemus discovered that the nymph was in love with a handsome young mortal named Acis, he slew Acis, after which the grief-stricken Galatea immortalized her lover by causing a spring of fresh water to bubble up from the earth.

SEE ALSO: Cyclopes

Galen
(A.D. 129–199)

A Greek physician who became the leading medical practitioner of the Roman Empire. Galen not only made a number of important medical advances himself, but he also collected, analyzed, and utilized the work of the best doctors of the past. He especially fell back on the advice and followed the philosophy of Hippocrates and other members of the Cos medical school, who endeavored to separate medical theory from religion and treat disease as a natural phenomenon governed by natural laws. Galen hailed from Pergamum in western Asia Minor and came from a wealthy family that stressed the importance of education. His father encouraged him to love learning and become a critical thinker. Encouraged by his father, Galen studied for a while with an anatomist who lived in Pergamum, then began traveling widely in search of new medical knowledge. In about 157 he returned to Pergamum and worked as a surgeon to gladiators. Eventually he struck out for Rome, where he was appalled by the incompetence of many Roman doctors. In such conditions, the brilliant Galen quickly made his mark and rose to become personal physician to the emperor Marcus Aurelius. Galen also attended Aurelius's son Commodus and the latter's three successors, including Septimius Severus. It is perhaps ironic that, quite inadvertently, Galen contributed to a steady decline in medical science in the centuries that followed. His skills as a doctor, researcher, observer, and writer were so great that later Greek, Roman, and medieval European physicians regarded him as an infallible

Galen, the foremost medical practitioner of the Roman Empire, delivers a lecture to the emperor and his courtiers in Rome's Temple of Concord. MARY EVANS PICTURE LIBRARY

authority and saw no need to carry on investigations of their own. So medical experimentation largely ceased for over a thousand years. Galen's surviving works include, among many others, *The Affectations and Errors of the Soul, Exercise with a Small Ball, The Pulse for Beginners, The Art of Medicine*, and *The Best Doctor Is Also a Philosopher*. In the latter, he sums up his whole approach to the study of medicine and to knowledge in general:

> The fact that we were born later than the ancients, and have inherited from them arts which they developed to such a high degree, should have been a considerable advantage. It would be easy, for example, to learn thoroughly in a very few years what Hippocrates discovered over a very long period of time, and then to devote the rest of one's life to the discovery of what

remains. . . . There is nothing to prevent us, not only from reaching a similar attainment, but even from becoming better than him. For it is open to us to learn everything which he gave us a good account of, and then to find out the rest for ourselves. (*The Best Doctor Is Also a Philosopher* 56–57, 62)

SEE ALSO: doctors and medicine; Hippocrates; Pergamum

gambling

Gambling was extremely popular among the ancient Greeks, a leisure activity perhaps almost as widespread as athletics. As remains the case today, people bet on sporting events of all kinds, although cockfights were particularly popular. Games of chance were also widespread among both adults and children. In his

Lysis, Plato describes children playing "odd or even" with tokens. (In "odd or even," a player guessed whether an opponent was holding an odd or even number of tokens.) In another common game of chance—knucklebones—players wagered on the number of tokens that, after being thrown into the air, would land on the back of someone's hand (or inside a given space). In addition, dice games were popular. The dice (*kyboi*) were usually made of terracotta, bone, or wood and, like modern versions, had six faces. Numbers or names were painted or scratched onto the faces. When using three dice, which was common, the best possible throw (called "Aphrodite's throw") was three sixes; the worst throw was three ones.

SEE ALSO: athletics

Ganymede

In Greek mythology, a brother of Priam, king of Troy. Homer claimed that Ganymede was so good-looking that the gods sent an eagle to bring him to Mt. Olympus. There the lad became a servant to these divinities. In another myth, Zeus put Ganymede in the sky as the constellation of Aquarius, the water carrier, while the eagle that had brought the boy to Olympus became the constellation of Aquila.

SEE ALSO: Zeus

Gelon of Gela
(ca. 540 B.C.–478 B.C.)

A noted tyrant (dictator) of the Greek cities of Gela and Syracuse, both in southern Sicily, he served as a cavalry commander under Hippocrates, tyrant of Gela. In about 490 B.C., after Hippocrates' death, Gelon used military force to take over the city's government. In 485 the ambitious

Gelon attacked and captured Syracuse and transplanted half of Gela's population to the larger city. Five years later, when Persia invaded mainland Greece, the Carthaginians (who had made an agreement with the Persians) invaded Sicily. Gelon defeated them at Himera in northern Sicily, making him a heroic figure throughout the Greek world. In 478 B.C. he died and was succeeded by his brother, Hiero I.

SEE ALSO: Battle of Himera; Hiero I; Syracuse

Geography

A large treatise completed by the Greek geographer Strabo in about 7 B.C. Of the seventeen books composing the work, the first two serve as an introduction. The other fifteen books cover the geography, history, economic activities, and often the major plant and animal life of Spain, Sicily, Greece, Asia Minor, the regions near the Black Sea, Palestine, Arabia, Persia (Mesopotamia), India, Egypt, and North Africa (to the west of Egypt). Like the third-century B.C. Greek scholar Eratosthenes, from whom he got much of his geographical information, Strabo pictured Earth as a sphere having a single large land mass in its northern hemisphere. This land mass was surrounded by water, thought by many to be the Ocean of mythology. The *Geography* is often picturesque and entertaining as well as informative, which explains why abridged versions of it were used as schoolbooks in medieval Europe.

SEE ALSO: Greece, geography of; Strabo

Geometric Period

As determined by modern scholars, a period (and style) of ancient Greek pottery and art lasting from about 900 to 700 B.C.

SEE ALSO: pottery

geometry

The Greeks borrowed a certain amount of mathematical knowledge, including basic geometrical concepts, from the Egyptians and the Babylonians and then developed complex formulas and proofs for these concepts.

SEE ALSO: *Elements*; Euclid; science

giants

In Greek mythology, a race of large, human-shaped beings who arose from the blood droplets that fell to Earth after the Titan Cronos castrated his father, Uranus. The main mythical giants (or Gigantes) included Eurymedon, Alcyoneus, Porphyrion, Ephialtes, Pallas, Enceladus, Mimas, Polybotes, Hippolytus, and Gration. The principal myth in which the giants appear was the one in which the Earth-goddess Gaia enlisted their aid in her failed attempt to overthrow Zeus, leader of the Olympian gods. The classical Greeks often depicted the giants' attack on the gods, called the Gigantomachy, in art and literature. For another kind of mythological giant, **see** Cyclopes; *Odyssey*.

SEE ALSO: Cronos; Zeus

glass

Two main forms of glass were either used or made in Greece in ancient times. The first, faience, consisted of crushed quartz or sand that was made into a paste and then coated with colored glazes. (Blue and green glazes were the most popular, although other colors were sometimes used.) Faience objects were produced in Egypt in the third millennium B.C., and the Minoans in Crete adopted the process in the early second millennium B.C. Faience bowls, cups, vases, beads, and figurines were imported to Mycenaean sites on mainland Greece a few centuries later.

Semitransparent and transparent glass objects were produced in Egypt in the mid-second millennium B.C., and some were exported to Minoan and Mycenaean towns. Three basic methods were employed to make these glass objects. In the first, sand was melted at high temperatures until it turned into molten (liquid) glass. With the aid of a metal handling rod, the glassmaker dipped a pottery core into the molten glass, a layer of which adhered to the core. Other layers might be added. Then, after the glass had cooled and hardened, the artisan poked a pointed tool through an opening in the object to break up and remove the core material, leaving the glass shell intact. The other two methods were "cold cutting," in which glass bars were cut into various shapes when still soft; and "molding," in which the artisan poured molten glass into a mold and allowed it to dry.

These techniques were largely lost at the close of Greece's Bronze Age, but they reappeared later. Glass and faience items began to be imported into Greece again in the sixth century B.C. and grew increasingly more common in the centuries that followed. It is unclear how many of these were imported from Egypt and other foreign lands and how many were manufactured locally in Greece. What is more certain is that, because such objects were independently crafted, they long remained mainly expensive luxury items. This changed somewhat after the invention of glassblowing in Syria in the first century B.C. Glass could now be mass produced, bringing down the price, although the clearest and most finely decorated glass objects remained expensive.

SEE ALSO: jewelry; pottery

Golden Fleece

In Greek mythology, the skin of a fabulous ram, which the hero Jason and his Argonauts were charged with retrieving.

SEE ALSO: *Argonautica*; Jason, 1; Medea

Gorgias (dialogue)

A dialogue written by Plato circa 380 B.C. and named after the famous sophist Gorgias, whom Plato knew. The speakers are Socrates, Gorgias, Polus, and Callicles. Gorgias defines rhetoric, the art of persuasive speech (or oratory), and asserts that it is a critical area of learning because leaders can use persuasive oratory to get local populaces to do their will. The characters then consider whether using one's skill this way is just or right. Socrates, who presents Plato's own view, argues that the just approach is for a leader to consider what is right for his people rather than to manipulate them to further his own agenda.

SEE ALSO: Gorgias; Plato

Gorgias
(ca. 483 B.C.–385 B.C.)

One of the best known of the Greek sophists, traveling teachers who dispensed knowledge for a fee. Born in the Greek city of Leontini in Sicily, Gorgias in his sixties served as ambassador to Athens and there made a positive impression on the locals with his moving public speeches. Among his few surviving works are the *Encomium of Helen* and *Defense of Palamedes*, in which he states that a skillful orator can successfully support and defend any argument, whether it is right or wrong. Some Greeks saw this as ethically objectionable, including Plato, who named a dialogue after Gorgias; in this work, Plato's old mentor Socrates squares off with Gorgias over the proper way to use the art of public speaking. Gorgias's ideas and style strongly influenced the orators Isocrates and Antiphon as well as the historian Thucydides.

SEE ALSO: *Gorgias* (dialogue); Isocrates; sophists

Gorgons

In Greek mythology, ugly and frightening female monsters who turned anyone who gazed on them to stone. The Gorgons, who were said to have sprung from the union of the sea gods Phorcys and Ceto, were three in number and bore the names Stheno ("Strength"), Euryale ("Wide-Jumping"), and Medusa ("Ruler"). Supposedly they were originally beautiful maidens, but in time they became hideous creatures with repulsive features, including tusks, animals' legs, and snakes for hair. Some ancient accounts said that all three Gorgons could turn people to stone, but others suggested that only Medusa was able to do so. The most famous story about the Gorgons is the one in which the hero Perseus hunts down and kills Medusa and uses her severed head to turn some of his human enemies to stone.

SEE ALSO: Medusa; Perseus, 1

Gortyn

An important city in south-central Crete, located on the northern rim of the productive plain of Mesara. Gortyn (or Gortyna) was settled some time during Greece's Dark Age, perhaps by people from the southern Peloponnesus on the mainland. Not much is known about Gortyn before the seventh century B.C., to which the city's earliest surviving inscriptions date. The most famous example is an inscribed rendition of the city's law code, dating from about 450 B.C. It is widely viewed as the single most valuable surviving source of Greek law produced before the Hellenistic Age. In the late first century B.C. Gortyn became the capital of the Roman province of "Crete and Cyrene."

SEE ALSO: Crete; epigraphy; laws and justice

government

Forms of government varied widely across the Greek lands in the roughly two millennia in which the ancient Greeks stood in the forefront of the march of Western civilization. Modern scholars generally conclude that Bronze Age Minoan and Mycenaean kingdoms were ruled by kings, supported by leading well-to-do aristocrats. These large-scale monarchies disappeared with the collapse of Bronze Age society in the twelfth century B.C.; and in the Dark Age that followed, government in Greece seems to have been smaller-scale and more local in nature. Each village had a leader called a *basileus*. Although this is sometimes translated as "king," a more accurate description would be "chief" or "headman" of a town or small region. Such a leader likely met with a few advisers and assistants in a council (*boule*) to decide policy for the whole community. These men probably also submitted their decisions to an assembly of the fighting men, who gave their approval.

A major development in the evolution of government in Greece occurred in the early Archaic Age, when the land's many isolated communities rapidly grew into full-blown city-states. The Greeks called the city-state the polis (plural, poleis). Various poleis developed differing local governments and traditions. In most of these states, power passed from the hands of local chieftains to ruling councils composed of several community leaders (at first exclusively aristocrats). This form of government is known as oligarchy, from a Greek word meaning "rule of the few." Some states, most notably Corinth, kept their oligarchic councils for several centuries. In contrast, many other Greek poleis tried new forms of government. One of these was tyranny. Common in the late 600s and throughout the 500s B.C., it was typified by an ambitious man who acquired dictatorial power by gaining the support of the common people against the ruling aristocrats. A number of tyrants at first enjoyed widespread popularity, initiated large building projects, and supported the arts.

However, tyranny as a governmental form did not last long in Greece. Most tyrants, along with most oligarchic councils, were steadily replaced by representative citizen bodies, mainly assemblies, that sought to assume governing authority themselves. Leading this trend toward more democratic government was Athens. There, in 594 B.C., the aristocrats and common people, who were on the brink of civil war, called on a prominent citizen named Solon to create a compromise. He instituted a system in which the local assembly had more authority and nonaristocrats were better able to climb the social and political ladder.

Following this trend toward more popular control of government, Athens launched the world's first true democracy in about the year 508 B.C. The Assembly's powers were greatly expanded. In addition to directly electing some public officials, it had the sovereign authority to declare war, make peace, create commercial alliances, grant citizenship, found colonies, allocate public funds for construction and other projects, and decide foreign policy. The existing Council (the Boule), which prepared the agenda for the Assembly, was increased from four hundred to five hundred members. The members of the Assembly debated and voted on the legislative bills prepared by the Council and could add amendments to a bill or send it back to the Council to be reframed. The Council also saw to it that the Assembly's directives were carried out by overseeing subcommittees (boards of councilors). These boards closely supervised the archons, public officials who actually ran the city on a day-to-day basis.

Athens's open democracy inspired other Greeks, who instituted similar democratic governments in the years that followed. One glaring exception was Sparta, which had two kings who ruled jointly. They were not all-powerful monarchs, however, as a group of five elected citizens, called ephors ("overseers"), outranked them in all but military and religious affairs. There was also an assembly of fighting men and a council (the *gerousia*, or "elders") that prepared its agenda. The exact balance of powers between these various governmental branches is still uncertain and is often disputed by scholars.

Although democracy, and to a lesser extent oligarchy and Sparta's unique system, remained in place in some Greek states into the Hellenistic Age, that era was dominated by several large kingdoms set up by the successors of Alexander the Great. These kingdoms featured absolute monarchies, with kings and royal courts. At least in these places, therefore, government in Greece had come full circle by reverting to the form that had dominated the area in the Bronze Age.

SEE ALSO: Athens; citizenship; laws and justice; polis

Graces

In Greek mythology, three minor goddesses who personified beauty, charm, and grace and enhanced the comforts and enjoyments of life. Their names were Euphrosyne, Aglaia, and Thalia. Greek artists frequently portrayed the Graces on vases and in wall paintings, often placing them alongside images of the Muses, minor goddesses of the fine arts, or of Aphrodite, goddess of love.

SEE ALSO: Aphrodite; Muses

grave goods

Weapons, clothes, food, grooming items, and other objects placed in a grave or tomb for the use of the deceased in the afterlife.

SEE ALSO: burial customs; Underworld

Greco-Persian Wars

A series of invasions and battles in the period from 490 to 479 B.C. in which the Greeks fought and defeated the Persians, whose empire was then the largest and most powerful on earth. (Some modern historians include as part of these wars the intermittent encounters between the two peoples in the decade before and the decades following this period, including the battles of Lade in 494 B.C. and Eurymedon in the 460s B.C.) These conflicts were not sudden occurrences but rather grew out of steadily increasing interaction and frictions between the Greeks and the Persians as the latter tried to expand their territory and influence westward in the late sixth and early fifth centuries B.C.

The Ionian Rebellion

First, in the 540s B.C. Persia's King Cyrus II gained control of the Greek cities of Ionia, the western coastal region of Asia

A Spartan phalanx (at right) smashes through the Persian lines in the pivotal battle of Plataea, fought in 479 B.C. North Wind Picture Archives

Minor. For years to come these cities were ruled by Greek puppets approved by the Persians. Then, in 512, one of Cyrus's successors, Darius I, led an army across the Bosphorus Strait into Europe. He had heard that Scythia, the sparsely populated region lying west of the Black Sea, possessed much gold, and he aimed to subdue the Scythians. Though Darius was unable to conquer the area, he did manage to overrun Thrace, lying north of the Aegean Sea and directly bordering the Greek lands. To support these expeditions, Darius demanded silver and other commodities from the Ionian Greeks and forced Ionian soldiers to serve in his army. Discontent over this situation steadily grew in the Ionian cities until they launched a major rebellion in 499. A leading citizen of Miletus, Aristagoras, traveled to the Greek mainland and enlisted the aid of Athens and Eretria in southwestern Euboea, which sent ships and supplies to help the beleaguered Ionians. In 498 a raiding party of Milesians and Athenians burned Sardis, Persia's local provincial capital. Hearing this, Darius was outraged that what he viewed as a group of puny, barbaric towns occupying the fringes of the civilized world had dared to challenge him, and he vowed to take revenge on the Athenians and the Eretrians. But first he dealt with the Ionians by sending a large fleet of warships, which crushed a united Ionian fleet near Lade (north of Miletus). Then a Persian army captured Miletus, and the rest of the Ionians either fled or conceded defeat.

The Persians Invade Greece

Darius had not forgotten his pledge to seek vengeance on Athens and Eretria. In 490 B.C. he sent a large fleet of ships, commanded by his nephew, Artaphernes, and a general named Datis, across the Aegean. The Persians first besieged and captured Eretria, then sailed southwest and anchored near the plain of Marathon, situated about 25 miles (40km) northeast of Athens. There, roughly twenty thousand Persian troops faced off against nine thousand Athenian hoplites, supported by perhaps a thousand soldiers from Athens's tiny neighbor Plataea. On or about September 12, the Greeks surged across the plain and decisively defeated the invaders. The surviving Persians returned in humiliation to Asia Minor, and Athens reveled in its newfound image as Greece's savior. The victorious "men of Marathon" were honored as national heroes and thereafter became models of the valorous Greek defending his home and way of life against the vile "barbarians" (then a common Greek term for non-Greeks).

At this point the vast majority of Greeks seem to have assumed that the Persian menace had been permanently eliminated. But the Athenian general Themistocles correctly foresaw that the enemy would return in much larger numbers and urged his countrymen to initiate a program of naval preparedness. As Plutarch says in his biography of Themistocles, "The Athenians built a hundred triremes [oared warships]. . . . After this he continued to draw the Athenians little by little and turn their thoughts in the direction of the sea. He told them that . . . with the power they would command in their fleet they could not only drive off the barbarians, but become the leaders of all Greece." (*Life of Themistocles* 4) Themistocles' warnings about further Persian incursions proved right. Although Darius died in 486 B.C. before he could avenge his loss at Marathon, his son Xerxes led a massive invasion force to Greece in 480. It may have numbered two hundred thousand combat infantry and cavalry, eight hundred to one thousand ships manned by at least 150,000 oarsmen and sailors; and a huge company of support personnel and camp followers numbering well over one hundred thousand. Faced with possible annihilation, most of Greece's leading city-states put aside their differences and prepared to fight. Themistocles hurried to assemble a united Greek fleet; meanwhile, to buy time for him, a small force of land troops fortified the pass of Thermopylae, through which the Persians would have to pass to reach southern Greece. Outnumbered by more than twenty to one, the Greeks, commanded by the Spartan king Leonidas, held the pass for three days and slaughtered up to a tenth of Xerxes' soldiers. But the Greeks were finally outflanked, and the Persians continued southward, reaching Athens in September 480 B.C. Xerxes ordered his men to burn the city (which was deserted because the inhabitants had evacuated). Soon afterward, however, an allied Greek fleet delivered the Persian navy a humiliating defeat in the Salamis strait west of Athens. The astonished Xerxes hastily returned to Asia Minor. But he left his son-in-law, Mardonius, with more than a hundred thousand troops to finish off the Greeks. Once more the king was guilty of both overconfidence and underestimating the abilities of his enemy. In the following spring Greek warriors from across the mainland converged on the Persians near Plataea and nearly annihilated them. Meanwhile, at Mycale in Ionia the Greeks achieved still another victory, thereby liberating the Ionians from the Persian yoke.

The Delian League

In the aftermath of these epic battles,

which had saved Europe from eastern domination, the Greeks, led by Athens, formed the Delian League, an alliance of city-states intended to protect Greece from further Persian attacks. The league's forces engaged Persian armies from time to time, battles in which the Greeks were always victorious. The long-term consequences of the Greco-Persian Wars were that no Persian army ever again entered Europe or posed a credible threat to the West. In contrast, the Greeks were filled with confidence and vigor, especially the Athenians, who soon produced a cultural outburst that has awed and inspired the world ever since.

SEE ALSO: Battle of Eurymedon; Battle of Marathon; Battle of Mycale; Battle of Plataea; Battle of Salamis; Battle of Thermopylae, 1; Darius I; Ionia; Leonidas; Themistocles; Xerxes

Greece, geography of

Overall, Greece is divided into two broad geographical regions—the mostly mountainous mainland and several clusters of islands lying on its eastern and western flanks. The mainland, which juts downward from the Balkans into the Mediterranean Sea, features several rugged mountain ranges. Mt. Taygetus, in the southern Peloponnesus, rises to 7,897 feet (2,407m); Mt. Parnassus, rising north of the Gulf of Corinth, reaches 8,061 feet (2,457m); and in northern Greece, Mt. Olympus, the land's tallest peak, is 9,570 feet (2,917m) high. Interspersed among the highlands are a few small fertile plains where a majority of ancient Greeks lived. Among the most important of these were the plain of Messenia, in the southern Peloponnesus; the Argive plain, in the northwestern Peloponnesus; the Lelantine plain, lying between Eretria and Chalcis on Euboea;

two small plains in Boeotia, north of Athens; and two larger plains farther north in Thessaly. The main island groups were the semiarid Cyclades, lying north of Crete; the Ionian Islands, off the mainland's western coast; and a long string of islands stretching along the western coast of Asia Minor.

The nature of these major geographical areas had a profound influence on Greece's history. First, the many separate valleys and islands promoted the growth of fiercely independent city-states (poleis), each of which developed its own local and often distinct dialects and social and political customs. Meanwhile, the scarcity of farmland provided a perennial motive for disputes among the city-states. Some coastal cities tried to solve the problem of lack of arable land by becoming skilled sailors, traders, and colonizers. A few, such as Athens, Aegina, and Corinth, grew rich through trade, while others, such as Eretria and Chalcis, spread their influence by establishing colonies.

Another geographical factor affecting Greece's history consisted of the range of high mountains lying north and northwest of Mt. Parnassus, along Thessaly's southern flank. These proved particularly strategic because they had only a few narrow passes. This made them fairly easy to defend against armies attempting to invade the prosperous poleis of the southern mainland, the pass of Thermopylae being the most famous example.

SEE ALSO: colonization; Cyclades; Olympus, Mt.; seafaring

Greece, history of

Modern scholars generally view Greek history as starting in the Bronze Age (ca. 3000–ca. 1100 B.C.), the era in which the people who lived in the region used tools

This is how Athens may have appeared at the height of its power and influence in the fifth century B.C. NORTH WIND PICTURE ARCHIVES

and weapons made of bronze. It remains somewhat uncertain exactly when the first Greeks arrived in mainland Greece. Available evidence suggests that people speaking an early form of Greek appeared in the area in the early to middle second millennium B.C. They are called Mycenaeans, after their chief fortress-town of Mycenae in the northeastern Peloponnesus. Other fortified cities or small kingdoms that they established on the mainland included Tiryns, Thebes, Pylos, Orchomenus, and Athens. The palaces and other major structures in the centers of these towns were surrounded by formidable stone walls up to ten feet thick.

The Mycenaeans were long culturally influenced, and maybe militarily dominated as well, by the Minoans, a non-Greek-speaking people who lived on Crete and other Aegean islands. The Minoans

built palaces, too, the largest being at Knossos in northern Crete. These were larger in scale and more splendid than those of the mainlanders. But like the Mycenaean versions, the Minoan palaces seem to have been the central focus of a collective form of agriculture. It may be that farmers contributed their products to palace officials, who then redistributed them among the populace. The Minoans also traded with peoples across the eastern Mediterranean sphere, including the Egyptians, and controlled the seaways around Greece.

By 1400 B.C. or so, however, Minoan power had declined, partly because of the devastating effects of the eruption of the volcano on the island of Thera, north of Crete. As a result, Mycenaean warlords were able to conquer the Minoan areas and gain control of the local seaways. For about two more centuries, the Mycenaeans prospered, partly by raiding the coasts of Asia Minor. One of these raids may have been the basis for the famous legend of the Trojan War, which was preserved in oral traditions and became the subject of the *Iliad* and the *Odyssey*, epic poems attributed to the eighth-century B.C. bard Homer.

The Dark and Archaic Ages

The Mycenaean Age came to an end between 1200 and 1100 B.C., when, for reasons that are still somewhat uncertain, the Aegean sphere and many parts of the Near East endured a series of major upheavals. Most of the major Mycenaean strongholds were destroyed and never rebuilt. Across most of Greece, writing, record keeping, large-scale political organization, and other aspects of advanced civilization all but vanished. The region entered what scholars call the Dark Age (ca. 1100–ca.800 B.C.), during which the Minoan-Mycenaean world steadily passed into legend and the surviving Greeks more or less forgot their heritage. Poverty was widespread. And most people identified themselves only with the particular isolated valley or island where they lived. They dwelled in wooden or stone houses clustered in small villages, each dominated by a local chieftain (*basileus*).

In time some of these scattered villages grew into large towns. Each came to dominate the affairs of a valley, island, or other local region and served as the nucleus of a new political entity that began to rise across Greece—the city-state, or polis. In what scholars call the Archaic Age (ca. 800–ca. 500 B.C.), the emerging city-states evolved differing local governments and traditions and came to think of themselves as tiny separate nations. As many of these cities grew increasingly

prosperous, Greece steadily and rapidly rose from its backward state. Trade and commerce revived and reading and writing, which had disappeared during the Dark Age, reappeared. In addition, monumental (large-scale) architecture developed; Panhellenic (all-Greece) shrines, oracles, and athletic games, including the Olympics, arose; and a number of cities established colonies along the shores of the Aegean, Black, and Mediterranean seas. Archaic times also witnessed a great deal of political experimentation. The rule of local chieftains gave way to aristocratic councils (oligarchies), tyrannies (dictatorships), and eventually democracies.

The first of the Greek democracies appeared in Athens at the beginning of the Classical Age (ca. 500–323 B.C.). And numerous Greek states adopted some version of democracy during this period. Under such a system, the state was controlled by an assembly made up mostly of a class of independent farmers. They became not only the economic backbone of the typical city-state but also the source of its military strength. These men formed a citizen militia that defended their property and city against would-be aggressors, most often neighboring poleis. The heavily armored infantry soldiers in these militias were called hoplites; they fought in a special formation known as a phalanx, most often composed of eight ranks, or rows, of soldiers, one aligned behind another.

The Classical Age and Rise of Athens

These local farmer-warriors encountered their greatest test shortly after the opening of the Classical Age. In 490 B.C. and again ten years later, the Persian Empire (centered in modern-day Iran and Iraq), then the most powerful realm on earth, attacked Greece. To meet this threat, most of the Greeks, who normally feuded among themselves, united; and in a phenomenal display of courage and fighting skill, they drove the Persians away in a series of epic battles.

Following the end of the Greco-Persian Wars in 479 B.C., Athens emerged as the most influential state in Greece. And in this capacity it spearheaded the creation of the Delian League, an alliance of more than a hundred city-states designed originally to protect Greece from further Persian incursions. Over time, however, the Athenians transformed the league into their own lucrative maritime empire. Under the direction of Pericles, the dominant Greek political figure of the mid-fifth century, much of the wealth that flowed from that empire into Athens's coffers went into public building projects designed to beautify the city and make it the wonder and envy of Greece. Accordingly, Pericles oversaw the construction of the magnificent Parthenon temple, dedicated to Athens's patron deity, Athena, atop the city's Acropolis.

However, Athens failed to maintain the tremendous momentum that allowed it to dominate Greek affairs during the mid-fifth century B.C. Its archrival, Sparta, which possessed the finest land army in Greece (while Athens had the strongest navy), viewed Athenian ambitions and aggressions with increasing alarm. So after several decades of mutual distrust and small-scale fighting, the two states finally came to death grips in the most devastating conflict the Greeks had ever known—the Peloponnesian War, which began in 431 B.C. In the words of Thucydides, the contemporary Greek historian who chronicled the war:

If both sides nourished the boldest

hopes and put forth their utmost strength for the war, this was only natural. Zeal is always at its height at the commencement of an undertaking; and on this particular occasion the Peloponnesus and Athens were both full of young men whose inexperience made them eager to take up arms, while the rest of Greece stood straining with excitement at the conflict of its leading cities. (*The Peloponnesian War* 2.8)

The Spartan and Theban Hegemonies

The war drew in most of the city-states, which allied themselves with either Athens or Sparta. It dragged on for twenty-seven grueling years and ultimately proved ruinous for all involved. Athens was forced to surrender in 404 B.C., ending its cultural golden age and dominance of Greece. The Greek city-states now entered a period of political and military decline in which their disunity and rivalry continued. Sparta dominated Greek affairs at first, but its leaders proved inept administrators who employed bullying tactics that alienated other Greeks and inspired much anti-Spartan opposition. The climax of this opposition occurred in 371 B.C. when Thebes shocked the Greek world by crushing Sparta's phalanx at Leuctra (near Thebes in Ionia). The Thebans then invaded the Peloponnesus. With their backing, many of the local cities, which had long followed Sparta out of fear, threw out their Spartan-backed regimes and instituted democracies.

The Theban hegemony (dominance) of Greece was relatively short-lived, however. In the mid-300s B.C., Macedonia, a disunited, culturally backward kingdom in Greece's northernmost sector, suddenly became united and powerful under the capable leadership of King Philip II. Desiring to make himself master of all Greeks,

Philip launched a series of diplomatic maneuvers and military campaigns that gained him control over much of northern and central Greece. Then, in the summer of 338 B.C., he and his eighteen-year-old son, Alexander (who would later be called "the Great"), defeated a coalition of city-states led by Athens and Thebes.

The victorious Philip wanted to fashion a confederacy of Greek states; so he called for a meeting of delegates from many mainland and island poleis and forced them to create a federal "Hellenic League," with himself as its supreme leader. He also began preparing them for a large-scale invasion of Persia. However, in 336 B.C. he was assassinated, and Alexander ended up leading the expedition. In 334 Alexander entered Asia Minor at the head of a small but formidable army of Macedonians and city-state Greeks. And in the course of only a decade, he conquered the entire Persian realm, which stretched from Egypt in the west to India in the east. Shortly after leaving India and returning to the Persian capital of Babylon, Alexander died unexpectedly (possibly of alcohol poisoning) at the age of thirty-three. Modern scholars mark the year of his passing, 323 B.C., as the end of the Classical Age and the start of the Hellenistic Age.

The Hellenistic Age

Hellenistic means "Greek-like" and here refers to the veneer of Greek language and customs that Alexander and his generals had imposed on the eastern cultures they had conquered. After Alexander's death, these generals, who became known as the Successors, waged a series of large-scale, bloody wars for control of his kingdom. Finally, by about 280 B.C., three major new Greek kingdoms had emerged. The Ptolemaic kingdom, founded by Ptolemy, consisted mainly of Egypt and parts of nearby Palestine; the Seleucid kingdom, established by Seleucus, encompassed most of the rest of the Near East; and the Macedonian kingdom, created by Antigonus Gonatas (grandson of Alexander's general Antigonus), consisted of Macedonia and portions of the Greek mainland. Among the smaller but still influential states of the day were the kingdoms of Pergamum in western Asia Minor and Epirus in northwestern Greece; the Aetolian League in western Greece and Achaean League in the Peloponnesus, federations of cities that had banded together for mutual protection; and some powerful independent city-states, notably the island of Rhodes off the coast of Asia Minor and Byzantium near the strait leading to the Black Sea.

The Hellenistic states made a number of notable scientific, artistic, and social achievements. Greek scientists, particularly those working in the Ptolemaic capital of Alexandria, made significant strides in anatomy, astronomy, mathematics, and other fields. The era's prevailing spirit of intellectual experimentation and individual expression found other outlets in the arts, as poets, sculptors, and painters achieved levels of vividness and realism unknown in prior ages. There was also an increased interest in the intellect, emotions, and political rights of the individual person within society. This benefited women, who in many Greek states gained a number of civil rights, including the right to inherit property and divorce their husbands at will. (They did not gain the rights to vote or hold public office, however.)

Sadly for the Greeks, the cultural progress they made in Hellenistic times was ultimately overshadowed by the fact that they failed to learn the lessons of their past disunity and wars. The successor-states almost incessantly engaged in disputes and destructive conflicts that drained their resources and energies and left them weak and vulnerable to attack from the outside. In the mid-third century B.C., as they quarreled, in faraway Italy the Romans were rapidly rising to prominence. Rome soundly defeated the maritime empire of Carthage (centered in Tunisia, in northern Africa), then turned on the Greek states of the eastern Mediterranean. In 197 B.C., in the climax of the Second Macedonian War, a Roman army demolished the Macedonian phalanx at Cynoscephalae in central Greece. And the results of the Greco-Roman battles and wars of the next few decades were the same. By 146 B.C. the Romans had gained control over most of the Greek lands.

The Ptolemaic kingdom remained independent, but it was already a second-rate power. And in the following century, with its vast stores of grain and royal treasure, Egypt became a prize coveted by the ambitious leading Romans of the day. Cleopatra VII, the last ruler of the Ptolemaic dynasty, allied herself with two of these men—Julius Caesar and Marcus Antonius (Mark Antony). In the end, Caesar was assassinated and his adopted son, Octavian (later Augustus, the first Roman emperor) defeated Antony and Cleopatra. After Cleopatra and Antony committed suicide in 30 B.C., Octavian annexed Egypt and made it a Roman province.

It was the Romans, therefore, and not the Greeks, who subsequently went on to unite the whole Mediterranean world into a vast commonwealth administered by one central government. The Romans were greatly impressed and influenced by Greek culture, however, and by absorbing much of it they ensured that the Greek cultural legacy would survive. But more than nineteen centuries would pass before the Greeks enjoyed self-rule again.

SEE ALSO: Alexander III ("the Great"); Athens; Cleopatra VII; government; Greco-Persian Wars; Macedonia; Minoans; Mycenaeans; Peloponnesian War; Rome; Sparta; Successors; Thebes; weapons and warfare, land; weapons and warfare, naval; weapons and warfare, siege

Greek language

Modern scholars identify Greek as one of several so-called Indo-European tongues that are all related, having descended from a common ancestor spoken in the Caucasus region (what is now southern Russia) in the third millennium B.C. or earlier. Thus, Greek is distantly related to a number of Italic, Germanic, Celtic, Slavic, and other languages that long ago radiated outward from that area. The earliest group of Greek speakers, known today as the Mycenaeans, entered mainland Greece from the north in about 2000 B.C. or perhaps somewhat later. They imposed both themselves and their language on the natives. However, a number of linguistic roots from the region's pre-Greek tongue became familiar aspects of Greek. Notable, for instance, are the originally non-Greek endings -sos, as in *Narkissos* (today, Narcissus), -thos, as in *Korinthos* (Corinth), and -ene, as in *Athene* (Athena).

At first the Mycenaeans were illiterate. Toward the end of the Bronze Age, however, they developed a script that English archaeologist Arthur Evans (who excavated the palace at Knossos in Crete) named Linear B. This was to distinguish it from Linear A, a script used by the Minoans to express their own language, which was unrelated to Greek. Linear B is composed of about ninety signs, each a vowel-consonant combination, with a few pictograms (picture signs) thrown in. About five thousand tablets bearing Linear B inscriptions have been discovered so far. This complex script was not suited to creating literature and was instead used almost exclusively for administrative accounts, inventories, and lists of people. At first archaeologists did not know that Linear B was a written form of Greek, although some suspected that this might be the case. In 1952 English scholar Michael Ventris proved it, and the scholarly consensus today is that the Mycenaeans adopted the script from Linear A to express their own tongue.

After the collapse of Mycenaean civilization in the twelfth century B.C., the Greek language remained in use, but what little literacy had existed before vanished. Also, the Dark Age that followed witnessed migrations across the Greek sphere of peoples speaking different dialects of Greek, which fell into large groupings, including Dorian, Aeolian, and Ionian. From the latter eventually developed the Attic dialect, centered in the Athenian territory of Attica. These dialects were similar enough that Greeks everywhere were able to understand one another without any difficulty.

Helping to ensure that this linguistic unity would be preserved was the return of writing sometime in the early Archaic Age. This time the Greeks borrowed a smaller, more practical alphabet from the Phoenicians. (The Greek word for *letters* was *phoinikia*, literally meaning "Phoenician things.") One problem was that the Phoenicians had only consonants, which made communication somewhat imprecise. The consonant combination *mt*, for instance, could stand for *moat, mute,* or *meet,* and the reader had to consider the context of the discussion to identify the specific meaning. The Greeks solved this problem by adding vowels, the symbols for which were Phoenician consonants not used in Greece. The new alphabet therefore combined simplicity with precision and flexibility, making it very suitable for expressing ideas, and the natural outcome was a rapid growth of written literature. Among the first literary works the Greeks committed to writing were poems, including Homer's epics.

For a long time, Greek literary works retained the diverse flavors of the traditional major dialects. And often this was done in a formal, artificial manner. For example, it became a literary convention to express the works of Homer and other epic poets in a formalized combination of the Aeolian and Ionian dialects. In the early Hellenistic Age, however, largely influenced by Macedonian attempts to unify the Greeks politically and otherwise, most of the older dialects declined in use in favor of koine, a version of the Attic dialect. The Athenian Xenophon was the first widely popular writer to employ koine exclusively. This form of Greek was subsequently used to produce Greek versions of the Old and New Testaments. Whatever dialect was expressed in writing, spoken Greek remained a clear, flexible, and melodious language that remained, along with Latin, one of the two principal tongues of the known world for the rest of antiquity.

SEE ALSO: Homer; Mycenaeans; writing materials

grooming

Evidence for grooming items and practices in ancient Greece comes partly from artistic renderings (on vases and cups and in wall paintings) and partly from archaeological finds (of combs, mirrors, makeup containers, and so forth). It is probably safe to generalize that, with a few exceptions, most Greeks were well groomed, just as they paid attention to regular bathing and wearing of clean clothes.

Regarding hairstyles, in the Classical Age the average man wore a beard (*pogon* or *hypene*), which he kept well trimmed. Some men wore mustaches with their beards, but no one wore a mustache by itself. In the early Hellenistic Age, the clean-shaven look became popular, although older men still sometimes grew beards. Greek men generally had long hair (often shoulder length) in Archaic times, but following the Greco-Persian Wars they began cutting it shorter (except boys, who kept their hair long until they were in their teens). A notable exception was Sparta, where most men sported long hair in the Classical Age and beyond. (In his *Histories*, Herodotus tells how the Persian king Xerxes was nonplussed when one of his spies reported that the Spartans stationed in the pass of Thermopylae were fussing with their long tresses in preparation for battle.)

Women in the Classical period normally grew their hair long but wore it layered in various ways on top of the head. Hairnets, combs, or a cloth band (*sakkos* or *sphendone*) kept it in place, although on formal occasions some or all of the hair might be allowed to hang down across the back or breast. In Hellenistic times, these headbands went out of fashion and, though women's hair was still long, it was kept in place by curling or waving it. (One exception was slaves' hair, which as a rule was short.) It also became popular to dye the hair, especially blond; and sometimes wigs were worn to achieve the same effect. Another common custom was to remove body hair, including pubic hair, by plucking it with tweezers or singeing it with a flame.

Greek women, both housewives and prostitutes, made liberal use of cosmetics, including makeup, skin oils, perfumes, and other products to enhance the way they looked and smelled. The fashion was to make one's complexion appear pale (probably to make the social statement that a woman was financially well off enough to avoid working outside in the sun). To achieve this effect, women employed powdered white lead (*psimythion*), which people made by soaking lead in vinegar and scraping off the residue that formed on it. It was also customary to add a bit of red rouge (*phykos*), made from mulberries or other plants, to the cheeks. Dark eyeliner was derived from soot or charcoal. Apparently, however, some Greek men were old-fashioned and preferred that their wives go without makeup (although it is unknown how well or often this was enforced). Xenophon observed, "The gods have made horses attract horses, cows cows, and sheep sheep. Human beings are no different. They find an unadorned human body the most attractive." (*Oeconomicus* 10.7–8) Women (and sometimes men) also used perfumes, often made by soaking flowers in olive oil. And common grooming instruments, besides tweezers and combs, included bronze razors, wooden or metal toothpicks to clean the teeth, manicure kits, and mirrors made of highly polished bronze or other metals.

SEE ALSO: baths and bathing; clothing; jewelry

gymnasia

In ancient Greece, public or private facilities where men went to wrestle or train for various athletic events.

SEE ALSO: athletics; baths and bathing; palaestrae

Hades

God of the Underworld, realm of the dead. Later references to the Underworld itself as Hades are incorrect; the ancients sometimes called it the "house of Hades," but the name Hades by itself designated only the god. Another misconception about Hades (also known as Plouton) was that he was an evil character. The Greeks did view him as dark, grim, unsympathetic, and a punisher of evil, but not as evil or unjust himself. Thus, he should not be equated with the Christian devil. Nevertheless, he was widely feared, so people considered it unlucky to speak his name aloud. Partly for that reason, and also because he had no interest in the living, no one actually worshipped Hades. Also, he appeared in very few myths. One famous myth in which he played a central role was the one in which he abducted Persephone, daughter of the goddess Demeter, desiring to make the young woman his bride and queen of the Underworld. Demeter was furious and forced Hades to allow Persephone to spend part of each year on the surface with her mother.

SEE ALSO: Demeter; Persephone; Underworld

Halicarnassus

A Greek city in Caria, in southern Asia Minor, said to have been settled circa 900 B.C. by people from Troezen in the southeastern sector of mainland Greece. Halicarnassus became subject to the Persians in the sixth century B.C., and its queen, Ar-

Two of Jason's Argonauts battle the Harpies, hideous monsters who were known for making people's food inedible. AKG-IMAGES/ PETER CONNOLLY

temisia I, was praised by the Persian king Xerxes as one of his wisest advisers. Nevertheless, she fought with the other Greeks against him at the Battle of Salamis in 480 B.C. After the Persians were defeated, Halicarnassus joined the Delian League and became an Athenian ally. Later, Alexander the Great took charge of the city, and following his death a series of different Hellenistic states administered it until it became part of the Roman province of Asia in the late second century B.C. Halicarnassus was famous as the birthplace of two leading Greek historians—Herodotus (fifth century B.C.) and Dionysius (first century B.C.).

SEE ALSO: Delian League; Herodotus

Harpies

In Greek mythology, ugly, vile, birdlike creatures, also known as "Snatchers," that stole people's food or covered it with a sickening stench, rendering it inedible. The

Greeks sometimes called them "Zeus's Hounds" because from time to time he was known to send them to punish humans. The Harpies figure prominently in the famous myth about Jason and the Argonauts and the quest for the Golden Fleece.

SEE ALSO: *Argonautica*

heating and lighting

The principal devices the Greeks used to light their homes were oil lamps—small, shallow ceramic vessels that burned wicks fueled by olive oil—and candles. People frequently set the latter in multiple-candle holders called candelabra. Torches were employed chiefly for outdoor lighting. The household hearth was a major source of heat in the average house, but people also obtained heat from the metal braziers they used for cooking. A brazier put out less heat than the hearth, but it was portable and could be moved from room to room.

SEE ALSO: houses

Hecataeus
(died ca. 476 B.C.)

An important early Greek historian and geographer born in Miletus in Asia Minor. After extensive travels through Persia, Egypt, and Greece, he created a map of the world showing the Mediterranean Sea in the middle, surrounded by land, and the legendary circular, outer Ocean enclosing all. His younger contemporary, the historian Herodotus, seems to have incorporated many of Hecataeus's observations into his own famous work, the *Histories*, without giving the author proper credit.

SEE ALSO: Herodotus; historical writing; Ocean

Hecate

An ancient and somewhat mysterious Greek goddess who was sometimes identified with Artemis, partly because both were seen as fertility goddesses. Most Greeks held that Hecate could bring people good fortune. But they also associated her with ghosts and demons, and people who practiced sorcery or black magic called on her to empower them.

SEE ALSO: Artemis; religion

Hector

In the legend of the Trojan War, and in Homer's *Iliad*, the eldest son of Priam, king of Troy, and the most formidable of Troy's fighters. After saying good-bye to his wife, Andromache, and their young son, Hector went out to confront the Greeks. In the fray, he slew Patroclus, friend of the mighty Greek warrior Achilles, and in response Achilles met Hector in single combat outside the city walls. Achilles killed Hector and dragged his body behind his chariot as he rode around the city. Later, when his anger had subsided, Achilles agreed to give Hector's body to Priam for a proper burial.

SEE ALSO: Achilles; *Iliad*; Troy

Hecuba

In Greek mythology, the wife of Priam, king of Troy. Hecuba (or Hacabe) gave Priam nineteen children, including Hector, Paris, Cassandra, Helenus, and Troilus. Although she plays a relatively small role in Homer's *Iliad*, Hecuba appears more prominently in Euripides' *The Trojan Women*, in which, following Troy's fall, she becomes a slave of Odysseus, king of Ithaca. Another of Euripides' plays, *Hecuba*, deals with the unjust deaths of Hecuba's son Polydorus and daughter Polyxene and how the mother exacts her revenge.

SEE ALSO: Euripides; Priam; Troy

Helen

In Greek mythology, a daughter of Zeus and a mortal woman, Leda, and the sister of the heroes Castor and Polydeuces. Helen, who was known for her ravishing beauty, married Menelaus, king of Sparta. She became a central character in the legendary Trojan War when Troy's Prince Paris either persuaded or forced her to leave Sparta and go with him to Troy. In retaliation, Menelaus and his brother, Agamemnon (king of Mycenae), formed a coalition of Greek kingdoms for a military expedition against Troy. After the Greeks won the war and sacked Troy, Menelaus took Helen back to Sparta. In most ancient accounts, she thereafter led a relatively uneventful life.

SEE ALSO: *Helen* (play); *Iliad*; Menelaus; Paris

Helen (play)

A tragedy by Euripides, first performed in Athens in 412 B.C. For his unusual plot, the playwright turned to an alternate legend about Helen. Instead of going with Paris to Troy, Helen is taken by the god Hermes to the court of the king of Egypt, while the woman who accompanies Paris to his native city is only a phantom. The play opens after the fall of Troy. Suddenly Teucer, one of the Greeks who fought at Troy, arrives and informs Helen that the war is over. Then her husband, the Spartan king, Menelaus, appears and tells how he was blown off course by a storm and shipwrecked off the Egyptian coast. Menelaus is at first confused because he thought

he had reclaimed Helen after Troy's demise. Now he finds that that woman was only a phantom. The real Helen tells Menelaus that the Egyptian king is presently demanding that she marry him. Helen and Menelaus trick the king into providing them a ship and manage to escape. The happy ending is unusual for a Greek tragedy and exemplifies Euripides' innovation and tendency to be unconventional.

SEE ALSO: Helen; Menelaus; Troy

Helenus

In Greek mythology, and in Homer's *Iliad*, a Trojan prince who had the ability to see into the future. Helenus used his gift of prophecy to warn his brother Paris that going to Sparta would end up causing much grief and destruction. But Paris did not listen, and his abduction of Helen, queen of Sparta, soon ignited the Trojan War. During that conflict Helenus was captured by the besieging Greeks and used his prophetic powers again, telling them that they must rescue the warrior Philoctetes, who had been stranded on an Aegean island. (They did so, as told by Sophocles in his play *Philoctetes*.) Following the sacking of Troy, Helenus married Andromache, the widow of his brother Hector, and established a small kingdom in northwestern Greece.

SEE ALSO: Paris; *Philoctetes*; Troy

Helicon, Mt.

The principal mountain range in Boeotia, located in the east-central portion of the Greek mainland. In Greek mythology Mt. Helicon was where the Muses (goddesses of the fine arts) dwelled. Both Mt. Helicon and the Muses figure prominently in the opening of Hesiod's epic poem the *Theogony*, the writing of which the poet claimed the Muses had inspired: "With the Heliconian Muses let us start our song. They hold the great and godly mount of Helicon, and on their delicate feet they dance around the darkly bubbling spring and round the altar of the mighty Zeus. ... The Muses once taught Hesiod to sing sweet songs, while he was shepherding his lambs on holy Helicon." (*Theogony* 1–5, 25–27).

SEE ALSO: Boeotia; Hesiod; *Theogony*

Helios

In Greek mythology, the god of the Sun, who was usually pictured as driving a flaming chariot across the sky each day. At night, Helios supposedly crossed back to his starting point in the east by riding in a golden cup on the waves of Ocean, a legendary river that encircled the world's land masses. From his lofty vantage in the sky, the god could see and hear people and events on earth, so both gods and humans frequently asked him to report what he had witnessed. The best-known myth associated with Helios involved his mortal son, Phaëthon. The young man wanted to drive his father's chariot across the sky, and the god reluctantly gave his permission. But then Phaëthon lost control of the flaming vehicle and Zeus, leader of the gods had to kill the boy with a thunderbolt. Historically, Helios was the patron god of the island city-state of Rhodes. After Demetrius, son of Alexander's Successor Antigonus, failed to take Rhodes in one of the most famous sieges of antiquity, the Rhodians constructed a towering bronze statue of Helios at the entrance to their main harbor. It became known as the Colossus of Rhodes and was included

in the list of the Seven Wonders of the Ancient World.

SEE ALSO: Rhodes; Seven Wonders of the Ancient World; weapons and warfare, siege

Hellas

The name the ancient Greeks used to describe their land. They called themselves Hellenes, or "Sons of Hellen," after Hellen, the mythical founder of the Greek race.

SEE ALSO: Greece, history of

Hellenica

A history of Greece written by Xenophon in the early fourth century B.C. The work's narrative begins in 411 B.C., during the last years of the Peloponnesian War, the point at which Thucydides' book describing that war breaks off. Books 1 and 2 of the *Hellenica* cover the years 411 to 403 B.C., including Athens's defeat by Sparta and the rule of the Thirty Tyrants in that city. Later, Xenophon describes Spartan operations against the Persians and the rivalry between Sparta and Thebes. The *Hellenica* ends with the Battle of Mantinea in 362 B.C. and Xenophon's famous observation that this great but indecisive battle left Greece in a more divided, uncertain state than it had been in before. Though valuable for its descriptions of many events in the years it covers, the work suffers from a number of omissions as well as from the author's tendency to inject his personal biases.

SEE ALSO: historical writing; Xenophon

Hellenistic Age

As determined by modern scholars, the period of ancient Greece lasting from 323 B.C. (the year Alexander the Great died) to 30 B.C. (the year Cleopatra VII, last of the independent Hellenistic monarchs, died). For the major events and figures of the period, **see** Greece, history of.

SEE ALSO: Pergamum; Seleucid Empire; Successors

Hellespont

The narrow, historically strategic strait separating Europe from Asia, it is now called the Dardanelles. The Persian king Xerxes I crossed it to invade Greece in 480 B.C., and the Macedonian conqueror Alexander the Great crossed it in the opposite direction during his invasion of Persia in 334 B.C. The Hellespont was also the site of the defeat of the Athenian navy in 405 B.C. by the Spartan general Lysander.

SEE ALSO: Battle of Aegospotami; Greco-Persian Wars; Lysander

helots

The formerly free inhabitants of the Greek state of Messenia, who were enslaved by the Spartans in the 600s B.C. The helots were treated harshly, partly because they greatly outnumbered native Spartan citizens, who worried constantly that the slaves might rebel. They actually did so in 464 B.C., after an earthquake had leveled most of the buildings in Sparta. It took the Spartans almost five years to completely quell the uprising. Thereafter the helots were treated even more cruelly than before. In addition to the beatings they would receive for breaking even minor rules, they were subjected to state-supported murder committed by young men in military training. As Plutarch tells it, "Periodically, the overseers of the young men would dispatch them into the countryside . . . equipped with daggers and basic rations, but nothing else. . . . At night, they made their way to roads and murdered any helot whom they caught. Frequently, too, they made their way through the fields, killing the helots who stood out for their physique and strength." (*Life of Lycurgus* 28) The helots were finally rescued from their plight by the Thebans, who liberated them after defeating the Spartans at Leuctra in 371 B.C.

SEE ALSO: Messenia; slaves and slavery; Sparta

Hephaestos

The Greek god of fire, the forge, and the patron of craftspeople (also spelled "Hephaestus"). In one legend, Hephaestos's mother, Hera, was upset that he was born with a lame leg, so she threw him off Mt. Olympus into the sea. Fortunately for the child, the sea nymph Thetis found him and raised him secretly in a cave. Later, Hephaestos returned to Mt. Olympus and became the gods' master craftsman. He not only fashioned palaces and made suits of armor for them, but also, at Zeus's order, he created Pandora, the first woman. Hephaestos supposedly worked at a forge on Mt. Olympus, but other ancient tales claimed he had another forge under a volcano on the Aegean island of Lemnos, where his cult was unusually popular.

SEE ALSO: Hera; Pandora; Zeus

Hera

In Greek mythology, the sister and wife of Zeus, leader of the Olympian gods. Her chief symbols were the peacock and the pomegranate. Worship of Hera was widespread among Greek women, who viewed her as their major protector as well as a protector of marriage and childbirth (although a minor goddess, Eileithyia, eventually came to be more strongly associated with childbirth). One famous myth about Hera held that she was one of the six original children of the Titans Cronos and Rhea (the others being Hestia, Demeter, Hades, Poseidon, and Zeus). Another legend claimed that Zeus decided to marry Hera after seeing her walking in the woods and becoming consumed with desire for her. Other popular myths told how she helped the hero Jason search for the Golden Fleece; how she was furious at the Trojan prince Paris for failing to choose her as the most beautiful goddess in a contest, and so took the side of the Greeks against the Trojans in the Trojan War; and how her jealousy drove her to punish some of the many lovers her husband, Zeus, carried on with behind her back.

SEE ALSO: Cronos; Paris; Zeus

Heracles

In Greek mythology, a mortal (but to some degree superhuman) son of Zeus, and the most famous of all human heroes and strongmen. He is better known today as Hercules, his Roman name. Greeks everywhere worshipped him or commemorated his deeds and adventures, which were described in dozens of major and minor myths. In one of the more famous of these stories, he accompanied Jason and the Argonauts in their search for the Golden Fleece. In another, Heracles liberated the Titan Prometheus from the mountaintop where he had been chained at Zeus's order.

By far the most renowned of Heracles' feats, however, were his so-called Twelve Labors. He performed these as a penance for the crime of slaying his own wife and children in a fit of temporary insanity. In the first labor Heracles killed the Nemean Lion—a monster that was impervious to weapons—by strangling it; in the second, he destroyed another monster, the nine-

For his second labor, the hero Heracles fights and kills a frightening nine-headed serpent, the Hydra. © BETTMANN/CORBIS

headed Hydra, using sword and fire; in the third, he captured alive a fabulous stag with horns of gold; in the fourth, he snared a large and vicious boar that was terrorizing villagers and farmers; in the fifth, he cleaned the stables of Augeas, king of Elis, which were buried in the wastes of thousands of cattle; in the sixth labor, Heracles drove away a flock of huge birds that were terrorizing a Greek town; in the seventh, he traveled to Crete and captured a savage bull roaming that island; in the eighth, he corralled a herd of man-eating horses; in the ninth, he fetched the girdle of Hippolyta, queen of the Amazons; in the tenth, he captured the cattle of a monster named Geryon (who had three bodies and three heads); in the eleventh, he collected a treasure trove of golden apples; and in the twelfth and final labor, he descended into the Underworld and captured Cerberus, the monstrous three-headed dog that guarded its entrance.

In the years following his completion of the Twelve Labors, Heracles performed many other formidable deeds, but eventually, after he had been badly burned by the caustic blood of a centaur (a creature half man and half horse), he opted to end his mortal life. His friends placed him on a large funeral pyre and set it ablaze, after which the gods raised him into heaven in a column of smoke and granted him eternal life.

See Also: *Argonautica*; centaurs; Zeus

Heraclitus
(ca. 540 B.C.–480 B.C.)

A Greek philosopher born at Ephesus in Asia Minor. Only fragments of his writings have survived, and most of these suffer from a lack of context and explanation and so are difficult to interpret. Heraclitus (or Heracleitus) seems to have felt that life and the world are in a state of constant change and are therefore uncertain and hard to comprehend. Still, he advocated that some kind of unity and stability exists beneath the surface. He also held that the main physical element of nature (the *physis*) is fire, which sometimes transforms itself into elements like earth and water. "All things are exchanged for fire," he writes "and fire for all things, as wares are exchanged for gold, and gold for wares. . . . Fire lives in the death of earth, and air lives in the death of fire. Water lives in the death of air, and earth in that of water. Fire coming upon all things will test them, and lay hold of them." (*On Nature* 15–19)

See Also: philosophy; science

herm

A bust of the god Hermes, divine messenger and patron of travelers. It was a common custom to place such a bust, often resting on a pedestal, outside the front entrance of a house or other building. The folk belief was that the statue would help keep evil or bad luck from entering.

See Also: Hermes; religion; roads

Hermes

In Greek mythology, the messenger god and patron of travelers, merchants, thieves, literature, and athletics. It was thought that Hermes also guided the souls of the dead to the Underworld. His symbol was a herald's staff, and Greek artists usually portrayed him wearing winged sandals and a wide-brimmed, winged hat. Hermes appears in a number of myths, usually carrying out various tasks for Zeus or other gods. At Zeus's request, for example, he intervened in a serious quarrel between the god Dionysus and the goddess Hera. During the Trojan War, Hermes helped arrange for the transfer of Hector's corpse from Achilles, who had slain Hector, to Hector's father, King Priam. Hermes also aided the Greek hero Odysseus during the latter's ten years of wandering.

See Also: *Odyssey*; Zeus

Hero of Alexandria
(flourished first century A.D.)

A noted Greek inventor who lived and worked in Alexandria, Egypt. Hero (or Heron) designed and built a number of toylike mechanical devices that at the time astounded people. They included mechanical birds that sang when someone poured water into a container, a device in which a model of the hero Heracles fought a monster, and mechanical puppet theaters with moving dancers. But though he tinkered with such gadgets, Hero was also a brilliant engineer who penned several well-written books discussing mechanical principles, including *Pneumatics*, in which he describes air pressure and how it can displace water. Hero also created an early version of the steam engine. He suspended a hollow metal ball above a pot of boiling water, and when steam from the water caused the ball to spin, any objects connected to the ball (such as miniature human figures) moved. Most people viewed the invention as a mere toy, and neither Hero nor anyone else applied it to industry. In a more practical vein, Hero designed some lethal catapults and other large artillery pieces.

SEE ALSO: Alexandria; science; weapons and warfare, siege

Herodas
(ca. 300 B.C.–250 B.C.)

Hailing from Miletus, in Asia Minor, Herodas (or Herondas) became known for writing mimes—short, dramatic narratives containing colorful and often humorous observations of city life. Only seven have survived complete. Although some may originally have been performed by actors, most seem to have been intended for private dramatic readings.

SEE ALSO: theater and drama

Herodotus
(ca. 485 B.C.–ca. 425 B.C.)

A Greek historian who hailed from Halicarnassus in southwestern Asia Minor and wrote a detailed account of the Greco-

Persian Wars—the *Histories*, now viewed as the oldest surviving conventional historical work. The book covers not only the main events of the Persian invasions of Greece in 490 and 480 B.C. but also the backgrounds and cultures of the peoples involved. Herodotus gathered his information mostly by traveling for years throughout the eastern Mediterranean world. He visited Babylon, Egypt, Phoenicia, and many other lands, making his book a valuable source of information about these places in his era. Not all of what he recorded was accurate, for he frequently simply repeated what the locals told him. To his credit, however, he was sometimes critical of claims of supernatural events and tried hard to present a comprehensive picture that incorporated a wide range of facts and opinions. "So much for what the Persians and Phoenicians say," he asserts at the start of his narrative. "I have no intention of passing judgment on its truth or falsity. I prefer to rely on my own knowledge. . . . I will proceed with my history, telling the story as I go along of small cities no less than that of great. . . . Knowing that human prosperity never abides long in the same place, I shall pay attention to both alike." (*Histories* 1.7–8) For his efforts, Herodotus later earned the nickname "the Father of History."

SEE ALSO: Greco-Persian Wars; historical writing

Herophilus
(early third century B.C.)

One of the leading medical researchers of the ancient world. Herophilus studied at the famous medical school at Cos in western Asia Minor, then moved to Alexandria, Egypt, and there founded the Alexandrian medical school. Fortunately for him, the Ptolemies (the Greek rulers of Egypt) permitted him to dissect dead human bodies, which was illegal in most other Greek states. So he was able to make numerous discoveries about anatomy that would have been otherwise impossible. His studies and descriptions of the liver, brain, nerves, ovaries, and fallopian tubes were groundbreaking and influenced later doctors and medical researchers, including Galen.

SEE ALSO: Alexandria; doctors and medicine; Galen

Hesiod
(flourished ca. 700 B.C.)

An early Greek epic poet whose works, like those of Homer, strongly influenced the way later Greeks viewed the gods and natural forces. Born in a small town in Boeotia, Hesiod was a hardworking shepherd and farmer. He claimed (in the opening verses of his great epic *Theogony*) that the Muses (goddesses of the fine arts) appeared to him on the slopes of Mt. Helicon and granted him the ability to express himself in verse. *Theogony* goes on to describe the creation of the universe, the gods, and humanity. In his other major work, the *Works and Days*, Hesiod recalls how, after his father died, the poet and his brother, Perses, divided the family estate between them, but Perses took more than his fair share. Later in the work, Hesiod calls on his brother to make amends and learn the value of hard work. (Beyond these incidents, little else is known about Hesiod's life.) The rest of *Works and Days* offers advice on planting crops and other rural activities.

SEE ALSO: Helicon, Mt.; Muses; *Theogony*; *Works and Days*

Hestia

In Greek mythology and religious worship, the goddess of the hearth, a major symbol of home and family life. Because it held controlled fire, which made civilized life possible, the hearth was seen as essential to the continued prosperity of the family; similarly, every Greek town had public hearths thought to maintain the public good. For these reasons, Hestia was widely worshipped as a protector of civilized life. According to legend, she was among the daughters of the Titan Cronos, who swallowed her right after she was born. Later, however, her brother Zeus forced Cronos to vomit her back up. For the rest of eternity, she remained a virgin and expected the priestesses who attended her temples to be virgins as well.

SEE ALSO: Cronos; religion; Zeus

hetairai

In ancient Greek society, courtesans, or high-class prostitutes. Their names (also spelled *hetaerae*) translates literally as "companions," which reflects the fact that they provided men with companionship, including stimulating conversation, as well as sex. In Athens they were most often foreigners who charged high fees to entertain men either in rented houses or rooms or in the men's homes. To ensure that they could hold their own with men in discussions about politics, history, art, and other subjects, *hetairai* acquired impressive educations. And because society discouraged female independence and denied most women formal educations, the courtesans were the most economically independent women around and were far better educated than the average man. The most famous of the *hetairai* was Aspasia, who became the mistress of the Athenian statesman Pericles in the mid-fifth century B.C.

SEE ALSO: Aspasia; Pericles; women

Hiero I
(early fifth century B.C.)

A dictator who ruled the Sicilian Greek city of Syracuse from about 478 to 466 B.C. He defeated the Etruscans (who lived in north-central Italy) in a naval battle in 474 and founded several colonies in Sicily and southern Italy.

SEE ALSO: Etruscans; Syracuse

Hiero II
(ca. 306 B.C.–215 B.C.)

King of the Greek city of Syracuse from about 270 to 215 B.C., a reign that was largely peaceful and prosperous. Hiero made an alliance with the Romans, who were rising to power in Italy, and backed them in their wars with Carthage. Hiero also gave financial support to the famous Syracusan inventor Archimedes.

SEE ALSO: Archimedes; Syracuse

Himera

A Greek city in northern Sicily. Settlers from Messina, who were themselves of Euboean origin, founded Himera in about 648 B.C. In the 480s B.C. Carthage invaded Sicily with a large force, and a major battle took place near Himera. Aided by troops from Syracuse in southeastern Sicily, the Himerans burned the Carthaginians' ships and defeated their army. However, in 409 B.C. another Carthaginian force invaded Sicily and destroyed Himera. The survivors settled at a spot about 7 miles (11km) away, which was thereafter also sometimes called Himera.

SEE ALSO: Carthage; Syracuse

Hipparchus
(late sixth century B.C.)

One of the two sons of Pisistratus, an Athenian tyrant. After his father's death, Hipparchus ruled jointly with his older brother, Hippias. The two autocrats became increasingly unpopular until Hipparchus was assassinated, after which Hippias's rule became even more tyrannical.

SEE ALSO: Hippias; Pisistratus

Hipparchus
(ca. 190 B.C.–ca. 125 B.C.)

A Greek astronomer who was born at Nicaea in Asia Minor but lived and worked mainly on the island of Rhodes. Most of Hipparchus's treatises have not survived. But the *Almagest* of the second-century A.D. Greek astronomer Claudius Ptolemy summarizes many of his contributions, including the creation of a catalog of more than eight hundred stars. Hipparchus positioned them on the celestial sphere using degrees of latitude and longitude, a system he invented. Hipparchus also developed the science of trigonometry.

SEE ALSO: astronomy

Hippias
(late sixth century B.C.)

The elder son of the Athenian tyrant Pisistratus and brother of Hipparchus, with whom Hippias jointly ruled Athens for a few years, beginning in 527 B.C. Hippias was a just ruler at first, but he steadily became more autocratic and unpopular. Hipparchus was cut down by assassins in 514, and when the Spartans invaded Attica in 510, Hippias fled and took refuge at the court of Darius I, king of Persia. Hippias dreamed of regaining power in Athens, and to that end he accompanied the Persians when they landed at Marathon in 490. But the unexpected Athenian victory ended that dream.

SEE ALSO: Battle of Marathon; Hipparchus, 1

Hippocrates of Cos (late fifth century B.C.)

A renowned Greek doctor who became known as "the Father of Medicine." Little is known about his life, except that he established a medical school on Cos (an island lying southwest of Asia Minor). It is possible that Hippocrates composed some of the school's surviving medical writings, known as the Hippocratic Corpus, although many, if not all, of these may have been written by his students and successors. The Hippocratic scholars were notable for their realization that disease has natural rather than supernatural causes.

SEE ALSO: doctors and medicine

Hippolytus

In Greek mythology, the son of Theseus, a Bronze Age king of Athens. In a popular myth, Theseus's second wife, Phaedra, fell in love with and made advances toward the grown-up Hippolytus. The young man turned her down, but Theseus came to believe that his son had propositioned Phaedra, so he exiled Hippolytus, who died shortly afterward.

SEE ALSO: *Hippolytus* (play); Theseus

Hippolytus (play)

A tragedy by Euripides, first presented in Athens circa 428 B.C. As the play begins, the grown-up Hippolytus discovers that

A surviving bust of Herodotus, one of ancient Greece's most famous historians.
SCALA/ART RESOURCE, NY

Phaedra, the second wife of his father, Theseus, king of Athens, has fallen in love with the young man. Hippolytus resists her advances and denounces her. Phaedra is so distraught by his rejection that she hangs herself, but not before writing a note to Theseus in which she falsely accuses Hippolytus of propositioning her. When Theseus reads the note, he curses his son and banishes him. Soon afterward, Hippolytus is mortally wounded in a chariot crash, and Theseus learns the truth of his son's innocence too late.

SEE ALSO: Euripides; Hippolytus; Theseus

historical writing

The discipline or art of historical writing, formally called historiography, was among the many literary genres that the Greeks originated and perfected in the Classical and Hellenistic periods. The first important Greek historian was Herodotus (fifth century B.C.). His *Histories*, describing the Greco-Persian Wars and the cultures of the peoples who fought in them remains the oldest-known surviving conventional historical work. Despite its reams of valuable information, however, the book contains a good deal of second- and third-hand accounts, hearsay, and other unreliable data. In contrast, Herodotus's younger contemporary, the Athenian Thucydides, produced the first modern-style history book. In this detailed account of the first twenty years of the Peloponnesian War, the author includes (with rare exceptions) only his own eyewitness accounts or those of people he has personally interviewed. Though not as skilled a historian as Thucydides, Xenophon (428–354 B.C.) penned important chronicles of the final years of the Peloponnesian War and a number of crucial conflicts of the fourth century B.C. Another notable Greek historian of that century was Theopompus, who wrote a detailed account of the exploits of Macedonia's Philip II. (The work has not survived, but it was used as a source by many other later ancient writers.) In the second century B.C. the historian Polybius recorded for posterity the rise of Rome, its destruction of Carthage, and its campaigns against the Greeks. Like Thucydides, Polybius tried to deal strictly with verifiable facts. And he contributed much to the development of historiography by dissecting and analyzing historical methods, including his own. "It is not a historian's business," he writes,

> to startle his readers with sensational descriptions, nor should he try, as the tragic poets do, to represent speeches which might have been delivered [but

remain only hearsay]. . . . It is his task first and foremost to record with fidelity what actually happened and was said, however commonplace this may be. . . . Making first-hand inquiries . . . is the historian's most important duty. . . . [He should] question as many people as possible, believe such witnesses who are trustworthy, and prove himself a good judge of the reports that reach him. (*Histories* 2.53, 12.4c)

Some Greek historians of lesser stature— for example, Ephorus (fourth century B.C.), whose works are lost—were less interested in accuracy and more concerned with making moral judgments about historical figures. These are the writers who most impressed and influenced later Roman historians such as Livy.

SEE ALSO: Herodotus; Polybius; Thucydides, 2; Xenophon

Histories

A renowned history text composed by the fifth-century B.C. Greek historian Herodotus, often called "the Father of History."

SEE ALSO: Herodotus; historical writing

Homer (middle to late eighth century B.C. ?)

The most respected and revered of the ancient Greek poets, and according to tradition, the author of the greatest epic poems ever written—the *Iliad* and the *Odyssey*. The *Iliad* describes a series of incidents in the tenth and final year of the legendary Trojan War; the *Odyssey* tells about the wanderings of Odysseus, one of the Greek kings who fought at Troy in the ten years following the city's demise. Homer's birthplace is uncertain, but he may have hailed from the Ionian island of

Chios, which claimed him as a native son. Although nothing is known about his life, later ancient Greeks were sure that he was a real person, and most modern scholars agree. Still, some Greek Hellenistic scholars proposed that the *Iliad* and the *Odyssey* may not have been written by a single person. This became part of a tradition of Homeric criticism, which continues today. It revolves around the so-called Homeric question, which seeks to know if Homer was indeed a real person, if he did write both epics, and if the characters and events he described were real, imaginary, or a combination of the two.

While scholars continue to argue over the Homeric question, the vast majority have come to believe that the *Iliad* and *Odyssey* were composed a little at a time by a series of poets. In this view, Homer's contribution was the greatest because the Greeks had rediscovered writing during his lifetime; and committing the poems to writing (perhaps by dictating them to a scribe) would have allowed for the addition of more complex detail and imagery than was customarily transmitted by oral means.

What is more certain is that Homer's epics came to exert a profound influence on Greek culture and thought, as well as Roman and European thought and literature, in the ages that followed. As noted scholar Michael Grant points out, the Homeric poems supplied the ancient Greeks

> with their greatest civilizing influence, and formed the foundation of their literary, artistic, moral, social, educational, and political attitudes. For a long time no histories of early times seemed at all necessary, since the *Iliad* and *Odyssey* fulfilled every requirement. They attracted universal esteem and reverence, too, as sources of general and practical wisdom, as argu-

> ments for heroic yet human nobility and dignity, as incentives to vigorous . . . manly action, and as mines of endless quotations and commentaries, the common property of Greeks everywhere. (*The Rise of the Greeks*, p. 147)

Homer's works were also major sources of information about the Greek gods and their powers, likes and dislikes, and so forth. In addition, the two epics were studied and often partially memorized by Greek schoolchildren. Today, Homer's writings are still major topics of study and analysis in college history and literary courses.

SEE ALSO: *Iliad*; poetry; *Odyssey*

Homeric Hymns

A major and influential collection of Greek poems dating from the eighth to sixth centuries B.C. Their attribution—*Homeric*—comes from the early assumption that Homer penned them. However, Greek scholars working in Alexandria in Hellenistic times determined that most or all of the hymns in the collection were written by various unknown Archaic poets following Homer's death. Modern scholars agree with this assessment.

Each of the thirty-three hymns is addressed to a specific god. Some are fairly short and may have been intended as warm-ups, so to speak, to prepare audiences for presentations of longer poems such as the *Iliad* and the *Odyssey*. Other hymns in the collection are longer, however, and may have been recited by themselves at religious festivals or other public gatherings. Whether short or long, these works provided the Greeks with valuable details about the deities they worshipped. In this respect, one of the richest mines of mythological and religious facts is the

"Hymn to Demeter," which tells how Demeter's daughter, Persephone, was abducted by Hades, king of the Underworld. The "Hymn to Apollo," which describes how that god seized control of the famous oracle at Delphi, is another gem in the collection. Its graceful verses include this one:

> And thence Apollo went speeding swiftly to the mountain ridge, and came to Crisa, beneath snowy [Mt.] Parnassus, a foothill turned toward the west. A cliff hangs over it from above, and a hollow, rugged glade runs under. There the lord Phoebus Apollo resolved to make his lovely temple, and thus he said: "In this place I am minded to build a glorious temple to be an oracle for men, and here . . . both they who dwell in the rich Peloponnesus and the men of Europe and from all the wave-washed isles [will come] to question me. And I will deliver to them all counsel that cannot fail [to be truthful], answering them in my rich temple." (*Homeric Hymns* 3.280–292)

Other hymns in the collection address Dionysus, Hermes, Aphrodite, Ares, Artemis, Athena, Hera, Asclepius, Pan, Poseidon, Hestia, Helios, the semidivine Heracles, and other deities.

SEE ALSO: Delphi; Homer; and the names of the individual gods

hoplite

In Greece and other parts of the ancient Mediterranean world, a heavily armored infantry soldier who most often fought in a phalanx formation.

SEE ALSO: weapons and warfare, land

houses

The size, building materials, and layout of ancient Greek houses varied according to the type of house and the financial means of the owners. Most rural Greeks lived in modest huts, some erected individually on farms, others clustered together in small villages for mutual security. Such huts were made of wood, fieldstones, sun-dried clay bricks, or a combination of these materials. A typical hut had one, two, or three rooms featuring floors composed of hard-packed dirt covered by flagstones or straw mats. A fire for heating and cooking blazed in a stone-lined hearth in the main room. Well-to-do people could afford larger, more comfortable country homes, usually called villas. The average villa had five to ten rooms that surrounded a central courtyard, which was open to the sky and elements. It was also common for a villa to have a stone tower, into which the occupants could retreat in times of danger.

The townhouses in Greek urban centers like Athens resembled rural houses in some ways. A townhouse usually had a stone foundation and walls made of sun-dried clay bricks, which were reinforced with wooden timbers when possible. Because space in the cities was at a premium, the houses were packed side by side along narrow, winding streets. The fronts of these dwellings were usually plain and whitewashed, each with a single door and no more than one or two small windows. The only decoration in the front of a townhouse was a herm, a bust of the god Hermes, which tradition held would keep evil from entering the house.

The layouts of Greek townhouses varied considerably. Many had rooms grouped around a small central courtyard, often with stairs leading to a second story that overlooked the yard. Others featured a long central hallway, the *pastas*, which had doorways leading to most of the dwelling's rooms. Poorer homes had as few as two rooms, but the average house had four to seven small rooms. Only a few had more, as a majority of Greek houses, including those of rich people, were fairly modest in size by modern standards.

With few exceptions, individual rooms in Greek homes were also small. In the larger homes, which had two stories, most or all of the bedrooms were upstairs. Tiny cubicles for the family slaves were also on the second floor, although it was also common for slaves to sleep on the roof. The rooms on the ground floor typically included an exedra, a sitting area with one or perhaps two sides open to the inner court; a central workroom where family members gathered; and an *andron*, a special dining room in which the man of the house entertained his male friends. It appears that up until the beginning of the mid-fifth century B.C. most Greek townhouses lacked formal kitchens. People did their cooking on braziers, metal containers that burned wood or charcoal; or they cooked over a stone-lined hearth located in the central workroom. By the early fourth century B.C., however, most townhouses did have small kitchens located off the main room. An average kitchen had wooden storage bins for fruit, bread, and kitchenware, and wooden tables for food preparation.

As for bathrooms, the poorest houses had none. The residents used chamber pots, which they emptied by hand into ditches, cesspools, or sewers outside. Many larger homes did have formal bathrooms with toilets. Some of those excavated by archaeologists were located beside the central workroom in order to take advantage of the residual heat from the hearth. One house, excavated at Olynthus on the Chalcidic peninsula, featured a surprisingly modern-shaped toilet made of terra-cotta (baked clay). Its wastes drained into a narrow terra-cotta channel that connected to the city's sewers. Some bathrooms also had terra-cotta tubs for bathing, most of which were a bit smaller than modern versions. People used buckets of water to fill a tub, work done by slaves in households that could afford to keep slaves. The dirty water drained to the outside through a terra-cotta channel recessed in the floor. Another common fixture of Greek bathrooms was a small basin for washing the hands and face.

SEE ALSO: baths and bathing; building materials and methods; family; heating and lighting; slaves and slavery; water supplies

hunting

In prehistoric Greece, and perhaps well into the Bronze Age (ca. 3000–ca. 1100 B.C.), hunting was likely primarily a necessary means of obtaining food and protecting family and community from wild beasts. Evidence shows that lions and wild boars still roamed mainland Greece in the Bronze Age and perhaps in the Dark Age as well. A vivid depiction of a boar hunt in Homer's *Odyssey*, which may have been passed down orally from those times, has preserved what such outings were like:

> As soon as rose-fingered early Dawn appeared, they went off to the hunt, with Autolycus' sons and dogs, as well. And Lord Odysseus left with them. They climbed up steep, tree-covered Mount Parnassus, and quickly reached its windy gullies. By this time, [the rays sent by the god] Helios had just begun to strike the fields, rising from deep streams of gently flowing Ocean. The beaters reached a clearing. The dogs went first, ahead of them, following the tracks. Behind them, came Autolycus' sons, with Lord Odysseus in their group, close to the dogs. He

was holding up his long-shadowed spear. Now, right there a huge wild boar was lying in a tangled thicket—it was so dense the power of watery winds could not get through, none of Helios' rays could pierce it, and the rain would never penetrate. There were fallen leaves in piles around the place. The sound of rustling feet from men and dogs, as they pushed on the hunt, came round the beast, and he charged from the thicket to confront them—his back was really bristling, eyes flashing fire—as he stood at bay before them. Odysseus rushed in first, his strong hands gripping the long spear, keen to strike the boar. But the beast got the jump on him and struck him above the knee, charging at him from the side, a long gash in his flesh sliced by its tusk, but it didn't reach Odysseus' bone. But then Odysseus struck the boar, hitting it on its right shoulder. The bright point of his spear went clean through, the boar fell in the dust, squealing, and its life force flew away. (*Odyssey* 19.429–454)

Even when large wild boars became scarce in Greece in the Archaic Age, the hunting of dangerous animals still occurred from time to time because packs of wolves persisted in the hills well into the Classical Age.

Meanwhile, although some poorer folk still hunted rabbits, deer, ducks, and other game to feed their families, for the most part hunting became a sport in the Classical and Hellenistic ages. The larger hunts were a province of the well-to-do, who could afford horses, hunting dogs, and elaborate traps. Hunters used bows and arrows, slings, spears, hatchets, knives, nets, and even clubs, depending on the prey and situation. The most common method was trapping, for which diverse kinds of traps were devised, including a spring-loaded trap described by Xenophon that was effective at catching deer:

> If the trap catches the front leg of the deer, he will be taken quickly, for the trap will strike every part of his body and head as he tries to run. But if the trap catches a hind leg, the drag of the trap will also interfere with the whole body. Sometimes the clog [wooden stake to which the trap was attached] is caught in the fork of a tree, and unless the cord breaks, the deer is captured then and there. But whether you overtake the deer in this way or wear the animal down, do not approach it, for if it is a stag it will gore you with its antlers or kick you. If it is a doe, it will kick. (*On Hunting* 9.19–20)

Another kind of trap, the pit trap, consisted of a deep pit with steep sides and tree branches and brush placed over the top to camouflage it. An unwary animal stepped onto the loose branches and fell into the pit. Then the hunters lowered a cage into the pit and used a hunk of meat or other food to coax the beast inside the cage. Perhaps in late Hellenistic times and certainly in Greece's Roman period, many of the bigger hunting expeditions lost their sense of sport; in these outings, beaters and horsemen first drove frightened animals into fenced-in enclosures, after which the rich, lazy "hunters," safely positioned outside the enclosures, fired arrows or other missiles at the helpless creatures.

SEE ALSO: athletics; food and drink; *Odyssey*

Icarus

The son of the mythical inventor and craftsman Daedalus. In a famous story set in Crete, the father and son donned wax wings and flew high into the sky. Icarus went too near the sun, however, which caused his wings to melt, sending him plummeting to his death.

SEE ALSO: Daedalus

Ictinus
(flourished ca. 450 B.C.–420 B.C.)

A prominent architect who was best known for designing the Parthenon temple in Athens, in collaboration with another architect, Callicrates, and the great sculptor Phidias.

SEE ALSO: Parthenon; Phidias

Ida, Mt.

A large mountain in northwestern Asia Minor situated near the legendary city of Troy. A number of noteworthy mythical incidents supposedly took place on the slopes of Mt. Ida, including the Judgment of Paris, in which the Trojan prince presided over a beauty contest involving the goddesses Athena, Hera, and Aphrodite. Later, during the infamous Trojan War, Zeus frequently sat on Mt. Ida's summit to observe the clashing armies below.

SEE ALSO: Paris; Troy; Zeus

Ida, Mt.

The tallest peak on the island of Crete. According to legend, some nymphs raised the young Zeus in a cave beneath the

As the champion warriors Achilles and Hector fight before Troy's walls, the god Apollo warns Hector that he is in mortal danger. MARY EVANS/EDWIN WALLACE

mountain. Many caves, some quite large, do riddle Mt. Ida and its foothills, and archaeological evidence shows that at least two of them were used as places of worship by the Bronze Age Minoans.

SEE ALSO: Crete; Minoans; Zeus

Iliad

Homer's great epic poem about a series of events that took place in the tenth year of the legendary Trojan War. The title of the work comes from Ilium (or Ilion), an alternate name for Troy. In the opening of the poem, Homer brilliantly sums up the core cause of the tumultuous and bloody events that are to follow. These happenings all revolve around the wrath of the Greek warrior Achilles, who has had a serious falling out with Agamemnon, commander of the Greek army that is besieging Troy: "Rage—Goddess, sing of the rage of Peleus's son Achilles, murderous, doomed, that cost the Greeks countless losses, hurtling down to the House of Death so many sturdy souls, great fighters' souls, but made their bodies carrion, feasts for the dogs and birds. . . . Begin, Muse, when the two [men] first broke and clashed, Agamemnon, lord of men, and brilliant Achilles." (*Iliad* 1.1–8) As Homer tells it, Achilles and Agamemnon "broke and clashed" over a woman. Agamemnon took as his mistress Chryseis, daughter of one of Apollo's local priests, and the god unleashed a plague on the Greek camp as a punishment. To halt the plague, Agamemnon gave the girl up. But then he seized Briseis, one of Achilles' mistresses. For this affront, Achilles went to his tent and refused to come out and fight. Without Achilles to lead them, the Greek troops were demoralized and suffered several defeats. Led by Hector, a prominent Trojan prince, the Trojans drove the Greeks back to their camp on the beach and set fire to some of the Greek ships. Fear and hopelessness now gripped the Greeks: "All their best were struck by grief too much to bear. . . . The Greeks' hearts were torn inside their chests. Distraught with rising anguish, Atreus's son [Agamemnon] went ranging back and forth, commanding heralds to sound out loud and clear and call the men to muster. . . . They grouped on the meeting grounds, [their] morale broken." (*Iliad* 9.3–14)

It looked as though the Greeks might have to abandon the siege and return to Greece. Yet even in the face of this potential shame, the mighty Achilles still would not leave his tent. Then his close friend Patroclus had an idea that he hoped would rally

the Greek forces. Patroclus asked Achilles for permission to borrow the latter's armor; and having donned that gleaming coat of bronze, Patroclus sallied forth and led many of his fellow Greeks directly at the Trojan ranks. Thinking that Achilles himself was back in the war, the Trojans were struck with fear and fled in disarray. Even Hector at first was caught up in the rout. But then the god Apollo, who supported the Trojan cause, appeared to him in human form and said: "Hector, why stop fighting? Neglecting your duty!. . . Up with you—fast! Lash those pounding stallions straight at Patroclus!" At this, Hector furiously reentered the fray and, per Apollo's order, lunged directly at Patroclus, who jumped down from his chariot to meet the oncoming threat. The two warriors

> strained to slash each other with ruthless bronze. . . . Patroclus charged the enemy, fired for the kill. . . . [But then] the spear in his grip was shattered . . . and his shield with straps and tassels dropped from his shoulders. . . . Disaster seized him, his fine legs buckling. . . . Hector [saw] the great-hearted Patroclus trying to stagger free . . . and came rushing into him . . . and rammed his spear-shaft home, stabbing deep in the bowels, and the brazen point came jutting straight out through Patroclus's back. Down he crashed, [and] horror gripped the Greek army. (*Iliad* 16.841–845, 885, 911, 930–935, 952–959)

Thus, once again the tide of battle had turned. But when great Achilles learned of his friend's ignoble end, he suddenly forgot about his grudge against Agamemnon. Donning a new suit of armor forged for him by the god Hephaestos, Achilles led the Greeks in a tremendous offensive that pushed the Trojans back. Finally, Achilles and Hector met in single combat. And after a fantastic struggle between these men, the two greatest warriors in the world, Hector finally fell. "Death cut him short," Homer movingly tells it. "The end closed in around him. Flying free of his limbs, his soul went winging down to the House of Death, wailing his fate, leaving his manhood behind." (*Iliad* 22.425–428) Achilles then elicited a burst of horror and pity in the ranks of Trojans who were watching by tying Hector's corpse to the back of his chariot and dragging it through the dust.

Following Achilles' victory over Hector, the Greeks held funeral games to honor the dead Patroclus. Then Troy's King Priam went to see Achilles and begged for him to give up Hector's body so that the Trojans could give it a decent burial. Achilles, his great anger and desire for revenge now dissipated, was so moved by the old man's words that he took Priam's hand: "And overpowered by memory, both men gave way to grief. Priam wept freely for man-killing Hector, throbbing, crouching before Achilles' feet as Achilles wept himself, now for his [own] father, now for Patroclus once again, and their sobbing rose and fell throughout the house." (*Iliad* 24.594–599) The *Iliad* ends with Priam returning to Troy with Hector's body, which the Trojans solemnly burned on a large funeral pyre. Afterward they placed the bones in a golden chest "and lowered the chest in a deep hollow grave, and over it piled a mound of huge stones. . . . And once they heaped the mound, they turned back to Troy, and gathering once again they shared a splendid funeral feast in Hector's honor. . . . And so the Trojans buried Hector, breaker of horses." (*Iliad* 24.936–944)

SEE ALSO: Achilles; Agamemnon; Hector; Homer; Troy

incubation

A practice common across the Greco-Roman world in which a sick person slept in a temple in hopes that the local god or goddess would appear in a dream and reveal the means of a cure.

SEE ALSO: doctors and medicine

industry

The ancient Greeks had no heavy industry in the modern sense—that is, large-scale manufacturing businesses or units. Rather, their version of industry was centered in small individual workshops in which clothes, weapons, pottery, jewelry, statues, and other products were created by hand by various kinds of craftspeople. A great many of the workers were slaves (most well trained), although free Greeks routinely worked alongside slaves. Perhaps because so much industrial labor was done by slaves, as a rule upper-class Greeks viewed such work as necessary but also low class and beneath their dignity. "I could not say for certain where the Greeks got their ideas about trade [and work]," Herodotus remarks.

> [But] I have observed that . . . almost all foreigners reckon craftsmen and their descendants as lower in the social scale than people who have no connection with manual work. Only the latter [i.e., those who do no manual labor], and especially those who are trained for war, do they count amongst the nobility. All the Greeks have adopted this attitude, especially the Spartans. The feeling against handicraft is least strong in Corinth. (*Histories* 2.167)

The crafts that can be viewed as making up Greece's industrial base included metalworking, glassmaking, ceramics (pottery making), painting (pottery, furniture, murals), woodworking, leather work, stonemasonry and sculpture, jewelry making, spinning and weaving, clothes making, the production of papyrus scrolls, the production of weapons, and so on.

SEE ALSO: building materials and methods; glass; jewelry; metalworking; painting; pottery; quarries; spinning and weaving

inhumation

Burial of the dead, which was common in the Greek lands in certain historical periods.

SEE ALSO: burial customs

inscriptions

Words or messages carved or scratched into stone, metal, or some other durable material.

SEE ALSO: epigraphy; Greek language

Io

In Greek mythology, a young woman who had a love affair with Zeus, leader of the Olympian gods, and as a result endured the wrath of Zeus's divine wife, Hera. As a young woman, Io served as a priestess in one of Hera's temples. But then Zeus seduced Io behind Hera's back, and it did not take long for Hera to find out what was happening. Hoping to keep his wife from punishing the girl, Zeus turned Io into a white calf, but Hera saw through the disguise and sent gadflies to sting the calf. The flies drove Io out of Greece and she ended up in faraway Egypt, where Zeus changed her back into a woman and they had a son together.

SEE ALSO: Hera; Zeus

Ion

In Greek mythology, the founder of the Ionian branch of Greeks, who inhabited western Asia Minor. Ion, a grandson of Hellen, who established the Greek race, became king of the northern region of the Peloponnesus and renamed the inhabitants Ionians, after himself. But soon afterward he was killed while helping the Athenians fight a neighboring state. Many years passed, and finally a rival band of Greeks drove the Ionians eastward across the Aegean Sea. The area they settled then became known as Greek Ionia. In his play about Ion, Euripides drew on a different myth that claimed that the legendary young man was an illegitimate son of the god Apollo.

SEE ALSO: Asia Minor; *Ion* (play); Ionia

Ion (play)

A play by Euripides, first presented in Athens circa 412 B.C. In the myth on which the play is based, the god Apollo seduced Creusa, daughter of Erechtheus, king of Athens, and the young woman gave birth to a child. Named Ion, he was taken by the god Hermes to Delphi for safekeeping and grew up there. As the play opens, Ion has grown into a young man, and Creusa is now married to a man named Xuthus, who goes to Delphi to ask the famous oracle why he and his wife have not been able to have children. The oracle tells Xuthus that he must accept as his son the first person he meets as he leaves the temple. It is Ion whom Xuthus encounters. When the two men return to Athens, Creusa grows suspicious of Ion (not realizing he is her son) and tries to kill him. When the attempt fails, she seeks sanctuary at Apollo's temple and there discovers Ion's true identity. Athena, Athens's patron goddess, now steps forward to make it clear that the young man is the rightful heir to the Athenian throne. Also, the goddess foretells, Ion will sire an important branch of the Greek race, which will be called the

Ionians in his honor.

See Also: Apollo; Athena; Ion

Ion (playwright)
(ca. 490 B.C.–421 B.C.)

A noted playwright born on the island of Chios. His plays, all tragedies, have not survived, but they won prizes at the drama festivals in Athens, where Ion eventually made his home. What has survived are portions of his memoirs in quotes by later ancient writers. Ion was an example of the many talented Greeks who immigrated to Athens in the fifth century B.C., helping to produce that city's now famous golden age.

See Also: Chios; theater and drama

Ionia

The Greek-controlled central part of the western coast of Asia Minor, including Samos, Chios, and numerous other islands near that coast. According to legend, in the dim past the Ionian Greeks, who had originally inhabited mainland Greece, were forced to migrate across the Aegean Sea by the invading Dorians. This myth seems to have been based partly on real, large-scale population movements that occurred during Greece's Dark Age. By roughly 950 B.C. large numbers of Ionian Greeks had migrated to Asia Minor. There they established many towns, twelve of which came together in an alliance, the Ionian League, in about 700 B.C. (The twelve were Miletus, Priene, Ephesus, Myus, Teos, Chios, Samos, Colophon, Phocaea, Erythrae, Clazomenae, and Lebedus.) In the two centuries that followed, the Ionians became highly prosperous through wide-ranging trade; established colonies across the Mediterranean sphere; built large, splendid temples (that utilized a new architectural style—the Ionian); and fostered a burst of intellectual activity that produced the noted philosopher-scientists Thales, Anaximander, and Anaximenes. The Ionians, particularly the residents of Chios, also claimed the great epic poet Homer as their native son.

In the mid-500s B.C. most of the Ionian cities fell under the control of Lydia, a non-Greek kingdom occupying much of western Asia Minor. Lydian domination was brief, however, because in 546 B.C. the Persian Empire defeated and absorbed Lydia and its domains, including the Ionian cities. The Ionians were not happy under Persian rule and rebelled in 499, but the Persian navy crushed an allied Ionian fleet at Lade (near Miletus) in 494. Only when the Persians were driven entirely out of the Aegean region in 479 after the battles of Salamis, Plataea, and Mycale, did the Ionians regain their freedom.

Many of the Ionian cities now joined the Delian League, a vast alliance of Greek states controlled by Athens. But because the Athenians treated many of their allies like vassals, several Ionian poleis, including Miletus, Ephesus, and Chios, backed Sparta against Athens in the Peloponnesian War (431–404 B.C.). Ionia did not fair well under Spartan domination, however, nor from another brief period of Persian control in the mid-fourth century B.C. Alexander the Great liberated the Ionians during his march through Asia Minor in the late 330s B.C., after which the region enjoyed much prosperity in the Hellenistic Age. Pergamum, in northern Ionia, became a small but splendid kingdom that featured architectural wonders and the second-largest library in the known world. In the late second century B.C. Ionia, including Pergamum, became part of the expanding Roman realm.

See Also: Asia Minor; Chios; Ephesus;

Greco-Persian Wars; Miletus; Pergamum; Samos

Ionian Sea

A term often used in antiquity to describe the Adriatic Sea, lying between Italy and the Balkan Peninsula. It also denoted the southern extension of that waterway, bordering northwestern Greece and encompassing the islands of Corcyra, Cephallenia, and Ithaca.

SEE ALSO: Greece, geography of

Ionic order

One of the three main architectural styles employed in ancient Greece, it was characterized by columns whose capitals (tops) featured scroll-like curves.

SEE ALSO: architectural orders; Erechtheum; Ionia

Iphicrates
(died ca. 355 B.C.)

An Athenian military general known for his innovative use of *peltasts* (light-armed, javelin-wielding soldiers) in battle. Iphicrates had his *peltasts* discard all armor and wear the lightest outfits possible. (The light leggings he designed thereafter became known as *iphicratides*.) He also trained these men to make repeated attacks on a small phalanx, especially on its flanks, thereby wearing down the heavily armored hoplites, who could not chase down the lightly clad javelin men. The crucial test of Iphicrates' new tactics came circa 390 B.C., when his *peltasts* assaulted and defeated a Spartan *mora* (a battalion of six hundred hoplites) near Corinth. According to Xenophon:

> As the javelins were hurled at them, some of the Spartans were killed and some wounded. . . . The [Spartan commander] then ordered the infantry [hoplites] in the age groups 20 and 30 to charge and drive off the attackers. However, they were hoplites pursuing peltasts at a distance of a javelin's throw, and they failed to catch anyone, since Iphicrates had ordered his men to fall back before the hoplites came to close quarters. But when the Spartans . . . turned back again from the pursuit, Iphicrates' men wheeled around, some hurling their javelins again from in front, while others ran up along the flank [of the phalanx], shooting at the side unprotected by the shields. (*Hellenica* 4.5.14–16)

Some 250 Spartan hoplites were killed and the rest fled, which shocked the Greek world because the Spartan infantry was thought to be nearly invincible. Not surprisingly, the use of *peltasts* thereafter became more common in Greek warfare.

SEE ALSO: Sparta; weapons and warfare, land

Iphigenia

In Greek mythology, the daughter of Agamemnon, king of Mycenae. As told in Euripides' play *Iphigenia at Aulis* and other ancient accounts, Agamemnon, who was in command of the Greek troops bound for Troy, needed favorable winds to get the ships on their way. So he sacrificed Iphigenia to the goddess Artemis, who then supplied the needed winds. Agamemnon's wife, Clytemnestra, never forgave her husband. As he left for Troy, she plotted her revenge, which she carried out when he returned from Troy ten years later (as described by Aeschylus in his play *Agamemnon*).

SEE ALSO: Agamemnon; Clytemnestra; *Iphigenia at Aulis*

Iphigenia at Aulis

A tragedy by Euripides, first presented in Athens in 405 B.C., shortly after the playwright's death. On the eve of the Trojan War, the Greek fleet, commanded by Agamemnon, king of Mycenae, is anchored at Aulis (on Boeotia's eastern coast) waiting for the wind to come up. Agamemnon hears that an oracle has declared that the winds will never come unless the king sacrifices his daughter Iphigenia to the goddess Artemis. Agamemnon does not want to kill his daughter, but he finally decides that it must be done. When the great warrior Achilles finds out about the impending sacrifice, he is outraged and prepares to fight the other Greeks to protect the girl. But then Iphigenia herself averts bloodshed by volunteering to go through with the ceremony. She does not desire to see the Greeks killing one another instead of their enemies, the Trojans. Later, on the sacrificial altar, as the priest swings his ax at Iphigenia, she disappears and, in her place, a dying deer materializes. As the long-awaited wind begins to blow, filling the ship's sails, everyone realizes that Artemis has taken Iphigenia to heaven.

SEE ALSO: Agamemnon; Artemis; Euripides

Iphigenia in Tauris

A tragic play by Euripides, first produced in Athens in 412 B.C. or shortly before. The plot deals with Iphigenia's tenure as a priestess of the goddess Artemis in the land of Tauris, located on the northern coast of the Black Sea. The action takes place in the years following the maiden's near-death as a sacrifice to ensure that the Greeks headed for Troy would obtain good winds for the voyage. (Aeschylus's version, *Agamemnon*, indicates that she died in the sacrifice. Euripides here follows an alternate version of the myth, in which Artemis saves Iphigenia at the last moment and transports her to Tauris.) In the play, some Greeks land in Tauris, and Iphigenia is called upon to sacrifice her own brother, Orestes. Refusing to do so, she tricks the local king; she and Orestes successfully escape, taking a carved image of Artemis with them.

SEE ALSO: Euripides; Iphigenia; *Iphigenia at Aulis*

Iris

In Greek mythology, the goddess of the rainbow. Because the ancients often viewed rainbows as bridges connecting heaven and earth, one of Iris's roles was to carry messages from the gods to humans. Iris was also the wife of Zephyrus, the West Wind, and a sister of the frightening Harpies, whom she protected from Jason and his Argonauts in the famous myth about the quest for the Golden Fleece.

SEE ALSO: Harpies; Jason

Isaeus
(ca. 420 B.C.–ca. 350 B.C.)

Little is known about the life of this Athenian orator, except that he was a student of the noted orator Isocrates and a teacher of Demosthenes, greatest of the Greek orators. As a *logographos*, or professional speechwriter, Isaeus composed about fifty speeches. Eleven survive complete, along with fragments of another. The eleven texts all deal with court cases involving inheritance and provide valuable information about inheritance laws and customs in ancient Athens.

SEE ALSO: Demosthenes; laws and justice

The Egyptian goddess Isis, depicted here in an Egyptian wall painting, was adopted by the Greeks in the fourth century B.C. © GIANNI DAGLI ORTI/CORBIS

Isis

In Egyptian mythology, and in Greek religious worship in the Hellenistic Age and beyond, a prominent goddess of fertility, marriage, and motherhood. As originally envisioned by the Egyptians, Isis was the sister and wife of the god Osiris and the mother of the god Horus, whom the Greeks called Harpocrates. Isis's cult and worship was established by Egyptian traders at Athens's port town, Piraeus, by the mid-fourth century B.C. Soon afterward, in the wake of Alexander's conquest of the Persian Empire, including Egypt, worship of the goddess spread across the Greek world in early Hellenistic times. The Greeks usually identified Isis with Aphrodite, the traditional Greek goddess of love, although some associated Isis with the divine Greek mother figure Demeter. Indeed, the rituals and beliefs of Isis's cult were similar to those of mystery religions with which the Greeks were already familiar, especially the cult of Demeter, centered at Eleusis in western Attica. All shared features such as formal initiations for newcomers, forms of baptism, teachings stressing virtuous behavior, and the promise of eternal salvation for those who had led virtuous lives.

SEE ALSO: Demeter; Egypt; Osiris

Isles of the Blessed

In ancient Greek mythology and religion, a pleasant, idyllic part of the Underworld set aside for human heroes, also called Elysium.

SEE ALSO: Underworld

Isocrates
(436 B.C.–338 B.C.)

A noted Athenian orator and pamphleteer, best known for championing the cause of Greece's conquest of Persia, whose society and rulers he portrayed as corrupt and inferior. Isocrates studied rhetoric (public speaking) with the skilled orator Gorgias and later established his own school of rhetoric. Isocrates also composed speeches for court litigants, six of which survive. His political pamphlets, for which he is most famous, called for all Greeks to unite against Persia and free any and all Ionian Greek cities then under Persian control. In his *Panegyricus* (380 B.C.), he argues that what Greece needs is an enlightened monarch, a sort of benign dictator, who can bring about the Greek unity he feels is needed. When the ambitious Macedonian ruler Philip II rapidly took control of much of Greece in the 340s, Isocrates felt he might be the great unifier he had envisioned. In the *Address to Philip* (346 B.C.), Isocrates urges Philip to launch an anti-Persian crusade:

> Since the others [i.e., other Greek leaders] are so lacking in spirit, I think it is opportune for you to head the war against the [Persian] King. And, while it is only natural for the other [Greeks] ... to cleave fondly to that state in which they happen to dwell, it is your privilege, as one who has been blessed with untrammeled freedom, to consider all Hellas [Greece] your fatherland ... and to be as ready to brave perils for her sake. ... I assert that it is incumbent upon you to work for the good of the Greeks, to reign as king over the Macedonians, and to extend your power over the greatest possible number of the barbarians [Persians and other non-Greeks]. For if you do these things, all men will be grateful to you, the Greeks for your kindness to them ... and the rest of the nations, if by your hands they are delivered from barbaric despotism and are brought under the protection of Hellas. (*Address to Philip* 127, 154)

Historians think that this pamphlet and other writings by Isocrates may have inspired Philip to begin planning an invasion of Persia. (Because Philip was assassinated in 336 B.C., his son, Alexander, ended up making the great campaign a reality.) But though Isocrates desired to see Philip unite the Greeks, the orator did not want to see this accomplished through naked conquest, especially of Athens, Isocrates' beloved native city. So when Philip defeated Athens and its coalition of city-states at Chaeronea in 338, the disillusioned Isocrates, then ninety-eight, starved himself to death.

SEE ALSO: Persians; Philip II; rhetoric

Isthmian Games

Important athletic and musical contests held every two years as part of a major religious festival of the sea god Poseidon at his sanctuary on the Isthmus of Corinth. For details on these and other similar competitions in ancient Greece, **see** athletics.

Italy

The Greeks heavily colonized both the Italian mainland and the island of Sicily (lying southwest of the Italian "boot") between about 750 and 550 B.C. On Sicily, the major cities included Syracuse, Catana, Naxos, Gela, and Acragas. The mainland cities were grouped into two general regions. The first was the fertile plain of Campania, near the Bay of Naples. There, Cumae, founded by people from Euboea, was the principal Greek settlement. The second region was southern Italy, where the cities of Taras (called Tarentum by the Romans), Sybaris, Locri, Rhegium, Siris, and Croton grew up. So many Greek cities were established there that the region became known as *Megale Hellas* (*Magna Graecia* in Latin) or "Great(er) Greece." Many of the southern Italian Greek cities fell under the influence of Syracuse in the 400s B.C. But this situation was short-lived. In the early 200s B.C., the rapidly expanding Latin city-state of Rome swiftly absorbed all of these Greek cities. Ironically, the Romans had already been indirectly affected by Greek culture. During the colonization period, the Greeks had exerted powerful religious, military, and other cultural influences on the Etruscans, who lived in the region north of Rome. And the Etruscans had passed these influences on to the Romans.

SEE ALSO: colonization; Etruscans; Syracuse; Tarentum

Ithaca

A small island in the Ionian group, off the western coast of Greece. In Greek mythology, especially in Homer's epics, the *Iliad* and the *Odyssey*, Ithaca was the site of the kingdom ruled by the hero Odysseus.

SEE ALSO: Odysseus; *Odyssey*

Jason

In Greek mythology, the leader of the famous quest to find the fabulous Golden Fleece (the hide of a magical ram that could talk and fly). Jason's father, Aeson, was the rightful king of Iolcos in Thessaly. But while Jason was a baby, Aeson's half brother, Pelias, stole the throne and Jason's mother, fearing for the child's safety, sent Jason to be raised by the civilized centaur Chiron. As a young man, Jason returned to Iolcos and laid claim to the throne. Pelias pretended to agree with this claim and said he would abdicate the throne, but only after Jason fulfilled a dangerous task that would prove his worthiness to be king. That task was to retrieve the Golden Fleece from the faraway land of Colchis. (Pelias was certain that Jason would fail, of course.) The events of Jason's quest for the Golden Fleece were told by Apollonius of Rhodes in his *Argonautica*. Jason's exploits following his return to Greece were the subject of Euripides' great play *Medea*.

SEE ALSO: Apollonius of Rhodes; *Argonautica*; Medea; *Medea* (play)

Jason of Pherae (reigned 385–370 B.C.)

A noted tyrant of the Greek state of Pherae in Thessaly. In a period in which alliances and power centers were rapidly shifting in Greece, Jason attempted to raise Thessaly to a major power. And to elevate his prestige as a ruler, he negotiated the treaty between Thebes and Sparta after the former defeated the latter at Leuctra in 371 B.C. But Jason's dreams for himself and his country never came to fruition because he was assassinated the following year.

SEE ALSO: Battle of Leuctra; Thessaly

jewelry

Ornate and finely made jewelry dates back to the Bronze Age in Greece. The Mycenaeans wore large gold necklaces and earrings and other jewelry, and a few gold workshops of that period have been found. In the Classical Age, lighter, more graceful necklaces came into vogue. Throughout this period and the Hellenistic centuries that followed it, in addition to necklaces and earrings, Greek women regularly wore rings; brooches and pins for fastening clothes; bracelets; anklets; headbands; and armbands (worn between the elbow and shoulder when the arm was free of a tunic or outer wrap). Also, necklaces featuring small hanging figurines of animals were common. Gold remained widely popular for fine jewelry, which was also made from silver, precious and semiprecious stones, and glass. Cheaper "costume" jewelry utilized materials such as iron, bronze, and lead.

Most metal jewelry was made from thin sheets of metal or wire, although a few items were cast in molds. To fashion a piece of sheet metal, the artisan heated an ingot of metal until it was soft and then beat it with a hammer until it had flattened down to the desired thickness. The sheet could then be either hammered across or into a wooden mold or cut up into strips. Rolling such a strip between two stones or metal plates created a wire, which could be twisted into various shapes or cut up into smaller pieces.

SEE ALSO: metalworking

Jews

Greeks and Jews had little or no contact and, in fact, scant knowledge of each other before the 300s B.C. Writing in the late sixth century B.C., the Jewish prophet Ezekiel mentions Greek Ionian traders in Palestine (although he calls where they are from "Javan" rather than Greece). And the fifth-century B.C. Greek historian Herodotus lists Jews (whom he calls "Palestinian Syrians") among the sailors conscripted by the Persian king Xerxes I for the invasion of Greece in 480 B.C. More concrete contact between the two peoples began when Alexander the Great took control of Palestine, Syria, and Babylonia, which had a small Jewish population, during his conquest of the Persian Empire in the 330s B.C. For a long time afterward, the Jews in the region were ruled by Hellenistic kings of the Ptolemaic and Seleucid dynasties. And large Jewish enclaves grew up in Ptolemaic Alexandria and Seleucid Antioch.

Although all Jews rejected Greek polytheism, wealthier Jews often adopted Greek customs, including administrative practices, physical culture (exercise in gymnasia), and symposia (after-dinner drinking parties). Also, the Greek language became the lingua franca of the regions in which the Jews lived, and over time many Jews became increasingly less proficient in Hebrew. As a result, during the reign of King Ptolemy II Jewish scholars translated the Hebrew Old Testament into Greek, a version that became known as the Septuagint. This translation later played a key role in preserving Jewish culture and spreading Christianity (which developed from Judaism) in the Roman Empire.

In 198 B.C. the Seleucids wrested Palestine from the Ptolemies, and about thirty years later the Seleucid king Antiochus IV tried to convert the Jewish temple in Jerusalem into a Greek temple. This ignited a Jewish revolt that eventually ousted the Seleucids from Jerusalem. The Jews in the region were now free to govern themselves; however, not long afterward, in 63 B.C., the Romans, who had already overrun all of the Greek lands except Ptolemaic Egypt, captured Palestine.

SEE ALSO: Seleucid Empire

Jocasta

In Greek mythology, and in several of the plays of the fifth-century B.C. Athenian playwrights, the wife of Laius, king of Thebes, and mother of Oedipus. Jocasta thought Oedipus had died in infancy. When he grew up and appeared at the Theban court following Laius's death, she married him. Jocasta then bore Oedipus two sons, Eteocles and Polynices, and two daughters, Antigone and Ismeme. For more on Jocasta, **see** Oedipus; *Oedipus the King*; and, for the momentous events directly following her death, **see** *Antigone*; *Oedipus at Colonus*; *Seven Against Thebes*.

Knights

A comedic play by Aristophanes that was first produced in Athens in 424 B.C. and won the first prize in the Lenaea, one of the city's drama festivals. The play pokes fun at the leading Athenian politicians and generals of the day, including Cleon, Demosthenes, and Nicias. An Athenian gentleman named Demos (meaning "the people") has two slaves named Demosthenes and Nicias. A new slave, Paphlago-nian (who represents Cleon) gains the master's confidence and abuses the other two servants. Demosthenes and Nicias consider running away, but then they learn that an oracle has predicted that Paphlagonian will be foiled by a sausage seller. Just such a merchant soon appears and contends with Paphlagonian for Demos's favor. After much shifty maneuvering and squabbling, the sausage seller (who represents Athens's Assembly) is victorious and Paphlagonian is forced to leave.

SEE ALSO: Aristophanes, 1

Knossos

In Greek mythology, the capital of King Minos's kingdom in Crete, and in reality the leading Minoan city in Crete during

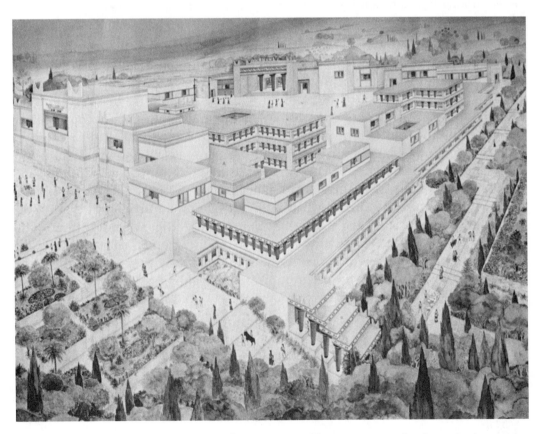

A reconstruction of the Bronze Age palace-center at Knossos accurately shows its impressive size and complexity. THE ART ARCHIVE/PRIVATE COLLECTION PARIS/DAGLI ORTI

Greece's Bronze Age. According to one famous myth, Minos had the inventor Daedalus build the labyrinth, a maze beneath the royal palace at Knossos (also Knossus, Cnossos, or Cnossus). Then Minos placed the Minotaur, a creature half man and half bull, in the labyrinth and fed it sacrificial victims obtained by force from Athens, on the Greek mainland. Eventually the Athenian hero Theseus sailed to Knossos, defeated its soldiers; and slew the Minotaur.

The mythical conflict between Knossos and Athens and Theseus's defeat of Knossos appear to have been based partly on real events. Modern archaeologists have shown that the site of Knossos, located about 4 miles (6.4km) from Crete's northern coast, was inhabited by the Minoans early in the Bronze Age and became the center of a thriving maritime empire. In the early 1900s British excavator Arthur Evans unearthed a huge, sprawling structure on the site. It seems to have served as both a palace and an administrative center for the villages and farms surrounding Knossos. Its hundreds of rooms, corridors, stairwells, and courtyards, covering 5.5 acres (2.2ha) in all, are complex and maze-like and could well have inspired the myth of Minos's labyrinth. (Also, the distorted memory of Minoan priests, who wore bull masks while conducting rituals, may have given rise to the legend of the monstrous Minotaur.) Among the artifacts found in the palace-center at Knossos are exquisite frescoes; a throne room with the throne still intact; and clay pipes that carried water to modern-style bathrooms.

Archaeological evidence also shows that Knossos and its environs were adversely affected by the eruption of the volcano on Thera (an island north of Crete) sometime around 1600 B.C. or shortly thereafter. Earthquakes and possibly a tsunami damaged the palace, though it was quickly restored to its former splendor. However, Knossos was sacked and burned circa 1400 B.C. and was never rebuilt. The culprits were the mainland Mycenaeans, who took over Crete at this time, an event that likely later gave rise to the myth about Theseus's military expedition to Knossos.

The long-abandoned site of Knossos was occupied once more when Dorian Greeks settled in Crete during the early years of Greece's Dark Age. A town grew up there, although the ruins of the palace-center were avoided and continued to decay. By the time the Romans took over Crete in 67 B.C., Knossos was an unimportant little town overshadowed by his neighbor and longtime rival, Gortyn.

SEE ALSO: Crete; Gortyn; labyrinth; Minoans; Minos; Thera; Theseus

koine

A dialect of Greek that came to be used widely across the Greek world in Hellenistic times. Koine, meaning "common tongue" first developed in the late fourth century B.C. and was based primarily on the Attic dialect, spoken in Athens and its immediate vicinity.

SEE ALSO: Greek language

kore

A kind of female statue popular in Greece in the Archaic Age.

SEE ALSO: sculpture

kouros

A kind of male statue popular in Greece in the Archaic Age.

SEE ALSO: sculpture

labyrinth

In Greek mythology, the maze built at Knossos by the legendary inventor Daedalus for Minos, king of Crete. Inside the labyrinth Minos put the frightening Minotaur, which fed on human flesh. Eventually the Athenian hero Theseus entered the maze, killed the beast, and, with the aid of Ariadne, Minos's daughter, found his way back out.

SEE ALSO: Daedalus; Knossos; Minotaur

Lacedaemon

The ancient Greek name for Sparta and its immediate environs, roughly equivalent to the term *Lakonike* (*Laconia* in Latin).

SEE ALSO: Sparta

Laconia

The Latin, and today more common, version of the Greek term *Lakonike*, denoting the region of the southeastern Peloponnesus dominated by Sparta.

SEE ALSO: Sparta

Laius

In Greek mythology, a king of Thebes and the father of the famous and tragic character Oedipus. After the reign of Amphion and Zethus (two of Zeus's mortal sons) ended in Thebes, Laius ascended the throne. He and his wife, Jocasta, ordered a servant to leave their infant son, Oedipus, outside to die. But the servant gave the child to a shepherd, who took Oedipus to Corinth to be raised. As a young man, Oedipus headed back to Thebes and on the way slew an old man on the roadside who refused to let him pass. Only years later, after Oedipus had married Jocasta and had children by her, did he learn that the old man on the roadside was his own father, Laius. These sordid and tragic events are the subject of Sophocles' immortal play *Oedipus the King*.

SEE ALSO: Jocasta; Oedipus; *Oedipus the King*

Lamian War

Fought in Greece between 323 and 322 B.C., the conflict arose soon after the death of Alexander the Great in June 323. Seeking to shake off Macedonian rule, Athens led a coalition of city-states that besieged Alexander's regent, Antipater, in the town of Lamia in Thessaly. Eventually Antipater got the upper hand, and the rebels were defeated at Crannon (also in Thessaly).

SEE ALSO: Alexander III ("the Great"); Antipater

Lapiths

In Greek mythology, a group of early Greeks who settled in Thessaly. They are famous for their war with the centaurs (creatures half man and half horse).

SEE ALSO: centaurs

Laws

A prominent dialogue by Plato and the last and longest of his many works. The dialogue's sentences are lengthy and complex, and it appears that much of the manuscript remained as yet unedited when the author died while in the midst of writing it. The three speakers are a Cretan named Cleinias, a Spartan named Magillus, and an unnamed Athenian man. Cleinias is the leader of a commission charged with the task of establishing a new city in Crete. In the course of the conversation, the men discuss the best way to set up a constitution and law code for the new city. Much of the narrative is dominated by the Athenian, who details numerous laws covering property, slaves, education, religious worship, marriage, and other aspects of civic society. Many of these laws appear to be what Plato viewed as well suited to an ideal, well-organized, and efficient society.

SEE ALSO: Plato

laws and justice

Almost nothing is known about laws and justice in the Greek lands before 700 B.C. In the Dark Age and early Archaic Age, when most Greek villages were run by chieftains who were advised by councils of elders (including religious leaders, large landowners, and others), these pillars of the community likely dispensed justice. A vague memory of what may have been a public trial from this period has survived in a small passage in Homer's *Iliad*, in which Hephaestos, god of the forge, creates new armor for the warrior Achilles. On the shield, the god carves a scene in which

> the people massed, streaming into the marketplace, where a quarrel had broken out and two men struggled over the blood-price for a kinsman just murdered. One [vowed] payment in full; [but] the other spurned him … so both men pressed for a judge to cut the knot. The crowd cheered on both [litigants], but a herald held them back as the city elders sat on polished stone benches. … Each [litigant] leapt to his feet to plead his

case in turn. Two bars of gold shone on the ground before them, a prize for the judge who'd speak the straightest [truest] verdict. (*Iliad* 18.580–592)

Early Law Codes

Before writing began to appear in Greece in the late 700s B.C. (thanks to the recent introduction of a new alphabet borrowed from the Phoenicians), the laws were not written down. Instead, these codes of acceptable behavior, which must have differed somewhat from one Greek community to another, were memorized by one or more citizens and passed along by oral means. The first-known written Greek law code was that of a lawgiver named Zaleucus in Locri, a Greek town in southern Italy, in about 662 B.C. (The Spartan lawgiver Lycurgus may have lived during this same period. However, it remains uncertain whether he was a real person. In any case, he supposedly ordered that his laws be kept in oral form, and the result was that Sparta's laws were not written down until centuries later.) Little is known about Zaleucus's laws except that they were said to be harsh. And some modern scholars think he may have supported the principal of *lex talionis*, or "an eye for an eye." The same sort of harsh law code was instituted in Athens a few years later, circa 625, by a man named Draco. About his legal code, Plutarch writes, "Under the Draconian code, almost any kind of offense was liable to the death penalty, so that even those convicted of idleness were executed, and those who stole fruit or vegetables suffered the same punishment as those who committed sacrilege or murder. This is the reason why, in later times [someone remarked that] Draco's code was written not in ink but in blood." (*Life of Solon* 17) Because they were so severe, Draco's laws caused unrest among the Athenians; and a generation later, in 594 B.C., the statesman Solon discarded them, keeping only the one dealing with homicide, and issued many new, fairer laws. Among these was one that forbade people from enslaving those who owed them money (a practice called debt bondage). "He also forbade people to abuse [one another] in temples, courts of law, public offices and during games or festivals," Plutarch recalls.

> The penalty was a fine of three drachmas to be paid to the injured party and two more to the public treasury. . . . Solon was also much admired for his law that dealt with wills. Before his time wills were not permitted and the whole estate of the deceased was bound to remain within his family. Solon, however . . . [allowed] any man who had no children to bequeath his property to whomever he chose. (*Life of Solon* 21)

These and Solon's other laws were carved onto wooden tablets and placed on public display in Athens's Agora; Plutarch said that most were still there some six centuries later in his own day.

Courts and Juries

Solon also seems to have made changes in the courts, although the exact nature of most of these reforms is unclear. More substantial changes in the Athenian court system occurred in the decades following the institution of full democracy in that city (circa 508 B.C.). In the 460s the radical democrats, led by the reformer Ephialtes, mentor of Pericles, greatly increased the size and powers of juries. In the new system, each year six thousand men thirty years old or older were chosen by lot (random drawing) to serve as jurors (*dikastai*). A large proportion of them were elderly. Later, Pericles pushed through legislation allowing jurors to be paid a

daily fee, which ensured that even the poorest Athenians who wanted to serve could do so (since otherwise the poor could not take time away from their jobs to serve). This stipend then became a sort of old-age pension for the elderly poor. In the courts in which these jurors served, there was no judge. Nor were there lawyers or detectives or investigators to gather evidence, so the litigants gathered their own evidence and witnesses and pleaded their own cases before the jurors. Those litigants who felt they lacked the competence to write and deliver their own court speeches hired professional speechwriters (*logographai*), some of the more famous of which included the orators Antiphon, Lysias, Isaeus, and Demosthenes.

Penalties in the Athenian courts were usually prescribed by law. But in some cases the prosecutor (i.e., the litigant bringing the complaint) was allowed to suggest a penalty. The defending litigant could propose a different penalty, and the jurors then decided which sentence to impose. This is what occurred in the famous trial of the philosopher Socrates in 399 B.C. His jury, numbering roughly five hundred men (as women were not allowed to sit on juries), voted twice, the first time to decide his guilt or innocence, the second time to determine his punishment. In such cases, the jury's decision was final and there were no appeals. Socrates received the death penalty after being found guilty of corrupting the city's young people with his "dangerous" teachings (a trumped-up charge). Other common penalties included exile, imprisonment, partial or full loss of citizenship, confiscation of property, and monetary fines. No matter how small the fine, until it was paid in full the offender and all of his descendants were barred from voting, holding public office, or sitting on juries. Also, to discourage frivolous prosecutions, a prosecuting litigant had to pay a fine if fewer than one-fifth of the jurors voted in his favor.

It is unknown how many other Greek states had legal systems like that of Athens (from which the vast bulk of the surviving evidence comes). But because many of these states did adopt Athenian-style democracies in the Classical Age, it is likely that courts in those places were similar. It is also likely, however, that there were local differences in laws, jury selection, and the nature and severity of penalties.

See Also: Draco; government; Lycurgus, 1; Pericles; Solon

Lemnos

An island in the northeastern Aegean Sea. Homer described it as a source of food for the Greeks who besieged Troy. According to Herodotus, the original inhabitants of the island were Pelasgians (non-Greeks who supposedly occupied the region before the arrival of Greek-speakers). A long inscription found on Lemnos bears Etruscan letters and was at one time cited as evidence that the Etruscans (an early Italian people) originated on Lemnos. However, more recent evidence suggests that the opposite is more likely (i.e., that some Etruscans from Italy may have at one time landed on or traded with Lemnos). After the Athenian general Miltiades seized the island in about 500 B.C., it remained mainly under Athenian control thereafter.

See Also: Etruscans; Miltiades

Leonidas
(ca. 540 B.C.–480 B.C.)

A Spartan king renowned for commanding the Greek soldiers who fought to the

Leonidas's Spartans slaughter thousands of oncoming Persian soldiers who are attempting to capture the pass of Thermopylae. North Wind Picture Archives

death defending the pass of Thermopylae against the invading Persians in 480 B.C. Little is known about his life before he became one of Sparta's two jointly ruling kings except that he belonged to the Agiad royal house and married a woman named Gorgo and had a son by her named Pleistarchus. Most of Leonidas's reign was fairly uneventful.

But in 480 B.C. a huge Persian army, led by King Xerxes, crossed the Hellespont and marched southward through the Greek mainland. Delegates from many of the southern Greek city-states, Leonidas among them, met near Corinth to decide how best to defend themselves. They decided to fortify the pass of Thermopylae, which seemed a natural place to set up a defensive position because, as Herodotus explains, it was very narrow. "The pass," he says, is "fifty feet (15m) wide; elsewhere, both east and west of Thermopylae, it is still narrower. . . . The Persians would be unable in the narrow pass to use their cavalry or take advantage of their numbers." (*Histories* 7.126) The plan was for a small Greek force to hold off the enemy while the Greek states assembled larger armies to fight the Persians. That force, commanded by Leonidas, consisted of three hundred picked Spartan troops, about twenty-seven hundred men from Sparta's Peloponnesian neighbors, and a few thousand soldiers from Thebes, Thespiae, and other states lying west and north of Athens.

Only a few days after Leonidas and his troops fortified the pass, the Persian army approached from the north. When someone asked him why he was willing to pit so few men against so many, he replied: "If you think that I should rely on numbers, then not even the whole of Greece is enough, since it is a small fraction of their horde. But if I am to rely on courage, then even this [small] number is quite adequate." (Quoted in Plutarch, "Sayings of the Spartans." in *Moralia* 223) This prediction proved accurate. For three days the tiny band of Greeks prevented the huge Persian army from making it through the pass. In fact, it began to look as if Leonidas and his small brigade of troops might be able to hold the pass indefinitely. But then a local Greek named Ephialtes, perhaps a sheep herder, agreed to show the Persians a little-known mountain path that led to the rear of the Greek position. On the morning of the fourth day, Leonidas realized that he was about to be outflanked. With only a few hours to spare, he sent the bulk of the Greek troops away to spare them for later battles. With his three hundred Spartans and a few hundred Thespians and other volunteers, he remained at his post in hopes of delaying the enemy as long as possible. When the Persians finally closed in on all sides, he and his men fought with courage and determination that has become legendary. Herodotus's gripping account reads:

> The Greeks under Leonidas, knowing they were going to their deaths . . . put forth all their strength and fought with fury and desperation. By this time most of their spears were broken. . . . In the course of the fight Leonidas fell. . . . There was a bitter struggle over [his] body. Four times the Greeks drove the enemy off, and at last by their valor rescued it. . . . [Finally they] took up a position . . . on the little hill at the entrance to the pass. . . . Here they resisted to the last, with their swords, if they had them, and, if not, with their hands and teeth, until the Persians . . . finally overwhelmed them with [arrows]. (*Histories* 7.225–227)

After the battle Xerxes located Leonidas's body and ordered the head severed and placed on a pole, while the body was crucified. Afterward, Leonidas's sacrifice became an inspiration to other Greeks, both ancient and modern; and today an enormous bronze statue of him stands near the spot where he and his comrades gave their last measure of devotion to Greece.

SEE ALSO: Battle of Thermopylae, 1; Greco-Persian Wars

Lesbos

A Greek island perhaps best known as the homeland of the female poet Sappho. At 630 square miles (1,632 sq. km), Lesbos, located off the northwestern coast of Asia

Minor, is the largest island in the eastern Aegean Sea. The first residents may have been of Trojan stock. (Troy was located only a short distance north of Lesbos.) The island's main city was Mytilene, a port on the southeastern coast that became highly prosperous through trade with Lydia, Egypt, and mainland Greece during the Archaic Age. Lesbos fell to the Persians in 527 B.C. and took part in the failed Ionian rebellion against Persia (499–494). After the expulsion of the Persians from the region in 479, the Lesbians joined the Athenian-controlled Delian League. But toward the close of the Peloponnesian War, the Spartans occupied the island. In the two centuries that followed, Lesbos endured the domination of a succession of outside powers, including the Persians once more, then Alexander the Great's Macedonians, then Antigonus I (one of Alexander's leading Successors), then the Ptolemies (the Greek rulers of Hellenistic Egypt), and finally the Romans in the 190s B.C.

SEE ALSO: Delian League; Mytilene; Sappho

Leucippus
(flourished ca. 500 B.C.–470 B.C.)

A pre-Socratic Greek philosopher-scientist who, along with Democritus, introduced the atomic theory. Little is known about Leucippus's life, and even his birthplace is uncertain. Also, regrettably, all of his written works, including the *Great World System*, which was famous in antiquity, are lost. Later ancient writers summarized his ideas, including Aristotle, who writes, "Leucippus [says] that all things are composed of indivisible bodies [atoms], and that these are finite both in number and in their various shapes; and that compounds get their different characters from the shape and arrangement of these

constituents." (*On Generation and Corruption* 314a)

SEE ALSO: Democritus; science

Libation Bearers, The

A tragic play by Aeschylus, first performed in Athens in 458 B.C. The work is the second part of the playwright's mighty trilogy, the *Oresteia*, about the mythical evil doings in the cursed House of Atreus. In the first play of the trilogy, *Agamemnon*, Clytemnestra, queen of Mycenae and Argos, and her lover, Aegisthus, assassinate her husband, King Agamemnon. Seven years pass and then the action of *The Libation Bearers* begins. Now in charge of the kingdom, Clytemnestra and Aegisthus treat Clytemnestra's daughter, Electra, like a servant because she still harbors a grudge against them for murdering her father. Then Electra's brother, Orestes, who has been living in a foreign city the last seven years, arrives. He and Electra reunite and immediately begin planning to avenge Agamemnon's death. With the aid of his close comrade Pylades, Orestes slays Aegisthus and Clytemnestra. Only moments later the palace doors open, revealing the bloody corpses to the servants and other people gathered outside. Before Orestes has time to gather his wits and claim the throne, it becomes clear that the frightening Furies (flying creatures that hunt down murderers) are swiftly approaching. Orestes flees for his life. (The story continues in the third play of the trilogy, the *Eumenides*.)

SEE ALSO: Agamemnon; Electra; Orestes

libraries

The Greeks did not have books in the modern sense until the fifth century B.C., but when they came into fashion they spread quickly. The word for book was at first *biblos*, which most often referred to a papyrus roll. The first Greek libraries were private collections of these rolls that appeared in Athens (and perhaps other Greek cities) in the fourth century B.C. The largest early collection belonged to the famous Athenian philosopher Aristotle. Larger libraries open to scholars and members of royal families (but usually not the public) first appeared in the next century in the large Hellenistic kingdoms. The first two Ptolemaic kings collected books from around the known world and housed them in the largest library of ancient times, the so-called Great Library at Alexandria. This institution may have held as many as five hundred thousand rolls (the equivalent of about one hundred thousand modern books) at its height; the second-largest ancient Greek library—at Pergamum—had about two hundred thousand rolls. Many smaller Greek towns also had libraries, often in or near local gymnasia. Many of the Greek library collections later passed into the hands of the Romans, who also established libraries of their own in imitation of the Greeks.

SEE ALSO: Alexandria; Pergamum; writing materials

Library of History

For this important historical work by the first-century Greek Diodorus Siculus, **see** Diodorus Siculus.

Linear B

A kind of script used for keeping inventories by the Bronze Age Mycenaeans, who, it is now known, spoke an early form of Greek.

SEE ALSO: Greek language; Knossos; Mycenaeans

liturgies

In ancient Athens and an unknown number of other ancient Greek city-states, a system (*leitourgiai*, or "the people's burdens") in which the government asked well-to-do members of the community to help pay for public activities and institutions. Such subsidies ensured that at least some of the wealth concentrated in the hands of a few individuals would benefit society as a whole. The most common liturgies were those that paid for play production in the yearly drama festivals, the construction of statues and monuments, distribution of food at religious festivals, and the outfitting and maintaining of ships for the city's navy. The backer of a play, for example, was called a *choregus*. In fifth-century B.C. Athens, a *choregus* spent an average of three hundred to fifteen hundred drachmas to produce a single play. (To put this in perspective, in this era an average Athenian worker earned from one to two drachmas per day.) Some *choregoi* spent three thousand drachmas or even more to put on a play. Despite the great cost, most of these men took pride in this duty, partly because it could bring them considerable prestige. In a speech delivered in court, one former drama patron bragged, "I won first prize at the Thargelia [a festival of Apollo held in May] with a men's chorus, having spent 2,000 drachmas. In the archonship of Glaukippus [410 B.C.] I spent 8,000 drachmas on Pyrrhic dancers at the Great Panathenaea [religious festival], and I won first prize as choregus with a men's chorus at the Dionysia [drama festival], spending 5,000 drachmas." (Quoted in Lysias, *On a Bribery Charge* 21). In the case of the wealthy citizens who supported the navy, each year the state selected a few hundred of them, in rotation, from a master list and charged each with maintaining one trireme (warship) for the coming season. The government provided the ship and paid the rowers. The backer paid the vessel's officers, took care of repairs, and in some cases commanded the ship. (If he had no naval experience, he followed the advice of the veteran helmsman). In the late fifth century B.C. during the debilitating Peloponnesian War, the Athenian government could no longer find enough well-to-do men of military age to assume this duty, so it had two men pool their resources to support each ship. Later, in 340 B.C., the state increased it to four or more men per ship. Finally, in early Hellenistic times, Athens eliminated the naval liturgy altogether.

SEE ALSO: government; theater and drama; weapons and warfare, naval

Locris

The name of two regions in the central part of mainland Greece. Eastern Locris, situated along the coast of the Euboean strait, near Boeotia, established a colony in southern Italy in the seventh century B.C. At first the strategic pass of Thermopylae (in south-central Greece) was under the control of the eastern Locrians, but they were eventually obliged to cede it to the larger state of Thessaly. Western Locris, along the northern coast of the Gulf of Corinth, early developed a reputation for piracy and cultural backwardness. After losing their port of Naupactus to Athens in about 460 B.C., the western Locrians took the Athenian side in the Peloponnesian War, but the eastern Locrians backed Sparta in the conflict.

SEE ALSO: Greece, history of

Long Walls

Erected between 461 and 456 B.C., the Long Walls connected Athens's walled urban center to its port town of Piraeus, some 4 miles (6.4km) distant. Most of the barrier consisted of two walls running parallel to each other and separated by roughly 600 feet (180m). The noted Athenian statesman Pericles oversaw their construction in order to protect Athens from attack (mainly by Sparta) while giving it safe access to the port and life-giving shipping lanes beyond. Predictably, the building of the Long Walls angered the Spartans, and existing tensions between the two city-states escalated. The walls certainly kept the Spartans out during the Peloponnesian War (431–404 B.C.). In that conflict, the Athenians often huddled behind these grand fortifications and watched the Spartans pillage Attica's farms. When the Athenians surrendered at the end of the war, the victors forced them to tear down the walls.

SEE ALSO: Peloponnesian War; Pericles; Sparta

Lucian
(ca. 115 A.D.–ca. 181 A.D.)

A noted Greek writer of more than eighty speeches, stories, essays, and dialogues. Outside of the fact that he hailed from Samosata, Syria, little is known about his life except that he eventually settled in Athens, where he did some legal work and teaching. Of his many literary works, the most famous are his dialogues and fantastic tales. Most of these are satires that ridicule serious literary works and characters. For example, his *True History*, now his best-known work, is a spoof of serious travelers' tales that were widely popular in ancient times. Lucian's travelers are sucked up into a giant waterspout and end up on the moon, where they find that the king of the moon is quarreling with the king of the sun over rights to colonize Jupiter. The travelers then return to Earth and visit the Isles of the Blessed (the section of the Underworld in which the souls of heroes and other noteworthy humans dwell). There they meet Homer, who reveals that he wrote the *Iliad* in haste, with no thought to structure or literary quality. Another spoof by Lucian, *Dialogues of the Gods*, pokes fun at familiar myths. In one section, the Titan Prometheus, whom Zeus had chained to a rock on a mountainside as a punishment for giving fire to humanity, makes a deal with the king of the gods. Prometheus, who can see into the future, warns Zeus that sleeping with a certain goddess will cause him much trouble, and in return, Zeus agrees to free the Titan from his chains. In the same irreverent spirit, Lucian's *Dialogues of the Dead* takes place in the Underworld, where Hermes, Heracles, Achilles, and other mythic characters offer critiques of human civilization in Lucian's day. Much of the biting humor in Lucian's works is reminiscent of the satirical plays of the fifth-century B.C. comic playwright Aristophanes, who strongly influenced Lucian.

SEE ALSO: Aristophanes, 1; Homer; Prometheus

Lyceum

A philosophical school established by Aristotle in about 335 B.C. It was located not far outside Athens's city walls in a grove sacred to the god Apollo. Around 286 B.C. the Lyceum moved into the urban center, where the school's second director, Theophrastus, had donated some buildings. The new setting included a colonnaded walkway, or *peripatos*, which gave the institu-

tion a new name—the Peripatetic School.

SEE ALSO: Aristotle

Lycurgus
(seventh century B.C. ?)

A noted Spartan lawgiver who may or may not have been a real person. Even in ancient times, little could be confirmed about his life and deeds. "Generally speaking," Plutarch said in the first century A.D., "it is impossible to make any undisputed statement about Lycurgus the lawgiver, since conflicting accounts have been given of his ancestry, his travels, his death, and above all his activity with respect to his laws and government." (*Life of Lycurgus* 1) According to tradition, at least, Lycurgus established Sparta's government and its social organization, including its regimented military training system, the *agoge*. In the Classical Age, the Spartans remembered Lycurgus with great respect and reverence. They still kept a short inscription (the "Great Rhetra") they believed he had written.

SEE ALSO: government; laws and justice; Sparta

Lycurgus
(ca. 390 B.C.–ca. 325 B.C.)

A prominent Athenian orator, statesman, and writer of the second half of the Classical Age. Lycurgus studied with the noted orator Isocrates and afterward put what he learned to good use by prosecuting several citizens he viewed as wrongdoers. Of the powerful court speeches he composed for these legal battles, only one, *Against Leocrates*, survives. He also served as a financial officer for the Athenian government in the years following the city's defeat at Chaeronea (338 B.C.) by Macedonia's King Philip

II. Lycurgus became extremely influential in this period and involved himself in many constructive public projects, including a building program that refurbished temples; the creation of a literary compilation of the plays of Aeschylus, Sophocles, and Euripides; and the sculpting of statues of those playwrights.

SEE ALSO: laws and justice; Philip II; theater and drama

Lydia

A short-lived but wealthy, powerful, and influential kingdom centered in the inland sector of western Asia Minor in the seventh and sixth centuries B.C. Lydia was the first non-Greek nation that directly involved itself in Greek political and cultural affairs. An early Lydian king, Gyges, heard about the oracle of Apollo at Delphi and sent gifts of friendship to the sacred sanctuary there. One of his successors, King Croesus, admired the Greeks so much that he adopted many Greek customs. He actually consulted the Delphic Oracle on more than one occasion. Still, Croesus also attacked the Ionian Greek cities in the 550s B.C. and turned them into subject states of Lydia. This marked the height of Lydia's power, however, for barely a decade later Croesus was defeated by the Persian king Cyrus II and the region became a Persian province. The former Lydian capital of Sardis now became the Persian province's capital. The region of Lydia was captured by Alexander the Great during his conquest of Persia in the 330s B.C., and after Alexander's death the Seleucid Empire administered the area. Later still, in the early second century B.C., the former Lydia was absorbed by Rome. Lydia's greatest contribution to the ancient world was its introduction of the art of coinage (ca. 635 B.C.), which

the Greeks and others then readily adopted.

SEE ALSO: Asia Minor; Croesus; Sardis

lyre

A harplike musical instrument, typically with seven strings, plucked with the fingers or a pick and used to accompany singers or poetry recital in ancient Greece. The smallest, simplest versions, with gut strings stretched across a tortoise shell, were played by any well-to-do person. Large wooden lyres called kitharas, sometimes inlaid with gems and precious metals, were played by skilled professionals.

SEE ALSO: music and dance

lyric poetry

Originally, verses intended to be sung to the accompaniment of a lyre or other instrument.

SEE ALSO: music and dance; poetry

Lysander
(ca. 445 B.C.–395 B.C.)

A renowned Spartan admiral who played a leading role in defeating Athens in the Peloponnesian War and administering that city in the conflict's aftermath. Lysander defeated the Athenians at Notium (on the Ionian coast north of Samos) in 406 B.C. and then attempted to cut off Athens's access to the life-giving Black Sea grain route by attacking the Athenian navy in the Hellespont. There, at Aegospotami in 405, he won a decisive victory that virtually ensured that Athens would no longer be able to prosecute the war. Sailing southward, Lysander blockaded Athens's port, Piraeus, and the following year accepted the Athenian surrender. Under the command of Lysander, the Spartans then forced the Athenians to tear down the Long Walls and install a pro-Spartan

The Spartan fleet, commanded by Lysander, sails into the harbor at Piraeus in the dramatic climax of the Peloponnesian War. TIME LIFE PICTURES/GETTY IMAGES

oligarchic council—the infamous Thirty Tyrants, headed by Critias. Later, in 395, Lysander was killed in a battle against the Thebans.

SEE ALSO: Battle of Aegospotami; Peloponnesian War; Sparta

Lysias
(ca. 458 B.C.–ca. 380 B.C.)

A famous Athenian orator who reportedly composed some eight hundred speeches, about a quarter of them for court litigants. Twenty-three survive complete. The son of a wealthy metic (foreigner living in Athens), Lysias had a thriving shield-making enterprise with his brothers. But when Athens lost the Peloponnesian War and the Thirty Tyrants began their reign of terror, Lysias and his brothers were at-

tacked and their property was confiscated. Lysias barely escaped with his life. After the overthrow of the tyrants and restoration of democracy the following year, he prosecuted one of them, Eratosthenes. In his speech to the jury, Lysias described the crimes against his family, saying in part:

My brother Polemarchus had received from the Thirty their customary order—to drink [poison] hemlock. This was before they had stated any reason for which he had to die—so far was he from having a trial and a chance to defend himself. When he was carried out dead from the prison, they refused to allow his funeral to take place. . . . They had confiscated our property. . . . They held vast sums of [our] silver and gold, bronze jewelry and furniture . . . [and] one hundred and twenty slaves [who had been

employed in the shield-making shop].
(*Against Eratosthenes* 17–19)

Following the trial, the verdict of which is unknown, Lysias was destitute. To support himself, he became a *logographos*, a writer of court speeches. Supposedly he turned out at least two hundred of these speeches in the following two decades and thereby became famous and well-to-do. He also composed funeral orations and other kinds of speeches and personally delivered one of them at Olympia, something then viewed as a high honor. Lysias's writing is distinguished by its directness, simplicity, conciseness, and clarity. And his court speeches are extremely well organized and persuasive.

SEE ALSO: laws and justice; Peloponnesian War; Thirty Tyrants

Lysimachus
(ca. 360 B.C.–281 B.C.)

One of Alexander the Great's leading Successors, who, following Alexander's death in 323 B.C., fought one another for control of his vast empire. Lysimachus started out as a member of Alexander's Companion cavalry and steadily rose through the military ranks to become a general. When Alexander died, Lysimachus became governor of the territories of Thrace and northwestern Asia Minor and married Nicaea, daughter of Antipater, another Successor. In 315 Lysimachus joined with Seleucus, Ptolemy, and other Successors against Antigonus; and several years later, in 301, Lysimachus was part of another coalition of Successors that overwhelmingly defeated Antigonus at Ipsus. By this time Lysimachus had taken the title of king of Thrace and western Asia Minor. And after seizing parts of mainland Greece in the 280s, he was for a brief time the most powerful

Successor. But in 282 Seleucus defeated and killed Lysimachus in battle and absorbed his lands in Asia Minor into the growing Seleucid realm.

SEE ALSO: Alexander III ("the Great"); Battle of Ipsus; Ptolemy I Soter; Seleucus

Lysistrata

A comic play by Aristophanes, one of his best and most popular, first performed in Athens in 411 B.C. At this time the Peloponnesian War was not going well for Athens. Less than two years before, thousands of Athenian soldiers had been killed or captured in the climax of the disastrous Sicilian expedition; and Sparta had recently made an anti-Athenian alliance with the Persians. There was, therefore, a strong desire for peace among the war-weary Athenian populace, and Aristophanes took advantage of this situation in concocting the play's humorous plot and antics.

As the play opens, the title character, whose name means "she who disbands armies," organizes the Athenian women. They go on a sex strike and then seize control of the Acropolis and the city's treasury, strategies designed to force their husbands to make peace with Sparta. At first the city's men resist the notion of ending the war, and the old men making up the play's chorus attempt to storm the Acropolis; but a second chorus, composed of old women, drives them away with buckets of water. Suddenly a Spartan herald appears and says that his countrymen are also tired of war and are ready to make peace. Urged on by the feisty Lysistrata, the Athenian and Spartan negotiators reach a deal and everyone celebrates by having a banquet.

SEE ALSO: Aristophanes, 1; Peloponnesian War; theater and drama

Macedonia

A kingdom of northern Greece, centered on the Thermaic plain, which stretches westward from the city of Thessaloniki. (Modern historians often use the term *Macedon* to denote the kingdom as a political state and the term *Macedonia* to describe the kingdom more generally as a region or cultural entity.) Little is known about the Bronze Age inhabitants of Macedonia. In the Dark Age and early Archaic Age, they were overrun by migrating Dorians, Thracians, and other tribal groups who spoke dialects of Greek.

During the Archaic Age, while Athens, Thebes, Corinth, and other major city-states of southern Greece were rising to power and creating a sophisticated culture, the Macedonians remained outside the Greek cultural mainstream and were politically divided and militarily weak. The chief reason for said division and weakness was a long-standing internal disunity. The kingdom was roughly divided into two portions—a spacious, hilly interior and the flatter, well-watered Thermaic plain near the Aegean coast. Traditionally, the inhabitants of the two regions did not get along. The first important Macedonian king, Perdiccas I, established his capital on the plain, at Aegae (modern Vergina), sometime in the seventh century B.C. He also founded the Argead dynasty, a family that was destined to rule the kingdom for many generations to come. But Perdiccas and his immediate successors were unable to gain control of the highland regions.

Much later King Archelaus I (reigned 413–399), made some limited, though significant, strides toward uniting the kingdom and bringing it into the Greek cultural mainstream. He moved the capital from Aegae to nearby Pella, but he retained Aegae as a ceremonial center and royal burial site. Archelaus invited numerous leading Greek artists and writers, including the playwright Euripides, to come and live at his court. The king also seems to have established some tenuous control of some of the highland regions. But his efforts came to naught, for when he died the country quickly reverted to its traditional backward, disunited state.

It was one of Archelaus's immediate successors, Philip II (reigned 359–336 B.C.), who finally united the country and put it on the Greek and world maps, so to speak. With amazing speed, Philip brought the feuding highland and lowland regions together and turned Macedonia into a strong, centralized state with a powerful professional standing army, the first that Europe had ever seen. He then decided to try to unite all of mainland Greece under his leadership. His conquests culminated in a sweeping victory over a coalition of major city-states at Chaeronea in 338 B.C. Two years later, however, he was assassinated, and his son, Alexander III (later called "the Great"), became king of Macedonia. Alexander led the Macedonians and Greeks in the conquest of the Persian Empire (334–330 B.C.), and it seemed as though a Macedonian ruler might soon control the entire known world. But when Alexander died suddenly at the age of thirty-three (in 323 B.C.), his great empire fell apart, and his Successors fought over control of Macedonia for nearly half a century.

Finally, in the 270s B.C., Antigonus II

Gonatas, grandson of Antigonus I (one of Alexander's leading Successors) founded a stable Macedonian dynasty. The new Macedonian kingdom, which incorporated the old realm and parts of mainland Greece, prospered as one of the three major Hellenistic Greek states until the early second century B.C. Then Macedonia went to war against Rome, and King Philip V was decisively defeated by the Romans at Cynoscephalae in 197 B.C. Philip's son, Perseus, tried to reverse the kingdom's decline, but a Roman army crushed his forces at Pydna in 167, imprisoned him, and dismantled his realm. A few years later the Romans annexed the region outright and made it part of their rapidly growing empire.

SEE ALSO: Alexander III ("the Great"); Antigonus II Gonatas; Perseus, 2; Philip II; Philip V

Madness of Heracles

A tragic play by Euripides (also called simply *Heracles*), first performed in Athens circa 420–417 B.C. In the play, the famed hero and strongman Heracles (whom the Romans called Hercules) descends into the Underworld to capture Cerberus, the monstrous dog that guards the entrance to that dark realm. In his absence, a man named Lycus slays the king of Heracles' native city of Thebes. Lycus now threatens to kill Heracles' wife, Megara, and children. Fortunately for the family, Heracles returns from his trip and saves his family, killing Lycus in the process. But then the goddess Hera, who dislikes Heracles, orders Lyssa, goddess of madness, to make the strongman temporarily insane. In that frenzied state, he kills his wife and children. When he comes to his senses, he is naturally overcome with despair and considers suicide. At that moment, however,

Heracles' friend, the Athenian king Theseus (who slew the monstrous Minotaur), appears on the scene and argues that the murders were the fault of Hera, not Heracles. In the conclusion of the play, Theseus leads Heracles away toward Athens, where, Theseus says, "I will purify your hands from blood and provide you money and a house, and give you those possessions which my citizens gave me when I had killed the Minotaur." (*Madness of Heracles* 1322–1325)

SEE ALSO: Heracles; Minotaur; Theseus

Maenads

Also known as the Bacchae, the legendary maenads were fanatical female worshippers of the fertility god Dionysus. According to popular myths, they dressed in animal skins and roamed the countryside, singing, dancing, and killing and dismembering animals. In some stories they were female counterparts of male satyrs (rural characters who were half human and half goat). The most famous portrayal of these wild and dangerous maidens was that penned by Euripides in his play *The Bacchae*.

SEE ALSO: *Bacchae, The*; Dionysus; Orpheus

magic

Magic was practiced by the ancient Greeks, but it remains unclear to what degree and how much such practices overlapped with standard religious rituals. In general, in religious rituals people appealed to the gods to make something happen, whereas in magic people tried to make it happen themselves through some kind of supernatural means. It appears that magic and magicians were more common in early times—the Bronze and Dark ages. Certainly magicians and witches abound in the rich collection of myths that originated in those periods. For instance, the god Hermes and goddess Hecate were said to be skilled in magic, and Orpheus and Melampus were famous mythical human magicians. Well-known legendary witches or sorceresses included Circe (in Homer's *Odyssey*) and Medea (immortalized in Euripides' most famous play, named for her).

Magic may have been less widely practiced in the Classical and Hellenistic periods. Evidence shows that educated Greeks came to associate certain kinds of magic with quacks, con men, and/or culturally backward people. Plato and a number of other philosophers saw magic as an abusive practice that should be punished. Still, many Greeks were superstitious to one degree or another, and some apparently believed that magic rituals were effective. These rituals included chanting words and phrases thought to have supernatural power; manipulating objects (metal, wood, plants, animal parts, and many others) in set ways; destroying a person's fingernails, hair, or clothing for the purpose of bringing him or her harm (called sympathetic magic); wearing amulets to ward off evil; calling on the spirits of the dead for help (necromancy); and manipulating various magical spells or objects in an effort to acquire someone's love.

SEE ALSO: religion

Magna Graecia

A Latin term meaning "Great(er) Greece," it referred to the large group of Greek cities that sprang up in Italy in the eighth, seventh, and sixth centuries B.C.

SEE ALSO: colonization; Italy

Mantinea

A city located on the Ophis River in the southern region of the Peloponnesus. Mantinea sent some five hundred men to help Sparta's King Leonidas fortify the pass of Thermopylae against the invading Persians in 480 B.C. During much of the rest of that century, the Mantineans had troubled relations with two neighbors to the south—Tegea and Sparta. In 385 B.C. the Spartans dammed the Ophis, causing considerable destruction in Mantinea, which then came under Spartan control. But following Sparta's defeat by Thebes in 371, the Mantineans enjoyed independence once more and joined the new Arcadian League. Later Mantinea joined the Achaean League. Finally, in the second century B.C., the city, along with the rest of southern Greece, became subject to Rome.

SEE ALSO: Achaea; Arcadia; Battle of Mantinea

Mardonius

A Persian general who accompanied King Xerxes during the latter's invasion of Greece in 480 B.C. and commanded the Persian army in the Battle of Plataea.

SEE ALSO: Battle of Plataea; Greco-Persian Wars; Xerxes

marriage and divorce

In the Archaic and Classical ages, the majority of marriages in Athens, and presumably in most other Greek states, were arranged by fathers or other male family members, so many young brides and grooms did not know each well before their wedding night. Although romantic love, as it is known today, did exist, it was less common and/or not taken seriously by most people. Another custom common

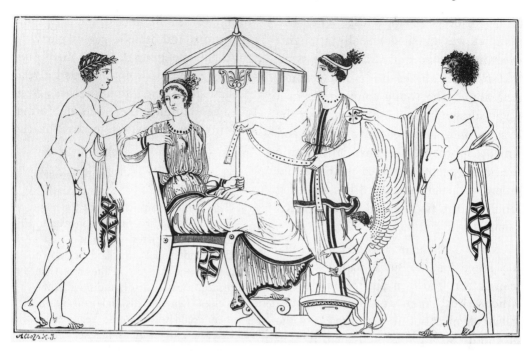

A drawing copied from an ancient Greek vase painting shows a young woman preparing for her wedding celebration. NORTH WIND PICTURE ARCHIVES

in ancient Greece but rare today was marriage between relatives. In Athens, from which most of the surviving evidence about ancient Greek marriage comes, it was acceptable for a half brother to marry his half sister; and marriages between male and female cousins and uncles and nieces occurred regularly. In large part, this was done to perpetuate family ties and keep any dowry monies within the immediate family. The dowry consisted of a sum of money, often substantial, given to the groom by the bride's father for the young woman's maintenance during the marriage. The negotiations over the dowry were conducted by the father and/or other leading men in the family. (The bride-to-be's father was her legal guardian, or *kyrios*, and her husband became her *kyrios* following the marriage.) The social ramifications of dowries could in some cases be far-reaching. For example, fathers of

minimal means might avoid raising many daughters because they could not afford to supply many dowries. So they were more likely to expose (leave outside to die) unwanted baby girls. Also, a man who was heavily in debt might view marriage to a woman with a substantial dowry as a way to raise needed funds. But if he used up the dowry money, he could be in trouble; if he later wanted a divorce, he was expected to return the dowry to his father-in-law.

As for the wedding celebration (*gamos*) in Athens, no complete or detailed descriptions have survived. But a general picture can be pieced together from various ancient sources. First, the two families offered a sacrifice to the deities who protected marriage, and the young woman gave up her toys and other childhood possessions. The families then decorated their homes with garlands and enjoyed a feast at the bride's father's house. When the banquet was finished, usually at night, everyone formed a wedding procession that marched to the bride and groom's new home. The young couple rode in a wagon drawn by mules or oxen, with the relatives and guests following on foot and singing appropriate hymns. On reaching the house, people showered the bride and groom with nuts and dried figs and sang loudly as the two headed for the bridal chamber.

Many of the marriages that began this way lasted for life. But as happens today, many others ended in divorce. In classical Athens, both men and women could initiate divorce, but the legal aspects of the procedure strongly favored men. A man who wanted a divorce could simply order his wife out of the house, and she usually returned to her father's house. A woman who desired a divorce had to get a male relative (or some other male citizen) to request permission from a government official. On the other hand, a woman's father could call for a divorce if he had evidence that her husband was abusing her or misusing her dowry. In the vast majority of divorces, the man got custody of the children. One of the main causes of divorce was adultery (*moicheia*), which was seen as a very serious offense because it cast doubt on the legitimacy of the children and brought shame on the entire family. A woman who committed adultery was disgraced, sometimes for the rest of her life, which made it difficult for her to find a second husband.

Marriage and divorce customs in most other Greek states were likely similar to those in Athens. But those in Sparta seem to have been a glaring exception (although very little is known about Spartan divorces). In Sparta, according to Plutarch,

young women paraded nude in public processions and athletic games partly to attract the attentions of young men. After a young man and woman formed a relationship and a marriage union was agreed to by the families, there was no formal wedding ceremony. Instead, Plutarch writes:

> The custom was to capture women for marriage. ... The so-called "bridesmaid" took charge of the captured girl. She first shaved her head to the scalp, then dressed her in a man's cloak and sandals, and laid her down alone on a mattress in the dark. The bridegroom ... first had dinner in the messes [i.e., with his male comrades], then would slip in, undo her belt, lift her and carry her to the bed. After spending only a short time with her, he would depart discreetly so as to sleep wherever he usually did along with the other young men. And this continued to be his practice thereafter. ... He would warily visit his bride in secret ... apprehensive in case someone in the house might notice him. His bride at the same time devised schemes and helped to plan how they might meet each other unobserved at suitable moments. It was not just for a short period that young men would do this, but for long enough that some might even have children before they saw their own wives in daylight. (*Life of Lycurgus* 15)

SEE ALSO: children; family; women

Massalia

Today the prominent port city of Marseille, on France's southern coast, Massalia (or Massilia) was established circa 600 B.C. by settlers from Phocaea in Greek Ionia (western Asia Minor). In time, the Massalians began trading with the natives of Gaul (now France) who lived along the Rhône

River. In exchange for grain and tin, the Greeks taught the local Gauls how to cultivate grapes and olives. Successful and prosperous, Massalia soon established colonies of its own on the coasts of Spain. This brought them into trade rivalry with Carthage, which controlled much of the western Mediterranean sphere. And it is not surprising that the Massalians made an alliance with Rome and backed the Romans against the Carthaginians in the Second Punic War (218–201 B.C.). Massalia remained independent until 49 B.C., when the powerful Roman general Julius Caesar captured it during his civil war with his chief rival, Pompey, whose side the Massalians had taken.

SEE ALSO: Carthage; Phocaea; Rome

Medea

In Greek mythology, an exotic sorceress who helped Jason and the Argonauts acquire the Golden Fleece, had children by Jason, and ended up murdering those children. Medea was the daughter of King Aeetes of Colchis (a city on the Black Sea), who had custody of the fleece. As told by Apollonius of Rhodes in his *Argonautica*, she fell in love with Jason and betrayed her father by making it possible for the Argonauts to steal the fleece. Medea then accompanied Jason in the voyage back to Iolcos in Thessaly where Jason's quest had begun. Eventually Medea and Jason were forced to flee from Iolcos to Corinth, where Euripides' play *Medea* picks up their story. Finding out that Jason no longer wants her and is planning to marry the daughter of the Corinthian king, the enraged Medea slays that king, his daughter, and her own children.

SEE ALSO: *Argonautica*; Jason; *Medea* (play)

Medea (play)

A tragic play by Euripides, first presented in Athens in 431 B.C. The play opens in Corinth, where Medea and Jason have recently fled with their two young children. (Hoping to help put Jason on the throne of Iolcos in Thessaly, she had engineered the killing of the reigning king, Pelias. But then Pelias's son, Acastus, accused Jason and Medea of murder and drove them from the city.) Medea has just discovered that Jason has decided to cast her aside and marry Glauce, daughter of Creon, king of Corinth. While Medea is hatching a scheme to get revenge on Jason, Creon tells her that she must take her children and leave Corinth. Jason offers Medea no pity, saying that her troubles are of her own making. She angrily reminds him that he could not have obtained the Golden Fleece if she had not risked everything and betrayed her own father. But Jason remains firm in his decision to marry Glauce.

Medea now puts her terrible plan in motion. She sends Glauce a beautiful crown and a dress spun of golden threads, pretending that these are wedding gifts. In reality, they are coated with poison. When the princess dons the crown and dress, the poison burns away her flesh, and when Creon tries to help her, the poison kills him, too. Then Medea slays her own children, believing this will cause Jason to be destroyed by grief. After committing these horrendous crimes, she escapes to Athens, where the local king Aegeus (father of the famous hero Theseus) gives her refuge.

SEE ALSO: *Argonautica*; Creon; Medea; Jason

Medusa

In Greek mythology, the most famous of the Gorgons, female creatures so hideous that anyone who gazed on them turned to stone. Some ancient myths claimed that Medusa started out as a lovely young woman, but then she had a sexual encounter with Poseidon, god of the seas, inside one of the goddess Athena's temples. The angry goddess punished the girl by turning her into a frightening gargoyle with skin like dried leather and hair made up of live snakes. One of the most famous of the Greek myths tells how the Greek hero Perseus slew Medusa by cutting off her head. At the time, she was pregnant with two of Poseidon's offspring, Pegasus, the flying horse, and a lowly creature named Chrysaor. Both managed to make their way out of her dead body.

SEE ALSO: Gorgons; Pegasus; Perseus, 1

Megara

A small but important Greek city located between the northern edge of the Saronic Gulf (an inlet of the Aegean Sea) and the Isthmus of Corinth. One of Greece's most ancient towns, it was founded during the Bronze Age and may for a while have been controlled by nearby Athens. Later, in Archaic times, the Megarans, now independent, established colonies on the island of Sicily and along the coasts of the Black Sea. By 500 B.C. Megara had joined Sparta's Peloponnesian League. And it was partly because of Athens's naval blockade of Megara in 432 B.C. that Sparta declared war on Athens, initiating the devastating Peloponnesian War. In the early third century B.C. Megara became part of the Macedonian kingdom, but in 243 the city joined the Achaean League.

SEE ALSO: Achaea; Peloponnesian War

Melos

One of the southernmost islands of the Cyclades group (lying north of Crete), Melos was known for its wide, deep harbor. It was also renowned for its supplies of obsidian (dark volcanic glass used to make weapons and cutting tools). Sometime in Greece's Dark Age (ca. 1100–800 B.C.), Sparta colonized Melos, and the island subsequently sent ships and troops to fight the Persians at the Battle of Salamis (480 B.C.). The Melians desired to remain neutral during the Peloponnesian War, but Athens refused to accept this and sent an army, which devastated the island, killed all the Melian men, and enslaved all the Melian women and children. Near the end of the war, Sparta liberated the island, which in the centuries that followed passed into the hands of the Macedonians and eventually the Romans.

SEE ALSO: Battle of Salamis; Cyclades; Sparta

Memorabilia

A major work by Xenophon the title of which is usually translated as *Memories of Socrates*. It was inspired in part by the author's former, youthful relationship with Socrates, the famous philosopher who was executed in Athens in 399 B.C. The work consists of four books, the first of which vigorously refutes the charges the Athenian government had brought against Socrates. Later Xenophon expounds on Socrates' sterling character, his views on education and various philosophical concepts, and his loyalty to his friends. It is interesting to note that Xenophon's descriptions of Socrates' opinions on some philosophical topics differ somewhat from those of Plato, who, as a young man, also associated with Socrates.

SEE ALSO: Plato; Socrates; Xenophon

Menander
(ca. 342 B.C.–ca. 292 B.C.)

A Greek comic playwright who dominated the theatrical period known as the New Comedy (ca. 320s–ca. 260 B.C.). An Athenian by birth, Menander is credited with writing more than a hundred plays. The only one that has survived complete is *The Bad-Tempered Man* (first discovered in 1958), although fair-sized portions of *The Arbitration, The Samian Women, The Shorn Girl, The Shield*, and a few others have been recovered. In addition, more than nine hundred quotations from Menander's plays exist in the works of other ancient writers. His comedies are a good deal tamer and less political than those of Aristophanes, chief exponent of the raucous Old Comedy. Menander's plots typically revolve around domestic settings, featuring young lovers trying to get together and clever slaves outwitting their masters. After his death he became widely popular among Roman audiences, and his works became models followed by the early Roman playwrights Plautus and Terrence.

SEE ALSO: Aristophanes, 1; *Bad-Tempered Man, The*; theater and drama

Menelaus

In Greek mythology, and in Homer's *Iliad*, a king of Sparta and husband of Helen of Troy. Menelaus and his brother, Agamemnon, were the sons of Atreus, king of Mycenae. When he was a young man, Menelaus was among the numerous suitors who vied for the hand of Helen, a Spartan princess. She selected Menelaus over the others, and after her father, King Tyndareos, died, Menelaus became king of Sparta. Later, after Helen ran off with Troy's Prince Paris, Menelaus and Agamemnon assembled a large army of Greeks (commanded by Agamemnon) to get her back. After a ten-year siege, the Greeks sacked Troy and Menelaus brought Helen back to Sparta, where they then led a more or less uneventful life.

SEE ALSO: Agamemnon; Helen; Troy

Messenia

The southwestern region of the Peloponnesus. In Greek mythology, one of the two fertile plains making up Messenia's heartland and the site of the kingdom of Pylos, ruled by King Nestor, one of the Greek commanders in the Trojan War. (Archaeology has revealed that in the Bronze Age Pylos was a real kingdom with a Mycenaean palace-citadel.) Beginning in the eighth century B.C., the Messenians fell on hard times as neighboring Sparta launched two invasions of their homeland (one beginning ca. 730, the other ca. 650). The conquest was complete by about 620 B.C., and one result was that the Spartans virtually enslaved the surviving Messenians. For nearly three centuries, the latter, now referred to as helots, did forced labor for the Spartans and endured terrible abuses. Then, in 369 B.C., shortly after Sparta's defeat at the hands of the Thebans at Leuctra, Thebes liberated Messenia. With the help of the Theban leader Epaminondas, the Messenians built a new city, Messene, and enjoyed an extended period of liberty and prosperity. Later, Messenia had to defend itself against Macedonia and the Achaean League before all three fell under the control of Rome in the second century B.C.

SEE ALSO: helots; Peloponnesus; Sparta

metalworking

The Greeks manufactured a large variety of products from a few basic metals, the most important of which were copper, bronze (an alloy of copper and tin), iron, lead, gold, silver, and electrum (a mixture of gold and silver). In most cases, these metals were derived from ores (mixtures of rock and metal) by smelting (heating and melting) the ores in fires or furnaces. Once in liquid form, the metals were poured into molds to make ingots that could be transported to shops and there transformed into weapons, figurines, utensils, jewelry, coins, or other useful products. Gold and silver (derived from an ore called galena), widely viewed as the most precious metals, were often refined (separated from various impurities) using a technique known as cupellation. Workers first crushed the ore into small particles, then heated these in a pottery container. Eventually the impurities separated out, leaving the gold or silver in the bottom of the container. The gold or silver could then be made into ingots or hammered into thin sheets, which were cut to make jewelry and other decorative products. A common by-product of smelting and refining silver was the less valuable metal lead, used for ship anchors, metal building clamps, and cheap jewelry. Iron was the most difficult metal for the Greeks (and other ancient peoples) to work with because their furnaces were not hot enough to turn it into a liquid. So a blacksmith heated the iron into a spongy mass and then hammered it repeatedly (reheating it when necessary), thereby slowly forcing it into the desired shape. Where holes were needed, he jabbed the hot iron mass with a pre-made iron punch (pointed utensil). Common iron products included knives, swords, spearheads, and nails.

From the Bronze Age through Hellenistic times, bronze was the most prevalent metal used in Greece. The copper needed to make bronze came mostly from a common ore called malachite. Tin, which was derived from the ore cassiterite, was extremely rare in the Mediterranean world, and most tin had to be obtained through traders who had connections with the then-primitive peoples of northern France and southern Britain. To make figurines, bowls, plates, cups, utensils, coins, tripods, and a myriad of other bronze items, Greek craftsmen employed various traditional casting (molding) techniques. In the easiest method, they poured smelted bronze into a stone mold, let the alloy harden, then removed the mold. In contrast, the "lost-wax" method required first making a wax model of the desired object and covering the wax with clay. When fired in a furnace, the clay hardened while the wax melted away, leaving hollow spaces inside the clay. The metalworker then poured liquid bronze into these spaces, and when the metal solidified, he removed the clay. A third technique, hollow casting, was used for making large, hollow bronze objects such as busts and statues. The metalworker made a clay core, surrounded it with a wax model of the object desired, then covered the wax with more clay. When heated, the wax melted, leaving hollow spaces conforming to the shape and details of the original wax model. These spaces were filled with molten bronze. And when the bronze hardened, the clay was removed, revealing the finished statue.

SEE ALSO: industry; mining; trade

Metamorphoses

Composed by the Roman poet Ovid (43 B.C.–A.D. 17), a long verse narrative that became one of the chief written sources preserving the major Greek myths. The work features more than two hundred tales, a majority of them derived from

Greek mythology, which had a profound influence on Roman mythology and religion. Among the myths Ovid covers are those that deal with the creation of the universe and humanity, the repopulation of the world after a great flood, the establishment of the Greek city of Thebes, the seizure of the Delphic Oracle by Apollo, the story of Jason and the quest for the Golden Fleece, Theseus's slaying of the monstrous Minotaur, the tragic tale of Orpheus and Eurydice, the Calydonian boar hunt, the death of the famous hero Heracles (or Hercules), episodes from the siege of Troy, and many more.

SEE ALSO: Heracles; Jason, 1; Theseus

Metaphysics

A group of manuscripts and lecture notes (also called *On Metaphysics*) written by Aristotle and later compiled and titled by the first-century B.C. Greek scholar Andronicus of Rhodes. Aristotle's own name for the work seems to have been *Primary Philosophy*. Consisting of fourteen books, the work covers a wide spectrum of topics relating to the substance, or essence, of the visible, tangible world. Notably, Aristotle proposes that an "unmoved mover" set the universe in motion. This can be, and often has been, interpreted as God, although in Aristotle's view the mover took no interest in the universe once it had come into existence. The most useful and noble activity humans can perform, Aristotle contends, is to imitate the mover by developing their minds and engaging in creative thought.

SEE ALSO: Aristotle; philosophy

metics

In ancient Athens, resident foreigners, including both non-Greeks and Greeks from other city-states. Most metics (*metoikoi*) were merchants or craftspeople, including weapons makers, potters, metalsmiths, jewelers, and so on. They were not Athenian citizens, so they could not vote in the Assembly or hold public office. But they regularly made important contributions to the community, such as providing essential goods and services, paying taxes, serving as backers (*choregoi*) for theatrical plays, and fighting in the army when needed. In a surviving court speech, one of the best-known metics, the orator Lysias, lists some of his family's contributions to the community: "We had produced the required dramas at the public festivals. We had paid many contributions [taxes] to the [state] treasury. We had conformed to law and order, and had done every duty imposed on us. . . . We had conducted ourselves far-better as aliens in this country than they [the Athenian tyrants who confiscated the family's possessions in 404 B.C.] had as natives." ("Against Eratosthenes" 20–21)

SEE ALSO: citizenship; Lysias; theater and drama

Midas

In Greek mythology, a king whose greed for gold caused his downfall. Midas was the ruler of Phrygia in central Asia Minor. The satyr Silenus granted his wish that everything he touched would turn into gold. But to his horror, the king saw that he might starve to death because even his food became gold when he touched it. The god Dionysus allowed Midas to free himself of this curse by plunging into a river, whose sands turned gold as his power was washed away, and he renounced wealth and splendor from then on. Another popular myth told how Midas was given donkey's ears by the god Apollo for choosing Pan over Apollo in a musical competition in which Midas was the judge.

SEE ALSO: Apollo; Pan; Silenus

Miletus

The southernmost major city of Greek Ionia and the leading city of that region in the Archaic and Classical eras. The Bronze Age inhabitants of Miletus may have migrated there from Crete, as both Minoan and Mycenaean ruins have been unearthed on the site. In the Archaic Age, the small town of Miletus grew into a thriving city thanks to shipping trade facilitated by four excellent natural harbors. Milesian merchants reached as far as Egypt and southern Italy. In the seventh and sixth centuries B.C., the Milesians also expanded their horizons by establishing colonies—possibly as many as sixty—mostly on the coasts of the Black Sea, the Propontis, and the Hellespont. In the mid-sixth century B.C. Miletus came under the sway of the kingdom of Lydia. Only a few years later the Persians defeated Lydia and made Miletus and the other Ionian cities its vassal states. It was a Milesian, Aristagoras, who led the failed Ionian rebellion against the Persians, which collapsed in 494 B.C. As a punishment, the Persians sacked Miletus, enslaved its women and children, and shipped its men to a spot on the Tigris River (in modern-day Iraq). Following the Greco-Persian Wars, however, the city rebounded and joined the Athenian-controlled Delian League. In 412 B.C., near the close of the Peloponnesian War, the Milesians switched sides and backed Athens's enemy, Sparta. Miletus fell once more to the Persians in the following century, but soon afterward it became part of the empire of Alexander the Great, who had conquered Persia. In Hellenistic times, the kingdoms of Alexander's Successors vied for control of Miletus until the city was absorbed into the Roman province of Asia in 133 B.C.

SEE ALSO: colonization; Greco-Persian Wars; Ionia

Miltiades
(ca. 540 B.C.–489 B.C.)

A prominent Athenian general best known for defeating the Persians at Marathon in 490 B.C., Miltiades came from a wealthy and distinguished Athenian family. His father, also named Miltiades, established an Athenian colony on the Thracian Chersonese, the long peninsula making up the eastern shore of the Hellespont. The area quickly became a sort of mini-empire, with the elder Miltiades the local dictator. The younger Miltiades took charge of the region in 514 B.C., shortly after his father's death. The following year Persia's King Darius I invaded Scythia (lying west of the Black Sea), and Miltiades may have served briefly as a military adviser to the Persians. However, in 499, when the cities of Greek Ionia rebelled against Darius, Miltiades took their side, and when the revolt collapsed in 494, he had to flee the Chersonese. Returning to Athens, Miltiades was prosecuted for running a dictatorship in the Chersonese in Athens's name. But he was acquitted and soon won election as one of Athens's ten generals (*strategoi*). When the Persians landed at Marathon in 490, Miltiades was chosen by his fellow generals to lead the city's militia of hoplites against the invaders. In the wake of the stunning Athenian victory, Miltiades was for a time honored as a hero. As Herodotus puts it, "After the slaughter at Marathon, the already high reputation of Miltiades in Athens was greatly increased." (*The Histories* 6.133) But less than a year later Miltiades fell from favor when his siege of the island of Paros failed. Again

Miltiades leads the Athenians and Plataeans into battle against the Persians on the plain of Marathon in 490 B.C. AKG-IMAGES

he was prosecuted, and although this time he was found guilty, he died a few days later from complications of a wound suffered in the siege. His son, Cimon, later became a leading Athenian statesman-general.

SEE ALSO: Battle of Marathon; Cimon; *strategos*

Mimnermus (flourished late 600s B.C.)

A lyric poet hailing from the city of Colophon in Greek Ionia (in western Asia Minor). He excelled at writing elegies, which at the time were poems of love and lament intended to be sung to flute music. The ancient elegy continued to develop and eventually matured in the literature of Hellenistic Alexandria and the early Roman Empire. Of the few surviving fragments of Mimnermus's works, the best known reads in part:

> What, then, is life if love the golden is gone? What is pleasure? Better to die when the thought of ... the flattery of surrender [and] the secret embrace in the darkness ... are lost from my heart. These alone are such charming flowers of youth as befall women and men. But once old age with its sorrows advances upon us, it makes a man feeble. ... Such is the thing of sorrow God has made of old age. (unnamed fragment)

SEE ALSO: Ionia; poetry

mining

The Greeks avidly mined gold, silver, copper, iron, and lead, which they extracted from ores. One of the richest mining regions in the Greek world was at Laurium (or Laurion), located in the southeastern sector of the Attic Peninsula. Evidence suggests that the Bronze Age (Mycenaean) Athenians mined there and that the site was abandoned some time during the Dark Age. Operations resumed later, and the peak period of exploitation was in the Classical Age, when Athens struck rich deposits of silver at Laurium in an ore called galena. The miners, who were condemned criminals and slaves, were usually shackled and poorly treated. The noted traveler Pausanias reported that by his day (the second century A.D.) extraction of silver at the site had ceased. Other important Greek mining areas included the Aegean islands of Siphnos in the Cyclades, Thasos in the northern Aegean, and the hills of Thrace. Some mines consisted of little more than a few crudely excavated tunnels; but others, including those at Laurium, featured extensive horizontal or tilted galleries, often only three to four feet (1.2m) high, along with access shafts up to three hundred feet (90m) deep. The ores were carried to ground level by slaves or were raised by windlasses. Workers then placed the ores in furnaces to heat them up and extract the metals.

SEE ALSO: Athens; industry; metalworking

Minoans

A culturally advanced non-Greek-speaking people who inhabited Crete and interacted with the Mycenaean Greeks in Greece's Bronze Age. Beginning circa 2000 B.C. the Minoans (named by modern scholars after the mythical Cretan king Minos) built a sophisticated and prosperous civilization that supported itself through a combination of trade and agriculture. Minoan traders ranged as far as Egypt and Palestine and set up trading posts and small colonies on islands in the Aegean Sea. (The town of Akroteri, on the island of Thera, may have begun as one of these posts or colonies.)

On Crete itself, the Minoans built several large palace-centers. These sprawling structures served as administrative centers for the Minoans' collective agricultural system and as the focus of state religious worship. When he excavated the palace-center at Knossos in northern Crete in the early twentieth century, British archaeologist Arthur Evans found tablets bearing two separate writing systems. He called one script Linear A and the other Linear B. It was later shown that Linear A (which is still largely undeciphered) was a rudimentary written form of the Minoan language; Linear B was an expression of the early form of Greek spoken by the Mycenaeans.

In fact, it appears that the Minoans long exerted strong cultural and perhaps political influence over the Mycenaeans, who lived on the Greek mainland. The Mycenaeans adopted Minoan styles of dress and other customs. Eventually the Mycenaeans grew strong enough to invade and gain control of Crete, an event (or perhaps a series of expeditions) that occurred sometime in the 1400s B.C. Evidence suggests that part of the Mycenaeans' success was the result of a marked decline in Minoan power caused by the destructive effects of the huge eruption of the volcano on Thera in the century or so preceding the invasion of Crete. After the Mycenaean takeover of Crete, the surviving Minoans likely became Mycenaean subjects who, along with their masters, faded into obscurity and lost their heritage in the early Dark Age.

SEE ALSO: Akroteri; Atlantis; Crete; Knossos

Minos

In Greek mythology, a famous king of Crete. Legends said that Minos's wife had sex with a bull, giving rise to the monstrous Minotaur, a creature half man and half bull. To house the beast, Minos ordered the Greek inventor Daedalus to erect the mazelike labyrinth. Eventually the Athenian hero Theseus defeated Minos, captured his capital of Knossos, and slew the Minotaur. After Minos died, Zeus, leader of the gods, made him one of the judges of the Underworld. Minos's name also lives on in the term *Minoan*, coined in the early 1900s by British archaeologist Arthur Evans to describe the people who built a sophisticated civilization on Crete in the Bronze Age.

SEE ALSO: Crete; Daedalus; Knossos

Minotaur

In Greek mythology, a hideous, ferocious creature with a bull's head and a man's body that dwelled in a mazelike structure called the labyrinth. Ancient stories claimed that the Minotaur was the product of the mating of a bull with Pasiphae, wife of Minos, king of Crete. Minos confined the creature in the labyrinth, built by the Greek inventor Daedalus, and for a long time the Minotaur devoured Athenian captives fed to it by Minos. Finally Theseus, son of Athens's King Aegeus, sailed to Crete, made his way into the labyrinth, and destroyed the bull-man.

SEE ALSO: Daedalus; Knossos; Theseus

money

Although the Greeks did not have formal monetary currencies before the seventh century B.C., long before that they engaged in trade, earned livings, and supported both through barter (exchanging goods of comparable value). In time, many Greeks substituted generic instruments of value for some or all barter goods. The chief instruments were bars, ingots, or rods of metal, most commonly silver or iron. Several silver bars together composed a "talent" and a handful of iron rods (*oboloi*) made up a drachma. *Oboloi* remained in use as late as 500 B.C. (and even later in Sparta), although most Greek states began using coins in the early 500s B.C. after borrowing the idea from their neighbors, the Lydians, who seem to have invented it.

The first Greek state to mint coins was Aegina (an island in the Saronic Gulf, not far from Athens), in about 595 B.C. The Aeginetans had three silver coins—the obol, the more valuable drachma, and the still more valuable stater, which bore the image of the city's symbol, the turtle. Athens and Corinth soon developed coins of their own, and within a century or so most major Greek states were minting their own coins. Thus, there was no standard currency for all Greeks, and traders and travelers often had to exchange foreign currencies, a job done by local bankers in each state.

Many coins became not only instruments of value but also works of art and means of advertising the power and prestige of the minting cities. Anyone who saw an Athenian coin, for instance, knew where it came from because it was proudly stamped with the image of an owl, symbol of the city's patron goddess, Athena. Similarly, Corinth's coins featured the mythical flying horse Pegasus. In time, coins also came to show the faces of Greek rulers, especially the coins minted by the large Greek kingdoms in the Hellenistic

Age. The ones that survive are an important source of evidence for what these persons looked like.

Although no Greek money was ever minted for use by all Greeks, in the Classical Age Athenian currency was highly valued and accepted in trade and finance across most of the Mediterranean world. Athens's monetary system was based on the obol and the silver drachma. Six obols equaled one drachma, and one hundred drachmas were equivalent to one mina. Sixty minae (or six thousand drachmas) equaled one talent. Minae and talents were represented by bars of silver, as in earlier times, rather than by coins. Other common Athenian coins included the didrachm (equal to two drachmas), tetradrachm (four drachmas), pentadrachm (five drachmas), and diobol (two obols). The practical worth of these coins in the Classical Age varied over time and is now difficult to reckon. But in general, a rower in the Athenian navy or a common laborer or craftsman made one or two drachmas per day. Skilled workers, like doctors and sculptors, earned two to three times as much. A gallon of olive oil cost about five or six drachmas, a sheep about twelve drachmas, a medium-priced slave two hundred to three hundred drachmas, and a townhouse in Athens four hundred to one thousand drachmas depending on its size and condition.

SEE ALSO: banking; trade; weights and measures

Moralia

One of Plutarch's most important and influential works (along with his *Parallel Lives*), the *Moralia* (*Moral Essays*) consists of a large number of individual essays covering a wide range of subjects. Some, such as "On Busy-Bodies," "How to Distinguish a Flatterer from a Friend," and "Advice to Married Couples," deal with social or family issues. Others deal more directly with moral and/or philosophical issues, including religious ones. Among the more engaging of these are "On Superstition," "On the Delays of Divine Justice," and "On the Cessation of Oracles." A few of the essays in the collection were written by lesser-known writers shortly after Plutarch's death, including "On Fate," and "The Doctrines of the Philosophers." The *Moralia* survived antiquity and was widely read by educated people in late medieval times. First translated into English in 1603, it remains a treasure trove of information about the social and moral traditions of the Greco-Roman world in which Plutarch lived.

SEE ALSO: Plutarch

Muses

In Greek mythology, nine minor goddesses who supposedly inspired poets, musicians, painters, and other artists and intellectuals. Their names were Calliope, Clio, Euterpe, Melpomene, Terpsichore, Erato, Polyhymnia, Urania, and Thalia. Shrines dedicated to them existed all over Greece, the leading ones on the slopes of Mt. Olympus in Thessaly and Mt. Helicon in Boeotia. Greek writers and artists often invoked the aid or creative spirit of the Muses, as in the case of Hesiod in the opening lines of his *Theogony* and Homer at the start of his great epic the *Odyssey*: "Sing in me, Muse, and through me tell the story of that man . . . the wanderer [Odysseus]." (*Odyssey* 1.1–3)

SEE ALSO: Helicon, Mt.; Hesiod; Orpheus

Museum

A university-like institution built in Alexandria (in Egypt) by the early Ptolemaic rulers, it housed some of the greatest scientists and scholars of the ancient world.

SEE ALSO: Alexandria; Ptolemy, Claudius; science

music and dance

The ancient Greeks loved music and used it in one form or another in numerous areas of their lives. They sang and/or played music at religious festivals, especially in processions; at weddings and funerals; in plays, each of which had a chorus that sang or recited to music; in athletic and musical competitions; and even on the battlefield. One of the more common instruments that produced the music for these activities was the lyre, a type of harp that was played by plucking its strings with a small pick called a plectrum. Also popular was the *aulos*, a woodwind instrument. Similar to a modern oboe, an *aulos* had a thin reed that vibrated when the player blew on it. Because most Greek men learned to play the lyre in school, they could entertain themselves and others at parties and in other settings. The most talented musicians in a family probably played at weddings, birth celebrations, clan gatherings, and so forth. And as Xenophon described it in his *Symposium*, expert musicians were frequently hired for dinner and drinking parties. Some of the more accomplished players took part in public athletic competitions. Surviving vase paintings show *aulos* players providing musical accompaniment to the athletes as they ran, jumped, boxed, and wrestled. Also, the victory odes composed by poets like Pindar for winning athletes were performed by groups of musicians and singers. In addition, there were songs of praise, drinking songs, sad songs for funeral processions, and battle hymns sung by soldiers marching toward the enemy. Regarding the latter, the playwright Aeschylus describes the Greek sailors singing as they bore down on the Persian ships in the Battle of Salamis: "From the Greek ships rose like a song of joy the piercing battle-cry." Greeks standing on the shore then took up the tune. The sound of tens of thousands of voices raised in enthusiastic song disquieted the enemy fighters: "The Persians knew their error; fear gripped every man. They were no fugitives who sang that terrifying battle hymn, but Greeks charging with courageous hearts to battle." (*The Persians* 389–394)

Dancing often went hand in hand with music in ancient Greece. People danced at religious ceremonies, weddings, harvest celebrations, theatrical plays, feasts, and so forth. Many of these dances had colorful names, such as "The Itch," "Stealing the Meat," "Setting the World on Fire," and "Knocking at the Door." How most of these dances were performed has been lost. But some of the moves of a popular Spartan dance have survived in a passage from one of Lucian's works, appropriately titled *Dance*. And Plato describes the "warrior dance," a combination of athletics and artistic expression in which a team of nude young men carrying spears and shields went through a complex series of precision moves in unison: "The warrior dance . . . imitates the modes of avoiding blows and missiles by dropping or giving way, or springing aside, or rising up or falling down; [it] also . . . [features] the imitation of archery and the hurling of javelins, and all sorts of blows." (*Laws* Book 7)

SEE ALSO: education; lyre; theater and drama

A reconstruction of the Bronze Age citadel at Mycenae shows the so-called grave circle (lower right) and royal palace (upper left). AKG-IMAGES

Mycenae

Probably the leading city of the Mycenaean Greek civilization that thrived on the Greek mainland in the Bronze Age and the focus of numerous important myths that derive from that era. In fact, modern scholars named that ancient people after the town. Archaeological evidence shows that Mycenae, located in the northeastern Peloponnesus on the northern edge of the Argive plain, was inhabited by non-Greek-speakers in the late Stone Age and early Bronze Age. In about 2100 B.C. (or somewhat later) the Greek-speakers, now called Mycenaeans, arrived and in time erected a royal residence atop the local acropolis. In the 1600s and 1500s B.C. royal shaft graves (now labeled Grave Circles A and B) containing gold masks, finely wrought weapons, and other valuables, were dug on the hill.

In the period in which Mycenaean civilization reached its height—ca. 1400–ca. 1200 B.C.—an imposing stone palace-citadel surrounded by massive limestone walls rose on the acropolis. Particularly notable was the so-called Lion Gate. More than 10 feet (3m) high, the portal is topped by a monumental sculpture of two lions guarding a sacred pillar, an image that may have been prominent in Mycenaean royal or religious art. This mighty palace dominated the region and may have exerted political influence over other Mycenaean centers. It likely produced the rulers whose exploits gave rise to the familiar stories about the House of Atreus, Agamemnon, Clytemnestra, Electra, Orestes, and other famous mythical characters.

Like other Mycenaean towns, Mycenae was sacked and burned, perhaps more than once, in about 1200 B.C. and rapidly declined. The causes of this wave of destruction are still unclear. But a credible recent theory (by Vanderbilt University scholar Robert Drews) suggests that marauders from southeastern Europe invaded and looted the entire eastern Mediterranean region. By 1100 B.C. at the latest, Mycenae's citadel stood ruined and largely deserted. Thereafter much of it lay exposed. And in the Archaic and Classical ages many Greeks concluded that the enormous blocks of stone making up its walls were hauled into place by the Cyclopes, mythical one-eyed giants. Modern study of Mycenae began in the 1870s, when noted German archaeologist Heinrich Schliemann (who also excavated Troy) began excavating in and around the ruined fortress.

SEE ALSO: Agamemnon; Mycenaeans; Troy

Mycenaeans

The name used by modern scholars to describe the Greek-speakers who inhabited mainland Greece in the second half of the Bronze Age. The name comes from *Mycenae*, a town in the northeastern Peloponnesus where these early Greeks erected an imposing palace-fortress. The original homeland of the Mycenaeans is uncertain. But it appears that they came from somewhere north of the Greek peninsula and descended into it in waves beginning circa

2100 B.C. or somewhat later. They worshipped a strong male deity, Zeus, and over time built religious sanctuaries dedicated to him and other gods that were destined to survive the Bronze Age and enjoy worship in later eras of ancient Greece.

For centuries the Mycenaeans were illiterate and generally culturally backward in contrast to the Minoans, the non-Greek-speakers who held sway in Crete and the Aegean Islands. The mainlanders adopted Minoan styles of dress, artistic motifs, and other customs and ideas and may at one time or another have been politically subservient to the islanders. At first the Mycenaeans supported themselves almost entirely through agriculture and may have adopted a collective system similar to that of the Minoans. Most of the mainlanders were peasant farmers. In addition to the crops needed to sustain themselves, they produced a surplus, which the local ruler's officials collected, stored, and distributed as they saw fit. Eventually Mycenaean society supported a small class of craftspeople and merchants, whose labors were also regulated and exploited by the central administration. Overseeing everything was a leader called the *wanax*, perhaps the title used by the Mycenaean kings.

Apparently by the fifteenth century B.C., the Mycenaeans had established several small kingdoms in the southern reaches of the Greek mainland. Each was eventually dominated by a large palace-citadel built from huge limestone blocks. In addition to the most famous and perhaps most powerful one at Mycenae, these power centers included Tiryns, not far south of Mycenae; Pylos, on the southwestern coast of the Peloponnesus; Athens, on the Attic Peninsula; and Thebes and Orchomenus in Boeotia, north of Attica. Circa 1400 B.C.

armies from one or more of these kingdoms invaded Minoan Crete. They sacked Knossos and other Cretan towns and for about two centuries thereafter controlled the Aegean region. In this period, which marked their zenith, the Mycenaeans supplemented their agricultural system with seaborne trade, as they essentially took over some or all of the existing Minoan trade routes. In Egypt, painted images of Aegean merchants (whom the Egyptians called Keftiu) were retouched to show changes in costume, perhaps reflecting the Mycenaean takeover of Crete.

Mycenaean dominance of the Aegean sphere was relatively short-lived, however. Between 1200 and perhaps 1120 B.C. all of the Mycenaean palace-citadels were attacked and burned, never to be rebuilt. Some of the theories advanced by scholars to explain this upheaval include civil conflicts, economic collapse, and invasion by tribal peoples migrating from the north and east. Classical historian Robert Drews of Vanderbilt University contends that military innovations among the peoples living on the northern periphery of the eastern Mediterranean allowed them to defeat the chariot corps of the Bronze Age kingdoms and then pillage and loot at will.

What seems more certain is that, in the wake of the collapse of Greece's Bronze Age culture, garbled memories of the kings, queens, and other prominent figures of Mycenaean civilization inspired many of the characters in the now-familiar Greek myths. These included the stories about Agamemnon's sacrifice of his daughter Iphigenia, his subsequent murder by his wife, Clytemnestra, and her own death by the hands of her son Orestes. The most famous collection of these myths, surrounding the events of the Trojan War, may have been based on distorted recollections of one or more Mycenaean raids on the city of Troy in northwestern Asia Minor.

SEE ALSO: Agamemnon; Mycenae; Orchomenus; Pylos; Thebes; Tiryns

Myron
(flourished ca. 480 B.C.–430 B.C.)

One of the leading sculptors of Greece's Classical Age. Hailing from the Attic town of Eleutherae, Myron worked mainly in bronze, unlike his younger contemporary Phidias, who specialized in stone sculpture. Of Myron's many statues, the most renowned today is the *Discus Thrower* (*Discobolus*). The original is lost, but marble copies made by later ancient sculptors have survived. In ancient times, however, his most famous creation was a bronze cow that stood in Athens's Agora (or possibly on the Acropolis).

SEE ALSO: metalworking; Phidias; sculpture

mystery religions

Religious cults, such as that of the goddess Demeter, that featured secret ceremonies and/or initiations and promised salvation in the afterlife for devoted followers.

SEE ALSO: Demeter; Eleusis; Isis; Orphism; Osiris

Mytilene

The main city and port on the Greek island of Lesbos (situated near the northwestern coast of Asia Minor). Little is known about the original, non-Greek inhabitants. During Greece's Dark Age, the port became an important way station for colonizers moving from the Greek mainland to Asia Minor. And by the late seventh century B.C., at the height of the Archaic

Age, Mytilene had become one of the major cities of Greek Ionia. In this era the city became famous as the home of two great poets—Alcaeus and Sappho. In his works, Alcaeus describes the events surrounding the dictatorship of Pittacus (ca. 590–580 B.C.), who managed to keep the city's opposing factions from launching a civil war. (Pittacus was later called one of Greece's Seven Sages.) In the late sixth century B.C. Mytilene languished under Persian domination. But after the expulsion of the Persians in 479, the city rebounded and became a member of the Delian League. Later, during the Pelopon-nesian War, Mytilene rebelled twice against Athens, which dominated the league. During the second revolt, the Athenians voted to destroy Mytilene and ships and troops departed to carry out this grim mission. Soon, however, the Athenians had a change of heart and sent messengers to rescind the order. In Hellenistic times, Mytilene was ruled by various large Greek states, notably Pergamum. And when the Pergamene king Attalus III gave the Romans his kingdom in his will in 133 B.C., Mytilene became part of Rome's growing empire.

SEE ALSO: Lesbos; Pergamum; Sappho

Naxos

This largest member of the Cyclades (the island group lying north of Crete) is also the most fertile. Its fine local marble quarries made it an important source of statuary from the Bronze Age through Archaic and Classical times. During the Archaic Age the island was ruled by aristocrats and tyrants, but by the start of the Classical Age a democratic government had taken charge. The Persians sacked Naxos on their way to attack Athens in 490 B.C. But after the conclusion of the Greco-Persian Wars, the island recovered and joined the Delian League. Another Greek island-state—Rhodes—briefly had control of Naxos before Rome's subjugation of Greece in the second century B.C.

SEE ALSO: Cyclades; Delian League

Nemean Games

Important athletic and musical contests held every two years as part of a major religious festival of the god Zeus at Nemea, not far south of Corinth. For details on these and other similar competitions in ancient Greece, **see** athletics.

Neoplatonism

A philosophical school and movement that utilized a number of earlier Greek philosophical concepts, especially certain ideas expounded by Plato, and then added certain elements of mysticism. Established by Plotinus in the third century A.D., Neoplatonism was built mostly around a ver-

sion of Plato's ideal form of goodness. Plotinus and his followers proposed that the underlying substance of the universe is a sort of mystical chain of being, in a sense an ascending ladder of realities, with pure goodness—called the "One"—occupying the highest rung on the ladder. Just below this supreme level is "Mind," essentially thought or intellect, a high degree of which is needed to perceive and strive for the One. By applying oneself to learning and meditation in a very disciplined manner, Plotinus said, a human being might eventually attain the higher levels of the ladder of realities.

SEE ALSO: Plato; Plotinus

Neoptolemus

In Greek mythology, the son of Achilles, the leading Greek warrior who fought at Troy, and one of the soldiers who hid inside the Trojan Horse. Following Achilles' demise, the captured Trojan prince Helenus, who could see into the future, told the Greeks that their siege of Troy would fail unless Neoptolemus was present. The problem was that Neoptolemus was at that moment living on the Aegean island of Skyros. So a delegation of Greeks, the famous Odysseus among them, traveled to Skyros to fetch him. Later, after Neoptolemus and his comrades climbed out of the Trojan Horse and opened the city's gates for the Greek army, he found and killed Troy's ruler, Priam. On returning to Greece, Neoptolemus took two captives with him—Helenus and Andromache, widow of the Trojan hero Hector. One ancient myth claimed that Neoptolemus was eventually slain by Orestes, son of Agamemnon (leader of the expedition to Troy).

SEE ALSO: Achilles; Helenus; Troy

Nestor

In Greek mythology, as well as in Homer's *Iliad*, a king of Pylos (in the southwestern Peloponnesus) and one of the leaders of the Greek attack on Troy. Already an old man when the Trojan War commenced, Nestor acted as a senior statesman, adviser, and dispenser of wisdom to the other Greek leaders. After Troy's fall, he returned to Pylos. There, according to Homer in the *Odyssey*, Odysseus's son, Telemachus, came and questioned Nestor about Odysseus's whereabouts.

SEE ALSO: Odysseus; Pylos; Troy

New Comedy

A period of Greek, especially Athenian, theater and drama lasting roughly from the 320s to 260 B.C. Its chief practitioner was the comic playwright Menander.

SEE ALSO: Menander; theater and drama

Nichomachean Ethics

A celebrated treatise written by the Athenian philosopher and scholar Aristotle circa 350 B.C. The main points of discussion in the work are the proper uses of human activity and the nature of moral virtue. The main object of human conduct, Aristotle argues, should be the achievement of happiness, which he broadly defines as the attainment of an understanding of universal truth. Happiness can be attained by developing the intellect so that one can gain wisdom. Part of the happy, good life, Aristotle says, involves displaying moral virtue. This can be acquired by living always in moderation, seeking knowledge and truth, and practicing self-discipline. The treatise also argues that politics plays a key role in the attainment of happiness, for only through being active in politics can citizens create a society that makes striving for the happy life feasible.

SEE ALSO: Aristotle; Nichomachus

Nicias
(ca. 470 B.C.–413 B.C.)

An Athenian statesman best known for his opposition to the rabble-rousing politician Alcibiades and his failed leadership in the disastrous Sicilian expedition. Nicias grew wealthy from silver mining and in time became active in politics. Though a democrat and backer of Pericles' policies, he lacked Pericles' outgoing personality and tended to be timid around others. After Pericles died in 429 B.C., Nicias reluctantly became leader of the democratic party, which opposed the right-wing faction led by Cleon. Nicias opposed continuing to fight Sparta in the Peloponnesian War. But as long as the pro-war Cleon maintained a strong following, Nicias was unable to gain enough support for pursuing peace. In 422 B.C., however, Cleon died and Nicias was able to negotiate a peace treaty, which became known as the Peace of Nicias in his honor.

But the peace did not last long because the unprincipled Alcibiades, who hated both Nicias and the Spartans, got the Athenians to ignore Nicias's treaty and renew the war. Alcibiades also convinced the Assembly to send a military expedition to conquer Syracuse in Sicily. Although Nicias objected vehemently, he was overruled and became even more disturbed when his countrymen placed him in joint command of the expedition with Alcibiades. As Plutarch puts it, "The people considered that Nicias's experience made him all the more essential to the enterprise and that his caution would provide a most valuable safeguard against Alcibiades' dar-

A nineteenth-century painting depicts the Oreads: in Greek mythology, a group of mountain nymphs. GIRAUDON/ART RESOURCE, NY

ing." (*Life of Nicias* 12) On the way to Sicily Alcibiades defected to Sparta, however, leaving Nicias, an indecisive, mediocre general, in charge of the expedition. Partly because of Nicias's poor judgment (and partly due to rash decisions made by other Athenian generals), the venture turned into a catastrophe. The Athenian fleet was defeated in Syracuse's harbor, and the surviving sailors and soldiers were killed or captured while fleeing across the Sicilian countryside. Nicias was summarily executed.

SEE ALSO: Alcibiades; Cleon; Syracuse

Nicomachus

Little is known about the life of this son of the famous Athenian philosopher Aristotle. One of the latter's works—the *Nico-*

machean Ethics—bears the younger man's name. But it is unclear whether this was because Aristotle dedicated the work to his son or because Nicomachus edited it following Aristotle's death.

SEE ALSO: Aristotle; *Nichomachean Ethics*

Nike

The Greek goddess of victory. Ancient sculptors produced numerous statues of Nike, most often giving her wings. Among the leading examples of these sculptures was one erected at Delphi by the Athenians following the Greek naval victory at Salamis in 480 B.C.; a six-foot-tall (1.8m) statue of Nike mounted in the open hand of Phidias's great statue of Athena inside the Parthenon; and most famous of all, the Nike of Samothrace (now in the Louvre Museum in Paris), carved circa 200 B.C.

SEE ALSO: Parthenon; Phidias; Samothrace

novel

The Greek novel, forerunner of the modern novel, developed during the Hellenistic Age and became particularly popular in Greece's Roman Period (30 B.C.–A.D. 476).

SEE ALSO: Alexandrian and other Hellenistic Greek literature

nymphs

In Greek mythology and religion, minor Greek goddesses who inhabited or personified various aspects of nature. It was thought that most nymphs were the offspring of Zeus, leader of the Olympian gods, or the daughters of various Titans (the primeval race of gods defeated by the Olympians). For example, the Titan Atlas supposedly gave rise to three groups of nymphs—the Hesperides, Hyades, and Pleiades. And two other Titans, Oceanus and

Tethys, produced the sea nymphs called Oceanids. Other groups of nymphs included the Meliae (tree nymphs), Oreads (mountain nymphs), and Naiads (nymphs of lakes, rivers, and springs). Greek and Roman artists and writers usually pictured these deities as beautiful young women who traveled with and/or had love affairs with various other gods.

SEE ALSO: Atlas; Titans; Zeus

Nyx

In Greek mythology, one of the primeval natural forces that emerged from Chaos at the beginning of time. Nyx was also seen as the goddess of night. According to ancient accounts, she gave rise to Ker, god of doom; Thanatos, god of death; Nemesis, goddess of vengeance; Hypnos, god of sleep; Eris, goddess of strife; and the three Fates, deities thought to influence people's destinies. Nyx was also the mother of many nymphs (minor nature goddesses).

SEE ALSO: Chaos; Fates; nymphs

obol

A small silver Athenian coin (*obolos*) as well as a small measure of weight.

SEE ALSO: money; weights and measures

Ocean

In Greek mythology, but also in various works by Greek geographers, a river that supposedly encircled the land portions of Earth. All the world's rivers were said to flow, either above or below the ground, from the Ocean, and Greek writers spoke about exotic islands in the Ocean where weird or dangerous creatures dwelled.

SEE ALSO: *Geography*; Oceanus

Oceanus

A Titan who ruled the Ocean, a wide stream that the ancients thought encircled the land portions of Earth. Oceanus mated with his sister, Tethys, to produce numerous sea deities and nymphs, including some three thousand Oceanids. One famous myth about Oceanus involved his interaction with the renowned strongman Heracles. The god loaned Heracles a large golden bowl in which the man rode across the surface of the Ocean and reached a remote island inhabited by the monster Geryon.

SEE ALSO: Heracles; Ocean; Titans

Odes

A notable collection of poems honoring victorious athletes, composed in the fourth century B.C. by Pindar. Each ode bears one of four titles—"Olympian," "Pythian," "Isthmian," or "Nemean"—and a number (e.g., the "Fourth Nemean Ode" or the "Tenth Olympian Ode"). The names indicate which of Greece's four main athletic venues the honored athlete had competed in, and the numbers identify specific poems for specific athletes. Forty-five of Pindar's victory odes (*epinikia*) have survived. As a rule, the athletes or their families hired the poet to write them, and choirs, accompanied by musicians, performed them in the athletes' native cities. The poems are not only literarily valuable, but also contain numerous references to mythical characters, places, and events. In this passage, for instance, Pindar alludes to the famous episode in which Jason, who sought the Golden Fleece, yoked some fire-breathing bulls in a dangerous test imposed on him by Aeetes, king of Colchis: "When Aeetes dragged forth the metal plow . . . and the oxen who breathed from yellow nostrils a flame of burning fire, and hoof after bronze-shod hoof ripped up the burning ground, he [Jason], grasping the plow, harnessed the oxen's necks . . . and speechless through his grief, Aeetes howled in amazement at [Jason's] might." ("Fourth Pythian Ode" 222–241)

SEE ALSO: Jason, 1; Pindar; poetry

Odysseus

In Greek mythology, king of the island kingdom of Ithaca and the main character of Homer's *Odyssey*. Odysseus left his wife, Penelope, and young son, Telemachus, in Ithaca and accompanied Agamemnon, Menelaus, and other Greeks to Troy. The cleverest of these leaders, Odysseus thought up the idea of smuggling Greek soldiers into Troy by concealing them inside a hollow wooden horse. As Homer tells it, following the city's fall Odysseus's ships were blown off course and he wandered far and wide for ten years, having many harrowing and exotic adventures and encountering a number of gods along the way. Eventually Odysseus made it back to Ithaca and his family.

SEE ALSO: Ithaca; *Odyssey*; Penelope; Telemachus

Odyssey

One of the two great epic poems thought to have been composed by the eighth-century B.C. poet Homer and one of the world's most famous and beloved adventure tales. The story begins ten years after the Greeks—among them Odysseus, king of Ithaca—have sacked Troy. Odysseus is trapped on the uncharted island of Ogygia, where the nymph Calypso has kept him captive for seven years. Meanwhile, back in Ithaca, his wife, Penelope, and his now-grown son, Telemachus, are among only a few who believe he might still be alive. Several suitors vie with one another for Penelope's hand, each hoping to become king of Ithaca. Odysseus finally manages to escape from Calypso's island by building a raft. But then Poseidon, god of the seas, causes the raft to capsize. As Homer tells it, "The god of earthquake heaved a wave against him high as a rooftree and of awful gloom. . . . When [a] gigantic billow struck, the boat's big timbers flew apart. Odysseus clung to a single beam, like a jockey riding [a horse]." (*Odyssey* 5.365–371) After the tempest, Odysseus washes ashore in the land of the Phaeacians, a happy people ruled by King Alcinous. At a banquet given by Alcinous, Odysseus tells the story of the adventures he has had since departing Troy.

On the way back across the Aegean Sea, Odysseus recalls, he and his men stopped in the land of the Lotus-eaters, who ate a local fruit that made them lazy and forgetful. He had to forcefully drag his men away to keep them from staying there forever. Next, the band of Greeks arrived on the island of the Cyclopes (one-eyed giants), where Odysseus and some of his men became trapped in the cave of a Cyclops named Polyphemus. The giant killed and ate many of the captives. "No pity came from him," Odysseus remembers. "In one stride he clutched at my companions and caught two in his hands like squirming puppies to beat their brains out, spattering the floor. Then he dismembered them and made his meal, gaping and crunching like a mountain lion—everything: innards, flesh, and marrow bones. We cried aloud, lifting our hands to Zeus." (*Odyssey* 9.287–294) Finally, however, the resourceful Odysseus concocted a plan to blind Polyphemus and escape. Unfortunately for Odysseus, though, Polyphemus was a son of Poseidon, who later got revenge by sinking Odysseus's raft. As their journey continued, Odysseus and his companions had another encounter with giants, who destroyed eleven of Odysseus's twelve ships. The last surviving vessel made it to the remote island of the sorceress Circe. She changed Odysseus's men into pigs, while he himself was protected by a special herb provided by the god Hermes. After a year, Circe released the Greeks, who next landed on the shore of the Ocean (the river surrounding Earth). There, several shades (spirits), including those of Achilles and Ajax, greatest of the Greek warriors who fought at Troy, rose up from the Underworld and spoke with Odysseus. Ajax was still angry with Odysseus for acquiring Achilles' armor, which Ajax had badly wanted for himself, following Achilles' death at Troy. Odysseus called on Ajax's shade to let bygones be bygones. "But he [Ajax] gave no reply, and turned away, following other ghosts toward Erebos. Who knows if in that darkness he might still have spoken, and I answered?" (*Odyssey* 11.562–565) Finally, Odysseus and his remaining men barely made it past the monsters Scylla and Charybdis and the island of the Sirens, deadly female creatures whose songs lured sailors to their deaths. After the last of Odysseus's ships was destroyed and the rest of his men lost, he landed on Calypso's island and spent seven years there against his will.

Having enjoyed Odysseus's story about his eventful travels, the Phaeacians give him a small boat, in which he sails to Ithaca. Aided by the goddess Athena, he disguises himself as an old beggar and reveals his true identity only to his son, Telemachus, and a faithful servant. These three seal the exits of the palace's great hall, where Penelope's suitors have gathered. Then Odysseus throws off his beggar's clothes and reveals himself to the startled men, telling them, "You yellow dogs! You never thought to see me back from Troy. So you ate me out of house and home; you raped my maids; you wooed my wife . . . with no more fear of the gods in heaven than of the human vengeance that might come. I tell you, one and all, that your doom is sealed." (*Odyssey* 22.36–42) Odysseus, Telemachus, and the servant proceed to slaughter the suitors. Then Odysseus reveals himself to Penelope, and at long last they are reunited in their wedding bed.

SEE ALSO: Homer; *Iliad*; Penelope

Oeconomicus

A major treatise by Xenophon, best described as a guide for well-to-do Greek landowners to efficiently manage their country estates. The work opens with a dialogue between the philosopher Socrates (Xenophon's old mentor) and a man named Critobulus. But soon Socrates recalls a previous conversation between himself and a well-to-do farmer named Ischomachus, and this second dialogue makes up the bulk of the *Oeconomicus*. In the course of these conversations, the speakers discuss various key aspects of horticulture, gardening, and management of servants. But the highlight of the work (by modern standards) is a charming description of the duties and proper manners of a good Greek wife. The fictional character Ischomachus, who is a thinly veiled version of Xenophon himself, tells his young wife, "God, as I see it, directly made women's nature suitable for the indoor jobs and tasks, and man's nature suitable for the outdoor ones. For he made the masculine body and mind more capable of enduring cold and heat and travel. . . . So, my dear . . . we must recognize what God has assigned to each of us, and try our hardest to carry through our respective responsibilities." (*Oeconomicus* 7.19)

SEE ALSO: marriage and divorce; women; Xenophon

Oedipus

In Greek mythology, as well as several monumental plays by the fifth-century B.C. Athenian dramatists, a king of Thebes whose life fulfilled a terrible prophecy that foretold he would kill his own father and marry his own mother. Hearing this prediction, Oedipus, a prince of Corinth, tries to avoid committing such crimes by fleeing from Corinth to Thebes. There, he outwits the Sphinx, a monster that has been terrorizing the city, and the Thebans reward him by making him their ruler. He marries Jocasta, wife of the former king, Laius (who had recently been killed on a roadside), and has children by her. Eventually, however, Oedipus learns that Laius and Jocasta are his real parents. It was he, Oedipus, who had unwittingly slain Laius on the roadside. Thus, the awful events of the prophecy had indeed come to pass. Horrified, Oedipus blinds himself and goes into exile, accompanied by his faithful daughter Antigone. After he has wandered far and wide and suffered for many years, the gods finally forgive him for his sins and lift him up into heaven.

SEE ALSO: *Antigone; Oedipus at Colonus; Oedipus the King*

Oedipus at Colonus

A tragedy by Sophocles, first produced in Athens in 401 B.C., five years after it was written and four years after the playwright's death. The play begins with Oedipus, a blind beggar, wandering around the countryside. Once Thebes's king, Oedipus has gone into exile after learning that he unknowingly killed his own father and married his own mother. Now, attended by his loving daughter Antigone, Oedipus eventually reaches Colonus, a village near Athens. Seeing Oedipus as cursed, the local residents tell him to leave. But then Theseus, king of Athens, enters and promises to protect Oedipus and provide him a decent burial after his death.

Soon afterward Ismene, Oedipus's other daughter, arrives and describes the situation back in Thebes. Oedipus's sons—Eteocles and Polynices—are feuding and Polynices is preparing to attack the city. These facts are confirmed when Creon, Oedipus's brother-in-law, appears in Colonus. He has come to take Oedipus back to Thebes because an oracle has said that the curse afflicting the blind man has the

power to keep Thebes safe from assault. After Oedipus refuses to go, still another Theban arrives at Colonus—Oedipus's son Polynices. The young man asks his father to join him in his fight with Eteocles. But Oedipus curses both of his sons.

At this juncture, the sky suddenly grows dark, thunder can be heard, and Oedipus realizes that his end has finally come. He walks away into the countryside and eerily disappears, at which point the other characters realize that the gods have taken the unfortunate Oedipus to their bosom.

SEE ALSO: Antigone; *Oedipus the King*; Sophocles

Oedipus the King

A tragic play (also called *Oedipus Rex* or *Oedipus Tyrranos*) by Sophocles, first presented in Athens circa 429 B.C. What many critics through the ages have called the greatest tragedy ever written opens with the great city of Thebes threatened with a deadly plague. Creon, brother of the city's queen, Jocasta, has just come from Delphi, where the famous oracle claimed the plague was a divine punishment aimed at the murderer of Jocasta's first husband, King Laius. Laius had been slain on a roadside years before, shortly before Jocasta's present husband, Oedipus, king of Thebes, had arrived on the scene. Hearing what the oracle had said, Oedipus swears he will hunt down and punish this murderer and thereby save the city.

But then Oedipus's world begins to crumble. The blind prophet Teiresias informs him that he, Oedipus, is the killer he is looking for. At first Oedipus declares that this cannot be true. But then he hears Jocasta describing her former husband's death and realizes that the details of that event are suspiciously similar to those of an incident in which Oedipus himself had killed a man on his way to Thebes.

As Oedipus ponders this disturbing revelation, a messenger arrives from Corinth. The messenger reveals that Oedipus was not born in Corinth as everyone, including Oedipus, had assumed. In reality, he was the son of Laius and Jocasta, as a baby left outside to die but found by shepherds and taken to be raised by Corinth's king and queen. Realizing the terrifying truth, Oedipus screams like an animal and blinds himself. Meanwhile, unable to face the horrible reality that she has married her own son and had children by him, Jocasta hangs herself. The play ends with Creon ascending the Theban throne as temporary regent.

SEE ALSO: Antigone; *Oedipus at Colonus*; Teiresias

Old Comedy

A period of Athenian theater and drama lasting from roughly 450 to 404 B.C. The outstanding comic playwright of the era was Aristophanes.

SEE ALSO: Aristophanes, 1; Menander; theater and drama

oligarchy

In ancient Greece, a government run by a council or other small group of leading citizens, usually aristocrats. The word means "rule of the few" in Greek.

SEE ALSO: *Constitution of the Athenians*, 2; government; Greece, history of

olives and olive oil

Olives, which appear to be native to the Mediterranean region, were long one of Greece's three chief crops (the other being grains and grape vines). The Greeks used olive oil for numerous purposes and products, including fuel for oil lamps; the liquid base of skin oils and perfumes; the chief cooking medium; a foundation for many sauces; an important ingredient of a number of medicines; and a lubricant for oiling the body, both in athletic events and to keep the skin clean (by scraping off the oil and dirt). Olive oil from some cities was considered finer than oil from other cities. Among the best and most expensive vintages were those of the Aegean island of Samos, Cyrenaica (lying west of Egypt in North Africa), and the Athenian territory of Athens.

Olives grew in the ancient Greek lands mainly at low altitudes. Most Greek olive growers planted new olive trees using *premna*, slices of existing olive tree trunks, as opposed to the Roman method, which favored using cuttings. In most cases olives could be harvested only every other year, which meant that growers had to stagger their crops as well as supplement olive production with sheep pasturage or other agrarian activities to make ends meet. The olives were harvested mainly in the late fall and winter.

To obtain the oil from the harvested olives, people first crushed them. For many centuries this was done by grinding them in a bowl using a mortar and pestle. But eventually, perhaps by the end of the fourth century B.C., the Greeks began using a device called a *trapetum*, consisting of a large stone saucer in which two millstones revolved and crushed the olives. After that, they pressed the crushed olives to squeeze out the oil. Pressing was done either by putting the olives in bags and placing heavy weights on the bags, or by putting the olives in a mechanical press,

This is how the sacred sanctuary at Olympia looked in its prime in the last few centuries of the first millennium B.C. AKG-IMAGES

which employed a large wooden beam to squash them.

SEE ALSO: farming; food and drink; trade

Olympia

Situated in a picturesque country setting in the northwestern Peloponnesus, Olympia was the site of the Olympic Games, the most famous and prestigious athletic competition in the ancient world. Tradition claimed that the games began in 776 B.C. But archaeological evidence suggests that the area was used for sacred purposes earlier, perhaps before the Mycenaeans arrived in Greece in the Bronze Age; and it is possible that some form of athletic contests were held there earlier than the eighth century B.C.

Over time a meeting hall, treasuries (small structures containing gifts given to the gods by religious pilgrims), and numerous statues were erected at Olympia. But the site was dominated by the Altis, a huge walled enclosure sacred to Zeus, leader of the Olympian gods. There, temples of Hera and Zeus were built. The temple of Zeus, completed in the 450s B.C., contained the famous seated statue of the god carved by Phidias, a monument that inspired awe in those who saw it and came to be counted among the Seven Wonders of the Ancient World. (In the fourth century A.D. the Romans removed the statue to Constantinople, formerly Byzantium. There, it was accidentally destroyed in a fire in the following century.) The structures used in the Olympic Games, including an immense gymnasium, a stadium for footraces, and a hippodrome (dirt racetrack) for horse and chariot races, were located in a flat area near the Altis.

SEE ALSO: athletics; Elis; Seven Wonders of the Ancient World

Olympians

In Greek mythology, the group of major gods that dwelled atop Mt. Olympus in northern Thessaly. According to legend, Zeus, son of the Titan Cronos, led the Olympians in a great war against the Titans and defeated them. Besides Zeus, the traditional Olympians included his wife, Hera; Poseidon, lord of the seas; Apollo, god of prophecy; Athena, goddess of war; Ares, god of war; Hestia, goddess of the hearth; Aphrodite, goddess of love; Hades, ruler of the Underworld; Demeter, goddess of agriculture; Hephaestos, master of the forge; Artemis, goddess of wildlife; Hermes, the messenger god; and Dionysus, god of the vine and fertility. Some ancient sources list only twelve Olympians, possibly because Hephaestos and Hestia eventually left Olympus.

SEE ALSO: Olympus, Mt.; Titans; and the names of the individual gods

Olympias
(ca. 375 B.C.–316 B.C.)

The most important of the wives of King Philip II of Macedonia and the mother of Philip's son, Alexander III (called "the Great" following his death). Olympias was the daughter of Neoptolemus, king of Epirus (a kingdom in northwestern Greece). She and Philip wed in 357 B.C. The following year she gave birth to Alexander, and in 354 she produced a daughter, Cleopatra. Olympias became very close to her children while Philip was away on military campaigns, and it is possible that she tried to turn Alexander against his father. Some modern scholars think that mother and son may have been behind Philip's murder in 336, although definitive proof is still lacking. What is more certain is that Olympias eagerly pursued her own lust for power while her son was campaigning in Persia. She and Antipater, whom Alexander had left in charge of Macedonia, did not get along. Unable to get rid of Antipater, she returned to Epirus and ruled that kingdom (as regent for her young cousin) for several years. Alexander died in 323 B.C. and Antipater followed him four years later. Antipater's son, Cassander, now drove Olympias's leading supporters out of Macedonia, prompting her to muster an army and invade the country. Her intent was to rule there as regent of Alexander's infant son, Alexander IV. However, Cassander besieged her at Pydna and she was forced to surrender, after which he ordered her execution.

SEE ALSO: Alexander III ("the Great"); Cassander; Philip II

Olympic Games

The leading athletic festival and venue in the ancient Greco-Roman world, it took place every four years at Olympia in the western Peloponnesus.

SEE ALSO: athletics; Olympia

Olympus, Mt.

The tallest mountain in mainland Greece, and in Greek mythology the home of the Olympian gods (named after the mountain). Olympus, which consists of a range of peaks that are often snow-covered, towers to 9,570 feet (2,919m) in northern Thessaly, a few miles from the Aegean coast. The idea that the gods dwelled atop Olympus dated from very early times, when the frequent cloud cover on the peaks was associated with Zeus in his manifestation as a storm god. By the Classical Age, most Greeks believed that if the gods did exist, they lived in the sky or in a remote land rather than on Olympus.

SEE ALSO: Greece, geography of; Olympians; Zeus

Olynthus

A city on the Chalcidic peninsula, along the northern coast of the Aegean Sea. Olynthus (or Olynthos) was inhabited by natives of Thrace (the region lying north of the peninsula) until the era of the Greco-Persian Wars, when it came under the control of Greeks living on the peninsula itself. The city joined the Delian League in 454 B.C., but two decades later, near the start of the Peloponnesian War, it quit the league and joined with other northern Aegean towns in an independent federation. In the following century Olynthus became the subject of a series of speeches (the *Olynthiacs*) delivered by the Athenian orator Demosthenes, who urged Greeks everywhere to support the city against the aggressions of Macedonia's King Philip II. These pleas were ignored and Philip destroyed Olynthus in 348 B.C. In the twentieth century archaeologists uncovered the remains of more than five complete blocks of Olynthian houses, providing a great deal of knowledge about the layout and contents of ancient Greek houses.

SEE ALSO: Demosthenes; houses; Philip II

omens

Various natural or human-related happenings that in ancient times were interpreted as supernatural signs of impending important events, such as the birth of great rulers or defeat or victory in battle.

SEE ALSO: religion

On the Crown

A monumental speech composed and delivered by the Athenian orator Demosthenes in 330 B.C. The purpose was to rebut an attack by his rival, the orator Aeschines, who had recently accused Demosthenes of fostering policies detrimental to Athenian security and interests. In *On the Crown,* Demosthenes insists that he has always acted in Athens's best interests. He also vigorously attacks Aeschines, ridiculing his supposed humble background and accusing him of taking bribes from Macedonia's Philip II. Filled with forceful language and vivid imagery, the speech is today regarded as Demosthenes' finest work.

SEE ALSO: Aeschines; Demosthenes

On the Murder of Eratosthenes

A court speech composed by the Athenian orator Lysias sometime between 400 and 380 B.C. The defendant was an Athenian named Euphiletus, who was on trial for killing a man named Eratosthenes. The latter had seduced Euphiletus's wife, and according to Athenian law, Euphiletus had every right to slay the interloper, as long as he had no other motive for the killing. Eratosthenes' relatives had prosecuted Euphiletus for murder, claiming that he had secretly set up the entire situation leading up to the crime. Lysias's masterful speech slowly but effectively paints Euphiletus as a normal, unsuspecting husband who had been grossly deceived by the seducer, thereby creating sympathy for the defendant in the eyes of the jury. The verdict in the case is unknown, but most modern observers feel it is likely that Euphiletus was acquitted. (Modern scholars also note that the speech contains the most detailed surviving literary description of an average Athenian house.)

SEE ALSO: laws and justice; Lysias

oracles

Messages thought to have come from the gods; also the sacred sites where such messages were given, or the priestesses who delivered the messages.

SEE ALSO: Apollo; Delphi; Dodona

Orchomenus

One of the leading Mycenaean strongholds in Greece's Bronze Age. Located a few miles northwest of Thebes, Orchomenus was the chief town of Boeotia (the region lying north of Attica) until it was overshadowed by Thebes in the early Archaic Age. Famed German archaeologist Heinrich Schliemann excavated the site of Orchomenus in 1880 and found the remains of a Mycenaean palace-citadel and a rich royal tomb, both dating from the late Bronze Age. In Greek mythology, Orchomenus was ruled by a powerful aristocratic clan, the Minyans, who supposedly made the town famous for its wealth. In the Classical Age, now much greatly diminished in wealth and importance, Orchomenus supported its more powerful neighbor, Thebes, in the Peloponnesian War. However, the Orchomenians switched their allegiance and backed Sparta against Thebes in the early fourth century B.C. In retaliation, Thebes destroyed Orchomenus in 364 B.C. The town was rebuilt but in later centuries languished in obscurity.

SEE ALSO: Mycenaeans; Thebes

Oresteia

A trilogy of tragedies composed by Aeschylus in 458 B.C. and the only complete surviving ancient Greek theatrical trilogy. The three plays of the Oresteia are *Agamemnon, The Libation Bearers,* and *Eumenides,* together describing the final phases of the mythical curse of the House of Atreus. For synopses of the three plays, see under their titles.

SEE ALSO: Aeschylus; Electra, 1 and 2; Orestes; theater and drama

Orestes

In Greek mythology, the son of Agamemnon (king of Mycenae) and brother of Electra. Aided by Electra, Orestes killed their mother, Clytemnestra, to avenge Clytemnestra's recent murder of Agamemnon. But Orestes was unable to assume the throne because the vengeful Furies chased him out of Mycenae. He sought refuge in Athens, where the goddess Athena intervened and granted him a trial, in which he was acquitted. This ended the long and terrible curse of the House of Atreus. Orestes is a major character in several of the plays of the great fifth-century B.C. Athenian tragedians.

SEE ALSO: Electra; *Electra* (play by Euripides); *Electra* (play by Sophocles); *Eumenides; Libation Bearers, The; Orestes* (play)

Orestes (play)

A tragedy by Euripides, first produced in Athens in 408 B.C. As the play begins, Electra, daughter of the legendary Greek king Agamemnon, is nurturing her brother, Orestes, following the latter's murders of their mother, Clytemnestra, and her lover. The people of Argos are about to pass judgment on Orestes for these crimes. Suddenly Orestes' uncle, Agamemnon's brother Menelaus, passes through on his way back from besieging Troy, but he fails to help Orestes. Soon the Argives sentence the younger man to death, after which Orestes and Electra plot to kill Menelaus's wife, Helen, whom they blame for all their troubles. (Her abduction had ignited the Trojan War, which, among other things, had led to Agamemnon's murder by Clytemnestra.) Before Helen's murder takes place, however, the god Apollo intervenes. He calls for a halt to the violence and prophesies that Orestes will stand trial in Athens and eventually become ruler of Argos.

SEE ALSO: Agamemnon; Clytemnestra; Orestes

Orpheus

In Greek mythology, a poet and musician said to be so talented that when he played his lyre all people, animals, and even trees within earshot were entranced by his songs. Orpheus supposedly flourished in the generation before the Trojan War. His musical talent and skills derived from his parents—Apollo, god of prophecy and music, and the Muse Calliope. Orpheus was among Jason's Argonauts, the adventurers who sought the fabulous Golden Fleece. The musician's great moment on the voyage came when his singing drowned out the voices of the alluring but deadly Sirens, allowing the Argonauts to escape harm.

In his most famous myth, Orpheus married a lovely nymph named Eurydice. After she died from the bite of a poisonous snake, he followed her into the Underworld and performed some songs for Hades, lord of that dark realm. Hades was so moved by Orpheus's music that he allowed Eurydice to leave, on the condition that Orpheus must walk ahead of his wife and never look back at her until they had reached the surface. Unable to resist temptation, however, at the last moment Orpheus looked back, and Eurydice disappeared back into the darkness, never to return. Thereafter Orpheus lived as a hermit, until the Maenads (fanatic followers of the fertility god Dionysus), who were upset that he had stopped offering them sacrifice, tore him apart.

SEE ALSO: Dionysus; Hades; Underworld

Orphism

From late Archaic times on, a mystery religion based on some writings (now lost) attributed to the mythical musician Orpheus. The exact origins of Orphism, which appears never to have gained a wide or well-organized following, are unknown. But it began to gain a few adherents in Athens and the Greek cities of southern Italy in the 600s B.C. and remained on the fringes of Greek and later Roman religious practices for many centuries to come. Evidently its main belief was that all humans bore the collective guilt (a version of original sin) for the death of an obscure god named Dionysus Zagreus, who in the dim past had been murdered by the Titans. To expiate the sin, worshippers had to endure three rounds of reincarnation. In each lifetime, a person returned to earth as either a human or an animal; and if he or she led a virtuous life each time, the person was allowed to enter the Isles of the Blessed, the section of the Underworld reserved for heroes and other elites. Thus, like the Eleusinian Mysteries, Orphism held out the promise of happiness in the afterlife for a chosen few. Perhaps what kept the cult from gaining more followers was its strict code of behavior, which forbade eating meat, hunting, wearing wool, and in some cases heterosexual intercourse.

SEE ALSO: Demeter; Eleusis; Orpheus

Osiris

In Egyptian mythology, and in Greek religious worship in the Hellenistic Age and beyond, a prominent god of fertility who was often identified with the native Greek fertility god Dionysus. As originally envisioned by the Egyptians, Osiris had been an early Egyptian pharaoh. After he was killed and dismembered by his brother, Seth, Osiris's sister, Isis, found and buried his body parts, allowing him to become whole again and rise from the dead. Based on this story, worshippers came to see Osiris as a renewer of life during the normal rotation of the seasons, and various Greek mystery cults worshipped him alongside other fertility gods, including Dionysus and Isis.

SEE ALSO: Dionysus; Egypt; Isis

ostracism

A unique feature of Athens's early democracy, it was designed to prevent one leader from gaining too much power or to sideline a leader whose policies slowed the democratic decision-making process. The citizens met and each was given a pottery fragment called an *ostrakon*. On it a person scratched the name of the man he wanted to see removed from office. The exact manner of tallying the votes is unclear, but it appears that a minimum of six thousand had to be cast, and the person who received the largest number was exiled from Athens for a period of ten years. The banished man retained his property and citizenship, however. Among the more famous leaders who were ostracized were Aristides, Themistocles, and Cimon.

SEE ALSO: Aristides; Cimon; government

owl

The chief symbol of Athena, goddess of war and wisdom, and a logo adopted by the Athenians, who worshipped Athena as their patron deity. Artists frequently pictured an owl sitting on Athena's shoulder. In the fifth century B.C., Athens issued a silver drachma bearing the image of an owl. Not surprisingly, these coins came to be called "owls."

SEE ALSO: Athena; Athens; money

paean

A war song encouraging people to fight, or a battle hymn sung by Greek soldiers as they marched toward the enemy. The seventh-century B.C. Spartan poet Tyrtaeus was known for writing paeans (also spelled "paians").

SEE ALSO: music and dance; poetry; Tyrtaeus

paidogogos

A male slave or servant who accompanied his master's son to school. The *paedagogus* made sure the boy got there safely, observed his behavior in his classes, and if necessary disciplined him.

SEE ALSO: education; slaves and slavery

painting

The Greeks produced paintings of distinctive quality and beauty from the Bronze Age through the Hellenistic Age and beyond. The Minoans and the Mycenaeans made paint pigments from vegetable matter and used them to produce brightly colored, vibrant murals (wall paintings), especially frescoes (paintings done on wet plaster). These works depicted real people and animals moving through natural, informal settings. Wall paintings have been found in the ruins of the palace-center at Knossos in northern Crete and at Akroteri on the island of Thera (modern Santorini). These include some splendid examples now on display in Athens's National Archaeological Museum. One shows two

young boys in a friendly boxing match. Another depicts some women wearing elegant dresses and jewelry and casually gathering flowers. And still another captures a tableau of an island with one or more cities and several ships approaching or departing the shore.

After the fall of Greece's Bronze Age civilization, painting in the Dark Age and early Archaic period was confined mainly to geometric designs and primitive animal and human stick figures on pottery vessels. Over time the form of the figures became more realistic and the colors more vivid. Corinthian painters led the way. Pottery continued to be a major painting surface, but paintings were also done on wooden panels, leather, and textiles. Most

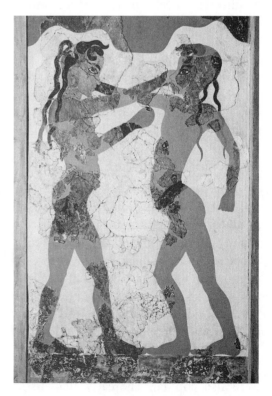

This Minoan painting of two young boys boxing was discovered on the island of Santorini (ancient Thera), located north of Crete. ERICH LESSING/ART RESOURCE, NY

of the nonceramic paintings disintegrated long ago, but a painting on a wooden plaque from Corinth circa 500 B.C. has been found. Its large range of colors, including flesh tones for human skin, suggest that by this time Greek painters were capable of more than the rather limited range of colors utilized in paintings on pottery. Early in the Classical Age Athens surpassed Corinth as the leading center of painting. Notable in this era was Polygnotus, who executed several huge wall paintings, the most famous depicting the fall of Troy, a work that graced the Stoa Poikile in Athens's Agora; and one that showed a panorama of the Underworld, displayed at Delphi. Polygnotus's method of portraying depth and distance was to place his figures at different levels in a painting. More realistic methods of achieving the illusion of depth, such as perspective and shading, began to appear in the latter years of the fifth century B.C. Pioneers of these methods include Apollodorus of Athens and Zeuxis, who hailed from southern Italy but worked for many years in Athens. It was said that Zeuxis's depictions of grapes were so realistic that they attracted hungry birds.

Indeed, in the fourth century B.C. and on into the Hellenistic Age, there was a steady development toward increased realism in Greek painting. Mythological scenes continued to be popular, especially in wall paintings in tombs; a magnificent example is a scene of Hades abducting Persephone into the Underworld, found in 1977 in one of the royal tombs unearthed at Vergina (ancient Aegae) in Macedonia. But paintings of real historical persons and events were also popular. The early Hellenistic Greek painter Philoxenos of Eretria appears to have produced an enormous wall mural showing Alexander the Great defeating the Persian king Darius III at Issus.

Although the painting itself has not survived, a copy of it, executed in mosaic tiles, was found in the ruins of the Roman city of Pompeii (buried and preserved by the eruption of Mt. Vesuvius in A.D. 79). The stunning use of shading and detail in this mosaic hints that by this time some Greek painters had achieved a level of proficiency rivaling that of Europe's Renaissance masters. Hellenistic paintings also portrayed realistic landscapes and trompe l'oeil effects, such as life-size, realistic-looking doors and windows painted on interior walls. Not surprisingly, Hellenistic Greek painters exerted a major influence on Roman painters in the centuries that followed.

SEE ALSO: Akroteri; Polygnotus; pottery; sculpture

palaestrae

In ancient Greece, wrestling schools or sections of gymnasia set aside for wrestling, boxing, exercise, and sometimes other athletic pursuits. Over time the palaestra took on a more or less standard form—a rectangular yard with a number of sand pits used for wrestling surfaces. The yard was typically surrounded by a building with colonnaded walkways on its exterior and rooms for dressing, bathing, and socializing on the interior.

SEE ALSO: athletics

Pan

In Greek mythology, lore, and religion, a woodland god who oversaw pastures and shepherds and their flocks. Artists and writers almost always portray Pan with a human upper body and a goat's legs, ears, and horns. They also show him playing a pipe with seven reeds (the syrinx, or panpipes), supposedly his own invention.

A son of Hermes, the messenger god, Pan was particularly popular in the picturesque countryside in and around Arcadia in the central Peloponnesus. Beginning in the fifth century B.C., worship of the god became more prevalent in Athens because of an incident that supposedly occurred shortly before the Battle of Marathon in 490 B.C. On his way to Sparta to ask for aid against the invading Persians, the Athenian runner Pheidippides encountered Pan. The god wanted to know why the Athenians had been neglecting his worship of late. The subsequent Athenian victory was partly attributed to Pan's help, so the Athenians instituted regular sacrifices to him.

SEE ALSO: Arcadia; Battle of Marathon; Hermes

Panathenaea

In ancient Athens, the most important and prestigious of the city's many annual religious festivals. Held over seven or eight days each July, the Panathenaea ("All the Athenians") was celebrated every fourth year with special pomp (the Greater Panathenaea). The Greater Panathenaea attracted visitors from a number of neighboring Greek states because its religious procession and sacrifices, feasts, and especially its musical and athletic contests were spectacular and colorful. One of the highlights of the festival, the sacred procession, featured marchers from all Athenian social classes and groups, including public officials, generals and soldiers, handsome elderly men carrying olive branches, children bearing trays and water jars, young virgins from the city's noblest families, selected metics bearing trays filled with pastries, freedmen carrying oak branches, and slaves leading the sacrificial animals. These marchers moved along the Panathenaic Way, which began at the Thriasian gate in the city's northwest wall, passed through the Agora, ascended the steps on the west slope of the Acropolis, and stopped in the open space between the Parthenon and the Erechtheum. There, the ceremony of the peplos, Athena's sacred robe, took place. After the robe had been presented to the goddess, sacrifices took place at her great altar, located near the eastern end of the Parthenon. A hundred cows and many sheep and other animals were slaughtered in the ceremony. Feasts followed, as well as athletic contests. Regarding the latter, some events, including many that were common at the Olympic Games, were open to all Greeks; other events, particularly the tribal competitions, were open only to Athenians.

SEE ALSO: Athena; Erechtheum; Parthenon

Pandora

In Greek mythology, the first human woman, fashioned of clay by Hephaestos, god of the forge. Zeus, who desired to punish the Titan Prometheus for giving fire to humans, gave Pandora to Prometheus's slow-witted brother, Epimetheus, who took her into his home even though Prometheus had warned him not to accept any gifts from Zeus. Once inside, she opened a box containing various evils, such as greed, hate, and envy, which escaped and permanently infected humanity.

SEE ALSO: Prometheus; women

panegyric

A formal speech praising a ruler, nation, or other entity. In the Classical and Hellenistic ages Greeks often delivered them at public festivals and games, including the Olympic Games. Sometimes they had political overtones or agendas. An example was the *Olympiacus,* delivered at the 388 B.C. Olympics by the Athenian orator Lysias, who called for Greek unity against foreign aggression. Lysias's younger contemporary, the orator Isocrates, also wrote panegyrics, although they were never delivered in public.

SEE ALSO: Lysias

pankration

An athletic combat event that combined moves from wrestling, boxing, and street fighting in an all-out brawl that often resulted in serious injury and sometimes even death. It may have resembled modern professional wrestling except that it was real rather than staged.

SEE ALSO: athletics

Paris

In Greek mythology, and in Homer's *Iliad,* a Trojan prince who instigated the Trojan War by abducting Helen, queen of Sparta. During the war Paris (sometimes called Alexander) engaged in single combat with Helen's husband, Menelaus; the latter would have defeated and slain Paris if Aphrodite, goddess of love, had not intervened. Paris, who was a skilled archer, also fired the arrow that struck Achilles' heel, killing that formidable Greek warrior. A poisoned arrow from the bow of another Greek, Philoctetes, finally slew Paris. Paris was also famous for acting as judge in a beauty contest among three Olympian goddesses, an episode known as the Judgment of Paris.

SEE ALSO: Achilles; Helen; *Iliad*; Troy

Parmenides
(early fifth century B.C.)

A noted pre-Socratic philosopher-scientist who established the Eleatic school of thought (centered in Elea, a Greek city in southern Italy). Parmenides, who visited Athens in the mid-fifth century B.C. and may have met the young Socrates, held that the ever-changing world that people perceive around them is not nature's true reality. Instead, reality, or "What Is," exists beyond the senses, is unchanging and indestructible, and can only be contemplated through mental concentration and reason. In his poem titled "On Nature" (divided into two parts—"The Way of Truth" and "The Way of Seeming") he states:

> There are many signs that What Is has no beginning and never will be destroyed. It is whole, still, and without end. It neither was nor will be. It simply is—now, altogether, one, continuous. How could you go about investigating its birth? . . . Necessarily, therefore, either it simply Is or it simply Is Not. Strong conviction will not let us think that anything springs from Being except itself. ("The Way of Truth" 7A)

Parmenides appears as a speaker in Plato's dialogue the *Parmenides,* and it is possible that the older thinker's ideas about human perceptions of reality influenced Plato's famous theory of forms.

SEE ALSO: *Parmenides* (dialogue); philosophy; Plato

Parmenides (dialogue)

A dialogue by Plato of uncertain date. It is also unclear whether the author uses the characters to expound his own views or to present various views of the philosophers Zeno and Parmenides, who appear in fictional form as two of the characters. Plato's old mentor, Socrates, is also a character. The main thrust of the piece is a criticism of Plato's own theory of forms (or ideas), which some modern observers have found strange. Many of the objections the characters raise about the theory resemble those of Plato's famous contemporary Aristotle.

SEE ALSO: Parmenides; Plato

Parmenio
(ca. 400 B.C.–330 B.C.)

A skilled military general and trusted friend of Macedonia's King Philip II. Parmenio was a key figure in many of Philip's early victories and in 346 B.C. negotiated with the Athenians on Philip's behalf. Following Philip's assassination in 336, Parmenio served as a leading general during Alexander's conquest of Persia, commanding the Greek left wings at the battles of Granicus River, Issus, and Gaugamela. But in 330, when Parmenio's son, Philotas, was implicated in a plot to kill Alexander, the latter ordered Parmenio's execution.

SEE ALSO: Alexander III ("the Great"); Battle of Gaugamela; Battle of Granicus River; Battle of Issus; Philip II

Parnassus, Mt.

The second-highest mountain in mainland Greece, located slightly north of the Gulf of Corinth. The tallest peak in the Parnassus range reaches a height of 8,061 feet (2,459m). Associated with the worship of Dionysus at first and later with that of Pan and Apollo, the slopes of Parnassus were viewed by all Greeks as sacred territory. These slopes featured a spring sacred to both Apollo and the Muses as well as the site of Delphi, home of Apollo's renowned oracle, situated between two cliffs (the Phaedriades, or "Shining Ones").

SEE ALSO: Delphi; Muses; Pan

Paros

The second-largest island (after Naxos) in the Cyclades group, lying north of Crete in the southern Aegean Sea. Paros was renowned for its excellent white marble and became an important producer of statuary. In the seventh century B.C. the Parians colonized Thasos, the northernmost Aegean island. Among the leaders of this effort was Paros's most famous native son, the poet Archilochus. Later, in 490 B.C., the Parians made the mistake of helping the Persians in the latter's attempt to subdue Athens. The Athenian general Miltiades tried to retaliate against Paros, but his siege of the island's main city (also called Paros) was unsuccessful. Following the Greco-Persian Wars, Paros joined the Delian League and remained a somewhat reluctant Athenian ally for more than a century. In Hellenistic times the island came under the control first of Macedonia, then of the Ptolemaic kingdom, and finally of Rome.

SEE ALSO: Archilochus; Miltiades; Thasos

Parthenon

The most famous and influential temple ever built by the Greeks, called by many modern experts the most perfect piece of architecture ever created. The Parthenon, dedicated to the goddess Athena (Athens's patron deity), was constructed atop the Athenian Acropolis in the 440s and 430s B.C. as part of a major building program initiated by the statesman Pericles. The structure was designed by the architects Ictinus and Callicrates and was decorated by Phidias, the greatest sculptor of the ancient world. In its prime it was 228 feet (69m) long, 101 feet (31m) wide, and 65 feet (20m) high, and it consisted of more than 22,000 tons (19,972 metric tons) of exquisite marble (mostly quarried at Mt.

As this reconstruction of the Parthenon in its heyday shows, the temple had eight columns across its front. Most Greek temples had six. NORTH WIND PICTURE ARCHIVES

Pentelikon, about 10 miles [16km] northeast of Athens's urban center). There were eight columns each on the front and back of the building and seventeen running down each side (counting the corner columns twice). The Parthenon's front (western) pediment featured a cluster of twenty-two larger-than-life-size statues engaged in the famous mythical contest between Athena and Poseidon for possession of Attica. The eastern pediment contained sculpted figures portraying Athena's dramatic birth from the head of Zeus. Running above the colonnade, beneath the building's roof, were ninety-two metopes, rectangular panels making up the Doric frieze. Each metope held a scene carved in relief by Phidias and his assistants. The western-facing metopes showed the Athenians fighting the legendary Amazons (a battle known as the Amazonomachy); the metopes on the temple's south side depicted the battle between the Lapiths and the Centaurs (the Centauromachy); the eastern metopes showed the mythical war between the giants and Olympian gods (the Gigantomachy); and the north-facing metopes depicted episodes from the Trojan War. High up on the inside of the outer colonnade (and difficult to see from ground level) was the Ionic frieze, which ran around the entire perimeter of the temple. It showed hundreds of figures taking part in the Panathenaic procession, a highlight of Athens's most prestigious religious festival. The outside of the Parthenon was originally painted in bright colors (mainly red, blue, and gold), which weathering long ago wore away.

Inside the temple was its main room, the *naos*, measuring 108 feet (33m) by 62 feet (20m), with a ceiling 43 feet (13m) high. A double colonnade (one row of columns standing atop another) divided the room into a U-shaped central area, flanked by narrow aisles. Standing inside this central area and completely dominating the *cella*'s interior was Phidias's great statue of the goddess—the *Athena Parthenos*, standing 38 feet (11m) tall. Made of ivory and beaten gold, the statue featured the aegis, the goddess's breastplate, on which Phidias carved the face of the Gorgon Medusa in ivory. In one hand, the statue held a six-foot-tall (1.8m) figure of Nike, goddess of victory, and in the other hand a huge spear.

At the time it was built, the Parthenon served not only as a religious shrine but also as a showcase of Athenian wealth and power. It was the crowning pinnacle of a myriad of Athenian achievements, prompting its sponsor, Pericles, to predict, quite correctly it turned out, "Future ages will wonder at us, as the present age wonders at us now." (Quoted in Thucydides, *The Peloponnesian War* 2.41)

The building remained largely intact for nearly two thousand years. Then, in 1687, during an artillery barrage between the Venetians and the Turks (who then controlled Athens), the Parthenon was shattered by a huge explosion. Further damage followed as the Turks used the Acropolis as a residential area and rich Europeans (notably England's Lord Elgin) carted away many of the surviving sculptures. Today, fortunately, the Parthenon is carefully protected and painstaking efforts are ongoing to preserve its remains for future generations. Still noble and awe-inspiring even in its ruined state, it symbolizes not only the tremendous vision and talent of its Athenian builders but also the greatness of ancient Greek civilization as a whole.

SEE ALSO: Acropolis; Athena; Elgin marbles; Pericles; Phidias; sculpture

Patroclus

In Greek mythology, and in Homer's *Iliad*, a comrade of the Greek warrior Achilles who donned Achilles' armor in an effort to fool the Trojans into thinking that Achilles had left his tent and reentered the fray. The plan worked, but in a way that Patroclus did not foresee. The Trojan prince Hector promptly slew him and only then did Achilles, driven by grief and anger over the loss of his friend, take up his weapons.

SEE ALSO: Achilles; *Iliad*; Troy

Pausanias (Spartan general) (ca. 467 B.C.)

A noted Spartan general who commanded a large segment of the Greek troops in their victory over the Persians at Plataea in 479 B.C. Soon afterward Pausanias recaptured Byzantium (near the entrance to the Black Sea) from the Persians. But then he was accused of plotting with Persia's King Xerxes against the Greeks. Though acquitted of this charge, Pausanias was later suspected of organizing a rebellion of Sparta's slaves, the helots, and died in disgrace.

SEE ALSO: Battle of Plataea; Greco-Persian Wars; helots

Pausanias (writer) (flourished ca. A.D. 150)

The author of one of the most famous and informative guidebooks of antiquity. Possibly hailing from Smyrna in Greek Ionia, Pausanias traveled widely, gathering information for his *Description of Greece* (or *Guide to Greece*). The work remains a valuable source of facts about the social customs, historical figures, myths, religious shrines, buildings, and art treasures of

Olympia, Sparta, Arcadia, Boeotia, Athens, Delphi, and other pivotal Greek places.

SEE ALSO: *Description of Greece*; Greece, geography of; Greece, history of

Peace

A comedy by Aristophanes, first produced in Athens in 421 B.C. At the time the Peloponnesian War, fought between Athens, Sparta, and their respective allies, was ongoing. And like other war-weary Athenians, Aristophanes was anticipating the conclusion of a peace treaty (the Peace of Nicias) in the near future. As the play opens, an Athenian grape grower named Trygaios, whose family has been suffering from war-related food shortages, decides to take matters into his own hands. He fattens up a dung-beetle until it is big enough to mount, and then rides it into the sky, hoping to petition the god Zeus to stop the war. Reaching heaven, Trygaios learns that Zeus is away and that the war god Polemos is temporarily in charge. Polemos has thrown the goddess Peace into a cave and threatens to lock her inside forever (thereby ensuring that the humans' war will never end). With the aid of the messenger god, Hermes, however, Trygaios manages to extract Peace from the cave. They bring her back to Greece, where most people celebrate the end of hostilities.

SEE ALSO: Aristophanes, 1; Peloponnesian War

Pegasus

In Greek mythology, a fabulous flying horse that was born from the dying body of Medusa, one of the hideous Gorgons. The most famous myth about Pegasus involved the human hero Bellerophon, who captured the flying steed using a magical bridle given to him by the god-dess Athena. Having tamed Pegasus, Belle-rophon rode the horse in a fateful encounter with the Chimaera, a dangerous monster that was terrorizing southern Asia Minor. Bellerophon slew the creature, but when he tried to ride Pegasus to the summit of Mt. Olympus, the flying horse bucked him off.

SEE ALSO: Bellerophon; Medusa

Pella

The capital city of Macedonia from the late 400s B.C. on, replacing Aegae (which remained the burial site of Macedonian royalty). Pella was located about 25 miles (40km) northwest of the seaport of Thessaloniki (established in the late fourth century B.C.).

SEE ALSO: Aegae; Macedonia; Thessaloniki

Pelopidas
(ca. 410 B.C.–364 B.C.)

A prominent Theban statesman and general who played an important role in that city's rise to power in the mid-fourth century B.C. In 379 B.C. Pelopidas commanded a group of Theban soldiers in a successful recapture of the city's acropolis (the Cadmea) from the Spartans, who had been occupying Thebes against the will of the local populace. Afterward Pelopidas joined with his friend and fellow general Epaminondas in preparing the Theban army to resist an attack by the Spartan infantry. Their efforts were successful, as the Thebans decisively defeated the Spartans at Leuctra in 371.

SEE ALSO: Battle of Leuctra; Epaminondas; Thebes

Peloponnesian League

An alliance of Peloponnesian cities established sometime in the sixth century B.C.

Sparta, Athens, and Their Allies

Macedonia

Lemnos

Thessaly

Aegean Sea

Persian Empire

Ionia

Thebes •

Andros

Corinth •

•Athens

Megara

'Delos

Sparta •

Naxos

■ Athenians and their allies

■ Spartans and their allies

□ Greek areas

Crete

Mediterranean Sea

Sparta dominated the organization, partly through intimidation, and led its members against Delian League states (led by Athens) in the Peloponnesian War (431–404 B.C.).

SEE ALSO: Delian League; Peloponnesian War; Sparta

Peloponnesian War

A long, debilitating conflict that involved and ultimately exhausted almost all the city-states of Greece and ended Athens's great age of imperialism and cultural greatness. The war pitted Athens and most of its Delian League allies against Sparta and its allies in the Peloponnesian League

(along with Megara, Thebes, and a few other non-Peloponnesian cities). Since the expulsion of the Persians in 479 B.C., Sparta and Athens had endured several decades of mutual distrust and small-scale fighting. The drift toward a wider conflict finally gained momentum in 433, when Athens and Corinth, a Spartan ally, entered into conflict over Corinth's former colony of Corcyra. The Corinthians begged the Spartans to intervene and put Athens in its place, but Spartan leaders were reluctant to act at this juncture. Then the Athenians blockaded the port of their neighbor, Megara, also a Spartan ally. This finally prompted Sparta to declare war in 431.

The Initial Strategies

As the great war commenced, it was recognized that Sparta had the best land army and Athens the best navy in Greece. So both sides were equally confident of victory; and as Thucydides, the chief historian of the war, reports, many young men across Greece were eager to fight:

> Both sides put everything into their war effort. This was natural enough. At the beginning of an undertaking, the enthusiasm is always greatest, and at that time both in the Peloponnesus and in Athens there were great numbers of young men who had never been in war and were consequently far from unwilling to join in this one. Meanwhile, all the rest of Greece hung poised on the event, as the two leading cities came into conflict. (*The Peloponnesian War* 2.8)

The initial strategies of the combatants were dictated by their individual military strengths. The Spartans planned to use their widely feared land troops to invade and devastate Attica. Anticipating this, the Athenians, led by Pericles, planned to retreat behind the Long Walls and rely on their fleets of cargo vessels and warships to keep them well supplied and safe. These strategies swiftly went into effect, as the Spartans led thirty five thousand troops (mostly Boeotians and other Spartan allies) into Attica and proceeded to destroy farms, houses, and crops. At first the Athenians only watched from behind the Long Walls. But soon they launched more than a hundred warships, which ravaged the coasts of the Peloponnesus. The Athenians also invaded the island of Aegina, a Spartan ally, and marched fourteen thousand troops into Megara. Thucydides remarks that it was "the biggest Athenian army that had ever taken the field." (*The Peloponnesian War* 2.31)

For a while, the conflict appeared to be a stalemate. The Athenians suffered heavy losses from a deadly plague that struck the city in 430 B.C., including their most experienced leader, Pericles, who died in 429. And in the same year, the Spartans besieged and destroyed Athens's neighbor, Plataea. However, Athens struck back, winning two major naval victories against fleets from Corinth and other Spartan allies. The Athenians also established a naval base at Pylos, only 50 miles (80km) west of Sparta, and defeated a small Spartan army sent to stop them. In Athens, the war hawk Cleon, who urged his countrymen to make bolder moves to achieve total victory, enjoyed popularity. But Cleon's aggressive policies backfired, as an Athenian invasion of Theban-dominated Boeotia failed miserably in 424. That same year, the Spartan general Brasidas captured the Athenian colony of Amphipolis in the northern Aegean. (The Athenians blamed the historian Thucydides, then a general charged with protecting Amphipolis, and banished him.) Cleon then led an expedition to free Amphipolis, and in the ensuing battle both he and Brasidas were slain.

The Sicilian Expedition

At this juncture, both sides had come to realize that total victory for either side was elusive and that further fighting would result only in more death and destruction. In March 421 B.C. the Athenian statesman Nicias brokered a peace treaty (the Peace of Nicias). But soon the energetic and unprincipled Alcibiades (foster son of Pericles) rose to prominence in Athens. Alcibiades fomented trouble among Sparta's Peloponnesian allies, including Mantinea, Elis, and Argos, who together fought the Spartans at Mantinea in 418 B.C. Sparta was victorious and soon retaliated against Athenian interference in its affairs by resuming hostilities. This pleased the ambitious Alcibiades, who envisioned himself leading Athens to total victory over its traditional rival.

The culmination of Alcibiades' influence and treachery came in 415 B.C., when he urged the Assembly to approve a daring expedition to the Greek city of Syracuse in Sicily. This, he said, would give Athens control of Sicily's considerable wealth, foodstuffs, and soldiers, and thereby create a decisive edge over Sparta and its allies. Nicias strongly objected, arguing that Alcibiades "was prepared to plunge the city into a difficult and hazardous war across the sea merely to satisfy his personal greed and ambition." (Quoted in Plutarch, *Life of Nicias* 12) To Nicias's disdain, however, the Athenian Assembly approved Alcibiades' audacious plan. The Athenians also placed Nicias in joint command of the expedition with Alcibiades. The two men led more than 130 warships, another 130 supply ships, and at least twenty-six thousand infantrymen, skirmishers, and sailors westward toward Syracuse. Along the way, however, Alcibiades turned traitor and joined the Spartans, leaving Nicias in charge of the venture. An indecisive, overly cautious person, Nicias seemed unsure of the best course of action. "For his strategy," Plutarch says, "he could offer nothing better than sitting idly at his base, cruising around the island, or drawing up plans, until the bright hopes with which the expedition had originally set out had faded, and the terror and dismay which the first sight of his fleet had caused the enemy had quite melted away." (*Life of Nicias* 14)

While the Athenians hesitated, a Spartan army commanded by Gylippus arrived and joined forces with the Syracusans. Nicias sent for reinforcements, which came; but their leader, Demosthenes, insisted on an immediate attack, which resulted in an Athenian defeat. Finally, inaction, poor judgment, and fear took their toll. In the fall of 413 the Athenian fleet was defeated in Syracuse's harbor, and the surviving sailors and soldiers had to flee across the Sicilian countryside. The Syracusans and Spartans gave chase and killed many of them. Nicias and Demosthenes were executed, and the rest of the Athenians were condemned to a living death as slaves in the Sicilian stone quarries. Athens's "sufferings were on an enormous scale," Thucydides writes. "Their losses were . . . total. Army, navy, everything was destroyed." (*The Peloponnesian War* 7.87)

The Tide Turns Against Athens

Despite these horrendous losses, however, the Athenians fought on. They were decidedly on the defensive, however. The Spartans set up a permanent base at Decelea, about 13 miles (21km) north of Athens's urban center, which allowed Spartan troops to control large parts of Attica year-round. Athens was now totally dependent on foreign supplies, especially grain from Greek cities on the coasts of the Black Sea. In 412 B.C. Sparta took advantage of this weakness by building its first navy, financed mostly by Persia's King Darius II, who was promised control of Greek Ionia in exchange. In the face of Spartan sea power, several members of Athens's alliance rebelled, including Chios, Ephesus, Miletus, and Rhodes. There was a brief resurgence of Athenian momentum beginning in 411, when, in a moment of desperation, the Athenians forgave Alcibiades and made him general once again. He delivered the Spartan navy a major defeat at Cyzicus in northwestern Asia Minor in 410 and captured Byzantium (near the entrance to the Black Sea) in 408. But when a capable Spartan commander, Lysander, won a victory over the Athenian navy, Alcibiades was forced to abandon his fleets. In 405 Lysander sailed 150 warships to the Hellespont, captured the town of Lampsacus, and then defeated a larger Athenian fleet at nearby Aegospotami. This cut off Athens's life-giving grain route; and after six months of siege by Lysander's forces, the city had no choice but to surrender, which occurred in April 404 B.C. The humiliated Athenians were forced to tear down the Long Walls, and Lysander installed a Spartan-backed oligarchy, the Thirty Tyrants. Athens's brief but glorious golden age, in which it had stood at the forefront of Greek and European civilization, was over.

SEE ALSO: Alcibiades; Battle of Aegospotami; Lysander; Nicias; Pericles; Syracuse

Peloponnesian War, The

A chronicle of the disastrous conflict that ravaged Greece between 431 and 404 B.C., written by the Athenian military general and historian Thucydides. The treatise, in eight books (in ancient times each filling a single papyrus scroll), was the first true work of history in the modern sense—that is, an unbiased account of events based on firsthand information. Thucydides reported only those events that he or someone he interviewed had witnessed firsthand. "With regard to my factual reporting of events," he says in the opening of the work,

> I have made it a principle not to write down the first story that came my way, and not even to be guided by my own general impressions; either I was present myself at the events which I have described or else I heard of them from eye-witnesses whose reports I

have checked with as much thoroughness as possible. . . . It may well be that my history will seem less easy to read because of the absence in it of a romantic element. It will be enough for me, however, if these words of mine are judged useful . . . [by] future [generations]. My work is not a piece of writing designed to meet the taste of an immediate public, but was done to last forever. (*The Peloponnesian War* 1.22)

Thucydides achieved this formidable goal. His great war chronicle became not only one of the most popular literary works both in later antiquity and the eras that followed (and is still widely read today) but also a model for all later Western historians.

In addition to the author's methods of and aims in writing the work, Book 1 of *The Peloponnesian War* provides a brief synopsis of Greek history up to the outbreak of the conflict and discusses the immediate causes of the war. Books 2 through 5 cover the events of the first ten years of fighting. Some of the highlights of this section include Pericles' magnificent funeral oration over the Athenian dead; a graphic description of the plague that struck Athens in 430 B.C., which Thucydides himself contracted but survived; a heart-rending recollection of Sparta's destruction of the small polis of Plataea; and the Peace of Nicias in 421. Books 6 and 7 describe the ill-fated Sicilian expedition, in which Athens lost hundreds of ships and tens of thousands of men. Book 8 tells about the Spartan capture of Decelea (north of Athens) and some naval warfare off the coast of Asia Minor, but it then breaks off in midsentence in a passage describing events in 411 B.C., seven years before the war's conclusion. It is unknown why Thucydides did not finish the work.

But Xenophon and other Greek historians honored his memory and achievement by starting their accounts of the war at the point where he left off.

SEE ALSO: historical writing; Peloponnesian War; Thucydides, 2

Peloponnesus

The large mountainous peninsula that makes up the southern third of the Greek mainland. The Peloponnesus (also Peloponnesos or Peloponnese) measures roughly 132 miles (212km) from north to south and 134 miles (215km) from east to west. Its name derives from *Pelopos nesos*, meaning "isle of Pelops," a reference to the mythical character Pelops, whose son, Atreus, supposedly established the House of Atreus, which later gave rise to Agamemnon, king of Mycenae, and Menelaus, king of Sparta. In fact, the real Mycenae appears to have been the chief Mycenaean Greek stronghold, rising to power between 1600 to 1400 B.C., during Greece's Bronze Age. After the fall of Mycenaean civilization, the peninsula was overrun by Dorians, who had migrated from the region north of Greece. Sparta and several other Peloponnesian centers retained Dorian customs well into the Classical Age. At the dawn of that pivotal era, the major regions of the Peloponnesus were Elis (in the northwest), which sponsored the Olympic Games every four years; Achaea (in the north, along the Gulf of Corinth); Arcadia (in the center); Argolis (in the northeast), where Argos held sway (Mycenae having been reduced to a mere village); Laconia (in the south), homeland of the militaristic Spartans; and Messenia (in the southwest), whose people were conquered and reduced to slavery by Sparta. Corinth, situated near the isthmus that joined the peninsula to central Greece,

was also a major Peloponnesian city in the Classical Age. In the last few decades of that era, Sparta declined in influence, thanks to the rise of Thebes under Epaminondas. Also, Messenia was liberated by Thebes and a new city—Megalopolis—was built in Arcadia. Early in Hellenistic times, ten towns in Achaea banded together into the Achaean League, which dominated the Peloponnesus until Rome dissolved the league in 146 B.C. In that same year, the Romans utterly destroyed Corinth as an object lesson to other Greeks who might contemplate resistance to Rome.

SEE ALSO: Achaean League; Arcadia; Corinth; Elis; Messenia; Mycenae; Olympia; Pelops; Sparta

Pelops

In Greek mythology, the namesake of the Peloponnesus and the founder of the family that later came to dominate the eastern part of that large Greek peninsula. Pelops's father, Tantalus, threw a feast for the gods. The main course was poor Pelops, who had been killed, cut into pieces, and cooked. But the gods saw through Tantalus's ruse. They restored Pelops to life and then cast a terrible curse on the family line—the so-called curse of the House of Atreus (named for Tantalus's grandson, Atreus). An alternate ancient account claimed that Pelops slew a local king, Oenomaus, and his chariot driver, Myrtilus. The latter then cursed Pelops and his descendants.

SEE ALSO: Agamemnon; Atreus; Peloponnesus

Penelope

In Greek mythology, and in Homer's *Odyssey*, the wife of Odysseus, king of the island kingdom of Ithaca. During the twenty years that Odysseus was fighting at Troy and wandering the Mediterranean seaways, Penelope dutifully waited for him while raising their son Telemachus. For a long time she refused to give in to demands by local aristocratic suitors that she choose one of them as her husband and king. Finally, Odysseus returned and slew the suitors, after which he and Penelope were reunited.

SEE ALSO: Odysseus; *Odyssey*; Telemachus

pentathlon

At the Olympic Games and many other ancient athletic competitions, a combination of five events: the running dash (called the *stade*), the running broad jump, the discus throw, the javelin throw, and wrestling. Each contestant had to perform all of these events in a single day.

SEE ALSO: athletics

Pentelikon, Mt.

A mountain in Attica, lying about 10 miles (16km) northeast of Athens's urban center. Mt. Pentelikon (or Pentelikos) rises to a height of about 3,600 feet (1,100m). The mountain was known for its large marble quarry, which produced the famous Pentelic marble used in the Parthenon and many other Athenian public buildings. Shimmering white when first quarried, Pentelic marble weathers to a warm golden brown.

SEE ALSO: building materials and methods; Parthenon; quarries

Perdiccas
(ca. 360 B.C.–321 B.C.)

A general under Alexander the Great and one of the latter's leading Successors. After Alexander sent Craterus, his closest associate, back to Greece in 324 B.C., Perdiccas became the young king's second in command. A year later, on his deathbed, Alexander entrusted Perdiccas with the royal seal, making him head of the council of Macedonian generals in Babylon. Soon, however, Perdiccas was at odds with three other powerful Successors—Antigonus, Antipater, and Ptolemy. While attacking Ptolemy in the Nile Delta in 321, Perdiccas suffered heavy losses and some of his own men mutinied and killed him.

SEE ALSO: Alexander III ("the Great"); Antigonus I; Antipater; Successors

Pergamum

During Greece's Hellenistic Age, a prosperous, culturally advanced Greek city and small kingdom located in northwestern Asia Minor, opposite the island of Lesbos. Pergamum (or Pergamon) began as a small town in the later years of the Classical Age and became part of the Seleucid kingdom following the wars of Alexander's Successors. A local leader named Philetaerus established a Seleucid-backed Pergemene dynasty circa 282 B.C.; it became known as the Attalid dynasty in memory of Philetaerus's father, Attalus. Philetaerus was succeeded by his nephew, Eumenes I, who ascended the throne in 263. A year later Eumenes led a revolt against the Seleucids, making Pergamum an independent state. Under his own nephew, Attalus I Soter ("Savior"), who ruled from 241 to 197, the kingdom came to control a fair proportion of western Asia Minor and became an influential cultural center. The Attalids were all generous arts patrons who encouraged and supported poets, intellectuals, painters, and sculptors. The city of Pergamum boasted the second-largest library in the ancient world, and the

Pergemene acropolis was a wonder to behold. Its highlight was the magnificent Great Altar of Zeus, later viewed as the pinnacle of Greek Hellenistic architecture and sculpture. The later Attalids, including Eumenes II (reigned 197–159), Attalus II (159–138), and Attalus III (138–133), extended friendship to Rome, which allowed the kingdom to continue thriving during the period when the Romans were conquering most of the other Greek lands. In fact, Attalus III actually bequeathed Pergamum to Rome in his will, and the kingdom became a Roman possession on his death in 133 B.C.

SEE ALSO: Attalids; libraries; Seleucid Empire

Periander
(reigned ca. 625–585 B.C.)

A famous and accomplished ruler of Corinth who was later remembered as one of the leading Greek tyrants. During Periander's reign Corinth acquired vast wealth from trade that ranged as far afield as Italy and Egypt. Periander also founded colonies on the coasts of the Aegean Sea (notably Potidaea) and the Adriatic Sea (notably Apollonia and Epidmanus). In addition, he oversaw the construction of a stone-paved road across the Isthmus of Corinth; this allowed merchant ships to be wheeled on large carts from the Saronic Gulf to the Gulf of Corinth, greatly reducing the time it took to travel from eastern to western Greece. The Corinthians charged tolls to other Greeks who used the road, adding to the city's growing wealth. Periander also supported the arts and launched large public building programs. Still, he was said to be suspicious of others and brutal to his enemies. When one of his sons died on the island of Corcyra, Periander sold three hundred Cor-

A bust of Pericles, who was repeatedly reelected strategos (general) and who helped lead Athens to cultural greatness in the mid-fifth century B.C. © CORBIS

cyraean boys into slavery. And rumors abounded that the tyrant killed his own wife, Melissa, and abused her body.

SEE ALSO: colonization; Corcyra; Corinth

Pericles
(ca. 495 B.C.–429 B.C.)

The leading statesman of Greece in the first half of the Classical Age and a champion of Athenian democracy and imperialism. Little is known about Pericles' early life because he kept a low public profile in those days. Plutarch claimed this was because Pericles looked like the former tyrant Pisistratus, and also because Pericles' head was abnormally long (and supposedly this is why he always wore a helmet when posing for portrait busts). Eventually Pericles did enter politics in the late

460s B.C., at first as a close associate of Ephialtes, leader of the radical democrats. The two men and their supporters opposed Cimon, leader of the pro-Spartan conservatives. In 461 Cimon was ostracized and banished, but Ephialtes was assassinated, leaving Pericles as the leader of the democrats. Pericles retained the position of Athens's most popular and influential statesman-general for the next three decades, swaying the Assembly with his effective oratory and guiding much of the city's domestic reforms and foreign policy.

On the domestic front, Pericles expanded the rights of the common people. He passed a bill providing pay for jurors, which made it possible for poorer people to take time away from their work to serve the state; and he got rid of rules that allowed only those who met certain financial qualifications to hold high office. He also employed thousands of citizens on large-scale public building projects that frequently lasted for years at a time. The climax of these programs came in the 440s and 430s B.C., when the Parthenon was erected atop the Acropolis and numerous other temples and public buildings began construction. These endeavors, along with increased democratic reforms, were designed not only to make the city more free, beautiful, and comfortable but also to transform it into Greece's showcase. "I declare that our city is an education to Greece," he declares in his famous funeral oration.

> Each single one of our citizens, in all the manifold aspects of life, is able to show himself the rightful lord and owner of his own person. . . . Athens alone of the states we know comes to her testing in a greatness that surpasses what was imagined of her. . . . Mighty indeed are the marks and monuments of our empire. . . . Future ages will wonder at us as the present age wonders at us now . . . for our adventurous spirit has forced our entry into every sea . . . and everywhere we have left behind us everlasting memorials of good. . . . This, then, is the kind of city for which these men . . . nobly fought and nobly died. . . . You should fix your eyes every day on the greatness of Athens and fall in love with her. (Quoted in Thucydides, *The Peloponnesian War* 2.40–43)

In foreign affairs, Pericles maintained strong anti-Spartan sentiments and policies and persuaded the Assembly to build the Long Walls to keep the urban center safe from Spartan aggression. These walls, he said, would also provide a secure corridor to the port town of Piraeus, keeping the city supplied with food and other necessary materials during an emergency. This move angered the Spartans, who saw both Pericles and Athens as overly ambitious and dangerous to the balance of power in Greece. They and other Greeks also criticized Pericles for moving the treasury of the Delian League from Delos to Athens and using large portions of the funds to pay for Athenian building projects. Meanwhile, Pericles endured frequent attacks at home by his conservative political enemies, who tried to discredit him by prosecuting his friends, the sculptor Phidias and the philosopher Anaxagoras, and Pericles' mistress, Aspasia. (Phidias and Anaxagoras left Athens and Aspasia was acquitted.) More enmity against Pericles resulted from his swift and harsh treatment of Delian League members who balked against Athenian authority. He led a large naval force against rebellious Samos in 440 B.C., for example, and reduced the island to a humiliated subject state. Pericles also spearheaded the alliance with Corcyra in 433 that pitted that former

Corinthian colony and Athens against Corinth, and the audacious and unpopular naval blockade of Athens's neighbor Megara the following year.

These heavy-handed tactics finally pushed the Spartans and their allies over the edge, and the disastrous Peloponnesian War erupted in 431 B.C. Pericles initiated a controversial strategy of herding his countrymen behind the Long Walls and allowing the Spartans and their allies to run amok destroying Athenian houses and crops. When a deadly plague struck Athens in 430, it spread rapidly in the crowded conditions behind the walls, and the following year Pericles himself contracted the disease and died.

SEE ALSO: Aspasia; Ephialtes, 1; Long Walls; Parthenon

Persephone

In Greek mythology, the daughter of the fertility goddess Demeter. Persephone (also known as Kore) was abducted by Hades, lord of the Underworld, and against Demeter's wishes Zeus allowed Hades to marry Persephone. However, Zeus also decreed that thereafter the girl could spend the months from planting until harvest (the fall, winter, and spring) with her mother on earth. Only in the summer did Persephone have to return to her husband in his dark, subterranean realm. The Greeks came to associate Persephone with corn planting and death, reflecting her contrasting residences and roles above and below the ground.

SEE ALSO: Demeter; Eleusis; Hades

Perseus

In Greek mythology, a human hero best known for killing the Gorgon Medusa, the sight of whom turned people to stone.

Helped by the goddess Athena, Perseus obtained winged shoes and a cap that turned him invisible. Using the shoes, he flew to the island on which the Gorgons dwelled, and after he donned the cap, Medusa could not see him and he was able to sneak up on her. He did not look directly at her, of course, for fear of becoming a block of stone. Instead, he saw the creature only in a harmless reflection in his shield and thereby slew her. Later in his life, according to various myths, Perseus became king of Tiryns in the northeastern Peloponnesus and founded the nearby city of Mycenae.

SEE ALSO: Gorgons; Medusa; Mycenae

Perseus
(ca. 213 B.C.–166 B.C.)

The last ruler of the kingdom of Macedonia and the elder son of King Philip V (reigned 221–179 B.C.). After the Romans defeated Philip in the Second Macedonian War (220–197 B.C.), Perseus harbored a deep dislike of Rome. After he became king in 179, he publicly pursued peaceful relations with the Romans, but behind the scenes he worked to maintain Macedonian power and prestige at Rome's expense. Tensions between the two nations increased until another war broke out. Perseus was defeated decisively by the Roman general Lucius Aemilius Paullus at Pydna in 168. Macedonia's government was dismantled, and Perseus was taken to Rome, where he died two years later.

SEE ALSO: Battle of Pydna; Macedonia; Philip V; Rome

Persians

A people who originated in Fars, a small region just north of the Persian Gulf in southern Iran, and in the sixth and fifth centuries B.C. created the largest empire the world had yet seen. Among the areas subjugated by the Persians was Asia Minor, which brought them into contact with the Ionian Greeks and in the years that followed the mainland Greeks as well. For the next two centuries, the histories of Greece and Persia were inextricably intertwined, as each held the other in contempt and frequently engaged in wars and political quarrels.

The Persian Empire was established in the 550s B.C. by a young aristocrat of Fars who ascended the local throne as Cyrus II. In fewer than eight years, he defeated the Medes, who then controlled most of Mesopotamia. Cyrus and his son and successor, Cambyses, expanded their realm until it included the entire Near East, including Egypt and Palestine, and stretched eastward through Afghanistan to the borders of India. Cyrus defeated Lydia, in Asia Minor, in 546, absorbing the Lydian-controlled Ionian Greek cities in the process. The Ionians disliked being subject to Persia, but there was little significant resistance until well after Cambyses' successor, Darius I, invaded Thrace (north of the Aegean Sea) in the late 500s B.C. In 499 the Ionians rebelled but were defeated in 494. During the insurrection, the mainland cities of Athens and Eretria helped the Ionians, raising Darius's ire, and he launched an expedition against the Greek mainland in 490. The Athenians defeated his troops at Marathon, an embarrassment but not a major hindrance to an empire as large and powerful as Persia's. Nevertheless, after Darius died in 486, his son, Xerxes I, saw the potential of capturing Greece as a foothold from which to launch a larger conquest of Europe. To that end, he led a huge army into mainland Greece in 480 B.C. This time the Persians were even more soundly defeated than before, and Xerxes returned to Persia.

After the Greco-Persian Wars, Xerxes and his immediate successors (Artaxerxes I, Xerxes II, and Darius II) continued to oppose the Greeks. Occasionally the two peoples met in battle, as when the Athenian general Cimon defeated a Persian army on the Eurymedon River in the 460s B.C. More often, Persian kings and governors intrigued with individual Greek states, trying to play Greek against Greek. During the latter stages of the Peloponnesian War, for example, Darius II helped the Spartans finance the war fleets that soon enabled Sparta to defeat Athens.

In the meantime, internally the Persian Empire grew increasingly weak as most of its rulers proved incompetent, self-absorbed, and ineffectual. Persian impotence became increasingly apparent to leading Greeks, including orators such as Isocrates (early fourth century B.C.), who urged his fellow Greeks to invade and subjugate Persia. Finally Macedonia's King Philip II decided to do just that. But with his unexpected assassination in 336 B.C., the task fell to his son, Alexander III, who in a mere decade reduced the mighty Persian realm to a huge Greek dependency. The last Persian king, Darius III, was killed by some of his own nobles while fleeing from Alexander. After Alexander's own untimely death in the Persian capital of Babylon in 323, the former Persian lands were divided among his Successors.

SEE ALSO: Alexander III ("the Great"); Artaxerxes; Cambyses; Cyrus II ("the Great"); Cyrus the Younger; Darius I; Darius III; Greco-Persian Wars; Xerxes

Persians, The

A tragedy by Aeschylus, first produced in Athens in 472 B.C. The *choregus* (financial sponsor) was Pericles, who would later become the leading statesman of Greece. The play centered on and commemorated the decisive Greek victory at Salamis eight years before, a battle in which the playwright himself fought. The action of the play takes place in Persia in 480. A chorus of Persian elders expresses worry that King Xerxes' invasion of Greece may not be successful. The king's mother, Atossa, also admits to being anxious. Then a messenger arrives and describes the devastating Persian defeat at Salamis. Soon the spirit of Xerxes' dead father, Darius, appears and suggests that the disaster is divine punishment for Persia's excessive arrogance. Finally, Xerxes enters, hears the bad news, and the play ends on a somber note.

SEE ALSO: Aeschylus; Battle of Salamis; Greco-Persian Wars

pets

Dogs, which were widely used for hunting as well as for companionship, appear to have been the favorite pets in Greece in most periods. Depictions of domesticated dogs in Greek art date back at least to 3000 B.C. Other common pets included weasels (which helped eliminate unwanted rodents), birds, goats, and mice. In contrast, pet cats appear to have been rare in Greece.

SEE ALSO: family; houses

Phaedo
(born ca. 418 B.C.)

A Greek philosopher who hailed from Elis (a city-state in the western Peloponnesus). As a young man Phaedo (or Phaidon) traveled to Athens and became a devoted follower of the eccentric philosopher Socrates. After the latter's execution in 399, Phaedo returned to Elis and established a

school there. Later Plato, another avid pupil of Socrates, named one of his dialogues after Phaedo.

SEE ALSO: *Phaedo* (dialogue); Socrates

Phaedo (dialogue)

An important dialogue by Plato, it is narrated by Phaedo, one of Socrates' young followers. The setting is Socrates' prison cell in the last few hours of the philosopher's life (after being sentenced to death by an Athenian jury). Socrates tells his gathered pupils that a true philosopher is one who is willing to die for his principles. A just person, he asserts, has nothing to fear from death because the gods will safeguard his soul. One of those present in the cell expresses his doubts about the survival of the soul after death, prompting Socrates to present a series of arguments supporting the idea that the soul is immortal. The condemned man also cites a myth that describes conditions in the afterlife. The work ends with a moving description of Socrates' courageous death, brought on by his drinking poison hemlock.

SEE ALSO: Phaedo; Plato; Socrates

phalanx

A battlefield formation in which soldiers stood in ranks (lines), one behind the other, and marched at an enemy army.

SEE ALSO: weapons and warfare, land

Pheidippides
(fifth century B.C. ?)

According to Herodotus, an Athenian runner who carried messages to Sparta and back just prior to the Battle of Marathon in 490 B.C. During this twenty-six mile run, Pheidippides (or Philippides) supposedly encountered the woodland god Pan, who asked why the Athenians had been ignoring him of late. Later stories claimed that the same runner fought at Marathon, then carried the message of victory back to Athens and dropped dead of exhaustion. The truth of this incident has often been questioned, but there is no doubt that it inspired the creation of the modern marathon race (twenty-six miles long), which was not an athletic event in ancient times.

SEE ALSO: Battle of Marathon

Phidias
(ca. 490 B.C.–ca. 425 B.C.)

A noted Athenian sculptor, best known for the giant statue of Zeus at Olympia and the magnificent sculptures on the outside and inside of the Parthenon. The great image of Zeus, which sat inside the god's temple in the Altis (sacred sanctuary) at Olympia, was later listed among the Seven Wonders of the Ancient World. Phidias (or Pheidias) also created the giant statue of Athena (the *Athena Parthenos*) that stood inside the *cella*, or inner chamber, of the Parthenon. His other famous works included a large bronze statue of the same goddess (the *Athena Promachos*) that stood outside between the Parthenon and the Propylaea on the Acropolis and a similar statue of Athena commissioned by the inhabitants of the island polis of Lemnos. Phidias was a close friend of the Athenian statesman Pericles, and in the late 430s B.C. the latter's political enemies tried to discredit him by accusing Phidias of stealing some of the gold intended for the *Athena Parthenos*. Although the sculptor was acquitted, he decided to leave Athens permanently. In 1958 archaeologists excavated Phidias's workshop at Olympia, where he produced the famous statue of Zeus. A bronze drinking cup found in the

ruins bears the inscription "I belong to Phidias."

SEE ALSO: Olympia; Parthenon; sculpture

Philip II
(ca. 382 B.C.–336 B.C.)

One of Macedonia's greatest rulers, one of the foremost military innovators of the ancient world, and the father of Alexander the Great. Philip was born the youngest son of King Amyntas III at a time when Macedonia was still a disunited, militarily weak, and culturally backward kingdom viewed with contempt by the major Greek city-states. In 359 B.C. Philip's brother Perdiccas, who had succeeded Amyntas, was killed in battle and Philip, then about twenty-two, inherited the throne. Despite his youth, Philip was a brilliant, energetic leader who succeeded in uniting the country's feuding factions and creating a large and effective national army. This new military organization greatly benefited from a series of military innovations that he initiated. One of his predecessors had introduced an elite cavalry corps of young noblemen—the King's Companions. Philip now trained the Companions to make frontal assaults on enemy infantry, a bold new tactic. He also made the traditional Greek phalanx more formidable by deepening it and increasing the length of the soldiers' spears. In addition, he improved on standard siege tactics, greatly reducing the time it took an army to capture a city.

Philip's new army was a potent tool for conquest. And it did not take long for him to begin using it against the major city-states of southern Greece, which he saw as politically outmoded. He dreamed of uniting them into a Panhellenic (all-Greek) confederation led by himself. In 357 B.C. he captured Amphipolis, about 70 miles (113km) east of the Macedonian capital of Pella, which gave him access to the rich gold and silver mines located north of that city. Then he seized Pydna, Potidaea, Methone, and other northern Aegean cities and absorbed their resources. Methodically and relentlessly he moved ever southward toward the major city-states, which failed to mount any significant attempt to stop him, either singly or together. Before the mid-340s B.C. only the Athenian orator Demosthenes called any urgent attention to the threat he posed. In 346 B.C. Philip entered southern Greece and took control of the religious sanctuary at Delphi. "The news stunned the Athenians," Plutarch later wrote. "No speaker dared to mount the rostrum, nobody knew what advice should be given, [and] the Assembly was struck dumb and appeared to be completely at a loss." (*Life of Demosthenes* 18) Demosthenes then organized a powerful anti-Macedonian alliance headed by Athens and Thebes. The big showdown came in the summer of 338 B.C. at Chaeronea (west of Thebes), where Philip, accompanied by Alexander, now eighteen, delivered the allies a decisive defeat.

The Greek city-states now faced the dawn of a new political order headed by Philip, who installed a Macedonian military garrison in Thebes and forced the Thebans, Athenians, and other Greeks to join a confederacy in which he bore the title captain-general. The member states would be mostly free to conduct their local affairs, he said, as long as they supplied him with soldiers, money, and other resources when he demanded them. In return, he would provide overall security for the Greeks. Next, Philip began preparations for a large-scale invasion of the Persian Empire. But in 336 B.C. a disgruntled Macedonian nobleman stabbed him to death, after which Alexander ascended the Macedonian throne and carried out his father's plans for conquest in Asia. In Alexander's hands, Philip's well-honed army went on to transform the Near East and open up seemingly limitless horizons for the Greeks.

See Also: Alexander III ("the Great"); Battle of Chaeronea; Demosthenes; Macedonia; Olympias

Philip V
(238 B.C.–179 B.C.)

The ruler of the Macedonian kingdom during the era when Rome first began making major inroads into Greece. Philip became king in 221 B.C., three years before Rome declared war on Carthage, initiating the epic Second Punic War. In 215, shortly after the Carthaginian general Hannibal had delivered the Romans their worst battlefield defeat ever, at Cannae, Philip, thinking Rome was doomed, made an alliance with Carthage. This turned out to be a serious mistake. The Romans won the war in 201 and almost immediately attacked Macedonia, launching what they called the Second Macedonian War (200–197). Philip's phalanx was crushed at Cynoscephalae in Thessaly, and he was forced to become a Roman ally. On his death in 279, he was succeeded by his son, Perseus.

See Also: Battle of Cynoscephalae; Macedonia; Perseus, 2

Philippics

A series of powerful speeches by the Athenian orator Demosthenes denouncing the aggressions of Macedonia's King Philip II, who was bent on conquering all of mainland Greece. Demosthenes delivered the first speech in 351 B.C., after Philip had overrun much of Thrace. "Observe, Athe-

This is a marble statue of Demosthenes, greatest of the ancient Greek orators and the author of the masterful Philippics. © BETTMANN/CORBIS

nians, the height to which the fellow's insolence has soared," Demosthenes thundered.

> He leaves you no choice of action or inaction; he blusters and talks big ... [and] he cannot rest content with what he has conquered; he is always taking in more, everywhere casting his net around us, while we sit idle and do nothing. When, Athenians, will you take the necessary action? What are you waiting for? Until you are compelled, I presume. ... If we refuse to fight now in Thrace, we shall perhaps be forced to fight here at home. ... Our business is not to speculate on what the future may bring forth, but to be certain that it will bring disaster, unless you face the facts and consent to do your

duty. (*First Philippic* 9–10, 50)

When these words seemed to fall mostly on deaf ears, Demosthenes continued to rail against Philip. The second and third speeches of the *Philippics* were delivered in 344 and 341, respectively. In the third speech, the orator calls on the Athenians to muster military forces to stop the Macedonian onslaught: "We must make provision for our defense ... with war galleys, funds, and men, for even if all other [Greek] states succumb to slavery, we surely must fight the battle of liberty." (*Third Philippic* 70–71) A fourth speech has survived, but most modern scholars are doubtful that Demosthenes composed it.

SEE ALSO: Demosthenes; Philip II

Philoctetes

In Greek mythology, a friend of the heroic strongman Heracles and one of the Greek warriors who fought at Troy. When Heracles was on his funeral pyre, he gave his mighty bow and poisoned arrows to Philoctetes' father, who subsequently gave them to Philoctetes. Later the younger man became king of Malis and commanded seven of the ships that sailed to Troy during the famous Trojan War. On the way across the Aegean, the Greeks stopped on the island of Lemnos. There, a snake bit Philoctetes, who complained so much of the pain that Odysseus and the other Greek commanders left him behind on the island. A few years later, however, they came back for him. Having reached Troy, Philoctetes used one of his poisoned arrows to kill Paris, the Trojan prince who had instigated the war.

SEE ALSO: Heracles; *Philoctetes* (play); Troy

Philoctetes (play)

A tragedy by Sophocles, first produced in Athens in 409 B.C. As the play begins, the Greek warrior Philoctetes is living alone on the Aegean island of Lemnos, where his comrades had abandoned him several years before. Suddenly two of these comrades, Odysseus and Neoptolemus, appear. They have come to take Philoctetes to Troy because they recently heard a prophecy saying that they could not win the war unless they retrieved Philoctetes and his bow and arrows (which originally belonged to the hero Heracles). At first Odysseus tries to trick Philoctetes into giving him the weapons. Odysseus wants to take them and abandon their owner again, but Neoptolemus sees this as unfair and wants to take Philoctetes back to Greece. Matters are settled when the spirit of the dead Heracles appears and informs Philoctetes that Zeus's plan is for him to go to Troy with his bow.

SEE ALSO: Philoctetes; Troy

philosophy

For the ancient Greeks, the term *philosophy* was usually a very broad one that incorporated various forms of scientific inquiry, along with ethical, moral, and social concerns, in an overall pursuit of knowledge. Thus, when Greek philosophy emerged in the Archaic Age, there was not yet a clear distinction between what today are seen as the separate disciplines of science and philosophy. Beginning with Thales of Miletus, circa 600 B.C., Greek philosophic endeavor was mainly concerned with trying to understand the underlying structure and principles of the universe (what the Greeks called the *cosmos*). In searching for the *physis*, the principal physical basis of nature, the Greeks largely removed the gods and other supernatural elements from the discussion. Thales, Anaximander, Anaximenes, Pythagoras, Empedocles, Democritus, Xenophanes, Anaxagoras, and others viewed nature as being governed by intrinsic, physical, and predictable laws rather than by the arbitrary whims of divine movers. Many Greek philosophers believed the gods existed, but they saw these beings as living far away and having little or no interest in humanity.

These early Greek thinkers are now called the pre-Socratics because they predate the Athenian philosopher Socrates (ca. 469–399 B.C.). His life and teachings marked the juncture where scientific conjecture began to become distinct from educated concern with the nature of ethical concepts such as goodness, wisdom, and justice, and how human beings should best apply them to improve themselves and society. Socrates left no writings of his own, but he strongly influenced later Greek thinkers, beginning with his young follower Plato (427–347 B.C.) and Plato's own student, Aristotle (384–322 B.C.). Like Socrates, both Plato and Aristotle were concerned with the concept of "goodness" (or virtue), including its derivation, forms, and how humans might come to use it to improve themselves. Plato examined whether goodness could be taught, for example. He and Aristotle also wrote extensively about the application of ethical concepts to politics and government, as in the case of Plato's ideal nation-state run by philosopher-kings, described in his *Republic*.

Neither Plato nor Aristotle concerned themselves solely with discussions of ethics and social and political reform; each man also produced a vast collection of works covering scientific topics such as astronomy and zoology. But a number of later Greek thinkers continued to deal with ethical concepts. Many Hellenistic Greek philosophers concentrated particularly on how these concepts might be applied in everyday life; and they and their followers sought to teach ordinary people how to cope with the many problems that plagued them and their society. Among these thinkers were Zeno, founder of the Stoic movement, and Epicurus, whose followers came to be known as the Epicureans. These and other schools of philosophical thought taught that fear, greed, dishonesty, and extravagance grow out of ignorance and can lead only to misery and misfortune; thus, a moderate, thoughtful, honest approach to life is best. These and other examples of Greek philosophy had a profound influence on Roman thinkers and later, after Rome's fall, on European thinkers.

SEE ALSO: Anaximander; Aristotle; Democritus; Eleatic school; Empedocles; Epicurus; Neoplatonism; Plato; Pythagoras; Skeptics; Socrates; Stoics

Phocaea

A Greek city located near the entrance of the Gulf of Smyrna (in western Asia Minor). The Phocaeans early became known for their skills as sailors, and they established several new towns on the coasts of the Aegean and Black seas. Their most celebrated colonies, however, were in the western Mediterranean. In the seventh and sixth centuries B.C., Phocaea founded Massalia (modern Marseille) on the southern coast of Gaul (France) and Alalia on the island of Corsica (off the western coast of Italy). In the 540s B.C. the Persians invaded Ionia, prompting many Phocaeans to migrate to their distant colonies. Following the Greco-Persian Wars and liberation

of the Ionian cities, Phocaea joined the Delian League. But in 412 B.C., during the Peloponnesian War, the city quit the league. In the Hellenistic Age, Phocaea fell under the domination of a succession of large Greek states, including the Seleucid and Ptolemaic empires and Pergamum, before Rome gained control of Asia Minor in the second century B.C.

SEE ALSO: Massalia

Phocis

A region of central Greece centered roughly on Mt. Parnassus, north of the Gulf of Corinth. In the early years of the Archaic Age, the Phocians controlled the sacred precinct of Delphi (home of the famous oracle). But in about 600 B.C. they lost control of the site to the Amphictyonic Council. During the Greco-Persian Wars, Phocis (or Phokis) was at first compelled to support the invading Persians but eventually defied them and joined the united Greek army at the Battle of Plataea in 479. In the 450s and 440s Phocis recaptured and lost Delphi more than once. The same thing happened in the middle of the following century, when a group of Phocians seized Delphi, igniting the Third Sacred War. The members of the Amphictyonic Council opposed Phocis until all involved were threatened by Macedonia's King Philip II. The Phocians subsequently joined the other Greeks in their unsuccessful fight against Philip at Chaeronea in 338 B.C. In the early second century B.C. Phocis joined the Aetolian League, but only a few years later Rome gained control of the region, along with the rest of southern Greece.

SEE ALSO: Amphictyonic Council; Delphi; Philip II

Phoenicia

A small coastal area in the eastern Mediterranean, corresponding roughly to modern-day Lebanon. It was the home of the famous Phoenicians, a prosperous seafaring people. Phoenician traders reached the Greek lands as early as 900 B.C., and a little more than a century later the Greeks adopted the Phoenician alphabet for use in expressing their own language. The Phoenicians profoundly affected the Greeks in other ways as well, especially by introducing them to a variety of Near Eastern artistic and mythological ideas. In addition, the Greeks learned a great deal about shipbuilding from the Phoenicians. Over the centuries the latter unsuccessfully fought both the Greeks and the Romans for control of Mediterranean shipping routes. By the first century B.C., Phoenicia had ceased to exist as a separate political and cultural sphere.

SEE ALSO: Carthage; Greek language; seafaring

Phoenician Women, The

A tragic play by Euripides, first produced in Athens sometime between 412 and 408 B.C. In the story, the women of the play's title have been sent by the king of the Phoenician city of Tyre to Delphi, home of Apollo's famous oracle. On their way, they stop in Thebes and watch the events of the play unfold. They see that Polynices, son of the former Theban king Oedipus, has arrived with an army, intent on deposing his brother, Eteocles, who refuses to share the throne with Polynices. Hoping to find a way to save the city, the residents of Thebes pay heed to the words of the blind prophet Teiresias. He says that Creon, Oedipus's brother-in-law, must sacrifice one of his sons. This is done, and the Thebans are able to drive the attackers away

from the city's walls. Then Eteocles and Polynices engage in single combat and slay each other. Their mother, Jocasta, is so distraught that she kills herself, after which Creon takes the throne and announces that Polynices' body will remain unburied.

SEE ALSO: Antigone; Jocasta; Teiresias

phratry

In ancient Athens and presumably many other Greek city-states, an extended kinship group that consisted of about thirty clans, each clan made up of a few individual family units. A phratry was similar to a modern religious congregation, except that the members of a phratry were related to one another. (However, sometimes people who had no family or clan were invited to become honorary members of a phratry, a form of social charity in Greek society.) Leaders of a typical phratry organized religious observances and celebrations, marriages and weddings, and various other religious and social gatherings for members of the group.

SEE ALSO: family; marriage and divorce; tribes

Phrygia

The central portion of Asia Minor, which underwent occupation by a long series of invaders over the centuries. Herodotus claimed that the original inhabitants of the region, called Briges, migrated there from Macedonia. By the early Archaic Age, the Phrygians, who spoke an Indo-European language distantly related to Greek, had created a centralized political state. But in about 700 B.C. the area was overrun by the Cimmerians, who came from somewhere in west-central Asia. About a century later Phrygia was absorbed by Lydia, and in the 540s B.C. the

Persians defeated Lydia and took over its territories, including Phrygia. The region remained under Persian control until Alexander the Great marched through in 333 B.C. It was in the Phrygian town of Gordium that he met the challenge of untying a thick knot (a feat that many others had failed to accomplish) by simply slicing through it with his sword. After Alexander's death Phrygia was disputed and occupied in fairly rapid succession by the Seleucids, the Gauls (a branch of Celts), the kingdom of Pergamum, and finally the Romans, who took over the area in the late second century B.C. The chief cultural contribution of Phrygia was the "Great Mother" goddess, Cybele, whose worship spread to Greece and Rome in the last few centuries B.C.

SEE ALSO: Asia Minor; Celts; Lydia; Seleucid Empire

Phrynichus
(late sixth century B.C.)

An early Athenian playwright credited with helping to establish the essentials of the genre of tragedy. Of his plays, only a few fragments are extant. Perhaps his most famous work was the *Fall of Miletus*, describing the capture of that Ionian Greek city by the Persians in 494 B.C. after the failed Ionian rebellion. According to Herodotus, the play's Athenian audience, who had friendly ties with the Milesians, "burst into tears." Afterward, "the author was fined a thousand drachmas for reminding them of a disaster which touched them so closely, and they [the authorities] forbade anybody ever to put the play on the stage again." (*Histories* 6.22)

SEE ALSO: theater and drama

Pillars of Heracles

The Strait of Gibraltar (or Pillars of Hercules), or, more specifically, the rocky hills resting on either side of that gateway from the Mediterranean Sea to the Atlantic Ocean. According to legend, the famous strongman Heracles created these hills while performing one of his twelve labors.

Pindar
(ca. 518 B.C.–ca. 438 B.C.)

The most famous and accomplished of Greece's choral poets, best known for his victory odes (*epinikia*) written to honor the victors of athletic events. Not much is known about Pindar's life. It seems that he was born near Thebes and had a house there and that he may have served as a priest in Apollo's cult at Delphi. Pindar traveled widely, often at the invitation of families and individuals who desired that he write odes for them. Perhaps the most famous instance was when Hiero I, king of Syracuse in Sicily, asked the poet to visit that city in 476 B.C. Pindar composed the 116-line "First Olympian Ode," now widely viewed as his masterpiece, to commemorate Hiero's victory in horse racing in the Olympic Games. Pindar died in Argos (in the eastern Peloponnesus) at the age of eighty and was long afterward fondly remembered by all Greeks. When Alexander the Great destroyed the city of Thebes in 335 B.C., he ordered that Pindar's house be spared.

SEE ALSO: music and dance; *Odes*; poetry

Piraeus

The port of Athens, lying about 4 miles (6.4km) west of the Athenian urban center. The docks and main port buildings were

A reconstruction of Piraeus in the mid-fifth century B.C. *shows the Long Walls stretching toward Athens's urban center.* NORTH WIND PICTURE ARCHIVES

begun circa 493 B.C. under the leadership of Themistocles, then an archon. Between 461 and 456 the statesman Pericles oversaw the construction of the Long Walls connecting Piraeus to the urban center. And in about 450, the architect Hippodamus of Miletus laid out a grid of streets for a proper town slightly inland from Piraeus's dock area. Eventually the combined town and dock area had several temples, two agoras, and two theaters. Some evidence suggests that at its height Piraeus could dock as many as 370 ships at a time, making it the largest port in Greece. However, it was badly damaged by the Romans in the early first century B.C., and many of its damaged structures were never rebuilt.

SEE ALSO: Aegina; Athens; Long Walls

Pisistratus
(ca. 600 B.C.–527 B.C.)

The most famous of the tyrants who ruled Athens in the sixth century B.C. Pisistratus, who came from an aristocratic Athenian family, first gained notoriety by leading an army against the neighboring city-state of Megara. At the time, Athens was gripped by political tensions, as the farmer-hoplite class resented that the aristocrats still held most governmental power despite the democratic reforms of Solon in the 590s B.C. Pisistratus took advantage of the situation by creating, in effect, a third faction, made up of common folk. He then convinced the Assembly to grant him a group of armed bodyguards. With these soldiers, he seized the Acropolis in about 560 and made himself tyrant (at the time defined as a benevolent dictator). Members of the other factions drove him into exile four years later, but he soon returned at the head of a small mercenary army, defeated a small force sent by the government to stop him, and reasserted his position as tyrant. Despite the forceful means he employed to keep himself in power, Pisistratus was a well-meaning and constructive ruler. He supported most of the reforms of Solon (to whom he was related by blood) and kept tax rates at reasonable levels. He also sponsored large-scale public building projects, made some religious festivals (notably the Panathenaea) more splendid, and patronized sculpture and the theater (invented in the later years of his reign). When he died, his sons, Hippias and Hipparchus, succeeded him.

SEE ALSO: Hipparchus, 1; Hippias; Solon

Plataea

A small city in southern Boeotia, near the border with Athenian-controlled Attica. The Plataeans early developed a friendship with Athens, and when the Persians landed at Marathon in 490 B.C., Plataea (or Plataiai) sent its entire army (perhaps six hundred men) to help the Athenians. Eleven years later Plataea became the site of the last major battle of the Greco-Persian Wars, when the Persian general Mardonius made a stand near the town against a large, united Greek army. In 431, shortly after the outbreak of the Peloponnesian War, Thebes, then a Spartan ally, attacked Plataea. Soon afterward the Spartans finished the job, completely destroying the town. It was rebuilt, but in 373 it met destruction again at the hands of the Thebans. A few decades later Plataea was rebuilt still again, this time by Alexander the Great.

SEE ALSO: Battle of Marathon; Battle of Plataea; Greco-Persian Wars; Peloponnesian War

Plato
(ca. 427 B.C.–347 B.C.)

One of the leading philosopher-scientists of the ancient world and the key conveyer of the ideas and teachings of his predecessor, Socrates, to later generations. The noted modern English philosopher Alfred North Whitehead once remarked that the entire Western philosophical tradition has been "a series of footnotes to Plato." (*Process and Reality*) Whitehead exaggerates a bit in order to make the point that all Western thinkers since Plato have either accepted some of his teachings or felt obligated to explain why they disagreed with them.

For a figure of Plato's great historical and literary importance, surprisingly little is known for certain about his life. Some facts were preserved in short biographies by later ancient writers, including Diogenes Laertius, who established that Plato was a member of a well-to-do Athenian family that traced its lineage back to the great lawgiver Solon. A bit more biographical information appears in the so-called *Seventh Letter* of Plato; it may or may not have been actually written by him, but most modern scholars think the data it contains is reasonably accurate. In the letter, Plato states, "In my youth, I went through the same experience as many other men. I fancied that if, early in life, I became my own master, I should at once embark upon a political career." However, Plato soon became disillusioned, first by the reign of terror of the Thirty Tyrants (404 B.C.), which his kinsman, Critias, led; then by the trial and execution of Plato's friend and mentor Socrates (399). Socrates, an eccentric philosopher who tried to get his fellow citizens to seek the truth and lead virtuous lives, had been the single-most important influence on the youthful Plato. The older man had taught Plato to question everything about himself as well as authority figures and the government. Thus, Plato was appalled when "those in power brought my friend Socrates ... to trial ... laying a most iniquitous charge against him. ... The result was that, though at first I had been full of a strong impulse toward political life ... my head began to swim." (*Seventh Letter*) His spirit temporarily crushed, after the execution Plato spent the next few years traveling around the Mediterranean region. After witnessing such great injustices in Athens, he hoped to find out how other societies and their rulers administered justice. More and more, he came to believe that such rulers should be guided by philosophers, who seek to know what is good and just, or that the philosophers themselves should rule. And thus he himself became a philosopher. In about 387 B.C. he returned to Athens, bought a plot of land, and on it established the Academy, a university-like school for higher learning. His idealistic goal was to produce a series of philosopher-statesmen who might transform society and the world. He spent the rest of his life at the school, where he produced an enormous collection of writings, all of which, fortunately, have survived.

Most of Plato's works are in the form of dialogues. In each, a group of people, Plato's old friend Socrates usually figuring prominently among them, discusses the pros and cons of an issue. One issue that recurs often in these writings is justice. The most detailed examination of that concept is in Plato's masterpiece, *The Republic*, which begins by trying to define what justice is and then describes an ideal government run by a fair and just philosopher-king. His longest single work (and his last), the *Laws* also explores an ideal society, although this one is less authoritarian than the one envisioned in *The Republic*. The other dialogues are shorter but no less perceptive and penetrating. The *Laches* explores the nature of courage, the *Charmides* discusses the qualities of temperance, the *Protagoras* tries to determine whether virtue can be taught, the *Symposium* explores the nature of love, the *Phaedo* addresses the question of whether the human soul is immortal, and the *Lysis* examines the nature of friendship. The *Timaeus* and the *Critias* are famous for their detailed descriptions of the legendary island-nation of Atlantis (based on information gathered in Egypt by Plato's ancestor, Solon). But the *Timaeus* is also much more—an ambitious attempt to survey the universe and discern how it formed as well as to determine humanity's place within it.

As crucial and enlightening as these discussions and ideas have been to generations of Western thinkers, perhaps most important of all was Plato's dramatic and thought-provoking vision of the nature of reality itself. In the dialogue *Parmenides*, as well as in *The Republic*, he presents his so-called theory of forms. By *forms*, he meant ideas or ideal constructions. The physical world perceived by the senses, he said, is in many ways an illusion because under its surface exists an invisible realm of pure ideas. The cosmos was constructed by a divine craftsman, Plato suggested, who made Earth and the heavens in perfect forms in his own mind's eye. In contrast, the visible, touchable versions of these things are only imperfect replicas of the original and ideal forms. Plato offered the analogy of a carpenter who visualizes in his mind the bed and table he plans to build. When actually making these items, the carpenter tries to reproduce his mental blueprints of them. But the limitations of his tools, materials, and skills keep the finished products from measuring up exactly to his mental pictures. "There are beds and tables in the world—plenty of them," Plato says, "but there are only two ideas or forms of them—one the idea of a bed, the other of a table. . . . And the maker of either of them makes a bed or he makes a table for our use, in accordance with the idea. . . . [The carpenter] cannot make true existence, but only some semblance of existence." (*The Republic* Book 10)

Taking this concept a step further, Plato held that even the forms themselves have an underlying principle that makes them possible—a form of goodness that might be described as the inherent goodness of the creator. The degree to which these ideas affected later thinkers cannot be overstated. Plato's questioning of the reality of sense perception and his connection of morality with religious notions of godhead influenced ancient Jewish thinkers, Roman intellectuals such as Cicero, the esoteric Neoplatonists of late antiquity, several early Christian thinkers, and numerous thinkers and writers of the European Renaissance.

SEE ALSO: Academy; Aristotle; philosophy; science; Socrates; and the individual names of Plato's works

Plotinus
(ca. A.D. 205–ca. 270)

A Greek philosopher who was the foremost exponent of a school of thought known as Neoplatonism. Born and educated in Roman Egypt, as a young man he traveled with the Roman army into Mesopotamia in an effort to learn about Eastern philosophies. Eventually he settled in Rome, where he gained a following as a philosophical teacher. His writings, which were intended only for use by his students, were later collected by one of them, Porphyry, who carried on Plotinus's teachings after the latter's death. For the essential tenets of the philosophy these men advocated, **see** Neoplatonism.

SEE ALSO: philosophy; Plato

Plutarch
(ca. A.D. 46–ca. 120)

A noted Greek moralist and essayist, the most famous biographer of antiquity, and one of the most widely read and influential Western writers. Plutarch, whose Greek name was Plutarchos, hailed from Chaeronea in Boeotia, where he was active in local government. He also served as a priest at Apollo's shrine at Delphi, became a Roman citizen, and traveled to Egypt and Rome. In addition, he somehow managed to turn out a huge corpus of essays and biographies, making him one of the most prolific authors in history. Plutarch's biographies were collected into his best-known work, the *Parallel Lives*, which covers the lives and achievements of some fifty famous Greek and Roman figures, including Solon, Cimon, Pericles, Alcibiades, Demosthenes, Alexander, Demetrius Poliorcetes, Pyrrhus, Coriolanus, Fabius Maximus, Julius Caesar, Marcus Brutus, and Marcus Tullius Cicero. (A few of Plutarch's biographies did not survive, most notably those of the Theban general Epaminondas and the Roman general Scipio Africanus.) These works are treasure troves of data about their subjects and about Greco-Roman history in general between 600 and 200 B.C. because Plutarch had access to many ancient historical works that are now lost. Moreover, his influence on later Western writers was profound. Sir Thomas North's sixteenth-century translation of the *Parallel Lives* was the main source for Shakespeare's plays *Coriolanus, Julius Caesar,* and *Antony and Cleopatra*. Also highly informative and widely read was Plutarch's *Moralia* (*Moral Essays*), a large series of tracts discussing social, moral, and literary issues. Indeed, in these essays, as well as in his biographies, Plutarch remained a stern moralist who judged as well as chronicled his subjects. Writing several generations after Rome had eclipsed the Greek world, he condemned the perpetual disunity of his Greek ancestors, saying bluntly, "Greece fought all her battles against and to enslave herself. Every one of her trophies stands as a memorial to her own shame and misfortune, and she owed her ruin above all to the misdeeds and the rivalries of her leaders." (*Life of Flamininus* 11)

SEE ALSO: biography; Greece, history of; *Moralia*

Pnyx Hill

The hill on which the Athenian Assembly met from the late sixth century B.C. on. It is situated a few hundred yards/meters west of the Acropolis, and in its prime it featured a speaker's platform that faced an open area, where the citizens congregated.

SEE ALSO: Athens; government

Poetics

One of Aristotle's more important works, it is essentially a critical analysis of poetry (including epic poems and dramatic plays) and to a lesser degree the arts in general. The author categorizes the various kinds of poetry according to the types of people

each kind depicts; for instance, he rates tragic characters as more substantial and noble than comic ones. He also traces the origins of tragedy and comedy and explores the various elements of each, including plot, character development, and catharsis (a purging of the emotions produced by effective poetry, drama, or art). Aristotle's examination of epic poetry includes a review of its proper form and a critical commentary of Homer and his epics. The *Poetics* exerted a strong influence on the later development of European poetry and drama.

SEE ALSO: Aristotle; poetry; theater and drama

poetry

Most ancient Greek poetry was meant to be recited or sung to musical accompaniment, most often the lyre (a small harp) but also other solo instruments or combinations of instruments. Professional poetry reciters, sometimes called rhapsodes, often traveled from region to region and recited verses, either for small groups of people or for larger groups during competitions staged during religious festivals. Before the fifth century B.C. the most popular works recited were those of epic poets like Homer.

Epic poetry was one of a few major categories of Greek poetry. A typical epic, for example Homer's *Iliad* or *Odyssey*, consisted of several thousand lines of verse and dealt with heroic, larger-than-life characters and themes, mostly relating to mythical times and events. In addition to Homer's epics, which first appeared sometime in the eighth century B.C., there were many others. The most famous were those making up the Epic Cycle, six of which dealt with elements of the Trojan War and its aftermath that Homer had not covered.

A painting on a red-figure vase depicts a musical competition involving a flute and lyre.
THE ART ARCHIVE/BIBLIOTHÈQUE DES ARTS DÉCORATIFS PARIS/DAGLI ORTI

Except for a few fragments, these works are lost, as are other works of the Epic Cycle that covered various mythological subjects and stories. One important early epic poem, the *Theogony* by Hesiod, did survive. It tells about the creation of the world and the early exploits of the gods.

Another major category of Greek poetry was lyric poetry. It consisted mainly of relatively short verses or songs, mostly about personal emotions and experiences and themes from everyday life. The term *lyric* refers to the fact that such poems were intended to be sung to the accompaniment of a lyre. A number of different forms of lyric verses developed featuring various meters (distinctive rhythms based on the number of short and long syllables in each line). One kind of lyric poetry, the elegy, was an effective medium for express-

ing personal feelings, the glories of war, tomb epitaphs, laments, and love songs. Early examples include poems by the Spartan Tyrtaeus and the Athenian Solon, among others. Some of Solon's verses, including the following one, describe his famous political reforms in Athens: "To the people, I have given just as much power as suffices, neither taking away from their due [rights], nor offering more. . . . The people will best follow its leaders if it be neither given undue liberty nor unduly oppressed. For excess bears arrogance whenever great prosperity attends on men whose minds are not well balanced." ("Salamis" 3–5) Much later, in Hellenistic times, the love elegy became widely popular. This earthy example is by the first-century B.C. poet Meleager: "The wine cup is happy. It rubbed against warm

Zenophila's erotic mouth. O bliss! I wish she would press her lips under my lips and in one breathless gulp drain down my soul." ("The Wine Cup.")

Lyric poetry also included choral odes. Initially, these were intended to be sung and danced to at religious festivals by choirs of men, boys, or girls. But over time such odes included any lyrics sung by a group of people and accompanied by musical instruments. There were many different types, including *paeans* (hymns praising Apollo and other gods), dithyrambs (songs describing the exploits of Dionysus and other gods), maiden songs (hymns sung by young women in religious processions), dirges (sad songs sung at funerals), wedding songs, and victory odes (*epinikia*). The fifth-century B.C. Theban poet Pindar gained a reputation as the master of the victory ode. He wrote a great many to honor winning athletes at Olympia, Nemea, and other major sporting venues. The following example celebrates the victory of Diagoras, a young boxer from Rhodes:

> Diagoras was twice crowned [with the wreath of victory]. At the famous Isthmus [of Corinth, site of the Isthmian Games], he was four times fortunate. . . . Six times he won at Aegina, and at Megara the stone record [listing victorious athletes] holds no other tale. Father Zeus . . . honor the rite of Olympian victory and a man who has found prowess in boxing. Grant him favor and joy from citizens and from strangers. ("Seventh Olympian Ode" 82–90)

Another kind of Greek poetry, iambic poetry, often sounded similar to lyric verse. However, the rhythm of iambic poetry was closer to human speech, and as a rule it was not sung or recited to musical accompaniment. For these reasons the lines in Greek drama were usually set in iambic meter. Iambic poetry was also frequently more witty, insulting, sarcastic, or moralistic than lyric poetry. One of the early masters of this genre was Archilochus, who lived on the island of Paros in the seventh century B.C. This example of his work uses humor to examine a popular stereotype: "I don't like a general who towers over the troops, lordly with elegant locks and trim mustache. Give me a stumpy soldier glaringly bowlegged, yet rockfirm on his feet, and in his heart a giant." ("My Kind of General")

SEE ALSO: Alexandrian and other Hellenistic Greek literature; Hesiod; Homer; *Iliad*; *Odyssey*; Pindar; theater and drama

polemarch

In Athens in the Archaic Age and early Classical times, an archon (city administrator) charged with commanding the city's army during wartime. Herodotus describes how the *polemarch* (or *polemarchos*) Callimachus influenced the decision to attack the Persians at Marathon in 490 B.C. In 487 B.C. the military authority of the *polemarch* was given to the ten elected generals (*strategoi*), and thereafter his job entailed mainly ceremonial state duties.

SEE ALSO: Callimachus, 1; *strategos*

polis

The name the Greeks used for the city-state. The poleis (the plural of *polis*) arose across mainland Greece and its nearby islands in the early to middle Archaic Age, and eventually there were hundreds of them in this region and on the coasts of Asia Minor and the lands surrounding the Black and Mediterranean seas. The average polis consisted of a central town, the urban center, which was often (though there were several exceptions) built around a central hill, or acropolis (meaning "the city's high place"). The farmland and villages around the town were also part of the polis. Although all Greeks, the residents of the various poleis developed differing local governments and customs as well as different forms of currency. Indeed, they thought of themselves as tiny separate nations, so they were fiercely independent, notoriously reluctant to unite, and frequently fought among themselves. The golden age, so to speak, of the polis was from about 480 to 330 B.C., when some of the major city-states—including Athens, Sparta, Thebes, Corinth, Miletus, and a few others—were among the leading political entities in the known world. In the wake of Alexander's conquests and rise of the Successor states in Hellenistic times, however, most poleis declined in power and influence.

SEE ALSO: government; Greece, history of; *Politics*

Politics

An important treatise in eight books by Aristotle. The central focus of the work is the city-state, or polis, which Aristotle sees as the best place for people to develop political institutions serving and benefiting both the community and individuals. Obtaining a decent, happy life for the citizens, he says, should be the main object of those governmental institutions. He talks about the prerequisites of citizenship and surveys different forms of government. Aristotle devotes considerable space to democracy and concludes that, while certain aspects of it are good, the ideal political system would be a limited democracy managed by a completely selfless

benevolent dictator, if such a person could be found.

SEE ALSO: Aristotle; government; polis

Polybius
(ca. 200 B.C.–ca. 117 B.C.)

One of the more important and influential of the ancient Greek historians, best known for his descriptions of the rise of Rome and the subsequent struggles between the Greeks and Romans. Polybius was born in Achaea (in the northern Peloponnesus) and was among the many Achaean hostages taken to Rome in 167 B.C. because the Romans wanted to ensure the good behavior of the Achaean League. Befriended by the Roman statesman and general Scipio Aemilianus, Polybius took an interest in Roman history and politics. And when Scipio annihilated the city of Carthage in the climax of the Third Punic War in 146 B.C., Polybius witnessed the destruction firsthand. Eventually Polybius compiled a voluminous history of Rome covering the period 220 to 146 B.C. The first five of the work's forty books are the only ones that have survived complete, but a number of fragments of the others have also been found. Polybius was an honest, thorough, and accurate historian who, like Thucydides, based most of his information on eyewitness accounts.

SEE ALSO: Achaean League; historical writing; Rome

Polycleitus
(flourished late fifth century B.C.)

One of the finest sculptors of the ancient world, famous for his idealized representations of the male body. Born in Argos in the northeastern Peloponnesus, Polycleitus utilized mainly bronze. Many of his statues of naked athletes stood in the sacred sanctuary at Olympia, including the renowned *Doryphorus* (*Spear Carrier*) and *Diadumenus* (*Ribbon Binder*). The *Doryphorus* immortalized the counterpoise stance of human statuary, in which the subject's weight rests on one leg projecting forward slightly from the other; this pose became standard among Western sculptors up to and beyond the Renaissance. Polycleitus's most famous work in antiquity was an imposing gold and ivory statue of the goddess Hera, which stood inside her temple at Argos. Some witnesses compared it favorably with Phidias's great statue of Zeus at Olympia.

SEE ALSO: metalworking; Phidias; sculpture

Polycrates
(reigned 540–522 B.C.)

Dictator of the island polis of Samos and one of the most famous and accomplished of the tyrants who ruled a number of Greek cities in the Archaic Age. At a time when other Ionian Greek cities were coming under Persian domination, Polycrates asserted Samian power by building a large navy, seen by Herodotus and Thucydides as a forerunner of Athens's naval empire in the following century. Using his warships, which were heavily armed with archers, Polycrates conducted raids of neighboring islands and the nearby Ionian coast. He also captured the island of Delos and expanded the scope of the athletic contests (the Delian Games) held there. Polycrates was a vigorous builder as well. He inaugurated the temple of Hera at Samos, then one of the largest and most splendid temples in the Greek world. Eventually the tyrant's audacity and aggressive military posture caught up with him, however. Some of his own sailors turned on him and convinced the Spartans

to attack Samos. Though he was able to survive this assault, Polycrates made the mistake of paying a visit to the Persian governor of Asia Minor, who murdered him. The Persians then confiscated his ships and used them against other Greeks.

SEE ALSO: government; Persians; Samos

Polygnotus
(flourished ca. 475 B.C.–447 B.C.)

One of the most talented and famous painters of ancient Greece. Although he hailed from the northern Aegean island of Thasos, Polygnotus spent most of his career in Athens, where he specialized in large murals depicting famous mythical events. These included paintings of the fall of Troy and Odysseus's encounters with a bevy of souls from the Underworld. Some were displayed in a stoa in the Athenian Agora and others at Apollo's sanctuary at Delphi. One of Polygnotus's greatest innovations was giving lifelike expressions to the human figures in his paintings. Although none of these works has survived, a few ancient writers have given thumbnail sketches of them. In his famous guidebook, for example, the later Greek traveler Pausanias describes Polygnotus's *Capture of Troy*, saying that it

> shows the fall of Troy and the Greeks sailing away. Menelaus's men are getting ready for the voyage [back to Greece]. There is a painting of the ship with a mixture of men and boys among the sailors. . . . [Some men] are taking down Menelaus's tent not far from the ship. . . . Helen herself is standing with Eurybates . . . [and] above Helen sits a man wrapped in a purple cloak, extremely melancholy. You would know it was [Trojan king] Priam's son Helenus even before you read the inscription. (*Guide to Greece* 10.25)

SEE ALSO: painting; stoa; Troy

Poseidon

In Greek mythology, the chief god of the seas. The brother of Zeus, Demeter, and Hades, Poseidon was called the "earth-shaker" because it was thought that he caused earthquakes. Poseidon was also seen as a skilled horse tamer, and the horse was one of his symbols. His other familiar symbols were the trident (three-pronged spear) and the dolphin. According to various ancient accounts, right after Poseidon was born, his father, the Titan Cronos, swallowed him, along with his brothers and sisters (except for Zeus), but fortunately vomited him back up later. After Poseidon reached maturity, he produced numerous offspring, including the minor sea god Triton; several giants, including Antaeus, Otus, and Ephialtes; the Cyclops Polyphemus, who was blinded by the Greek warrior Odysseus (as told in Homer's *Odyssey*); and Pelias, a mortal who usurped the throne of Iolcos in Thessaly from its rightful owner, Jason. Poseidon appears in many other myths. He is particularly conspicuous in Homer's *Iliad*, in which he takes the side of the Greeks against the Trojans. At the war's end, however, he punishes several of the Greek leaders after one of them (Ajax the Lesser) commits sacrilege in the local temple of Athena. According to legend, Poseidon also had a contest with that goddess over which of them would become the patron deity of Athens. He struck the Acropolis with his trident, creating a spring, but she planted an olive tree on the hill, and the Athenians judged her the winner.

Mythology aside, it appears that Poseidon, like Zeus, was a very ancient god that the Mycenaeans brought with them from the north when they entered Greece circa 2100 to 1900 B.C. Because the region they came from was landlocked, he may have originally been a god of horses, which would explain his close association with horses. Once the Mycenaeans established towns on the coasts of the Greek mainland, however, he took on his more important role of lord of the seas. And archaeologists have found his name mentioned often in the Linear B tablets dating from the late Bronze Age. From the Archaic Age on, sailors, fishermen, and merchants prayed to Poseidon to keep them safe when they were at sea; and survivors of shipwrecks sacrificed to him to give thanks. He had temples and shrines in coastal cities across the Greek sphere, but his most famous temple was on the Isthmus of Corinth, where the Isthmian Games, dedicated to him, took place.

SEE ALSO: Athena; *Odyssey*; Troy

Potidaea

A city established circa 600 B.C. by Corinth in a strategic spot on the Chalcidic peninsula (on the northern Aegean coast). It was originally intended as a Corinthian trading post to tap into trade routes running northwestward into Macedonia and Illyria and northeastward into Thrace and Scythia, but it soon became a prosperous, independent city. After the Greco-Persian Wars, the Potidaeans joined the Delian League, but they rebelled against Athens (which controlled the league) in 432 B.C., aided by their former mentor, Corinth. Athens sent troops, which besieged and eventually captured Potidaea. But after the Athenians lost the Peloponnesian War, the city became independent again, only to be seized in 356 B.C. by Macedonia's King Philip II, who sold the inhabitants into slavery. About forty years later Cassander, one of the Successors of Alexander the Great, erected a new town on the site, call-

This finely painted black-figure vase was made in about 600 B.C. LIBRARY OF CONGRESS

ing it Cassandrea after himself. In the 270s B.C. the city fell under Macedonian rule again, and when the Romans absorbed Macedonia in the second century B.C., Potidaea became a Roman colony.

SEE ALSO: Battle of Potidaea; Philip II

pottery

Pottery (or ceramics)—vessels and other objects made from baked clay—was produced in large quantity and in a wide range of styles throughout Greek history and is the most common artifact found in Greek archaeological sites. Greek pottery products included cups, bowls, plates, jugs, vases, buckets, bathtubs, ovens, coffins, cremation urns, cosmetic boxes, storage containers (amphorae), cooking pots, statues, lamps, roofing tiles, architectural decorations, theater tokens, and many others. Pottery was often painted, and because

painting styles and the shapes of pottery vessels were often distinct to certain eras and places, archaeologists can often date a site (a house, tomb, town, or whatever) by the kinds of ceramic items found there.

Examples of pottery objects dating from the late Stone Age (before 3000 B.C.) have been found in many parts of Greece. In the Bronze Age (ca. 3000–ca. 1100 B.C.), Minoan and Mycenaean pottery came in a wide range of shapes, colors, and styles of decoration. To differentiate and date the various types, archaeologists employ a scheme that breaks down into three sections, one for each of the major cultural spheres that existed in Bronze Age Greece. Pottery from Crete is called Minoan; pottery from the Cycladic islands lying north of Crete is called Cycladic; and pottery from the Mycenaean mainland is called Helladic. Each type breaks down into Early, Middle, and Late periods, and each period further breaks down into subperiods I, II, and III (e.g., Middle Minoan III or Early Cycladic II). Stone Age and Bronze Age Greek pottery is also sometimes named for the places where it is found or for mythical characters, for example: Kamares ware, Koumasa ware, and Minyan ware. In general, Bronze Age pottery was either unglazed or covered with a glaze made from crushed quartz (a technique known as faience). With the exception of larger jars for storage and pouring, most items were surprisingly thin and delicate. They were painted most often with abstract or stylized designs, including reeds, grasses, and flowers as well as marine plants and animals (the octopus being particularly popular).

In Greece's Dark Age (ca. 1100–800 B.C.), which followed the collapse of the sophisticated Minoan and Mycenaean cultures, ceramics were still produced. But

The funerary container above is in the geometric style and dates from ca. 750 B.C. © WOLF-GANG KAEHLER/CORBIS

overall they were of lower quality and utilized in a more limited range of decorative designs. From about 1050 to 900 B.C. (which scholars call the Protogeometric Period of Greek pottery), these designs were simple and uninspired, consisting mainly of abstract, repetitive arcs, half circles, concentric circles, and so forth. In the two centuries that followed (900–720 B.C., called the Geometric Period), the designs on pottery featured more geometrical patterns and shapes, including triangles, squares, cross-hatching, zigzags, and the familiar Greek key pattern. In about 800 B.C., coinciding with the beginning of the Archaic Age (and the last part of the Geometric Period), paintings on ceramics began to portray living things, including horses, birds, deer, and eventu-

ally people. By roughly 720 B.C. artistic styles from the Near East had begun to influence Greek art, including pottery painting. Modern scholars call this influence "Orientalizing." Typical subjects of ceramic paintings in the Orientalizing period included flowers, animals, mythical creatures, and abstract designs that had a Near Eastern flavor, which the Greeks saw as exotic.

In the late Archaic Age, probably between 625 and 600 B.C., Athenian potters introduced the "black-figure" style. It was so named because figures of people, animals, and objects were painted in black onto the natural reddish orange surface of the baked clay. The artist then used a pointed tool to etch details into the figures. An early master of the black-figure technique was Sophilos, the first potter known to have signed his work. Black-figure pottery reached its height of popularity between 550 and 525 B.C., when an unnamed artisan now called the Amasis Painter was working. It was in this period that the Athenians began awarding amphorae decorated in the black-figure style as prizes in the athletic games accompanying the Panathenaic festival.

In the last two decades of the Archaic Age and in the Classical Age that followed, the demand for ceramic vessels of all kinds increased and a new style of ceramics—the "red-figure" technique—became popular. The red-figure style reversed the black-figure approach by leaving the figures of humans and animals in the fired pot's natural reddish tone and rendering the background black. This allowed for the application of more realistic details, which were applied with a brush (although etching was still employed for certain fine details). Athenian artisans perfected the new style, among them the so-called Berlin Painter, who was particularly adept at painting human limbs and muscles. Another red-figure expert, the Brygos Painter, produced beautiful painted scenes on the bottoms of drinking cups. Other famous red-figure potters included the Andocides Painter, the Pan Painter, and the Meidias Painter. The subjects of the paintings on the pots ranged widely from mythological characters to everyday activities to erotic episodes. A variation of the red-figure style, the Kerch technique, which appeared in the fourth century B.C., utilized extra colors, especially yellow, gold, and white. Another style of ceramics that emerged in the Classical era, the "white-ground" technique, featured figures painted in delicate dark lines against a white background. White-ground paintings were most often used on *lekythoi*, pottery urns placed in tombs.

Regardless of the style of the painting used on pottery artifacts, the methods of making the pots themselves changed very little from the Dark Age through Classical times. A potter began with a wad of wet clay (*ceramos*) and shaped it on a flat wheel that turned around an upright vertical spindle. The artisan turned the wheel himself, using his hand or foot, or had a helper do it. After the piece had been properly shaped, the potter placed it outside to dry in the sunshine, and then, if possible, put it in a wood-burning kiln that reached temperatures approaching 1,000 degrees Fahrenheit (380°C). This imparted tremendous durability to the pot; indeed, ceramic items made this way more than two millennia ago are today displayed in museums around the globe and in many cases look practically new. But these finely painted pots became much less common in the beginning of Greece's Hellenistic Age (323–30 B.C.). In that period, most Greek pottery was made by working the wet *ceramos* into wooden molds having pre-carved patterns that resulted in raised relief decorations (such as swags of wreath).

SEE ALSO: industry; painting; Panathenaea

Praxiteles
(flourished ca. 370 B.C.–330 B.C.)

One of the most skilled and widely admired of the ancient Greek sculptors. Praxiteles, who hailed from Athens, was most famous for his statues of nude people, especially women, having ideal, often heroic physical attributes. His best-loved work, the Aphrodite of Cnidus, has not survived, but a later ancient copy of it did survive and now rests in the Vatican Museum. The original version of another celebrated statue by Praxiteles, which shows the god Hermes holding the baby Dionysus, was discovered in the late 1800s at Olympia.

SEE ALSO: sculpture

pre-Socratics

The Greek thinkers (philosopher-scientists) who preceded the fifth-century B.C. Athenian philosopher Socrates.

SEE ALSO: philosophy; science; Socrates

Priam

In Greek mythology, and in Homer's great epic poem the *Iliad*, the ruler of Troy during the famous Trojan War. Priam rebuilt the city after the Greek strongman Heracles had destroyed it (in revenge for Priam's father's refusal to reward Heracles for saving the life of a Trojan princess). Priam eventually had fifty sons, among them Hector, Paris, Helenus, and Polydorus. He also had fifty daughters, including Cassandra, Cruesa, and Polyxena. Nineteen of the children belonged to Hecuba, Priam's principal wife, who was queen of Troy during the war with the Greeks. Perhaps the most famous mythical episode featuring Priam involved his negotiations with the Greek warrior Achilles to recover the body of Hector after the latter had been slain by Achilles.

SEE ALSO: Achilles; Hecuba; Troy

Prometheus

In Greek mythology, one of the Titans (the first race of gods) and the creator of the human race. Prometheus's name means "Forethought," reflecting the fact that he had the power to see into the future. He was also known for his cleverness and his bravery, and both of these qualities came into play in the most famous myth associated with him. In it, Zeus asked Prometheus to decide how the humans should go about making sacrifices to the gods. Prometheus deceived Zeus by arranging for the gods to receive the bones and fat of the animals sacrificed and for the humans to keep and eat the meat. The angry Zeus responded by denying humans the knowledge of fire, but Prometheus took pity on them, stole fire from heaven, and gave it to them. In retaliation, Zeus had Hephaestos (god of the forge) chain Prometheus to a mountaintop, where a huge eagle (in some versions a vulture) ate his liver each day (after the liver had grown back each night). Eventually, the human hero Heracles set Prometheus free. The tragic playwright Aeschylus dramatized parts of this myth in his powerful play *Prometheus Bound*.

SEE ALSO: Heracles; *Prometheus Bound*; Zeus

Prometheus Bound

A tragic play by Aeschylus, first performed in Athens in about 460 B.C. and widely viewed as one of the greatest dramatic works ever written. The plot deals with the suffering and heroism of the Titan Prometheus, who angered Zeus by helping humans. Prometheus had created humanity, to whom he gave the physical form of the divine Olympians. Zeus had accepted this, but had forbidden Prometheus from giving the humans the secret of fire, which Zeus insisted must always remain an exclusive possession of the gods. However, Prometheus had a soft spot in his heart for the humans and wanted them to be able to make weapons to defend themselves from wild beasts and to learn various basic and essential crafts. These all required the use of fire, so he defied Zeus, stole some fire from heaven, and gave it to the humans.

As the play opens, it becomes clear that Zeus has found out about Prometheus's defiant and disobedient act. Enraged, Zeus tells his servants, the giants Force and Violence, to seize Prometheus and take him to the remote Caucasus region, far to the north of Greece. There, accompanied by Hephaestos, god of the forge, they bind the Titan to a jagged rock. Then they leave him there to suffer. All Prometheus has to do is admit that he was wrong to disobey Zeus, but the Titan flatly refuses. After Prometheus had suffered for many years, Zeus sends his messenger, Hermes, to offer him a deal. Zeus has heard a prophecy claiming that some day a son will be born to him, a child who will end up driving him off his throne on Olympus. Because Prometheus possesses the gift of foresight, he alone knows the identity of the woman who will become the boy's mother. If Prometheus will reveal the name of this woman, Hermes says, the king of the gods will free the Titan from his torments. But Prometheus rejects this offer. He knows that in the past he has served Zeus well and that taking pity on the humans and giving them fire was the right thing to do. The chained god asserts that Zeus's punishment is cruel and unjust and that he will never submit to his tyranny. Hermes warns Prometheus that if he does not submit to Zeus's will, he will never enjoy a single moment of sleep or relief. Each morning a huge, bloodthirsty eagle will swoop down and gnaw away at his liver. At night the organ will grow back, but the next day the eagle will return to repeat its grisly task, and this cycle will be repeated for all eternity. Even in the face of this terrible fate, the stalwart Prometheus refuses to give in. And because of this stubborn-

ness, Zeus becomes angrier than ever. As Prometheus bravely roars his continued defiance, the play comes to a shattering end as the rock and its chained prisoner collapse and disappear into the depths.

SEE ALSO: Aeschylus; Prometheus; Zeus

Propontis

The waterway lying between the Aegean and Black seas (today the Sea of Marmara). The main cities on its coasts were Byzantium and Chalcedon, situated on either side of the Bosphorus Strait.

SEE ALSO: Byzantium

Propylaea

The magnificent roofed gateway built on the western side of Athens's Acropolis between 437 and 431 B.C., at the height of the construction programs overseen by the statesman Pericles. The Propylaea (or Propylaia) was designed by the architect Mnesicles. Its center section opened onto the summit of the hill, facing the imposing Parthenon temple. The gateway also had wings containing rooms, the north wing housing an art gallery that featured paintings executed on wooden plaques.

SEE ALSO: acropolis; Parthenon; Pericles

Protagoras
(ca. 485 B.C.–ca. 420 B.C.)

The most famous of the ancient Greek sophists, men who taught rhetoric and other subjects for a fee. Protagoras is also sometimes seen as a philosopher. He was born in Abdera in Thrace and as an adult traveled to Athens, where he met the noted politician Pericles. It is possible that Protagoras also came to know the philosopher Socrates, though this remains uncon-

The World According to Ptolemy, ca A.D. 150

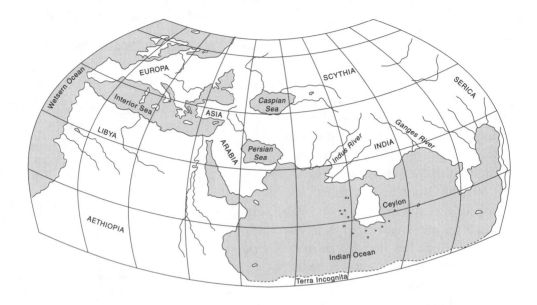

Steve Zmina

firmed. The main philosophical doctrine preached by Protagoras was that right and wrong do not exist. Rather, all aspects of reality are relative and determined by how people perceive them. He explored this idea in his treatise titled *Truth*, which bore the famous opening line, "Man is the measure of all things." Later, Plato made Protagoras a character in a dialogue named for the sophist, a work that explores the nature of goodness.

See Also: *Protagoras* (dialogue); Socrates; sophists

Protagoras (dialogue)

A dialogue by Plato in which the participants (Socrates and the sophists Protagoras, Hippias, and Prodicus) discuss the nature of virtue and the best way of obtaining it. Protagoras argues that good-

ness can be taught, like an intellectual discipline. The others end up agreeing and concluding that virtue is a form of knowledge. Protagoras also suggests that criminals should be rehabilitated so that they will end up doing good deeds, rather than merely be punished for past bad deeds.

See Also: philosophy; Plato; Protagoras

Ptolemy, Claudius (ca. 100 A.D.–ca. 178 A.D.)

One of the leading geographers and astronomers of ancient times (also known as Claudius Ptolemaeus). His maps were copied and recopied for many centuries following his death and strongly influenced the development of the modern science of cartography (mapmaking). Practically nothing of a definite nature is known about Ptolemy's personal life other than that he was an Egyptian by birth, a Greek by heritage, and a Roman by political status. So far as modern scholars can tell, he was not related to the Ptolemies who ruled Egypt in Hellenistic times. It is also fairly certain that he worked for at least a few years at the Museum in Alexandria. His masterwork, the *Guide to Geography*, was likely written between A.D. 150 and 160. It is divided into eight books, the first of which discusses the principles of applying mathematics to geography and map-making and also includes a thumbnail sketch of the length and breadth of the inhabited world. The next six books list the latitude and longitude of some eight thousand geographical locations. And the last book gives estimates for the longest day of the year in various latitudes and longitudes. Some of Ptolemy's statements and assumptions in the work are fairly accurate; others are grossly inaccurate.

Also influential for later generations was Ptolemy's great astronomical work, which he and his contemporaries referred to as the *Syntaxis*, or *Mathematical Compilation*. Later, in the ninth century, Arab scholars translated it from Greek into Arabic and called it *al-majisti*, meaning "The Greatest." Over time this mutated into *Almagest*, the title by which it is known today. The work is a long, complex, and elegantly crafted compilation of the prevailing astronomical views of Ptolemy's day, all based on the idea that Earth is the center of all things (the geocentric view). But though the Ptolemaic astronomical system was wrong, it was so well constructed, and its proofs so mathematically complex and convincing, that it was widely accepted as factual by medieval scholars. Also, the *Almagest*'s catalog of the latitudes, longitudes, and magnitudes (degrees of brightness) of 1,022 stars in forty-eight constellations continued as the standard reference work for sky maps in both the Western and Islamic worlds until the seventeenth century.

SEE ALSO: Alexandria; astronomy; science

Ptolemy I Soter
(ca. 366 B.C.–ca. 283 B.C.)

One of the leading Successors of Alexander the Great and the founder of the Greek Ptolemaic dynasty, whose members ruled Egypt for nearly three centuries. The son of a Macedonian nobleman, Ptolemy (TAW-luh-mee) was a close boyhood friend of Alexander, though Alexander was about ten years younger. Thereafter, Ptolemy remained among the crown prince's confidants and served on his general staff during the expedition against Persia, which began in 334 B.C. Ptolemy also wrote a detailed account of the expedition. Though it did not survive antiquity, the work was one of the major sources used later by Arrian and other chroniclers of Alexander's exploits.

Following Alexander's death in 323 B.C., Ptolemy took charge of Egypt and wasted little time in building a permanent power base there. To create an air of legitimacy, he sent agents to seize Alexander's body, which was on its way back to Greece from Babylon, and placed it in a golden coffin that eventually rested in a special shrine in the Egyptian capital of Alexandria. For a while Ptolemy ruled Egypt in Alexander's name while fighting several of the other Successors for territories in Palestine and other parts of the Near East. A few years after defeating Perdiccas (in 321), Ptolemy joined a coalition of these power brokers against Antigonus and his son, Demetrius. Though this alliance failed to get rid of that dynamic father and son duo, Ptolemy helped engineer a second coalition that soundly defeated them in the mammoth Battle of Ipsus in 301.

Now firmly entrenched in Egypt and having declared himself pharaoh (king) of that land, Ptolemy celebrated the victory at Ipsus by adding the title of Soter, meaning "Savior," to his name. He proceeded to rule the country the same way the Egyptian pharaohs had, as an absolute monarchy, which meant that the lives of average Egyptians did not change. In his splendid bastion of Alexandria, Ptolemy initiated construction of an immense palace complex and began building the Museum, a scientific research facility, and the Great Library, which quickly became the world's largest. When he died in his eighties, he was succeeded by his son, Ptolemy II Philadelphus.

SEE ALSO: Alexander III ("the Great"); Alexandria; Egypt; Ptolemy II Philadelphus; Successors

Ptolemy II Philadelphus
(reigned 283–246 B.C.)

The son of Ptolemy I Soter, founder of the Ptolemaic kingdom. Ptolemy II continued expanding the capital, Alexandria (which had been established by Alexander the Great a few decades before), and made it the premiere cultural center of the Mediterranean world. He finished work on the Great Library and Museum, which attracted leading scholars from far and wide. Ptolemy also inaugurated the towering Pharos lighthouse, which came to be seen as one of the wonders of the world. His first marriage was to Arsinoë, daughter of Lysimachus (one of Alexander's Successors). When she was exiled for plotting to assassinate him, Ptolemy married his own sister, also named Arsinoë, and with her established a ruler cult in which the two were worshipped as living gods. On the political-military front, Ptolemy periodically clashed with the Seleucid kingdom over disputed territories in Palestine and Asia Minor.

SEE ALSO: Arsinoë Egypt; Ptolemy I Soter

Ptolemy XII Auletes
(died 51 B.C.)

One of the last of the Ptolemaic rulers of Egypt, best known to posterity as the father of Cleopatra VII. The name *Auletes* means "the Piper" and derived from this king's skill as a flute player. An incompetent ruler, Auletes mismanaged the royal treasury, debased the coinage, and tried to make up for these mistakes by levying heavy new taxes, all of which drove most Egyptians to the brink of rebellion by 59 B.C. Then, when he was away, one of his daughters seized his throne. Desperate, he managed to get the military backing of a Roman governor, who restored him to power. Auletes remained unpopular, however, and died soon afterward, a miserable and hated man.

SEE ALSO: Cleopatra VII; Egypt

Pydna

A town on the northeastern coast of the Greek mainland, it was long controlled by Macedonia. The Macedonians and Athenians fought over it in the fourth century B.C. It later became famous as the site of the great battle in which the Romans defeated the Macedonian monarch Perseus in 168 B.C.

SEE ALSO: Battle of Pydna; Macedonia; Perseus, 2

Pylos

A town near the southwestern coast of the Peloponnesus that archaeological evidence indicates was the site of a Bronze Age

Mycenaean palace. However, it remains uncertain that, as Homer claimed, this was the seat of the kingdom of the legendary hero Nestor, one of the Greek leaders of the famous expedition to Troy. Pylos gained brief notoriety in 425 B.C. during the Peloponnesian War, when an Athenian army landed there and trapped and captured a small force of Spartans. Sparta recaptured Pylos in 409.

SEE ALSO: Nestor; Mycenaeans; Peloponnesian War

Pyrrhus
(319 B.C.–272 B.C.)

The most famous ruler of the Greek kingdom of Epirus in northwestern Greece and the first Greek general to wage a full-scale war against the Romans. Although Pyrrhus was a talented general, much of his political success was due to his connections with the right people. First, he was the son of a king of Epirus, Aiacides, and a second cousin of Alexander the Great. Also, after Aiacides was deposed and banished, along with his son, in 317 B.C., Pyrrhus served as an officer for the audacious military strongman Demetrius Poliorcetes, who married Pyrrhus's sister. Finally, Pyrrhus married Antigone, stepdaughter of Ptolemy I, king of Egypt. And Ptolemy helped him return to Epirus as its ruler (Aiacides having died by this time).

Once in power, Pyrrhus devoted most of his energies to trying to expand his kingdom's boundaries and prestige. This brought him into opposition with his old mentor, Demetrius, now ruler of Macedonia. Pyrrhus's most renowned military exploits, however, began in 280 B.C., when the Greek city of Taras (or Tarentum) in southern Italy begged him to help them fight the Romans. Crossing the Adriatic Sea with more than twenty-two thousand soldiers and about twenty battle elephants, he engaged the Romans in several large battles. In most of these encounters he won narrow victories. But his losses were heavy, and he is famous for a remark he made following the Battle of Ausculum: "One more victory like that over the Romans will destroy us completely!" (quoted in Plutarch, *Life of Pyrrhus* 21) This is the source of the term *Pyrrhic victory*, meaning an unduly costly win. Indeed, Pyrrhus finally realized that fighting the stubborn and relentless Romans was too costly and returned to Epirus in 275 B.C. Again he tried to expand into Macedonia and enjoyed considerable success. But then, allowing his attention to be diverted, he invaded the Peloponnesus and died in a street riot in the city of Argos.

SEE ALSO: Demetrius Poliorcetes; Epirus; Rome

Pythagoras
(flourished late sixth century B.C.)

A leading pre-Socratic mathematician and philosopher, best known for his theory that numerical relationships make up nature's underlying fabric. A native of Samos, Pythagoras migrated to Croton in southern Italy circa 531 B.C. and there set up a religious commune and philosophical school. He and his closest followers led an austere, monklike existence in which they practiced self-denial and refused to eat meat. In the intellectual sphere, they concluded that the gods had endowed the cosmos with an intrinsic scheme based on mathematics. For example, the Pythagoreans cited the fact that musical pitches repeat themselves in ascending and descending groups of eight (octaves) and that pressing on a lyre's string at its midpoint produces a tone an octave higher. In addition, Pythagoras and his followers attached mystical significance to the number ten; they pointed out that ten is the sum of the numbers one, two, three, and four, and that placing dots representing these integers in rows creates an equilateral triangle. Although they are generally credited with discovering that the square of the hypotenuse of a right triangle is equal to the sum of the squares of the other two sides (now called the Pythagorean theorem), this may have been known earlier to the Egyptians. The Pythagoreans also held that Earth is a sphere resting within larger (and invisible) cosmic spheres and that the soul is immortal. In addition, they promoted the idea of reincarnation.

SEE ALSO: astronomy; philosophy; science

Pytheas
(flourished late fourth century B.C.)

A Greek explorer from Massalia (in what is now southern France) who visited northern France, parts of the British Isles, the North Sea, and probably the island of Iceland.

SEE ALSO: explorers and exploration; Massalia

Pythia

A term denoting the oracle, or female priestess, who served at the sacred sanctuary of Apollo at Delphi and acted as a medium between the god and humans seeking divine guidance.

SEE ALSO: Apollo; Delphi; oracles

Pythian Games

Important athletic and musical contests held every four years as part of a major religious festival of the god Apollo at his sanctuary at Delphi in central Greece. For details on these and other similar competitions in ancient Greece,

SEE ALSO: athletics

quarries

Because Greek monumental architecture, exemplified by temples and other public buildings, primarily utilized stone, quarries were essential sources of building materials. The most common building stones were soft, easily workable ones (termed *poros*), limestone being the most popular of all. The most famous Greek limestone quarry was the one at Syracuse in Sicily, which produced tens of millions of tons of stone during antiquity. Also widely used were stone types that could be highly polished (termed *marmaros*), of which marble was the most popular. The leading marble quarries in the Greek world were on the islands of Paros, Naxos, and Chios; in Attica (including Mt. Pentelikon and Mt. Hymettus); and in a few spots in western Asia Minor. When possible, quarries were on the surface, where the stone could be directly and more easily manipu-lated; however, sometimes tunneling was employed, as in the case of some veins of marble in the Paros quarries.

Cutting the stone from the quarry bed was the most difficult, as well as the most crucial, phase of the quarrying process. In general, workers cut rectangular blocks that were slightly larger than needed (to allow for trimming and polishing). Mallets and chisels were used to cut grooves in the stone, thereby outlining the desired block. Then the workers employed picks to deepen the grooves and finally drove wooden wedges into the bottoms of the grooves and saturated them with water. As the wedges absorbed the water, they expanded, forcing the stone to crack, after which the workers used crowbars and other tools to finish freeing the stones. (Some harder stones, such as basalt, required iron wedges to be driven in by laborious pounding; conversely, sometimes metal saws or taut metal wires were used to cut through softer stones.) Once the stones had been freed from the parent rock, they were transported overland (or in some cases by ship) to the building site.

See Also: building materials and methods; mining; Paros; Pentelikon, Mt.

religion

The ancient Greeks were, with rare exceptions, devoutly religious and believed that their gods exerted a guiding influence in human affairs. Therefore, religion played a major role in Greek life, and religious rituals were associated with a wide range of public and private activities, including meals, in which a portion of the food was offered to the gods; birth and marriage ceremonies; and public meetings, which often began with an animal sacrifice and prayers. Indeed, the public dimension of religion was particularly important to the Greeks. They believed that the welfare of a community depended on obtaining and maintaining the goodwill and support of a god or gods. And not surprisingly, impiety (*asebeia*), lacking faith in or respect for the gods, was viewed as a crime, for if one person offended the gods, it might bring down their wrath on the entire community. Each Greek city-state worshipped a range of gods (*theoi*) and recognized Zeus as the leader of the Olympian divinities (originally thought to reside atop Mt. Olympus in northern Thessaly), but each also singled out a personal patron deity who supposedly watched over and protected that polis. For example, Hera (Zeus's wife) was the patron goddess of Argos; Athena (goddess of war and wisdom) watched over Athens; and Poseidon (lord of the seas) protected Corinth.

A New Religion Emerges

These and the other major gods were seen as having human form and attributes. And the myths about them, like the Greek language, acted as a unifying force, reinforcing the fact that all Greeks shared a common culture. The early epic poets Homer (in the *Iliad* and the *Odyssey*) and Hesiod (in the *Theogony*) played an especially important role in providing average Greeks with descriptions of these gods and their divine attributes and personalities. The origins of the Olympian gods and the religious customs surrounding them are still somewhat unclear. But archaeologists have found evidence that early versions of some of these deities (including Zeus, Poseidon, Dionysus, and Hermes) were worshipped by Mycenaeans in the Bronze Age. Some of the basics of worship, especially sacrifice (making offerings to the gods) apparently also originated in this period. The Greeks retained some of these deities and religious rituals in the Dark Age and Archaic Age, following the collapse of Mycenaean civilization. But overall, what amounted to a new religion had emerged by the late seventh century B.C. It featured open-air altars on which sacrifices were performed; large temples in which, it was thought, a god resided from time to time; cult images (statues) of the gods, usually set inside the temples; and public religious festivals to honor the gods. Perhaps the most famous and splendid of these festivals was Athens's Panathenaea, which climaxed in an enormous procession of the citizenry and a huge open-air sacrifice on the summit of the Acropolis.

Sacrifice and Prayer

In fact, sacrifice was the chief Greek religious ritual. It was based on the notion that the gods expected something in return for protecting and helping humans. The deities would provide a certain minimum level of good fortune, prosperity, and safety as long as people honored them, faithfully celebrated their festivals, and conducted proper sacrifices. The latter consisted of offerings of plants, liquids (mainly wine), and more commonly animals, including goats, sheep, birds, and cattle. Animal sacrifice usually followed set rituals. First, the worshippers draped flower garlands over the animal, called the victim, as they led it to the altar. Next, the person or persons conducting the ceremony poured water over the altar to purify it and sprinkled barley grains on the victim for the same purpose. Then a club was employed to stun the animal and a knife to cut its throat. The blood drained into a bowl and was sprinkled on the altar (and/or over the worshippers). Finally, people used axes and knives to butcher the victim, wrapped the bones and organs in the fat, and burned them. It was believed that the resulting smoke rose up to nourish and appease the gods. Then the worshippers divided, cooked, and ate the meat. Prayer, another important aspect of Greek worship, could be both public and private. A person generally prayed while standing, with his or her hands raised, palms upwards. Kneeling in prayer, which is common today, was seen as unworthy of a free person. Also, prayers were usually said aloud unless the worshipper had some special reason to conceal them.

Neither sacrifice nor prayers required special training in ancient Greece, so any person could lead such rituals. Home worship, centered on a small central altar, was led by the head of the household, while a clan or tribal leader or a state official led more public rituals. Any of these persons could be called a priest (*hiereus*), as could full- or part-time caretakers of temples and cults (religious congregations). Thus, there were no priests in the modern sense (full-time spiritual guides). Priestlike

individuals were also involved in divination, foretelling future events by reading and interpreting various kinds of divine signs, as there was a widespread belief in omens, signs of impending good or bad fortune. Certain events in dreams were also seen to foreshadow the future. The same individuals who claimed the ability to read omens sometimes interpreted oracles, which were a form of natural divination. Oracles were messages supposedly passed to humans from the gods. The most famous and revered oracles were those of Apollo at Delphi in central Greece and of Zeus at Dodona in northwestern Greece.

Beyond a general belief in the gods and rituals such as sacrifice, prayer, and divination, Greek religion had few set or universal beliefs and practices. There was no sacred text, like the Bible or Koran, for instance, nor any written moral creed. Similarly, Greek concepts of the afterlife varied widely. Many people believed that human shades (souls) spent eternity in the Underworld (ruled by Hades) wandering aimlessly across a dismal plain. But by the late Classical Age a large number of Greeks had turned to mystery religions, such as the cult of Demeter (the Eleusinian Mysteries), which promised members eternal happiness in Elysium (heaven or a pleasant part of the Underworld). The mystery cults became especially popular in the Hellenistic Age, which also witnessed the spread of Near Eastern gods, such as Osiris and Isis (from Egypt), through the Greek lands.

After Rome absorbed these lands in late Hellenistic times, the Greeks continued with their traditional worship, although in many places the gods and rituals came to be conflated or equated with Roman versions. This stemmed from the tremendous influence Greek religion had on the Romans. Though they saw the Greeks as politically and morally inferior to themselves, the Romans profoundly admired many aspects of Greek culture, particularly religious ones. Thus, the Roman god Jupiter came to be seen as equivalent to the Greek Zeus; the Roman Neptune to the Greek Poseidon; and so forth. The result was a "Classical" (Greco-Roman) form of worship that flourished in the Mediterranean world from the first century B.C. to the fourth century A.D., when the Christians, who had taken over the Roman government, tried to stamp out the old beliefs.

SEE ALSO: Athena; Delphi; Olympians; oracles; temples; Underworld; Zeus

Republic, The

A major literary work by Plato written circa 375 B.C. Consisting of ten sections (or books), *The Republic* (*Politeia* in Greek; *Respublica* in Latin) opens with a dialogue among the characters Socrates (Plato's old mentor), Cephalus (father of the orator Lysias), Cephalus's son Polemarchus, a sophist named Thrasymachus, and Plato's brothers, Adeimantus and Glaucon. Eventually Socrates dominates the conversation, and most of the work consists of his extended lecture about the rulers and institutions of an ideal political state, views that are obviously those of Plato himself.

First the speakers try to arrive at a definition for *justice*. Thrasymachus and Glaucon insist that justice is relative and that people will be unjust if it is to their advantage. But Socrates argues that justice should be pursued for its own sake, because it is good and will reward those who seek it. In an ideal state, he says, justice would always prevail. This launches his dissertation on a government administered

This is a Roman copy of a now lost bust of Plato, whose Republic *deals with the concept of justice and how rulers might achieve it.* HULTON ARCHIVE/GETTY IMAGES

by an honest, fair, and constructive ruler. Aiding this philosopher-king would be the "guardians," superior individuals who share their property with one another. These men would organize and guide two lesser groups of citizens—the "soldiers," who defend the community with their courage, and the "producers," who make things and perform menial labor. Members of each group would have their assigned duties and would have to perform them without question, giving thought only to the good of the greater community. Individuality and political and cultural innovation are discouraged in the Platonic state because they might lead to disorder. The result of these social groups working together for the common good, Socrates says, is a sort of harmony that constitutes justice in its purest form.

The narrative of *The Republic* also

dwells at length on the proper education of the elite guardians and their approach to knowledge. This affords Plato the chance to explain his "theory of forms," which contends that the world perceived by the senses is illusionary, made up only of imperfect replicas of invisible, divinely inspired forms. And only a few specially enlightened people will be able to appreciate this hidden world. In the seventh book of the work, Plato offers an analogy, today often called the "Myth of the Cave." In it, a group of individuals, representing ordinary, unenlightened people, are chained inside a dark cave. They incorrectly assume that the distorted images perceived by their senses in the cave are the real world because they are completely unaware that a wider, well-lit world of "reality" and "truth" exists beyond. They require an enlightened mind—that of a guardian—to lead them up into the daylight. Later in *The Republic*, Plato explains that the way to train the mind to see this light of truth is to master subjects that deal with abstract ideas, such as geometry and astronomy. Eventually this will lead to liberation of the soul.

SEE ALSO: government; philosophy; Plato

rhapsodia

In ancient Greece, poetry recitations, often accompanied by music, at religious festivals, athletic and dramatic contests, and other public celebrations. The performers, called rhapsodes, frequently competed for prizes. Homer's epics (the *Iliad* and the *Odyssey*) were the most popular subjects of these recitations, but various other epics, as well as lyric poems, were also presented.

SEE ALSO: Homer; music and dance; theater and drama

rhetoric

The art of communicating in public, persuasive speaking, or effective oratory. However one defined *rhetoric*, mastery of it was essential for any man who wanted to pursue politics or serve in government; this was because he had to convey his ideas and argue his beliefs and policies solely by oral means. The exact origins of rhetoric as a formal discipline are uncertain. But in the early Classical Age the itinerant teachers known as sophists promoted it, saying that skill in public speaking was a must for an educated man in a Greek democracy or any state in which people discussed community matters in assemblies or pleaded cases before juries. Late in the fifth century B.C. the orator Gorgias pioneered teaching rhetoric in a formal school setting, and such schools became popular in the century that followed as well as in Hellenistic times and the Roman Period. One of the more famous schools of rhetoric was that of the orator Isocrates, founded circa 390 B.C.

Formal rhetoric came to emphasize five fundamental steps for preparing a speech. First was "invention," in which the orator chose his subject and researched it. In the second step, "arrangement," he organized his facts logically, so that they followed a clear progression. Thirdly, he chose the most effective tone of voice to deliver the speech, a step called "diction." Then came "memory," in which the speaker used various tricks to memorize long tracts of material since reading from notes was unacceptable. Finally, the fifth step, "delivery," involved various vocal techniques and tricks used in the actual delivery of a speech. Influenced by the Greek orators, Roman politicians and orators adopted these same steps beginning in the first century B.C., and thereafter the study of rhetoric become an important part of the education of well-to-do Roman men as well as Greek men.

See Also: Demosthenes; education; sophists

Rhodes

One of the largest of the Greek islands located off the southwestern coast of Asia Minor and one of the leading naval powers of Greece and the Mediterranean world in the early Hellenistic Age. According to some ancient myths, the original inhabitants of Rhodes, the Telchines, had magical powers that allowed them to change the weather and cure disease. In reality, as archaeology reveals, in the Bronze Age the island was settled by people from Asia Minor, perhaps from the southern region of Caria. They may have been dominated by the Minoans, centered on Crete, or at least they adopted certain Minoan customs. After the fall of Greece's Bronze Age civilization, Dorians from the Peloponnesus settled Rhodes and founded its three principal cities—Lindus, Camirus, and Ialysus. Thereafter, Eastern influences filtering in from Asia Minor combined with Dorian Greek customs to produce a unique version of Greek culture. For example, the Rhodians imported an Eastern sun god as their national patron, but over time that deity became associated with the Greek sun god Helios. In the later Archaic Age, Rhodes grew prosperous from trade and established overseas colonies. The island fell to the Persians in 494 B.C., but the mainland Greeks liberated it a few years later and it joined the Athenian-controlled Delian League. Around 400 B.C. the three Rhodian cities combined their efforts to build a new capital, called Rhodos, which quickly became one of the leading seaports of the eastern Mediterranean.

That new city played a key role in the most famous episode in Rhodian history. After the death of Alexander the Great in 323 B.C., several of his Successors wanted either to control or to ally themselves with Rhodes because of its wealth and influence. In the spring of 305 B.C., one of these men, Demetrius, son of Antigonus, led a vast invasion force against the island and besieged the city of Rhodos. In a tremendous display of ingenuity, bravery, and sheer fortitude, the Rhodians withstood the onslaught and eventually forced Demetrius to withdraw. (Even though the siege failed, he still received the nickname of Poliorcetes, or "the Besieger.") After his embarrassing retreat, the overjoyed Rhodians celebrated their deliverance in a manner as spectacular as the assault itself. They gathered up the enormous amounts of bronze from the siege engines Demetrius had left behind, melted it down, and used it to build a giant statue of their patron, Helios. It became known as the Colossus of Rhodes and was listed among the so-called Seven Wonders of the Ancient World. The Rhodians' days of defiant independence were numbered, however; in the first century B.C. the Romans conquered the island and made it part of their growing empire.

See Also: Demetrius Poliorcetes; Helios; weapons and warfare, siege

roads

The Greeks did not have a complex system of paved roads, as the Romans eventually did. Instead, most Greek roads were narrow dirt or gravel tracks frequented by pack animals, horses, and human foot traffic and were not suitable for wagons and other wheeled vehicles. Wider, studier roads were sometimes constructed, leading from urban centers to nearby temples or shrines, to accommodate larger volumes of traffic. These roads either took advantage of natural deposits of limestone for their surfaces or were paved in blocks of limestone. Other noteworthy paved roadways included the one running across the Isthmus of Corinth, which was used for hauling ships (on large carts) from the Saronic Gulf to the Gulf of Corinth; and the stone-surfaced road stretching from Athens's urban center to the quarries at Mt. Pentelikon, on which the heavy marble blocks used in the Parthenon and the Propylaea (on the Acropolis) were transported. Many roads had ruts purposely cut in them to provide stability and traction for wagon wheels.

When roads crossed small rivers or gullies, bridges were used, but most were simple timber constructions that have long since disappeared. Occasionally, beginning in the fifth century B.C., Greek bridge builders employed stone piers (vertical supports) topped by stone lintels (rectangular slabs); but large bridges supported by stone arches were not erected in the Greek lands until the Roman period, when Roman engineers introduced more advanced road- and bridge-building methods. Also uncommon in Greece before the Roman period were milestones set up along the roadways. However, the Athenians placed herms (carved images of the god Hermes, patron of travelers) at intervals along Attica's roads beginning in the late sixth century B.C.

SEE ALSO: herm; Rome; trade

Roman Period

As determined by modern scholars, the period of ancient Greece lasting from about 30 B.C. (when Rome defeated and absorbed the Ptolemaic kingdom) to A.D. 476 (when the last Roman emperor was deposed). The Greek lands remained under Rome's control throughout the Roman Period.

SEE ALSO: Greece, history of; Rome

Rome

An Italian city-state that methodically created an empire during Greece's Classical and Hellenistic ages, conquered and absorbed nearly all of the independent Greek states, and went on to rule most of the known world. In the process, the Romans adopted many aspects of Greek culture and passed them on to later generations of Europeans. Rome began as a series of villages at a bend in the Tiber River (near Italy's western coast) circa 1000 B.C. (during Greece's Dark Age). The inhabitants spoke an early form of Latin, an Indo-European tongue. At first ruled by kings, in about 509 B.C. the Romans adopted a representative form of government, the Roman Republic, which had citizen assemblies that chose leaders and a legislature made up of well-to-do aristocrats—the Senate.

Rome's initial contacts with the Greeks occurred soon after Greek cities began to spring up in western and southern Italy in the eighth and seventh centuries B.C. Greek goods flowed northward into Rome, and Greek customs and ideas, including the alphabet and religious concepts, filtered in via the Etruscans, immediate neighbors of the Romans who, like the Romans themselves, were highly impressed by Greek culture. After the establishment of the Republic, the Romans began expanding their power and influence and fought wars with various Italian peoples, including the Greeks who lived in the southern part of the peninsula. By 265 B.C. Rome had absorbed these cities and become masters of most of Italy.

The Roman conquest of the Greek

lands lying outside of Italy began as a consequence of the bloody Second Punic War (218–201 B.C.), in which Rome fought and defeated the empire of Carthage (centered in North Africa). During the conflict the Macedonian kingdom, ruled by Philip V, became Carthage's ally; when Carthage lost the war, the Romans decided to punish Philip for interfering in their affairs. In 200 B.C. Rome launched an attack on Macedonia in which Europe's two most formidable and feared military systems met head-on. The Greeks still used the phalanx formation, which the Romans had long ago abandoned. Employing a more flexible and more mobile system involving smaller battlefield units (called maniples), the Romans decisively defeated Philip's forces at Cynoscephalae in central Greece. Not long afterward, in 191 B.C., the Romans also defeated the Seleucid ruler Antiochus III in the pass of Thermopylae, where Sparta's King Leonidas and his men had fought to the death against the Persians in 480 B.C. The following year, 190 B.C., the Romans defeated Antiochus again, at Magnesia in Asia Minor.

Many Greeks resented Rome's intrusion into the Greek sphere, and anti-Roman factions developed in Macedonia and in the Achaean League. The unrest culminated in another war in which a Roman army crushed Macedonia's new king, Perseus, at Pydna. This time, Rome dismantled the Macedonian kingdom and then moved against other Greek states, including the Achaean League, Epirus, Rhodes, Corinth, and others. In the span of a mere fifty-four years, the Romans reduced most of the independent Greek kingdoms and poleis to dependent states.

And in the first century B.C., Rome annexed Ptolemaic Egypt after defeating its last Greek ruler, Cleopatra VII, at Actium in western Greece in 31 B.C. The Mediterranean Sea had become in a sense a vast Roman lake.

The fall of Ptolemaic Egypt, marking the end of Greece's Hellenistic Age, also coincided with the demise of the Roman Republic, which had been rocked by a series of devastating civil wars in the first century B.C. Octavian (adopted son of the great Roman general Julius Caesar), the victor of Actium, created the more autocratic Roman Empire. And under the name of Augustus (the "Revered One"), he became the first of its long line of emperors (although he never actually called himself *emperor*). During the roughly five centuries in which these rulers controlled the known world, the Greek lands remained provinces of the empire. Meanwhile, many aspects of the societies of Greece and Rome merged to form what modern scholars call Classical (or Greco-Roman) civilization. Finally, the western Roman government, beset by internal decay and external invasions by tribal peoples from central and northern Europe, disintegrated in the fifth century A.D. The eastern Roman sphere, with Greece at its center, survived and became the Greek-speaking Byzantine Empire. An exotic mix of old Roman and new Greek culture, the Byzantine realm lasted until 1453, when the Ottoman Turks overran it.

SEE ALSO: Battle of Actium; Battle of Cynoscephalae; Battle of Magnesia; Battle of Pydna; Battle of Thermopylae, 3; Carthage; Etruscans; Italy

Sacred Wars

A series of conflicts waged over the control and protection of the sacred site of Delphi (home of the famous oracle of Apollo) in central Greece. The first war occurred in the early 500s B.C., when Delphi and its neighbor, Crisa, squabbled over Crisa's right to collect tolls from religious pilgrims visiting Delphi. Crisa was destroyed by soldiers from some of the states making up the Amphictyonic Council, the religious organization charged with protecting the Delphic shrines. The Second Sacred War took place in 448 B.C., when the city-state of Phocis (a member of the Amphictyony) seized Delphi. Sparta liberated the sacred sanctuary, but Athens soon restored it to Phocis. The third war (356–346 B.C.) pitted Phocis against the Amphictyony until Macedonia's king, Philip II, intervened, ousted the Phocians, and took their seats on the council.

SEE ALSO: Amphictyonic Council; Delphi; Phocis

Salamis

An island lying near the western coast of Attica. The narrow strait between the island and the coast was the site of the great sea battle in which the Greeks defeated the Persians in 480 B.C.

SEE ALSO: Battle of Salamis; Greco-Persian Wars

Samos

A Greek island situated about 2 miles (3.2km) off the western coast of Asia Minor, Samos was famous for its skilled sailors and local temples dedicated to the goddess Hera, who was the island's patron deity. Mycenaean Greeks occupied Samos in the Bronze Age. Later, in the Dark Age, Ionian Greeks migrating from the mainland settled the island. Samos became highly prosperous from trade in Archaic times (ca. 800–500 B.C.) and between 560 and 540 the Samians erected the largest Greek building of the era—a temple of Hera measuring 320 by 160 feet (98 by 49m). Then came the rule of Polycrates (540–522), a dynamic tyrant whose court attracted writers and skilled craftsmen from far and wide. Polycrates was killed by the Persians, who captured the island and installed a series of Greek puppet rulers. Following the defeat of Persia's King Xerxes in 479 B.C., however, Samos was liberated. The island then became one of the leading members of the Athenian-controlled Delian League. In 440 the Samians quit the league, and Athens responded by laying siege to their chief town. In the Peloponnesian War, Samos hosted an Athenian naval base, but when Athens surrendered in 404, the Spartans seized the island. Athens regained control in the following century. Later, in the early years of the Hellenistic Age, Ptolemaic Egypt took control of Samos. Finally, in 127 B.C., the island fell to Rome.

SEE ALSO: Ionia; Polycrates

Samothrace

A small oval-shaped island located in the northern part of the Aegean Sea. It was originally populated by people from Thrace (the land north of the Aegean), but in the Archaic Age settlers from nearby islands, probably Lesbos and Samos, took over and thereafter dominated Samothrace. In the fifth century B.C. Samothrace

A Roman copy of an original Greek bust depicts Sappho of Lesbos, the leading female poet of ancient Greece. THE ART ARCHIVE/ ARCHAELOGICAL MUSEUM ISTANBUL/DAGLI ORTI

joined the Delian League. Later, in Hellenistic times, the island became a frequent pawn in the many disputes among the large Greek kingdoms, until Rome absorbed all the Greek lands in the second century B.C.

sanctuary

In ancient Greece, a sacred site consisting of a temple and its surrounding grounds.

SEE ALSO: religion; temples

Sappho
(flourished late seventh century B.C.)

The most famous of the few female poets of ancient Greece. Sappho, who hailed from Mytilene on the island of Lesbos,

belonged to a local cult of Aphrodite, goddess of love. Sappho's lyric poems describe both her female friends in the cult and mythical characters, especially Aphrodite. Only two of these works survive complete, along with some fragments, but they are enough to show that Sappho's writing is direct, honest, and sometimes erotic.

SEE ALSO: Lesbos; Mytilene; poetry

Sardis

Situated some 40 miles (64km) inland from the Aegean coast, Sardis (or Sardes) was long the leading city in Asia Minor. In the seventh century B.C. it served as the capital of the kingdom of Lydia, which issued the world's first coined currency. In the 540s B.C. the city became the capital of Persia's Asia Minor province. And in 498 the Athenians, who were aiding the Ionian rebellion against Persia, burned Sardis (an act for which the Persian king Darius I retaliated by sending an invasion force to Greece in 490 B.C.). Alexander the Great took the city in 334, after which it passed to the Seleucid kingdom, then to the kingdom of Pergamum (ca. 180 B.C.), and finally to Rome (133 B.C.).

SEE ALSO: Battle of Marathon; Lydia; Persians

Saronic Gulf

An inlet of the Aegean Sea, bordering the western coast of the Attic peninsula. Three of Greece's leading trading cities—Athens, Aegina, and Megara—had ports in the gulf, making it one of the busiest waterways in the ancient Mediterranean.

SEE ALSO: Aegina; Piraeus

satyr plays

In ancient Greek drama festivals, short comic plays featuring the bawdy antics of

The Greenhaven Encyclopedia of Ancient Greece

satyrs, mythical creatures half man and half goat.

SEE ALSO: satyrs; theater and drama

satyrs

In Greek mythology, creatures that were half human, half goat (or half horse). They were associated with the god Dionysus and shared some of his traits, including mischief-making, drunkenness, sexual lust, and playfulness. The satyrs were often the subjects of artists and playwrights.

SEE ALSO: Dionysus; Silenus; theater and drama

science

The ancient Greeks were the first people in the world to develop a systematic approach to the study of science. Beginning in the seventh century B.C., Greek thinkers, best described as philosopher-scientists (because philosophy and science had not yet separated into distinct disciplines), sought the underlying principles of nature. In so doing, they largely removed the gods and other supernatural elements from scientific discussion. The heavenly bodies and other aspects of nature came to be seen as material objects obeying natural laws rather than as personalized beings.

Early Greek Scientists

The first period of Greek science is now called the pre-Socratic because it predated the fifth-century B.C. Athenian philosopher Socrates (who was more interested in ethical philosophy than science). The pre-Socratic Greek thinkers are usually grouped into two schools, or intellectual traditions. One was the Ionian, encompassing the Greek city-states clustered along the western coast of Asia Minor (what is now Turkey). The earliest

major Ionian scholar, Thales, who hailed from Miletus, borrowed some of his mathematical ideas from Egypt and astronomical ones from Babylonia. Unlike the Egyptians and the Babylonians, however, Thales tried to describe the workings of nature without resorting to supernatural or other powers outside of nature itself. He was the first person to refer to the known universe as the cosmos (from the Greek word for "order"), seeing it as ordered, rational, and comprehensible. Thales began the scientific tradition of searching for the *physis* (from which the word *physics* comes), nature's main underlying physical principle. For him, the *physis* was water, and he envisioned Earth as floating in a vast cosmic ocean of water.

Other early Greek thinkers proposed different concepts for the nature of the *physis*. One of Thales' students, Anaximander (ca. 611–547 B.C.), suggested that this substance was an eternal, unchanging, and invisible material that he called the "Boundless." The principal elements that make up everything in the universe—earth, water, air, and fire—he said, had arisen from the Boundless. Anaximander also proposed that the first living creatures came into being in water and that in time these creatures crawled onto the dry land and adapted themselves to their new surroundings, evolutionary concepts accepted by modern scientists. A later Ionian, Anaxagoras, had a significantly different view of the *physis*. He suggested that manifestations of all elements are present in all things in the form of tiny seeds that have existed from the beginning of time. Thus, the seeds of "hair" are present everywhere and give rise to hair in living things at appropriate times.

The second group of early Greek thinkers lived in some of the Greek cities of southern Italy. In about 530 B.C. the philosopher Pythagoras, a resident of the city of Crotona, established a school dedicated to the study of mathematics, astronomy, music, theology, and other subjects. The Pythagoreans differed from the Ionians in their choosing of numbers as nature's underlying principle, rather than material elements such as water or microscopic seeds. According to the Pythagoreans, natural objects are defined by precise geometric shapes and mathematical principles. They viewed the sphere as the most noble and perfect of the existing geometrical shapes and pictured Earth, the planets, and the heavens as consisting of a variety of spheres, often nesting within one another, a notion that profoundly influenced later Greek thinkers. The Pythagoreans also proposed that, because the heavenly spheres were part of a single, perfectly tuned mathematical scheme, these bodies must, like the strings of a lyre, produce harmonious musical effects. This is the derivation of the familiar expression "music of the spheres." Another pre-Socratic notion about the nature of the *physis* was rejected by most ancient thinkers, though it turned out to be essentially correct. The thinkers Leucippus and Democritus claimed that all matter in the universe is composed of tiny, invisible particles called atoms (from the Greek word for "indivisible"). At the time, this first atomic theory was just too novel and bold a concept to be accepted into the prevailing scientific mainstream.

A number of post-Socratic Greek thinkers began to develop a more definite system, or organized approach, to the study of science. Based in part on Socrates' system of searching for the truth by asking a series of questions (the Socratic method), his pupil Plato, and later, Plato's own student Aristotle, tried to apply what now looks like a primitive form of the scientific method. Science began to gain its own identity separate from that of philosophy and also to some degree to separate into subdisciplines, or branches, such as astronomy, biology, botany, physics, mechanics, and so on. Both Plato and Aristotle made proposals about the nature and workings of the heavens that became profoundly influential to later astronomers. Aristotle also made significant strides in the fields of biology and zoology. Among other things, he devised an ingenious system for classifying animals and observed the gestation of a chick inside its egg. Meanwhile, the emerging field of botany was dominated in this period by Aristotle's colleague and friend Theophrastus, who produced long, detailed writings about nearly all aspects of the plants known at that time.

Rise of Medical Science

Greek physicians and medical researchers also did important work in the Classical and Hellenistic periods. Highly respected medical schools arose, the two most celebrated at Cnidus and Cos (both located northwest of the island of Rhodes). These schools featured clinical research, classroom lessons, and practical apprenticeships. Students took a solemn oath to help the sick, to love humanity as dearly as their profession, and never to take a life or sexually abuse a patient. Overseeing the Cos school in the late fifth century B.C. was Hippocrates, who later came to be seen as "the Father of Medicine." He and his followers produced hundreds of writings on anatomy, surgery, treatment by diet and drugs, diseases of women and children, and medical ethics. By separating medical theory from religion and philosophy, they established medicine as a true scientific discipline. In the Hellenistic Age, the focus of new medical research shifted to Alexandria, where Herophilus, who had trained at Cos, established the Alexandrian medical school. He and his pupil Erasistratus made important strides, especially in anatomy, including descriptions of the motor and sensory nerves, the female ovaries, and the human digestive tract. About four centuries later, the Greek doctor Galen made more important studies of the human body and turned out large numbers of medical treatises.

Mechanical Geniuses

The Greeks also laid the foundations for the science of mechanics. The first major pioneer in this field was the third-century B.C. scholar Strato, who worked first in Athens and later in Alexandria. Like his noted predecessor Aristotle, Strato was fascinated by the concepts of force and motion and how they applied to everyday objects. Strato was one of the few later Greek thinkers who accepted Democritus's theory of atoms, saying that it satisfactorily explained how light could pass through water and how heat could flow from body to body. Strato's younger contemporary Archimedes was an even greater mechanical genius. Archimedes discovered important mathematical formulas pertaining to the volumes of spheres, cylinders, and other solid figures as well as the basic principles of floating bodies. He also experimented with levers, pulleys, and other simple machines, demonstrating their principles in large-scale applications, the most famous being devastating weapons of war. Meanwhile, one of Archimedes' contemporaries, Ctesibius (t'SIB-ee-us), invented the simple cylinder and plunger, the basis for numerous machines, both ancient and modern (including the cylinders and pistons in automobile engines).

As Archimedes had, Ctesibius, his pupil Philo of Byzantium, and the first-century A.D. inventor Hero of Alexandria designed large and lethal artillery devices, including huge catapults, dart throwers, and crossbows.

SEE ALSO: Archimedes; Aristotle; astronomy; Democritus; Galen; Hippocrates; Plato; Pythagoras

sculpture

The earliest examples of Greek sculpture were those of the Bronze Age Minoans and Mycenaeans. As a rule, they turned out small, elegant figurines rather than large-scale statues. The principal material was terra-cotta (baked clay), either unglazed or covered with a glaze made from crushed quartz (a technique known as faience). Sculpted objects were almost always painted, either with landscape motifs or abstract or stylized designs.

In the Archaic Age, the development of larger-scale sculptures paralleled the rise of monumental architecture in temples and other public buildings. Many Archaic statues were life-size, and their style was influenced somewhat by Egyptian models. These kouroi ("young men") and korai ("maidens") were typically static and formal, with their hands hanging stiffly at their sides, though they did have a certain elegance and charm. Over time these figures grew more realistic. An example from late Archaic times is the Anavysos kouros, now in Athens's National Archaeological Museum. It has more detail than earlier kouroi, including the depiction of tear ducts, although the body retains the traditional stiff, unimaginative stance.

In the early years of the Classical Age (ca. 500–323 B.C.), Greek sculpture underwent a major transition. The static and minimally detailed human figures of

Archaic times became much more realistic and began to achieve larger-than-life qualities of beauty, grace, and nobility. Modern scholars have come to call this style the Classical ideal. Free-standing statues graced the grounds of religious sanctuaries, and sculptors placed statues on temples and other monumental structures. The Parthenon's two pediments had many free-standing statues designed by the master sculptor Phidias, for instance. Other sculpted figures were carved in bas-relief (raised partly from the flat surfaces of the stones) in friezes on temples and other public buildings.

To make such monumental sculpted figures, the artists began with small clay models to work out conceptual details. Then came a full-size clay model, consisting of layers of clay applied to an inner wooden or metal frame. Copying these models, apprentice sculptors chipped away the initial layers from large stone blocks. Eventually the master sculptor himself took over and applied the final proportions and detail. The last step involved the application of accessories and colored paints. Metalworkers attached bronze spears, horse harnesses, and other details to holes the sculptors had drilled in the appropriate places. Then painters applied coatings of wax and bright colors, bringing the statues to life. The polished wax represented flesh, giving the effect of sun-tanned skin, while hair, lips, and eyebrows were painted a deep red.

The Classical approach of showing well-proportioned gods and heroes continued in Hellenistic times. The difference was that Hellenistic artists stressed realism even more as well as added more emotional and dramatic overtones. This dynamic new style reached its height in the great sculpted frieze winding around the base of the famous altar at Pergamum. This magnificent depiction of the mythical Gigantomachy (a battle pitting giants against the gods and their mortal helpers) contains seventy-five figures in all, each an artistic masterpiece. The figures appear to flow and writhe, imparting a startling impression of life and movement where none actually exists. This period of Greek sculpture had a profound influence on both the Romans and the artists of the Italian Renaissance.

SEE ALSO: Parthenon; Phidias; Praxiteles

Scythia

The name the Greeks used loosely to describe the large, sparsely inhabited region north of Thrace and bordering the Black Sea in the west and north. Scythia was often cited as the homeland of the Amazons, a legendary race of warrior women who had once launched a failed attack on Athens.

SEE ALSO: Amazons; Darius I

seafaring

The Greeks were one of the greatest seafaring peoples of antiquity, due in part to Greece's geography. The Greek mainland is extremely mountainous and has little arable land. In contrast, it features almost 2,000 miles (3,200km) of coastline and hundreds of offshore islands. As a result, the inhabitants of the mainland and islands were early drawn to the sea. Ships and seafaring provided a number of advantages, first and foremost the ability to move goods much faster and easier than was possible using carts or mules on land. Shipborne trade conducted throughout the Mediterranean and Black Sea spheres brought prosperity to Greece as a whole, but especially to a few leading naval powers, most notably Athens, Miletus, Corinth,

Greek triremes ply the Aegean seaways during the fifth century B.C., *an era in which Athens maintained a large navy to impose its will on other Greek states.* THE ART ARCHIVE/MUSEO NAVAL MADRID/DAGLI ORTI

Aegina, Samos, Rhodes, and Massalia. Ships were also a means of colonizing distant shores, and the Greeks established hundreds of new cities far and wide, particularly between 750 and 550 B.C. In addition, warships were potent tools for conquest, intimidation of enemies, and security. It was through naval power that Athens dominated the member states of the Delian League, for example, and that Sparta defeated Athens in the conclusion of the Peloponnesian War.

Whether they were warships or cargo vessels, Greek ships were made of wood and used both oar and sail power. Cargo vessels were wider and deeper than warships and had decks with spacious holds beneath, providing room for crewmen and passengers to sleep and cook. In contrast, warships—the most common type being the trireme—were long, narrow, and lacked holds. Most available space was devoted to benches for rowers, and there was little room to sleep or store supplies. As a rule, therefore, these vessels had to be beached each evening so the crew could go ashore.

Along with cargo ships, warships operated mainly in the period lasting from May through September. This was when rain and storms were least frequent and the seas calmest. When possible, sailors kept coastlines or other visible markers in view because compasses and similar naval aids did not yet exist. The stars could be used to navigate in open seas, but this method depended on clear weather and could be imprecise.

SEE ALSO: colonization; explorers and exploration; trade; and, for warships, including details about triremes, **see** weapons and warfare, naval

Seleucid Empire

The large realm established in the Near East in the early Hellenistic Age by one of Alexander's leading Successors, Seleucus. Under Seleucus's rule, a steady stream of Greek bureaucrats, army officers, and traders migrated into his empire, which covered much of Iran, Iraq, and parts of Asia Minor and Palestine. He built several new cities in that vast region, patterning them physically and culturally after Greek ones. Seleucus made one of these, Seleucia-on-the-Tigris (northeast of Babylon), his capital. The city also became a major nexus of trade routes passing through Mesopotamia and thereby drew both population and business away from Babylon, which went into decline.

Under Seleucus and his immediate successors, the kingdom became wealthy and powerful. However, this prosperity was not felt at all levels of society. As the Greeks continued to impose their culture on the region, a classist society emerged in which Greeks enjoyed higher social status and privilege than native Mesopotamians. Greek naturally became an important language in the region, one essential to government circles. Yet other languages, notably Aramaic and Akkadian, remained prominent, especially in regions where fewer Greeks settled. Also, Seleucus and his heirs recognized the importance of maintaining other facets of old Mesopotamian culture to make ruling this large and ancient land easier. They retained most of the old Persian bureaucratic structure and

dutifully supported and perpetuated the traditional temples and worship of the Persians, Babylonians, and other native peoples.

Such efforts to strike a practical balance between Greek and traditional Mesopotamian cultures were sometimes successful. However, the Seleucids' monumental experiment in nation-building was never completed. Less than a century after it was founded, the realm was in serious decline, partly because the Seleucid rulers incessantly fought with other large Greek kingdoms, draining human and material resources. Also, in 238 B.C. a group of nomadic Iranian tribesmen seized a large piece of the empire's eastern sector. Their leader, Arsaces, established the Parthian dynasty, whose aggressive rulers steadily chipped away at the Seleucid realm. The Seleucid realm was also hammered by the Romans, who decisively defeated the Seleucid ruler Antiochus III in the 190s B.C. By 63 B.C. all of Seleucus's once-great empire had been overrun either by the Parthians or the Romans.

SEE ALSO: Rome; Seleucus; Successors

Seleucus
(ca. 358 B.C.–281 B.C.)

One of the leading Successors of Alexander the Great and the founder of the Seleucid Empire. Seleucus commanded one of Alexander's key infantry units during the conquest of Persia. Following Alexander's death in 323 B.C., Seleucus at first seemed to support Perdiccas's attempt to hold Alexander's empire together. But soon Seleucus became heavily involved in the complex and destructive wars of the Successors, which tore that realm asunder. Eventually he became firmly entrenched in Babylon, took control of much of central and western Persia, and seized territory in

Syria, thereby creating the largest of the major Successor kingdoms. Seleucus was killed while trying to invade Macedonia in 281 B.C.

SEE ALSO: Alexander III ("the Great"); Antioch; Successors

Semonides (flourished seventh century B.C.)

A noted lyric poet, Semonides was born on the island of Samos but spent most of his life on the Cycladic island of Amorgos. Only one of his poems survives complete, a satire on women.

SEE ALSO: poetry

Septuagint

The Greek version of the Hebrew Old Testament, dating from the third century B.C.

SEE ALSO: Jews

Serapis

An Egyptian god introduced by King Ptolemy I shortly after he established a Greek dynasty in Egypt in the early third century B.C. Ptolemy's goal was likely to provide a deity that both his Egyptian and Greek subjects could appreciate and worship together. Thus, Serapis (or Sarapis) combined attributes of the traditional Egyptian god Osiris with those of some Greek gods, notably Asclepius, god of healing. After Ptolemy III erected a lavish temple to Serapis—the Serapeum—worship of the god spread beyond Egypt to other Mediterranean regions.

SEE ALSO: Asclepius; Osiris; Ptolemy I Soter

Seven Against Thebes

A tragedy by Aeschylus, first produced in Athens in 467 B.C. The subject is the ill-fated attempt of Polynices, son of Oedipus, to depose Oedipus's other son, Eteocles. Eteocles and Polynices had agreed to share the Theban throne, but Eteocles wanted to rule alone and shut his brother out. With the help of Adrastus, king of Argos, and five other military leaders (together making up the "Seven" of the play's title), Polynices assembles an army and prepares to attack Thebes. At first the attackers are unsuccessful. Eteocles and Polynices then engage in single combat and kill each other. Soon afterward a herald announces the decision of the regents who are in temporary control of the city. Eteocles will be given a proper funeral, but Polynices will be left unburied. Hearing this, Antigone, Eteocles' and Polynices' sister, says that she will defy the decree and bury her brother.

SEE ALSO: Antigone; *Antigone; Phoenician Women, The*

Seven Sages

A list of seven men chosen sometime in the sixth century B.C. as the wisest in all the Greek lands. The author or authors of the list are unknown. The seven men were the noted philosopher-scientist Thales; Pittacus, a famous ruler of Mytilene on the island of Lesbos; Bias, a diplomat who hailed from Priene in Ionia; the great Athenian lawgiver Solon; Cleobulus, a benign dictator of the island of Rhodes; Chilon, a shrewd Spartan public official; and Myson, a rural wise man mentioned briefly by the historian Herodotus. Some later Greek writers made alternative lists of sages, often deleting Myson and substituting other figures, such as the Corinthian dictator Periander or the philosopher Pythagoras.

SEE ALSO: Solon; Thales

Seven Wonders of the Ancient World

Seven notable structures first listed by the Greek writer and traveler Antipater of Sidon in about 130 B.C. They include the great pyramid of Khufu (called Cheops by the Greeks) at Giza in Egypt; the Hanging Gardens of Babylon, a series of gardens built on terraces in the royal palace of a Babylonian king in the sixth century B.C.; the large Greek temple of Artemis at Ephesus, on the Aegean coast of Asia Minor; the giant statue of Zeus at Olympia; the Mausoleum, a splendid tomb at Halicarnassus built for the ruler Mausolus by his wife, Artemisia; the Colossus of Rhodes, a towering statue of the sun god Helios erected on the island of Rhodes; and the Pharos, a skyscraper-like lighthouse constructed by the early Ptolemaic rulers in Egypt.

SEE ALSO: Ephesus; Olympia; Rhodes

shade

The spirit or soul of a deceased person.

SEE ALSO: Underworld

Sicilian expedition

One of the most important and influential incidents of the Peloponnesian War. The Athenians assembled a huge military force to attack Syracuse on the island of Sicily and suffered a crushing defeat.

SEE ALSO: Alcibiades; Peloponnesian War; Syracuse

Sicily

A large island (Sikelia in Greek) situated off the southwestern coast of Italy and the site of several influential Greek cities during the Archaic, Classical, and Hellenistic ages. Most of the Greek cities sprang up in the island's eastern portion during the eighth and seventh centuries B.C., including Gela, Catana, Leontini, Acragas, Himera, Naxos, and the largest and most powerful, Syracuse. Meanwhile, settlers from Carthage in North Africa colonized the island's western section. By about 500 B.C. the Greeks and Carthaginians had become bitter enemies. On several occasions the rulers of Syracuse led the other local Sicilian Greeks in attempts to oust the Carthaginians, including a major Greek victory at Himera in 480 B.C. But neither of the two peoples was able to take complete control of Sicily. Eventually Rome conquered both the Greeks and the Carthaginians and made the island a Roman province in the late third century B.C.

SEE ALSO: Battle of Himera; Carthage; Gelon of Gela; Peloponnesian War; Syracuse; Timoleon

Silenus

The best known of the satyrs, mythological creatures pictured as half man and half goat (or half horse). Greek artists routinely portrayed Silenus with the tail and ears of a horse, a pot belly, and a bald head. Some stories claimed he tutored the young Dionysus, the fertility god with whom he and other satyrs were often associated. Supposedly Silenus also had the gift of prophecy. He had many sons, called the Sileni. Along with him, they were favorite characters in the comedic satyr plays presented by Athenian playwrights.

SEE ALSO: satyrs; theater and drama

Simonides
(ca. 556 B.C.–ca. 468 B.C.)

A Greek poet who hailed from Ceos, an island in the Cyclades. Simonides wrote lyric poetry, including drinking songs, epitaphs for the dead, hymns, and humorous ditties. Only a few of these have survived, the most famous being his epitaph for the Greeks who fell at Thermopylae in 480 B.C., which opens with these words: "Tell them in Sparta, passerby, that here, true to their command, we lie." ("For the Spartans Killed at Thermopylae" 1–2).

SEE ALSO: Battle of Thermopylae, 1; poetry

Sisyphus

In Greek legend, a grandson of Hellen, founder of the Greek race. Sisyphus was said to have established the city of Corinth and the Isthmian Games, one of the four leading athletic competitions in the Greek world. In the most famous story about Sisyphus, he witnessed the abduction of Aegina, daughter of a river god, by Zeus. Sisyphus told Aegina's father what he had seen, and for this, Zeus tried to punish Sisyphus by sending Thanatos, god of death, to take the man down to the Underworld. The clever Sisyphus outwitted Thanatos, however, and trapped him in a prison cell. Later Sisyphus tricked Hades, god of the Underworld, too. Eventually Sisyphus paid a heavy price for his insolence. The gods condemned him to roll a heavy stone up a hill over and over again for eternity.

SEE ALSO: Hades

Skeptics

A group of Greek philosophers who argued that most knowledge is ultimately unattainable by humans. Thus, the best approach to life is to refrain from judging others, avoid extensive commitments, and strive as best as one can to achieve peace of mind.

SEE ALSO: philosophy

slaves and slavery

Slavery never became as widespread in Greece as it eventually became in Rome, which had the largest slavery institution of ancient times. Nevertheless, slavery existed throughout Greece's history, and slaves did a large proportion of the physical labor in all social areas and occupations in Greece. Like the Romans and other ancients, the Greeks accepted the existence of slavery as part of the natural way of things, a condition fully sanctioned by the gods. Even the slaves themselves thought slavery was a natural and inevitable situation, as evidenced by the fact that many of those slaves who earned their freedom bought slaves of their own. Society also saw slaves as lacking complete mental and moral abilities and as dishonest, lazy, or otherwise naturally deficient. For these reasons, it was thought that slaves could not be trusted and must be supervised whenever possible.

Most Greek slaves were non-Greeks, as it was generally viewed as improper to enslave other Greeks. (There were glaring exceptions to this rule, however, as when the Spartans enslaved their neighbors, the Messenians, creating a class of slaves called helots.) A majority of slaves were captured in wars or bought from slave traders, but some were bred in the home. The exact numbers of slaves who lived and worked in Greek homes and shops are uncertain, but it is likely that a household of moderate means had two or three slaves and a well-to-do family perhaps fifteen to twenty. A higher proportion of household slaves were women than men, partly because household tasks were seen as "women's work." Female domestic slaves helped with the spinning, weaving, sewing, cooking, and cleaning as well as nursed babies and watched over the family children. In many

A slave auction takes place in the Athenian Agora. Domestic slaves were generally well treated, whereas those who worked in Athens's mines were brutalized. © Bettmann/Corbis

Greek households, female slaves also had to perform sexual favors for the master. Today, such sexual exploitation is viewed as a serious form of abuse, but in the Greco-Roman world, like slavery itself, it was widely accepted as natural and inevitable. Male household slaves also had many important jobs. They ran errands, did much of the family shopping, accompanied the master's son to school, and guarded the women of the house when they went out in public. In national emergencies, some male slaves also fought alongside their masters in battle.

Not all Greek slaves worked in homes. They also labored in shops and other commercial enterprises as well as in agricultural jobs such as planting, harvesting, threshing, tending animals, and so forth. These slaves often worked side by side with their owners and/or members of the owner's family. In the Athenian territory of Attica, as well as in Boeotia and most other parts of Greece, slaves played mainly a supporting role in agriculture. In these areas, free peasant farmers generally preferred to work their own lands with only minimal help. A major exception was Sparta, where in the late Archaic Age and early Classical Age the helots did most of the agricultural work so that Spartan citizens could devote all their time to politics or the army.

In addition to privately owned slaves, there were slaves owned and exploited by the governments of Greek city-states. Aristotle describes some of the tasks performed by the slaves who worked for Athens's elected officials: "They keep watch to prevent any scavengers from depositing [manure and other refuse] within a mile and a quarter of the [town] wall. And they prevent the construction of buildings encroaching on and balconies overhanging the roads; and they remove for burial the bodies of persons who die on the roads."

(*Constitution of the Athenians* 50.2) Aristotle said that slaves also repaired the roads. In addition, after about 100 B.C. Athenian leaders delegated the job of overseeing weights and measures in the city's marketplace to slaves. Finally, many Athenian public slaves toiled in the state-owned silver mines at Laureum in southern Attica. These workers were treated with great cruelty. They were shackled day and night, forced to work in terrible conditions, and had no hope of gaining their freedom. The Spartan helots were also treated badly. They performed backbreaking work from sunup to sundown and endured beatings for the slightest infraction. Also, all over Greece it was common practice to torture slaves who gave evidence in court cases, based on the idea that the natural dishonesty of slaves would make them lie unless they were under duress.

By and large, however, the majority of Greek household, shop, and public slaves were usually well treated. It was not uncommon for household slaves to become trusted members of the family, for instance. This was partly due to human kindness but also to the fact slaves were seen as valuable property that could not be properly exploited when physically injured or emotionally upset. Therefore, though some masters did punish their domestic slaves, both custom and law usually prevented severe brutality. In Athens, for example, a free person who beat or killed another person's slave could be prosecuted. Another example of the generally decent treatment of household slaves is the common custom of paying them small wages, probably better described as periodic tips for good behavior. A slave could spend this money or save it up to buy his or her freedom, if, of course, the master would allow it.

Freeing a slave, called manumission, was often accomplished through a written contract. Several such agreements have survived, some carved onto the walls of public buildings. One disadvantage for a freed slave, or freedman, was that he or she had to work for the former owner for a set number of years. In the meantime, a freedman's social status was the same as that of a metic, which meant that he had no political rights and could not own land. Still a freedman was allowed to own a business, so he had at least the potential to become financially successful. This occasionally happened, the most famous example being a freedman named Paison who, at his death in the 370s B.C., was one of the richest men in Athens.

SEE ALSO: family; helots; metics; Sparta

Socrates
(ca. 469 B.C.–399 B.C.)

Arguably the most influential and pivotal of all the ancient Greek philosophers, whose ideas and methods profoundly influenced later Western thinkers. Most of what little is known about Socrates' life derives from the pens of Plato and Xenophon, who knew and came to revere him in their youth. It appears that Socrates was a fairly ordinary, middle-class Athenian citizen until he was in his thirties or forties. Then he had some sort of epiphany and drastically changed his lifestyle. Existing in self-imposed poverty and self-denial, he committed himself to defining and publicly promoting ethical concepts such as goodness and justice, even if they challenged traditional beliefs and institutions. Wandering the streets barefoot, he engaged his fellow Athenians in conversation, urging them to take stock of themselves and to seek justice and truth. Socrates guided such a session by asking a series of penetrating questions about a subject, and the person's answers became a sort of trail leading to the discovery of the core truth of that subject. This approach to learning became known as the Socratic method, in his honor. Plato later described what these encounters were like: "Anyone who . . . enters into conversation with [Socrates] is liable to be drawn into an argument; and whatever subject he may start, he will be continually carried round and round by him, until at last he finds that he has to give an account both of his present and past life; and when he is once entangled, Socrates will not let him go until he has completely and thoroughly sifted him." (*Laches* 187–188)

Although Plato and a number of other bright, sensitive young men came to respect and listen to Socrates, many other Athenians viewed the eccentric philosopher as a crank or a nuisance. Aristophanes and other comic playwrights ridiculed him. Also, some of his closest friends and supporters, including Alcibiades and Critias, eventually came to be seen as traitors to Athens and its democratic principles. For his association with them, along with other reasons, in 399 B.C. the Athenians tried Socrates and condemned him to death. Since he had committed no crime, the prosecution trumped up false charges, one claiming that he had corrupted Athens's youth through his teachings. Plato later summarized his mentor's dramatic speeches to the jury in the *Apology*. In another work, the *Phaedo*, Plato records how, after the trial, most of Socrates' closest friends watched him drink poison hemlock and die with courage and dignity. For excerpts from Socrates' court speeches, **see** *Apology*.

SEE ALSO: Alcibiades; philosophy; Plato

Solon
(ca. 640 B.C.–ca. 560 B.C.)

A lawgiver and social reformer who laid the groundwork for full-fledged democracy in Athens. Solon, a local statesman known for his honesty, wisdom, and fairness, came to the fore in 594 B.C. A violent class war between the wealthy, aristocratic faction and a coalition of the middle and lower classes was about to erupt, and a group of concerned citizens begged him to arbitrate a compromise. Solon instituted a series of sweeping reforms, among them cancellation of all debts (giving everyone a fresh start in life); elimination of the right of a creditor to enslave those who could not repay him; creating the *Boule* (Council), a group of four hundred men charged with preparing the agenda for the Assembly; repealing most of the harsh laws drafted earlier by the statesman Draco; and making wealth, rather than birth, the main qualification for holding political office. After enacting his reforms, which averted civil war, Solon traveled widely around the Mediterranean world and wrote lofty poetry, through which he expressed his political beliefs and explained his reforms. For a sample of Solon's verses, **see** poetry.

SEE ALSO: Draco; laws and justice

sophists

Beginning in the second half of the fifth century B.C., traveling teachers who, for a fee, taught young men how to speak in public and win political and other arguments. Some sophists (*sophistai*) also dispensed general knowledge of science and other disciplines. These men, whom some deridingly called wisdom-sellers, appeared on the scene partly in response to rapid social and political changes in Greece that opened up intellectual inquiry to all citizens rather than only a privileged few.

The sophists and their students hoped that their teachings would increase a person's chances of getting ahead in politics and business and thereby of acquiring money and success. But many people criticized them, seeing it as immoral to teach someone how to effectively argue both sides of a dispute. The earliest major sophist was Protagoras, who visited Athens and may have influenced the young Socrates.

SEE ALSO: education; Protagoras; *Protagoras*

Sophocles
(ca. 496 B.C.–406 B.C.)

A noted Athenian dramatist who wrote *Oedipus the King*, widely viewed as one of the greatest tragedies ever written. He was born in the small Athenian village of Colonus. Ancient writers claim that Sophocles wrote 123 plays, 7 of which have survived: *Ajax* (written ca. 447 B.C.), *Antigone* (ca. 441), *Oedipus the King* (ca. 429), *The Women of Trachis* (ca. 428), *Electra* (ca. 415), *Philoctetes* (ca. 409), and *Oedipus at Colonus* (406). Fragments of his satyr play, *The Trackers*, have also survived. Sophocles was highly skilled at characterization, and he was the first playwright to use a third actor, which increased the amount of character interaction in drama. He also reduced the importance of the chorus, fixing its size at fifteen members. The plots of Sophocles' plays usually revolve around central characters whose personal flaws (often called tragic flaws) cause them to make mistakes that adversely affect them, their families, and society as a whole. He won eighteen victories at the City Dionysia (Athens's main dramatic festival), more than any other playwright.

SEE ALSO: theater and drama; and the individual names of Sophocles' plays

Sparta

One of the two principal city-states of Greece from the seventh to fourth centuries B.C. and the home of Greece's most formidable and feared land army. Situated in Laconia in the southeastern Peloponnesus, Sparta was inhabited by Mycenaeans in the Bronze Age. Their small kingdom there seems to have been the source of various myths about King Menelaus, whose wife, Helen, was abducted by a Trojan prince, leading to the famous Trojan War. During Greece's Dark Age, Dorian Greeks overran Laconia, and circa 950 B.C. separate Dorian towns, and their rulers, came together to form a single state. This may be the derivation of the Spartan custom of having two kings rule jointly, one from the Agiad family, the other from the Eurypontid family. Over time the authority of these kings came to be overshadowed to some extent by various public officials. These included five ephors, the Council of Elders (*gerousia*), and an assembly (*apella*) made up of freeborn Spartans (*Spartiates*). After that, the kings' powers were limited chiefly to religious and military matters. It was the Spartan kings who led the city's soldiers into neighboring Messenia in the later eighth century B.C., conquered the region, and turned its inhabitants into Spartan slaves (the helots).

Sometime in the mid-600s B.C. Spartan society underwent drastic political and social changes, mostly built around the *agoge*, a highly regimented military training system designed to turn out machine-like soldiers. Young boys were separated from their families and thereafter lived in military barracks, endured grueling, unrelenting physical drills and survival tests, and learned to fight and kill. This new approach paid off for Sparta in short order. In the sixth and fifth centuries B.C., it emerged as the dominant power in the Peloponnesus and formed the Peloponnesian League, an alliance of the Greek states in that region. Sparta also assumed a leadership role (along with Athens) in the defense of Greece during the great Persian invasion of 480 to 479 B.C. A Spartan, Pausanias, commanded the allied Greek forces in the Battle of Plataea, and the Spartan king Leonidas became a hero to all Greeks by fighting to the death with his men at Thermopylae. Following the Greco-Persian Wars, Sparta became the staunch rival of Athens, and for decades each vied with the other for supremacy in Greece. The result was the Peloponnesian War (431–404 B.C.), in which the two states and their respective leagues of allies came to death grips. After winning the war, Sparta temporarily enjoyed the status of Greece's leading power. However, the Spartans were poor administrators and employed bullying tactics against other Greeks, which inspired widespread hatred and resistance. In 371 the Theban army, commanded by Epaminondas crushed the Spartan phalanx at Leuctra (near Thebes), instantly dispelling the myth of Spartan invincibility.

In the decades that followed, Sparta slipped into a steady decline in prestige and influence, remaining more or less isolated from Greece's political and cultural mainstream. By about 250 B.C. only seven hundred or so full Spartan citizens were left, greatly outnumbered by local slaves and resident foreigners (*perioikoi*), and Sparta found itself politically dominated by the Achaean League. In the 240s a young Spartan king, Agis IV, tried to reorganize the state and revive Spartan prestige, but he was killed in a local power struggle. By 146 B.C., when Rome took firm control of mainland Greece, Sparta had been reduced to a backwater hamlet with a total population of only a few thousand.

SEE ALSO: Battle of Aegospotami; Battle of Leuctra; Battle of Mantinea, 1 and 2; Battle of Plataea; Battle of Thermopylae, 1; education; government; helots; Leonidas; Lycurgus; Lysander; Peloponnesian War; women; weapons and warfare, land

Sphinx

In Greek mythology, a monster having the body of a lion, the head of a woman, and wings. In one famous story the Sphinx (or Phix) terrorized the citizens of Thebes until a young man named Oedipus arrived and outwitted the creature, which took its own life.

SEE ALSO: *Oedipus the King*

spinning and weaving

In ancient Greece spinning (making yarn) and weaving (fashioning the yarn into cloth) occurred mainly in the home and were among the major duties of women, both slave and free. Both activities were very labor intensive and time-consuming. Spinning utilized the spindle, a wooden stick up to 8 inches (20cm) long that was slightly thicker toward the lower end. A whorl, a small pottery or stone weight, was attached to the spindle to make it spin. The spinner also employed a distaff—a forked stick that held a bundle of fibers. She pulled a few fibers out of the distaff, tied them to the spindle, and then spun the spindle in such a way that the fibers twisted together to form a sturdy thread of yarn. After the yarn had been created, the woman wove it into a piece of fabric. She used a loom consisting of two vertical pieces of wood connected at the top by a horizontal beam, from which a row of vertical threads (the warp) hung. They were weighted at the bottom by more whorls. Using a heddle (a wooden rod), she moved the odd-numbered warp threads backward and forward while interspersing horizontal threads (the weft) between them. This produced a tight latticework of warp and weft threads, better known as a piece of cloth.

SEE ALSO: clothing; industry; women

stade

Also known as a *stadion*, an ancient Greek unit of length measuring six hundred Greek feet.

SEE ALSO: athletics; weights and measures

stoa

A common public building in ancient Greek cities, especially marketplaces, it was long and relatively narrow. The front of a typical stoa featured a walkway open to the street and covered by a roof held up by a graceful row of Doric or Ionic columns. To the rear of the walkway were a few or many small chambers that were most often used as shops or meeting places. The most famous stoa was Athens's Stoa Poikile, or "Painted Stoa," so named because it housed a series of large, impressive painted murals.

SEE ALSO: architectural orders; Athens; Polygnotus

Stoics

Members of a philosophical school (Stoicism) founded in Athens circa 300 B.C. by Zeno of Citium. The Stoics held that the universe is controlled by an intelligent force that manifests itself as reason and purpose.

SEE ALSO: philosophy; Zeno, 2

Strabo (ca. 64 B.C.–ca. 25 A.D.)

A prominent Greek traveler, geographer, and historian who flourished during the early years of Greece's Roman Period. Hailing from northern Asia Minor, Strabo migrated to Rome in 44 B.C., there studied philosophy and geography, and then traveled extensively, spending time in Egypt, Greece, and other parts of the Mediterranean world. Along the way he jotted down descriptions of the animals, plants, and cities he saw and interviewed the locals about their histories and customs, data that made their way into the text of his *Geography*, which has survived nearly complete. However, Strabo's other major work, a straight history text, has been lost.

SEE ALSO: explorers and exploration; *Geography*; science

strategos

In ancient Greece, a military general and statesman, often elected by a democratic assembly. In Athens, the *strategoi* (plural) were members of a board of ten generals (the Strategia). These generals served for a year, like many other public officials, but could be reelected immediately and for an unlimited number of terms. Much more than a military leader, an Athenian *strategos* was a leading politician who could initiate policy both in the Assembly and in the Council, which is why many Athenian decrees had the names of generals attached to them. The generals also carried out the Assembly's foreign-policy initiatives. When reelected repeatedly, as Pericles was in the mid-fifth century B.C., a popular general could become the most influential member of the community.

SEE ALSO: government; Pericles

Strato
(flourished early third century B.C.)

Hailing from Lampsacus in northwestern Asia Minor, the philosopher-scientist Strato (or Straton) studied at Aristotle's Lyceum, then moved to Alexandria, where he tutored the son of King Ptolemy I Soter. Strato's main scientific contributions were in the emerging field of mechanics, which deals with the effects of force and motion. He held that all objects have weight and explained how moving objects can accelerate.

SEE ALSO: science

Styx

In Greek mythology, a river marking the outer boundary of the Underworld.

SEE ALSO: Charon; Hades; Underworld

Successors

The general name given to Alexander the Great's leading generals and governors (and some of their sons), who fought one another for supremacy following Alexander's death in 323 B.C. Their rivalries, wars, and foundations of new cities and kingdoms marked the beginning of Greece's Hellenistic Age (323–30 B.C.). The principal Successors (in Greek, *Diadochoi*) were Perdiccas, Antipater, Craterus, Antigonus "the One-Eyed," Ptolemy, Seleucus, Eumenes, Lysimachus, Cassander (son of Antipater), Demetrius Poliorcetes (son of Antigonus), and Antigonus Gonatas (son of Demetrius

and grandson of Antigonus). Ultimately, the three most successful of these men were Ptolemy, who founded the Ptolemaic kingdom consisting of Egypt and parts of Palestine; Seleucus, who established the Seleucid kingdom encompassing most of the heart of the old Persian Empire; and Antigonus Gonatas, who created the Macedonian kingdom made up of Macedonia and most of the rest of mainland Greece.

SEE ALSO: Alexander III ("the Great"); Seleucid Empire; and the names of individual Successors

Suppliant Women, The (play by Aeschylus)

A tragedy by Aeschylus, first produced in Athens about 463 B.C. The women mentioned in the play's title are the Danaids, the fifty daughters of Danaus, son of the Egyptian king Belus and twin brother of Aegyptus. Aegyptus has fifty sons and wants them to marry the Danaids, but Danaus does not trust his brother and takes his daughters to Greece. Aegyptus's fifty sons follow the maidens to Greece and demand that the Danaids marry them. But the young women manage to get the protection of Pelasgus, king of Argos. He warns the fifty suitors to leave his kingdom or be prepared to fight.

SEE ALSO: Aeschylus; Danaus

Suppliant Women, The (play by Euripides)

A tragedy by Euripides, first presented in Athens in about 422 B.C. The play's events take place after the failed attack on Thebes by the Seven Against Thebes, led by Polynices (son of Oedipus) and Adrastus (king of Argos). The Thebans will not

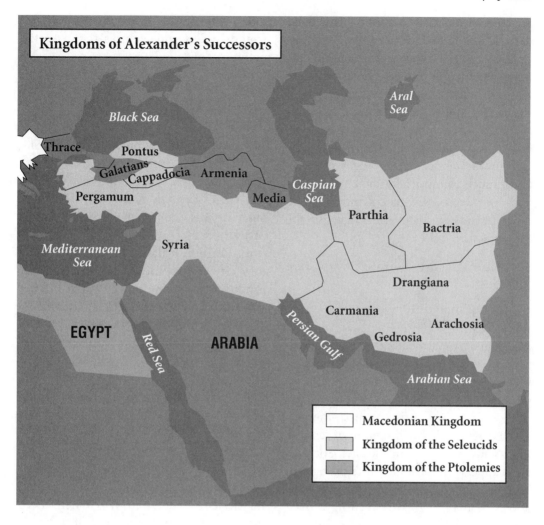

Kingdoms of Alexander's Successors

allow Adrastus to bury his dead, a decision most other Greeks view as unfair. Adrastus protests by marching with the mothers of his dead comrades to Eleusis (near Athens). At the shrine of the goddess Demeter they appeal to Theseus, king of Athens, to try to persuade the Thebans to rescind the decree. Theseus agrees to help, and after diplomacy fails, he defeats the Thebans in battle and sees that all bodies are given proper burial rites.

SEE ALSO: Euripides; *Seven Against Thebes*; Theseus

Sybaris

A Greek city situated in southern Italy, it was destroyed in the late 500s B.C. and later rebuilt and renamed Thurii.

SEE ALSO: Thurii

symposium

An after-dinner drinking party that played an important role in ancient Greek social life. Male heads of households invited their male friends and relatives, who met in the house's *andron*, a special dining room reserved for male gatherings. (During these parties, the household women were relegated to the "women's quarters" in another part of the house.) The guests usually reclined on couches as slaves served them wine and snacks. Common activities included singing songs, telling stories, discussing politics, and reciting poetry, sometimes supplemented by hired entertainers such as musicians, dancers, singers, and even acrobats. Greek symposia were made famous by Plato in his dialogue the *Symposium*.

SEE ALSO: family; houses; *Symposium* (dialogue)

Symposium (dialogue)

A dialogue by Plato dating from about 384 B.C. The setting is the house of the Athenian poet Agathon in 416 B.C. Agathon's guests include Phaedrus, Pausanias, the comic playwright Aristophanes, the beloved rogue Alcibiades, and of course Plato's mentor, the philosopher Socrates (who appears in most of Plato's dialogues). The main subject of the discussion is love, and each man begins by reciting a brief speech about the nature of love. Socrates then argues that the best form of love is that which leads people to contemplate beauty or seek wisdom. One of the most enlightening portions of the dialogue is the one in which Alcibiades describes, in fair detail, Socrates' wisdom as well as incidents from the philosopher's life.

SEE ALSO: Plato; Socrates; symposium

Symposium (work by Xenophon)

A work by Xenophon that ably captures the atmosphere of a typical Athenian drinking party. The imaginary gathering is set in 421 B.C. at the home of the Athenian politician Callias. The central figure is Socrates, who enjoys being the butt of his friends' jokes and lectures them on the nature of love.

SEE ALSO: Socrates; symposium; Xenophon

Syracuse

The chief Greek city on the island of Sicily, it played a prominent role in Greco-Roman political and military events from the fifth through third centuries B.C. Syracuse was established on Sicily's southeastern coast in about 733 B.C. by settlers from Corinth. It did not take long for the new city to become an important grain producer, supplying not only the mother city but many other Greek cities as well. The fifth century B.C. witnessed the rise of two dynamic tyrants in Syracuse, who asserted the city's growing military strength against Carthage's expansion in Sicily. The first of these strong rulers, Gelon (ruled 485–478 B.C.), defeated the Carthaginians at Himera in 480 and seized perhaps two-thirds of the island. His brother, Hiero I, succeeded him and extended Syracusan power into southern Italy by defeating the Etruscans at Cumae in 474. When Hiero died in 467, the Syracusans installed a democracy, which was still in place when the Athenians attacked Syracuse in 415 B.C., at the height of the Peloponnesian War. With the aid of Sparta, the Syracusans demolished the invaders two years later. Soon afterward the Carthaginians again posed a threat to Syracuse, and a new dictator—Dionysius—rose to meet it. His reign (405–367 B.C.) marked a high point of Syracusan military power and prestige. Syracuse was now the leading Greek city outside of Greece proper, and philosophers, writers, and artists from across the Mediterranean flocked to Dionysius's court. Syracuse declined under his son, Dionysius II, but rebounded under two stronger tyrants—Agathocles (317–287 B.C.) and Hiero II (269–215). However, Hiero's successor made the mistake of allying himself with Carthage, then fighting Rome in the Second Punic War. The Romans besieged Syracuse from 213 through 211. And despite the famous, ingenious defenses designed by the city's native son, the great scientist Archimedes, Syracuse was captured. For centuries thereafter it remained the leading Roman city on Sicily.

SEE ALSO: Archimedes; Dionysius I; Gelon of Gela; Hiero I; Hiero II

talent

In ancient Greece, a measure of currency equal to six thousand drachmas.

SEE ALSO: money

Tarentum

A Greek city founded by Sparta (the only colony the Spartans ever established) in the late eighth century B.C. on Italy's southern coast. (Its Greek name was Taras, but it is now more often referred to by its Latin name, Tarentum.) Thanks to its successful agricultural production and manufacture of well-made pottery and jewelry, Tarentum became the leading Greek city of southern Italy by about 450 B.C. Over time Italian peoples, especially the Romans, threatened Tarentum's existence, and in 280 B.C. the city appealed to King Pyrrhus of the Greek kingdom of Epirus for aid. Although at first successful against the Romans, Pyrrhus eventually decided his efforts were not worth it and he departed. That sealed Tarentum's fate, and it fell to Rome in 272 B.C.

SEE ALSO: colonization; Italy; Pyrrhus

Tartarus

An unpleasant section of the Underworld, where, according to a famous myth, Zeus imprisoned the Titans after defeating them. Early Greek writers said that the shades (souls) of bad people ended up in Tartarus, where some endured punishments.

SEE ALSO: Underworld

taxation

Methods and mediums of taxation varied widely in ancient Greece from era to era and place to place. It remains unclear whether the Bronze Age Minoans and Mycenaeans imposed taxes, but some evidence suggests that common folk had to contribute a portion of their crops to the central state. In Archaic times (ca. 800–500 B.C.) it became common in many Greek cities to levy taxes on noncitizens, for instance the metics in Athens. Foreigners also had to pay taxes to dock their ships and to conduct trade among the locals. Direct taxes on citizens or their property happened during emergencies or short-lived dictatorships but was generally viewed as improper. In this era and for centuries to come, however, everyone paid a sort of sales tax (*eponia*) on certain goods bought in the marketplace, usually 1 percent of an item's value. Also, in Athens, and likely in numerous other Greek cities, citizens did pay a more indirect sort of tax in the form of liturgies, mandatory financial support of public festivals and other institutions. Beginning in the fifth century B.C., there were also voluntary taxes, in which citizens, particularly wealthy ones, gave the state funds during wartime or other emergencies. During the Hellenistic Age, when large kingdoms became common in the Greek world, cities within those kingdoms were taxed by the central governments. Salt, perfumes, leather, and spices were among the more common goods taxed. With some exceptions, tax collectors were private parties that submitted bids to the state for the job. The tax men made their profits by collecting a little more than a person actually owed the state and pocketing the difference. It was not uncommon for unscrupulous collectors to gouge people, which gave tax collectors in general a bad reputation.

SEE ALSO: liturgies; money; trade

Tegea

A city in the east-central Peloponnesus, north of Sparta, Tegea coalesced from a group of local villages perhaps around 600 B.C. The Tegeans quickly became renowned as excellent soldiers, their army rated second only to that of the Spartans in the region. Tegea joined the Spartan-dominated Peloponnesian League sometime in the late 500s. And though relations with Sparta were sometimes strained in the early 400s, the city backed Sparta in the Peloponnesian War (431–404 B.C.). However, in the following century the Tegeans joined Thebes in its attempt to break Spartan power in the Peloponnesus. In Hellenistic times, Tegea changed political alliances frequently, alternating its support for the Achaean League and Sparta, until the Romans overran Greece in the second century B.C.

SEE ALSO: Achaean League; Peloponnesus; Sparta

Teiresias

In Greek mythology, a blind prophet who hailed from Thebes. It was said that to compensate for his lost sight, the gods gave him the gift of prophecy and a very long life span. The most famous of the several myths involving Teiresias is the one in which he reveals to the Theban ruler Oedipus that the latter had killed his own father and married his own mother.

SEE ALSO: Oedipus; *Oedipus the King*

Telemachus

In Greek mythology, and in Homer's famous epic poem the *Odyssey*, the son of the Greek hero Odysseus, king of Ithaca, and his wife, Penelope. When his father failed to return from the Trojan War, Telemachus searched for him in neighboring Greek lands, but to no avail. Eventually Odysseus made it back to Ithaca, where father and son had a moving reunion. Telemachus then helped Odysseus kill the suitors who had been demanding Penelope's hand in marriage.

SEE ALSO: Odysseus; *Odyssey*

temples

Each Greek city-state worshipped several gods, but it gave special devotion to a local patron deity who, it was believed, watched over the community. It seemed only natural, therefore, to provide the god with a suitable shelter within the city. Such shelters took the form of religious temples, which the Greeks viewed as sacred places, along with their surrounding grounds. (A temple and its grounds together made up the god's sanctuary.) A temple's altars were erected outside, often on the front steps, so as to respect the god's privacy, and no large-scale worship took place inside.

The earliest Greek temples were small hutlike structures made mostly of perishable materials, including mud bricks, wood, and thatch; not surprisingly, none have survived. But pottery models of such buildings show that each had a front porch with a triangular pediment (the gable formed by the slanted roof) supported by two or four thin wooden columns. Early in the Archaic Age, Greek architects added more and more columns, eventually creating a colonnade (row of columns) that stretched around the whole structure. A temple of this type, honoring the goddess Hera, was built on the island of Samos in the early eighth century B.C.

As time went on, Greek temples became more or less standard in design, each featuring a rectangular inner chamber, a row of columns supporting front and back porches, colonnades running down the sides, and a low-pitched roof forming a triangular pediment on each end. For a while the columns were made of wood. But when heavy roofing tiles began to be used, stone columns, which could better bear the added weight, came into use. By the middle of the sixth century B.C., all-stone temples were the norm everywhere in Greece. The most famous temples of the Classical Age were the ones erected in Pericles' ambitious building program in Athens in the late fifth century B.C., including the Parthenon, which many modern architects call the most perfect structure ever built.

SEE ALSO: architectural orders; building materials and methods; Erechtheum; Parthenon

Thales
(flourished ca. 600 B.C.)

The first-known Greek philosopher-scientist and the founder of the Ionian school of thought. According to tradition, he introduced geometry to the Greeks (based to some extent on Egyptian ideas) and proposed that nature's main underlying substance (the *physis*) is water.

SEE ALSO: philosophy; science

Thasos

The northernmost island in the Aegean Sea. Thasos is about 16 miles (26km) across and features low, rugged mountains punctuated by small fertile valleys. In the mid-600s B.C. the island was colonized by people from the Cycladic island of Paros. Among the first settlers was the famous poet Archilochus. The following two centuries saw Thasos prosper from its

exports of timber, wine, and ores from mines it exploited in nearby Thrace. In 477 B.C. the island joined the Delian League. It tried to secede shortly afterward, but the Athenians forced the Thasians to remain. With the help of Sparta, Thasos did manage to break away from Athens during the Peloponnesian War. In 340 B.C the island fell to Macedonia, but the Romans ended Macedonian control of the island at the beginning of the second century B.C.

SEE ALSO: Archilochus; Paros

theater and drama

Greek theater and drama first developed in Athens in the sixth and fifth centuries B.C. The exact origins of these arts are uncertain, but it appears that they grew out of the colorful rituals attending worship of the fertility god Dionysus. These rituals included the dithyramb, a special form of verse, which the worshippers sang and danced to. It seems that at first the dithyramb reenacted various myths about Dionysus's life and adventures, but as time went on the ceremonies expanded to include other gods as well as human heroes. A major advance occurred when priests began offering new versions of the accepted story lines, essentially making these men the first playwrights. Another source for drama was epic poetry, especially the epics of Homer, which roving bards recited and partially acted out in front of audiences.

Pioneering Actors and Playwrights

A major turning point in theatrical history was the institution of a large-scale annual religious festival—the City Dionysia (in Dionysus's honor)—in Athens in 534 B.C. The festival featured a contest for performers of both the dithyramb and the

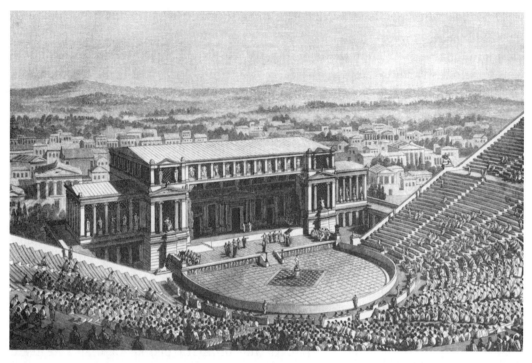

This is how scholars think the Theater of Dionysus, in Athens, looked in Hellenistic times. Only small sections of the facility have survived intact. © BETTMANN/CORBIS

epic poem. The first winner of the competition was Thespis, who supposedly transformed his presentation into the earliest version of a theatrical play. He added a chorus, whose members recited in unison some of the lines and also commented on the events of the story to heighten the dramatic effect. Thespis also originated the idea of impersonating, rather than simply telling about, the story's heroes. This made him in a sense the world's first actor. In addition, Thespis experimented with ways of disguising himself so that he could portray different characters in the same dramatic piece. His solution was to wear a series of masks, which became a standard convention of Greek theater.

In the century that followed, many writer-actor-managers picked up where Thespis had left off. Early pioneers, including Choerilus and Pratinus, produced many plays that did not survive, basing their subjects mainly on standard Greek myths and stories told in the *Iliad* and other epics. Under their guidance, the City Dionysia festival, covering several days in March, became a major annual holiday event that attracted spectators from far and wide, many of them from neighboring city-states. The Athenian government financed the theater building and its maintenance, paid fees to the actors, and provided the prizes for the dramatic contests. All other expenses of play production, including costumes, sets, musicians, and the training of the choruses, were the responsibility of the backers, called *choregoi*, well-to-do citizens whom the state called on to help support the festival. Meanwhile, the playwrights wrote the plays, trained the choruses, composed the music, choreographed the dances, and supervised all other aspects of production.

The dramatic competitions for which these productions were mounted started with some old-style dithyrambic presentations, a gesture to tradition. Then each of three playwrights presented three tragedies. The first comedies were performed in 501 B.C., but they were viewed as secondary to the tragedies until a few decades later. The actors wore elaborate masks and both white and brightly colored costumes. They also used props, including chariots, couches, statues of gods, shields and swords, and biers to display dead bodies. The settings were left mostly to the audience's imagination, and no solid evidence exists for the use of movable painted scenery like that in modern theaters. At the conclusion of the performances, an awards ceremony was held. The winners were chosen by a panel of ten judges, and the prizes consisted of crowns of ivy.

The audiences who watched these presentations came from all classes of the population (although slaves sometimes may have been excluded). Even poor people were able to attend often, after the democratic statesman Pericles created a special government fund to subsidize their theater tokens circa 450 B.C. The tokens looked like coins and were made of bronze, lead, ivory, or bone. Whether rich or poor, spectators reacted to what they saw on-stage in lively fashion, groaning or booing when they were displeased and applauding and cheering when they enjoyed the show.

Four Theatrical Giants

Four playwrights pleased audiences the most during the fifth century B.C., when Greek theater reached its height. The first of these artists was Aeschylus, who raised the art of tragedy to the level of great literature. One of his key innovations was the introduction of a second actor. Until his time, following the tradition established by Thespis, playwrights made do with one actor, limiting them to telling fairly simple stories with a few characters. Adding a second actor increased the storytelling potential because it made it possible to depict twice as many characters. Aeschylus also expanded the scope of drama by introducing the trilogy, a series of three plays related in plot and theme. The second great fifth-century B.C. playwright, Sophocles, introduced a third actor (and may also have employed a fourth toward the end of his career), which further increased the possible number of characters. Euripides, the third great playwright of the century, became famous for depicting ordinary people in highly realistic ways, including giving them speeches bristling with deep-felt emotion. Some Athenians saw this as innovative and compelling; others viewed it as too undignified for the tragic stage, which they felt should show more heroic, formalized, larger-than-life people and themes. Euripides was therefore far ahead of his time, and later scholars came to see him as the first playwright to deal with human problems in a modern way. The tragic playwrights also wrote satyr plays, which they presented alongside their tragedies. The plots and tone of satyr plays were silly and often bawdy, even obscene, as they spoofed the mythical characters of the tragedies. The fourth of the theatrical giants of the fifth century B.C. was the comic playwright Aristophanes. His plays marked the height of the most creative period for Greek comedy, usually called the Old Comedy, lasting from about 450 to 404 B.C. Aristophanes (and other comic playwrights) employed highly topical humor and poked fun at people of all walks of life, especially politicians and generals.

The era of extraordinary theatrical innovation in which Aeschylus, Sophocles, Euripides, and Aristophanes plied their trade ended in 404 B.C. when Athens surrendered to Sparta in the conclusion of the devastating Peloponnesian War. The City Dionysia and its drama competitions continued, as did a second, lesser dramatic competition, the Lenaea (held in January), about which little is known. But few noteworthy tragedies were written thereafter, perhaps because audiences' tastes had changed in the wake of Athens's defeat. Thereafter, comedies became the mainstay of Greek theater. The period lasting from the 320s to about 260 B.C. became known as the New Comedy. The most popular playwright of that era was Menander, whose works are more realistic but less topical, satiric, and inventive than those of Aristophanes.

SEE ALSO: dithyramb; Theater of Dionysus; and the names of individual playwrights

Theater of Dionysus

The most famous ancient Greek theater and the site of the renowned Athenian drama festivals. Dedicated to the fertility god Dionysus, from whose rituals drama first developed, the theater was situated near the southeastern foot of Athens's Acropolis. It was constructed in the early 490s B.C. after the wooden seating in the city's former theater (likely its first) collapsed, killing many people. The new theater featured a safer arrangement of stone seats set into the earth of the rising hillside. After a number of renovations over the years, this seating section, or *theatron*, eventually held as many as fourteen thousand playgoers. They looked down onto the orchestra, or "dancing place," where the actors performed. Behind the

orchestra rose the *skene*, or "scene building," which tripled as a backdrop for the stage action, a place from which actors could make entrances and exits, and a storage place for props. The Theater of Dionysus became the model for the many other theaters erected across Greece and other parts of the known world in the centuries that followed. Today the best preserved of all of them is the theater at Epidaurus in the eastern Peloponnesus, in which plays are still sometimes performed.

SEE ALSO: Dionysus; theater and drama

Thebes

The chief city of Boeotia (bee-OH-shya), the region of the Greek mainland situated north of the Athenian territory of Attica. Thebes played a central role in many of the pivotal events of Greece's mythology and history. A famous myth said that the city was founded in the dim past by Cadmus, a nobleman of the Phoenician town of Tyre. Other important myths dealing with Thebes and its leaders included the story of how Oedipus saved the city from a murderous monster, the Sphinx; how Oedipus became king and then fell from power when it was revealed that he had unknowingly killed his own father and married his own mother; and how his daughter, Antigone, met with tragedy. These and other tales were later collected into three epic poems (the *Oedipodia*, *Thebaïd*, and *Epigoni*), which provided inspiration for many of the plays of the great Athenian dramatists.

Regarding the real history of Thebes, it appears to have been an important Mycenaean settlement and probably the focus of one of the small Mycenaean kingdoms of the late Bronze Age. Long after the collapse of Mycenaean civilization, the city of Thebes slowly rose again to prominence.

In the 500s B.C. it exerted its power and influence over the smaller Boeotian towns surrounding it, forming a political alliance commonly called the Boeotian League. In the following century Thebes and its powerful neighbor, Athens, squabbled and clashed off and on, so it is not surprising that the Thebans supported Sparta in the Peloponnesian War. In the early fourth century B.C., however, Thebes and Sparta became enemies, and in 371 B.C. a Theban army commanded by the noted military innovator Epaminondas crushed Sparta's phalanx at Leuctra in western Boeotia. This vaulted Thebes into the overall hegemony of Greece, highlighted by several Theban military forays into the Peloponnesus that freed a number of local towns from Spartan domination.

But the Theban hegemony proved relatively brief. After Epaminondas's death in 362 B.C. in the Battle of Mantinea, Thebes became a far less vigorous and effective power. Its weakness became particularly apparent in 338 B.C. when Thebes and Athens formed an alliance designed to stop Macedonia's King Philip II from conquering southern Greece, but were decisively defeated by him at Chaeronea (west of Thebes). Philip immediately disbanded the Boeotian League. Under Philip's successor, Alexander, the Thebans launched an insurrection. Alexander easily put down the revolt and proceeded to destroy the city (sparing only the temples and the house of the poet Pindar). A few years later one of Alexander's Successors, Cassander, rebuilt Thebes. But it never regained its former power and influence.

SEE ALSO: Battle of Chaeronea; Battle of Leuctra; Battle of Mantinea; Boeotia; Epaminondas; Oedipus; *Seven Against Thebes*

Themistocles
(ca. 524 B.C.–459 B.C.)

A noted Athenian statesman-general and the so-called Father of Athenian Naval Supremacy. Throughout his long political career, Themistocles, who came from a well-to-do Athenian family, proved himself a farsighted individual and a controversial public figure. When he became archon in 493 B.C., for example, he foresaw that the Persians posed a serious threat to Athens and spearheaded the initial construction of Athens's docks and naval base at Piraeus. After the Battle of Marathon, in which he fought, Themistocles got involved in politics in a big way. A radical democrat, he was anti-Spartan and made many enemies among the city's conservatives, who favored closer relations with Sparta. These enemies tried several times to ostracize (banish) Themistocles. But they were unable to do so, and he dominated the Athenian political scene for more than a decade. His wise long-range military policies also saved Athens from destruction, for he persuaded the Assembly to build the largest fleet of ships in Greece. And this enabled the Greeks to defeat the Persians in the pivotal naval battle fought at Salamis in 480 B.C. After the war Themistocles rebuilt Athens's city walls (which the Persians had wrecked), which angered the Spartans. He also engineered alliances with some of Sparta's enemies. However, a new political rival, Cimon, who was pro-Spartan, managed to get Themistocles ostracized in about 472. In the years that followed, Themistocles traveled across Greece stirring up anti-Spartan sentiments. And under pressure from Spartan leaders, the Athenians finally accused him of treason. Ironically, his former enemies, the Persians, gave him refuge, and he died in a Persian town in Asia Minor.

SEE ALSO: government; Greco-Persian Wars; Sparta

Theocritus
(flourished early third century B.C.)

A leading Hellenistic Greek poet, he was born in Syracuse but as a young man immigrated to Alexandria, where he gained renown at the court of King Ptolemy II. Evidence suggests that Theocritus became a close friend of the poet Callimachus. Theocritus's major literary contribution was a series of poems describing pleasant countryside scenes in which shepherds played music while tending their flocks, a theme and style that heavily influenced later Roman poets. Thirty-one of his works have survived.

SEE ALSO: Callimachus, 2; poetry

Theognis
(flourished mid-sixth century B.C.)

A noted Greek lyric poet native to Megara (northwest of Athens). Many of Theognis's poems are bitter in tone and bemoan the social changes ongoing in his day, particularly the transfer of power from aristocratic families and councils to popular leaders and the rise in status of common folk. For example: "Now the noblest man will marry the lowest daughter of a base family, if only she brings in money [from a rich dowry]. ... No wonder our city's blood is polluted when noble men will couple with upstarts [commoners]." ("Eugenics")

SEE ALSO: poetry

Theogony

A long poem composed by the eighth-century B.C. Greek poet Hesiod. The work, the title of which means *The Lineage of the Gods*, recounts the major myths describing the origins of the Greek gods. In the beginning, Hesiod says, there was Chaos, from which sprang the deities Gaia (Earth), Tartarus (the darkest region of the Underworld), and Eros (Love). Gaia then produced Uranus (Sky), and in their turn these two coupled and gave rise to the first race of Greek gods, the Titans. The *Theogony* next describes how the leader of the Titans, Cronos, fathered the first Olympian gods, including Zeus, and how Zeus overthrew Cronos. In addition, Hesiod gives a detailed, colorful account of the war between the Titans and the Olympians, which the Olympians won. Later Greek writers, including the great Athenian playwrights, frequently drew on this material for characters and plots.

SEE ALSO: Hesiod; Titans; Zeus

Theophrastus
(ca. 370 B.C.–ca. 286 B.C.)

A noted Greek philosopher-scientist who pioneered the study of botany. Theophrastus hailed from the island of Lesbos and as a young man became a close friend and associate of Aristotle. Although Theophrastus's writings covered a wide range of subjects, the most important ones were the *History of Plants* and *Causes of Plants*, which describe hundreds of plant species, the effects of climate and cultivation on plants, plant diseases, and techniques of plant reproduction, including germination, budding, and grafting and growing cuttings. After Aristotle died, Theophrastus succeeded him as director of the Lyceum.

SEE ALSO: Aristotle; Lyceum; science

Theopompus
(ca. 376 B.C.–ca. 320 B.C.)

An important Greek historian who studied under the orator Isocrates and became a friend to the Macedonian rulers Philip II and Alexander III ("the Great"). Except for a few fragments, none of Theopompus's works have survived. But his *Hellenica*, which picks up the narrative of Greek history where Thucydides' *Peloponnesian War* leaves off in 411 B.C., and his *Philippica*, a massive world history with Philip's achievements a central theme, were used as major sources by later historians and writers, including Plutarch.

SEE ALSO: historical writing; Philip II; Plutarch

Thera

A small, crescent-shaped island lying about 70 miles (113km) north of Crete. In ancient times Thera (modern Santorini) was dominated by a large volcano, which erupted with stupendous force sometime between 1620 and 1450 B.C. The disaster crippled the Minoan civilization on Crete and may have inspired the famous myth of Atlantis.

SEE ALSO: Akroteri; Atlantis; Crete; Minoans

Theseus

In Greek mythology, an early king of Athens and that city's national hero. The son of King Aegeus, Theseus was raised in a foreign town (unbeknownst to Aegeus) and appeared at his father's court as a young man. Soon afterward, Theseus proved himself by sailing to Crete, defeating King Minos (who had been forcing Aegeus to send hostages to Crete each year), and slaying the monstrous Minotaur (which had been devouring the hostages). Later, after Aegeus died, Theseus became king and unified the scattered communities of Attica into a single Athenian state. Legends also claimed that Theseus married Hippolyta, queen of the Amazons, and

fought off an army of these warrior women who had come to Athens to recover her. (This battle, which the Greeks called the Amazonomachy, was a favorite subject of Greek sculptors and other artists in the Classical Age.) When an insurrection erupted in Athens, Theseus fled to the island of Scyros (northeast of Euboea), where the local king murdered him. In the early fifth century B.C. the Athenian statesman Cimon went to Scyros and found a large skeleton, which he and other Athenians believed was that of Theseus.

SEE ALSO: Aegeus; Crete; Knossos

Thespis
(late sixth century B.C.)

An Athenian poet who supposedly invented a number of key theatrical conventions, including acting, tragedy, and character masks. None of his plays has survived, but his name lives on in the term *thespian*, describing an actor or theater devotee.

SEE ALSO: theater and drama

Thessaloniki

The chief city of the Greek region and kingdom of Macedonia. One of Alexander's Successors, Cassander, established Thessaloniki (also Thessalonica or Salonica) in about 316 B.C., naming it after his wife (and Alexander's sister), Thessalonice. It did not take long for the city's port to replace that of Macedonia's capital, Pella, which had badly silted up. Thanks to extensive shipping and trade, Thessaloniki became large and prosperous, and the Romans made it the capital of their province of Macedonia-Achaea in 146 B.C. after their subjugation of Greece.

SEE ALSO: Cassander; Macedonia

Thessaly

A broad region of the northeastern Greek mainland, consisting of two fertile plains surrounded by rugged mountain ranges. The southern range was dominated by Mt. Oeta, whose main pass was Thermopylae (which led into Phocis and southern Greece), while in the north the towering Mt. Olympus separated the Thessalian plains from Macedonia. Most of Thessaly's Aegean coast was too rocky to make harbors, except along the northern rim of the Gulf of Pagasae (now the Gulf of Volos). There, the port of Iolcos (home city of the mythical Jason) thrived as a Mycenaean stronghold in the late Bronze Age. After the fall of Mycenaean civilization, a group of Greeks called the Thessaloi settled in the area and gave it their name. In the Archaic Age and early Classical Age, while the major southern city-states were experimenting with democracy and creating high culture, Thessaly remained more provincial and out of the cultural mainstream. It retained aristocratic rule, dominated by a few rich families. These prospered by growing grain and raising herds of cattle and horses. Indeed, the locals became famous for their horse farms and skilled cavalrymen. Thessaly came briefly under the sway of a tyrant, Jason of Pherae, in the late 370s B.C., but he was soon assassinated. And a few years later Macedonia's King Philip II seized the region. Macedonian domination continued until the second century B.C., when both Thessaly and Macedonia fell under Roman control.

SEE ALSO: Jason, 1 and 2; Olympus, Mt.

Thirty Tyrants

The most common name for the thirty men, all right-wing Athenians, who took control of Athens directly following its surrender to Sparta at the conclusion of the Peloponnesian War in 404 B.C. With the approval and backing of the Spartan general Lysander, they dismantled the city's cherished democracy and instituted an oligarchic dictatorship and reign of terror in its place. Prominent among these despots were Critias, a former follower of the philosopher Socrates, and Critias's nephew, Charmides. The tyrants murdered as many as fifteen hundred leading citizens and metics and confiscated their properties. Eventually, a resistance movement, led by Thrasybulus, overthrew the tyrants and reinstated the city's democracy in the fall of 403.

SEE ALSO: Critias; Lysander; Peloponnesian War

tholos

Originally a circular, underground stone tomb used to house the remains of Mycenaean royalty in the Bronze Age. A spectacular example still survives at Mycenae. It features conical stone walls that arch inward at the top, creating a chamber shaped like a beehive (hence the nickname of "beehive" for a *tholos* tomb). In the Classical Age, another kind of *tholos* became common in Greek cities—a circular building with its roof supported by a circular row of columns. The exact purpose of these *tholoi* is unknown, but they were sometimes used for state-supported banquets and other public functions.

SEE ALSO: burial customs; Mycenae

Thrace

The area situated north of the Aegean Sea, west of the Propontis (now the Sea of Marmara), and east of Macedonia. Thrace features three large rivers—the Nestes, Strymon, and Hebrus—that empty into

This ancient tholos, *a royal tomb, is located near the ruins of the Bronze Age palace at Pylos, in southwestern Greece.* © RUGGERO VANNI/CORBIS

the Aegean. The native Thracians originally spoke a non-Greek language, belonged to warlike tribes, lived in rural villages rather than large cities, and were culturally backward in comparison to most Greeks. Some of the Greek city-states and kingdoms either planted colonies in Thrace (as in the case of Athens's establishment of Amphipolis) or vied for control of it because it had rich gold and silver mines. The region also possessed plentiful supplies of timber, wheat, and people to enslave. Macedonia's King Philip II directly annexed Thrace in the 340s B.C. A generation later the area became the center of the kingdom ruled by Lysimachus, one of Alexander the Great's Successors. Finally, in the late second century B.C., Thrace became part of the Roman province of Macedonia.

SEE ALSO: Amphipolis; Chalcidice; Lysimachus

Thucydides
(ca. 500 B.C.–ca. 420 B.C.)

An Athenian politician who led the city's right-wing aristocratic faction against the policies of the liberal party of Pericles. The Athenians ostracized Thucydides in 443 B.C., forcing him into exile.

SEE ALSO: Pericles

Thucydides
(ca. 460 B.C.–ca. 400 B.C.)

A noted Athenian soldier and historian who penned the principal surviving chronicle of the bloody Peloponnesian War (431–404 B.C., although his account breaks off in 411). Thucydides, who came from a well-to-do Athenian family, may have been related to the noted conservative politicians Cimon and Thucydides. However, the younger Thucydides ended up supporting the liberal democratic faction led by Pericles, whom he quotes extensively in his history. The historian was elected general in 424 B.C., but he was relieved of duty and exiled after failing to stop the Spartans from capturing the strategic city of Amphipolis. At the war's end in 404, he was allowed to return to Athens and died there in about 400. Today Thucydides is widely viewed as the world's first great historian, as he was the first to follow a strict chronology and to describe events strictly in terms of human motivations and deeds. Also, he either personally witnessed the events he described or interviewed eyewitnesses. "My work is not a piece of writing designed to meet the taste of an immediate public," he states in an early passage, "but was done to last forever." (*The Peloponnesian War* 1.22). In the fullness of time, this goal was fulfilled.

SEE ALSO: Cimon; historical writing; Peloponnesian War; *Peloponnesian War, The*

Thurii

A Greek city established with the original name of Sybaris in about 720 B.C. by settlers from Achaea, in the northern sector of the Peloponnesus. The Sybarites became increasingly prosperous through both the raising of cattle and trade and became known for their wealth and love of luxury. In about 510 B.C. the people of a neighboring and rival Greek city, Croton, destroyed Sybaris by diverting the course of a local river and flooding it. The site was abandoned for a couple of generations. But in the 450s descendants of the former Sybarites returned. Accompanied by other Greeks, and supported by the Athenian leader Pericles, they erected a new city on the site and named it Thuria, now known in its Latin form—Thurii. In time the city became known for its ceramic vases. Its leaders became increasingly pro-Roman during the years when Rome was threatening the Greek cities of southern Italy; and, to the disdain of their Greek neighbors, in 282 B.C. the Thurians allowed Roman soldiers to occupy their city.

SEE ALSO: Peloponnesus

Timaeus
(ca. 356 B.C.–260 B.C.)

A Greek historian who was born in Sicily and immigrated to Athens in about 317 B.C. He wrote an extensive history of Sicily that is now lost except for a few fragments. Timaeus also appears to have originated the system of dating past Greek events by the Olympiads (four-year periods separating each successive session of the Olympic Games).

SEE ALSO: historical writing

Timaeus (dialogue)

One of the last dialogues composed by Plato and one of his most influential in later ages. It seems to have been conceived as a description of the origins and development of the universe and the human race. According to one of the main speakers in the work, Timaeus, the universe (including the stars, Earth, and the traditional Greek gods) was fashioned by a creator-god, the Demiurge, from the elements earth, air, fire, and water. The gods then created the bodies of humans, although the Demiurge made their souls. The dialogue also explores the nature of the soul and suggests that it goes through various stages of reincarnation. One of the most famous passages from the *Timaeus* is the one in which the character Critias briefly describes the lost continent of Atlantis, a subject Plato presented in more detail in another dialogue, the *Critias*. The ideas discussed in the *Timaeus* exerted considerable influence on Neoplatonist philosophy in late antiquity as well as on the Christians, who equated Plato's Demiurge with the creator-god of the Old Testament.

SEE ALSO: Atlantis; *Critias* (dialogue); Plato

Timoleon
(died 334 B.C.)

Born in Corinth, Timoleon was a noted local soldier and statesman chosen by his city to lead a small force of troops to Sicily. The expedition was a response to a call for aid by some of the citizens of Syracuse who were opposed to the harsh rule of a tyrant, Dionysius II. Timoleon drove away Dionysius and then proceeded to oust the tyrants who had been ruling several neighboring Sicilian Greek cities. The people of Sicily later remembered Timoleon as a brave, unselfish hero. His exploits were preserved for posterity in his biography penned by Plutarch a few centuries later.

SEE ALSO: Syracuse

Tiryns

An important Bronze Age Greek town lying about 9 miles (14.4km) south of Mycenae in the northeastern Peloponnesus. Tiryns (TEER-ins) originally lay on the edge of the sea, but due to coastal changes over the millennia, it now rests about 1 mile (1.6km) inland. In mythology, Cyclopes (one-eyed giants) erected the walls of the town's imposing fortress-citadel, and the hero Perseus reigned as one of its kings. In reality, the site of Tiryns was inhabited well before the Mycenaeans

entered the Greek peninsula. Whoever the town's early residents were, the Mycenaeans displaced or absorbed them, and in the late Bronze Age the town seems to have served as the port of the kingdom centered at Mycenae. After Mycenaean civilization collapsed in the 1100s B.C., Tiryns was reduced to an obscure village that survived for a few centuries until the people of nearby Argos destroyed it. The site of Tiryns was excavated by German archaeologist Heinrich Schliemann (who also dug at Troy and Mycenae) in 1884.

SEE ALSO: Argos; Mycenae; Mycenaeans

Titans

In Greek mythology, the earliest race of Greek gods, said to have come from the union of the primeval forces Gaia (Earth) and Uranus (Sky). The leading male Titan was Cronos, who overthrew his father and seized control of the universe. Other leading male Titans included Crius, Oceanus, Hyperion, and Iapetus. Among the chief female Titans were Rhea, Themis, Mnemosyne, Phoebe, and Tethys. Some of these beings gave birth to Titan children, including Prometheus (later famous for stealing fire from heaven); his brother, Epimetheus; and Atlas (who later came to hold up the sky). Also, Cronos and Rhea spawned children that eventually became a new race of gods, the Olympians, including Zeus, Poseidon, Demeter, and Hades. In a war the Classical Greeks called the Titanomachy, the two races of gods clashed for ten years until Zeus and his followers (including a few Titans) emerged victorious. Zeus then hurled the defeated Titans down into the depths of Tartarus (in the Underworld), where they remain confined for eternity. Following the conflict, a few Titans, among them Helios and Oceanus, continued to serve Zeus.

SEE ALSO: Cronos; Olympians; Prometheus; Zeus

trade

Along with the Phoenicians, the Greeks were the most ambitious, far-ranging, and successful traders of the ancient Mediterranean world. Modern archaeologists are able to detect and trace the extent of many of the old Greek trade routes through Greek-made pottery and metal artifacts found in the ruins of towns and buildings in Egypt, Palestine, Italy, North Africa, Spain, and numerous other locales. As early as the 1300s B.C., Mycenaean traders regularly sailed to the Lipari islands (near Sicily), Egypt, Cyprus, and Palestine, where they conducted exchanges of goods (the barter system). Most of these trade routes were probably abandoned for a while following the demise of Greece's Bronze Age cultures.

In the early Archaic Age, however, especially during the great era of Greek colonization in the eighth and seventh centuries B.C., new and even more extensive trade routes were established. Greek merchant ships reached all the coasts of the Black Sea as well as southern Gaul (now France) and Spain. In Spain they acquired tin (which the Greeks mixed with copper to make bronze), much of which seems to have come from southern Britain by way of Celtic trade connections. In exchange for tin, silver, and lead from the western Mediterranean; textiles, grain, and papyrus from Egypt; purple dye from Phoenicia; and timber and grain from Italy, Thrace, and the northern reaches of the Black Sea; Greek traders offered widely coveted Greek-made products. These included fine wools from the Ionian Greek cities, exquisite painted pottery from Corinth and Athens, and fine wines, olive oil, and marble. These same products were traded in the Hellenistic Age. But the many new Greek cities that sprang up in the Near East in that period allowed the Greeks to tap into ancient Mesopotamian trade routes stretching to Arabia, India, and other lands that the Greeks viewed as very remote and exotic.

Some Greek maritime trade was sponsored by local governments, especially in Hellenistic times, when the large monarchies (including the Seleucid and Ptolemaic empires) competed for the fattest shares of the international commercial markets. But more often, trade was privately financed by individual merchants and shippers, sometimes backed by businessmen who were willing to take the risk that a cargo would make a profit.

SEE ALSO: banking; colonization; industry; money; Phoenicia; pottery

tragedy

A literary form that exploits and develops serious, sober, and/or sad themes, classically involving a protagonist or hero whose so-called tragic flaw leads to his downfall (and who elicits both pity and fear in the audience). Ancient Greek playwrights, including Aeschylus, Sophocles, and Euripides, produced some of the greatest tragedies ever written.

SEE ALSO: theater and drama; and the names of the individual playwrights and their works

treasury

In ancient Greece, a small but ornate structure used for storing gold and other valuables. Treasuries were purposely built to look like miniature temples, with rows of columns and painted or sculpted decorations. The valuable contents of these structures frequently included offerings made to gods at major religious shrines. Treasuries were also intended to show off the wealth, power, and piety of the city-states that erected them. For these reasons, Athens and other leading states constructed treasuries at Apollo's sanctuary at Delphi (home of the famous oracle) and at Olympia (site of Greece's most prestigious athletic games).

SEE ALSO: Delphi; Olympia; temples

tribes

Large kinship groups (*phylai*; singular, *phyle*) dating back at least to Greece's early Dark Age and in some areas probably much earlier. Each tribe, which consisted of several hundred or several thousand people related by blood, broke down further into smaller groups—phratries and families. Each tribe had its leaders (*phylarchs*) and priests, who figured prominently in religious festivals and social gatherings attended by members of the tribe. When the Dorians entered Greece during the Dark Age, they were of three major tribes—the Dymanes, Pamphyloi, and Hylleis—and branches of these could be found in Dorian cities, such as Sparta, well into the Classical Age. Athens long had four traditional tribes. But when Cleisthenes introduced democracy circa 508 B.C., he replaced these with ten new tribes named after mythical heroes and organized them in such a way that each contained people from each of Attica's three general regions—the urban area, the coastal areas, and the inland areas.

SEE ALSO: deme; phratry

trireme

An ancient warship that had three banks of oars.

SEE ALSO: weapons and warfare, naval

Troas

The area of northwestern Asia Minor bordering the southern shore of the Hellespont strait (also called Troad). The chief town of the region was Troy, lying a few miles south of the Hellespont.

SEE ALSO: Asia Minor; Troy

Troezen

A town in the southeastern sector of Argolis in the Peloponnesus. In Greek mythology, Troezen was the birthplace of the Athenian hero Theseus and part of the kingdom of Diomedes, one of the Greek leaders of the expedition against Troy. In historic times, the town played a minor role in Greek affairs, except when it took in Athenian refugees escaping the oncoming Persians in 480 B.C.

SEE ALSO: Greco-Persian Wars

Troilus

In Greek legend, one of the sons of Troy's King Priam and Queen Hecuba. During the famous Trojan War, immortalized in Homer's *Iliad* and other ancient epics, Troilus died at the hands of the Greek champion Achilles. Later, a medieval romance—*Troilus and Cressida*—was loosely based on Troilus and other mythical characters, and this work, in turn, inspired Shakespeare's play of the same name.

SEE ALSO: Troy

Trojan Horse

According to Greek legend, after laying siege to Troy for ten years the Greeks tricked the Trojans by pretending to depart and leaving behind a huge wooden horse as an offering to the gods. Greek warriors hid inside the horse and climbed out by night after the Trojans had dragged it inside the city. The stowaways then opened the city's gates to the waiting Greek army.

SEE ALSO: Troy

Trojan War

The legendary ten-year conflict between the city of Troy (in Asia Minor) and an alliance of Greek kings bent on avenging the abduction of Sparta's Queen Helen by Troy's Prince Paris. The war was immortalized in ancient times in Homer's *Iliad* and other epics as well as in plays and other writings. For synopses of the events of the war, **see** *Iliad*; Troy. And for related details, *see* Achilles; Hector; Helen; Homer; *Odyssey*.

Trojan Women, The

A tragedy by Euripides, first produced in Athens in 415 B.C. The setting is Troy shortly after its fall to the Greeks. The Trojan men have been slain, and the grieving women nervously await news of their own fate. Finally a Greek herald enters and explains that Hecuba, Troy's queen, is to become a servant to Odysseus, king of Ithaca; Hecuba's daughter, Cassandra, will become the property of Agamemnon, the leader of the Greek expedition. Because she is a prophetess, Cassandra is able to foretell that some of the Greeks will meet unpleasant fates of their own in the near future. The herald also reveals that Andromache, wife of Troy's Prince Hector, has been assigned to the Greek warrior Neoptolemus. Then Menelaus, king of Sparta, enters to deal with his wife, Helen, who ran off with Troy's Prince Paris ten years before and has been living with the Trojans. Although he is ready to kill her, she pleads for her life and it becomes clear that he will spare her. As the captive women are led away, Troy is set to the torch.

SEE ALSO: Euripides; Troy

Troy

In Greek mythology and literature, a city besieged by the Greeks in the Age of Heroes, and, in reality, a prosperous Bronze Age town on the coast of northwestern Asia Minor. Modern scholars were uncertain whether Troy (or Ilium) was a real town until German archaeologist Heinrich Schliemann unearthed its remains in the 1870s. He uncovered a series of cities, dating from the late Bronze Age, one built on top of another. Schliemann concluded that the sixth city from the bottom was Homer's Troy. But more recent evidence indicated that the city now labeled Troy VIIa underwent a siege in about 1220 B.C., in the approximate time frame of the mythical Trojan War. In that era, Troy occupied a commanding position on a hill overlooking a small seaside plain. And scholars believe that the Trojans exacted tolls from merchant ships entering or leaving the nearby Hellespont (today called the Dardanelles). It is possible that one or more Mycenaean kings attacked the city so that they could exploit the region without Trojan interference; however, even if this happened, it remains unproven that it was the war that Homer and other writers described.

That mythical conflict was said to have lasted ten years. Led by Agamemnon, brother of Menelaus, whose wife, Helen, had been abducted by a Trojan prince, the Greeks erected a large camp on the beach side of the plain lying in front of Troy. At first the Greeks enjoyed success in fighting bands of Trojan warriors who left the protection of the city's towering walls and fought them in the plain. Still, the Greeks

In this modern painting, the victorious Achilles drags the body of his slain foe, Hector, around the Trojan citadel. AKG-IMAGES/PETER CONNOLLY

could not breach those mighty walls, so the war dragged on and on. Then, in the ninth year of the siege, Achilles, greatest of the Greek warriors, got into an argument with Agamemnon. Achilles retired to his tent and refused to fight. That lowered the spirits of his comrades, and the Trojans enjoyed a series of victories. Eventually Achilles patched things up with Agamemnon, reentered the fray, and in single combat slew Hector, greatest of the Trojan champions. Not long afterward, Troy's Prince Paris killed Achilles with an arrow. The fighting continued for many more months, until one of the Greek kings, Odysseus, conceived the idea of fooling the Trojans by pretending to leave. The Greeks left a huge wooden horse on the plain, supposedly an offering to the gods, and sailed their ships out of sight. However, Greek soldiers were hiding inside the horse, and after the Trojans dragged it into the city, these men climbed out and opened the gates. Under cover of darkness, the Greeks returned, swarmed into Troy, and sacked it.

SEE ALSO: Achilles; Agamemnon; Hector; Homer; *Iliad*

tyrants

In ancient Greece, ambitious men who seized dictatorial power in a number of major Greek cities in the 600s and 500s B.C. The most common method a tyrant (*turannos*) used to gain power was to exploit growing antiaristocratic sentiments among the lower classes. By the late Archaic Age, a large proportion of a Greek city's soldiers were farmers and others belonging to these lower classes, so with their help, a dictator could grab and maintain power. Among the more successful tyrants were Athens's Pisistratus, Samos's Polycrates, and Corinth's Periander. These men did not fit the now-familiar stereotype of a tyrant—a cruel or oppressive ruler—that developed later. Though they used unconstitutional means to gain power, many Greek tyrants were effective, generous rulers who sponsored public building projects and the arts. But their kind were not destined to remain long on Greece's political scene. By the start of the Classical Age, the citizens of Athens and other city-states had eliminated the tyrants and had taken control of their governments themselves.

SEE ALSO: Hippias; Periander; Pisistratus; Polycrates

Tyre

One of the leading Phoenician cities, situated just off the coast of what is now Lebanon. Joining the city to the mainland were some small rocky islands and an artificial quay, which together created two excellent harbors. A very ancient city, over the centuries Tyre either traded with or fought against the Egyptians, Assyrians, Babylonians, Persians, and Greeks, the most famous of the latter group being Alexander the Great. In 332 B.C., during his conquest of Persia, Alexander captured the city in the climax of a spectacular siege. After Alexander's death, Tyre first became part of the Ptolemaic Empire, then of the Seleucid Empire. Finally, in the first century B.C., the Romans incorporated the city into their new province of Syria.

SEE ALSO: Alexander III ("the Great"); Phoenicia

Tyrtaeus
(flourished seventh century B.C.)

The most famous of Sparta's poets. Tyrtaeus composed lyric poetry, often glorifying the warrior ethic that underlay Sparta's society and policies. "No man ever proves himself a good man in war," he writes, "unless he can endure to face the blood and the slaughter, go close against the enemy and fight with his hands. Here is courage, mankind's finest possession." ("The Spartan Creed" 6–7.) Some of Tyrtaeus's verses were battle hymns (paeans) that Spartan soldiers sung while marching into battle.

SEE ALSO: poetry; Sparta

Underworld

In Greek mythology and religion, the subterranean region where the shades (spirits) of the dead were thought to reside. Tradition held that the shades were led down into the Underworld, which the god Hades ruled, by another god, Hermes, although some ancient accounts (notably Euripides' play *Alcestis*) pictured Thanatos, god of death, performing this grim duty. The outer boundary of the Underworld was the River Styx, variously referred to as the "appalling river," "hated river," or "river of unbreakable oaths." On its shore, a cheerless boatman, Charon, ferried the shades across the dark waters. A frightening three-headed dog, Cerberus, guarded the area to make sure that no one tried to escape their fate. After the shades reached the far side of the river, they encountered the three judges of the dead—Minos, Rhadamanthys, and Aeacus. The extent of their authority and the manner in which they judged people are no longer clear (and even in ancient Greece stories about them varied widely).

What seems fairly certain is that most shades ended up spending eternity on the Plain of Asphodel, an ill-defined, colorless, and perhaps dreary (though not painful) region where they wandered aimlessly about. In contrast, the shades of a few fortunate people, most often kings, queens, or heroic warriors, went to Elysium (or Elision or the Isles of the Blessed), where they enjoyed sunlight, good food, and companionship. On the other hand, the shades of criminals went to the Underworld's lowest, darkest, and most unpleasant region—Tartarus. There they joined a bevy of monsters and other former enemies of the gods that had been confined in the depths since the Age of Heroes.

These were the basic concepts of the Underworld that became an integral part of Greek folklore and religion. However, beliefs about the afterlife varied widely in different parts of Greece in different times. The traditional Underworld described above was neither a heaven nor a hell in the modern sense (even Tartarus was not the equivalent of hell); it was simply a neutral sort of place where everyone ended up sooner or later. But though some people accepted this version of the afterlife as real and inevitable, others rejected it as mere fable; and a few, notably the followers of the philosopher Epicurus, proposed that the soul simply died with the body, and so there was no afterlife at all.

Most Greeks were unwilling to accept such a bleak and pessimistic outlook, however. At the same time, the traditional Underworld, with its grim boatman and monotonous Plain of Asphodel, seemed neither believable nor appealing. So in the Classical Age and the centuries that followed it, a number of mystery religions became increasingly popular because they offered a more hopeful and appealing vision of the afterlife than either the traditional view or the concept of eternal nothingness after death. The mystery cults, most famously Demeter's cult at Eleusis, promised admittance into Elysium or someplace like it for all worshippers, regardless of their class or stature in life. (This concept strongly influenced early Christian beliefs about the afterlife.) Meanwhile, a handful of Greek religious cults, including Orphism, promoted the concept of reincarnation, with the souls of good people being reborn as kings and heroes, and the souls of bad people ending up as slaves or animals.

SEE ALSO: Demeter; Hades; religion

Uranus

In Greek mythology, one of the conscious natural forces that predated the races of gods (the Titans and the Olympians). Uranus (or Ouranos), who was identified with the sky, sprang from the union of two other forces—Gaia (Earth) and Chaos (primeval disorder). Then Uranus and Gaia mated and produced the Titans.

However, Uranus was jealous of his children and worried that some of them might overthrow him, so he shoved them back inside Gaia. Not surprisingly, this caused her great discomfort, so she appealed to her son Cronos, who castrated Uranus with a sickle, sending his severed genitals splashing into the sea. The foam that formed in their wake soon gave rise to Aphrodite, goddess of love. And the blood droplets from the castration grew into the Furies (pursuers of criminals), the giants, and various nymphs (minor female goddesses).

SEE ALSO: Cronos; Gaia; Titans

villas

Large, comfortable country homes, usually having several rooms lining the perimeter of a central, open courtyard.

SEE ALSO: houses

vines and vineyards

Grapevines were cultivated and wines were produced from them in many parts of Greece as well as in numerous Mediterranean regions colonized by the Greeks.

SEE ALSO: farming

votive offerings

Gifts given to a god as a reward for a favor or favors the worshipper believed the god had performed.

SEE ALSO: religion

Wasps

A comic play by Aristophanes, first presented in Athens in 422 B.C. By this time, large numbers of poor, often elderly, Athenians were at least partially financially dependent on the small payments they received from the state for jury duty. *Wasps* was a biting satire on this indirect welfare system. The main character, Philocleon, is so addicted to serving on juries that his son, Bdelycleon, resorts to locking him in the house. One morning Philocleon's friends, who are also avid jurors, arrive as usual to take him to the courts. They are dressed as wasps to emphasize that they are prepared to sentence any criminals they might convict to stinging punishment. When the wasps try to help Philocleon escape, Bdelycleon stops them and a heated discussion about the value of jury duty ensues. Eventually, to prove a point, the son sets up a mock trial in which Philocleon is asked either to convict or acquit the family dog for the crime of stealing some cheese. The old man finds the dog not guilty.

SEE ALSO: Aristophanes, 1

water supplies

The earliest inhabitants of Greece got their water directly from streams and rivers, and in some areas streams remained an important source of water for drinking, cooking, and bathing throughout antiquity. However, during the Bronze Age the Minoans devised a system of baked clay pipes that channeled water from streams into the palace-centers (and perhaps other buildings). On the Greek mainland, where the Mycenaeans lived, evidence has been found of early versions of aqueducts, stone-cut or stone-lined channels that carried water from streams or lakes into human settlements. People also dug wells when and where they could.

In the Archaic, Classical, and Hellenistic ages, wells remained important sources of fresh water, especially in regions like Attica, which were dry and had few rivers and other natural waterways. In his biography of the Athenian statesman Solon, Plutarch remarks, "Attica cannot rely for her water upon rivers that flow all the year round, or upon lakes or abundant streams, but most of it comes from artificial wells. Solon therefore made a law that wherever there was a public well within a distance of half a mile, everyone should use that, but if the distance was greater, they should dig one for themselves." (*Life of Solon* 23) Another major source of fresh water was cisterns, basins or tanks that caught and stored rainwater, some underground (and coated on the inside with waterproof substances), others on rooftops. Both wells and underground cisterns were usually equipped with stone or terra-cotta lids to keep people and animals from falling in. When wells or cisterns were outside the house, the well-to-do installed clay pipes to bring the water in. People of average means had to rely on buckets and muscle power.

By contrast, in areas where streams, springs, and small rivers were more numerous, many townspeople got their water supplies from fountain houses. A fountain house was a small building that more often than not was built beside a stream. Water flowed from the stream into stone settling tanks inside, and from the tanks the water

A Macedonian phalanx is on the move in this reconstruction. The use of long battle pikes differentiated this version from the standard Greek phalanx. AKG-IMAGES/PETER CONNOLLY

trickled through clay pipes into bronze spouts protruding from an outer wall. Those who lived nearby filled their buckets from these spouts. Because they were public buildings, fountain houses were often splendidly decorated so that they looked much like miniature temples. Some fountain houses got their water from aqueducts rather than streams. An excellent example from the Classical Age was unearthed at Olynthus (on the Chalcidic peninsula, in the northern Aegean). This aqueduct carried water from the hills several miles away into the city, where the precious liquid was diverted to fountain houses. For the most part, however, the Greeks built few aqueducts during the height of their power, partly because they were very expensive to build; and only later, when the Romans took over and administered the Greek lands, did aqueducts become common in Greece.

SEE ALSO: baths and bathing; Minoans

weapons and warfare, land

Archaeological evidence shows that land weapons and warfare in Greece's Bronze Age in many ways resembled those in the Near East, with which both the Minoans and Mycenaeans had commercial and cultural contacts. In this period the Egyptians, Assyrians, Hittites, and other Near Eastern peoples utilized bronze swords and battle-axes, bronze-tipped spears, the bow and arrow (including the composite bow, which was more powerful than an ordinary bow), and war chariots. The Greek-speaking Mycenaeans had all of these weapons, although it is likely that the rarity of wide, flat plains in the region made large-scale chariot battles impossible. Probably the biggest such battles involved a few hundred chariots at best. As in the Near East, a warrior stood in his chariot and wielded a bow and/or spear. Meanwhile, foot soldiers supported the chariots and tried to kill charioteers who had fallen from their vehicles.

Following the collapse of Mycenaean civilization, warfare, like society itself, became smaller in scale and less organized.

No longer a major offensive weapon, the chariot became mostly a "prestige vehicle" that carried leading warriors to and from the battlefield, where they fought on foot. (Homer vividly depicts this practice in his *Iliad*.) Not much is known about weapons and their use in the Dark Age, except that the throwing spear (javelin) and the sword seem to have been the principal weapons.

Emergence of Hoplite Warfare

In the Archaic Age, however, the Greeks rapidly developed a new military system that revolutionized land warfare in Europe and made Greek armies the most formidable in the known world for centuries to come. By the seventh century B.C., with the rise of city-states across the Greek sphere, small citizen militias, manned mainly by independent farmers, had become widespread. In times of war, these men doubled as hoplites, heavily armored infantry soldiers. A hoplite's extensive array of arms and armor was collectively called the panoply, its key element being a shield, the *aspis* (or *hoplon*). It was about 3 feet (1m) in diameter, weighed about 17 pounds (8kg), and consisted of a wooden core reinforced on the outside by a coating of bronze (and/or layers of ox hide). The inside of the shield had a distinctive gripping system. The hoplite passed his left forearm through a bronze strip with a loop in the middle and grasped a leather handle with his left hand. This allowed him to let go of the handle and hold a spare weapon in his left hand without losing his shield; it also helped to relieve the burden of the shield's considerable weight. To protect his chest and abdomen, a hoplite wore a cuirass. Some cuirasses were made of bronze, but in time the most common version was the *linothorax*, made up of several layers of linen or canvas glued together to form a stiff shirt. The other elements of

the panoply included a bronze helmet, which had eye slits and breathing spaces for the nose and mouth; greaves, bronze lower-leg protectors, applied by pulling them open and clipping them on, in the manner of modern wrist cuffs; a thrusting spear about 7 feet (2m) long with an iron head; and a sword with an iron blade about 2 feet (.61m) long. The spear was the hoplite's principle weapon, and he used his sword mainly as a backup weapon if he lost or broke his spear.

The hoplites fought in a battlefield formation called the phalanx, made up of a long block of soldiers standing in ranks (lines), one behind the other. The average depth was eight ranks, but sometimes more or fewer ranks were used. At the Battle of Marathon (490 B.C.), most of the Athenian line featured four or fewer ranks; the Spartans often employed a depth of twelve ranks in their wings; and at Leuctra (371 B.C.), the Theban commander Epaminondas utilized fifty ranks in one of his wings. The Greek phalanx was an enormously effective offensive unit for two chief reasons. First, it provided each hoplite with a great deal of protection. When assembled in close order, about 2 to 3 feet (.6 to 1m) apart, the fighters' uplifted shields formed an unbroken protective barrier. Also, as the hoplites marched forward in unison, the formation took on a huge amount of forward momentum, which increased still further when it made contact with the enemy line. At this point, the hoplites in the front rank jabbed their spears at their opponents, while those in the rear ranks pushed at their comrades' backs, forcing them forward with irresistible force. (This maneuver was known as the *othismos*, or "shoving.")

The phalanx was particularly devastating when used against non-Greeks, as in the case of the many victories achieved by Greek armies over the Persians. In contrast, when two Greek phalanxes met head-on, the result was usually a gigantic shoving match that ended when one side became exhausted and retreated. The phalanx became even more formidable in the fourth century B.C., when Macedonia's King Philip II made the formation deeper and replaced the men's spears with long battle pikes (*sarissas*). The "Macedonian phalanx," as it came to be called, featured a largely impenetrable mass of iron spear points protruding from its front, prompting the Greek historian Polybius's famous remark, "So long as the phalanx retains its characteristic form and strength, nothing can withstand its charge or resist it face to face." (*Histories* 18.29)

Cavalry and Light-Armed Troops

The phalanx, in one form or another, remained the main tactical formation of Greek land armies throughout the Classical and Hellenistic periods. However, other kinds of soldiers supported the hoplites in secondary roles. The Greeks made little or no use of cavalry before the late fifth century B.C., and at first these horsemen were not used in shock action (direct charges on the infantry). This was partly because saddles were crude and stirrups did not yet exist, so staying on a swiftly moving horse was difficult, especially if the rider was loaded down with armor and weapons. Therefore, early Greek cavalrymen mainly protected the wings of the phalanx from enemy flanking movements or chased down escaping enemy troops after the battle was over. Mounted warriors finally came into their own under Philip II and his son, Alexander the Great, in the mid-fourth century B.C. Philip created a highly effective integrated arms system in which the phalanx, cavalry, and

light infantry all played key roles in battle. His elite cavalry corps consisted of young Macedonian noblemen—the "Companions" (*hetairoi*), who wore bronze armor and sometimes charged in a wedge-shaped formation directly into enemy infantry. Typically this tactic opened a hole in the enemy line large enough for the Macedonian phalanx to enter and do its work.

Both before and after Philip and Alexander, light infantry, or skirmishers, also played a role in Greek land warfare. Skirmishers, including archers, slingers, and *peltasts*, wore little or no armor. *Peltasts* carried small bundles of javelins, which they threw at the enemy and then ran away. The main tasks of skirmishers were to soften up the enemy before the charge of the phalanx and to protect the sides and rear of the phalanx. The armies of the Hellenistic Greek states of the era following Alexander's death in 323 B.C. featured these same elements—phalanxes, cavalry, and skirmishers—and often added battle elephants, which the Greeks first saw in use in Asia. Hellenistic leaders also used mercenaries in large numbers. It was common to hire archers from Crete, slingers from Rhodes, and *peltasts* from Thrace, for instance.

Despite the tremendous effectiveness of the Hellenistic Greek phalanxes and their supporting troops, the Greek military system had certain disadvantages that the Romans eventually took full advantage of. First and foremost, the phalanx was very rigid and inflexible, and if the ground was not flat and fairly free of trees and other obstructions, it fell apart and became almost useless. In the second century B.C., Roman military formations, which were smaller, more mobile, and more flexible, outmaneuvered and neutralized the Greek phalanxes, allowing Rome to defeat the

Greek kingdoms and city-states with amazing swiftness.

See Also: Alexander III ("the Great"); chariots; Epaminondas; Philip II; Rome; weapons and warfare, naval; weapons and warfare, siege

weapons and warfare, naval

Little is known about Bronze Age Greek ships and the degree to which they were employed in warfare, but evidence shows that the Minoans and Mycenaeans did have navies that they used to control the Aegean seaways. After they took over the Minoan sphere in the fifteenth and fourteenth centuries B.C., the Mycenaeans may have employed their ships not only for trade but also to carry troops for raids on cities on the shores of Asia Minor. The legendary Greek fleet that sailed to Troy, as described in Homer's *Iliad*, may be based on a memory of such expeditions. As for actual naval battles, a clue to their existence in the Bronze Age is a wall fresco found on the Aegean island of Thera (north of Crete), which depicts the conclusion of a naval battle fought between Aegean (presumably Mycenaean) ships and non-Aegean ones. Also, some graphic stone reliefs found in Egypt show a naval battle fought on Egypt's northern coast against invaders in ships, some of whom may have been Mycenaean Greeks.

More is known about naval warfare in Greece starting in the Archaic Age (ca. 800–ca. 500 B.C.). In the early years of that era the principal warship was the *pentekonter*, with fifty rowers who all sat on the same bank (deck level). This vessel had little room for storage, and the sailors had to sleep at their oars. The *pentekonter* was impractical for long voyages at sea, therefore, and captains stuck mainly to shorelines or hopped from one island to the next. Homer and other ancient writers often describe crews beaching their vessels each evening to search for food and other supplies and to make camp. In about 700 B.C. or so, the bireme appeared. It had two oar banks and was shorter, more powerful, and more maneuverable than the *pentekonter*. An even more formidable warship, the trireme (*triers*), came into use in the sixth century B.C. It had three banks of oars, was usually about 130 feet (40m) long, 18 feet (6m) wide, and carried a crew of about two hundred. This included 170 rowers, which in an Athenian trireme broke down into sixty-two men in the upper oar bank (the *thranite*) and fifty-four each in the middle and lower banks (*zygite* and *thalamite*, respectively). The crew also typically included a flute player who kept time for the rowers, a fighting force of ten (and occasionally up to thirty or more) hoplite marines (*epibatai*), four archers, and fifteen deckhands.

Like *pentekonters*, triremes lacked eating and sleeping facilities, which meant that they still had to be beached every day and were therefore impractical for long-term naval strategy. Naval strategy was therefore of a short-term nature, mainly concerned with how to win an individual battle. The tactics were fairly simple. Crewmen lowered the sails so that the vessels maneuvered solely by oar power during the fighting. The warships, which were equipped with bronze "beaks" on their prows, often tried to ram opposing ships and thereby sink them. One common maneuver was first to attack at an angle and sheer off the enemy's oars, leaving the ship disabled and that side of its hull open to ramming. Another tactic was to use grappling hooks or ropes to lock two ships together. The marines from one vessel then boarded the other and fought hand to hand. All of these tactics were employed in the great naval battle fought in 480 B.C. between the Greeks and Persians at Salamis, which the playwright Aeschylus (who fought in the battle) described in his play *The Persians*.

In the fourth century B.C. and on into Hellenistic times, larger warships appeared, among them "fours," "fives," "sixes," and so on (although most often these numbers likely referred to the number of men on an oar rather than to the number of oar banks). These big galleys could deliver much larger volleys of missiles (from archers, catapults, and mechanical dart throwers) than triremes could. But the main battle tactics were still, as in the past, ramming and boarding. The last ancient naval battle in which the fleet of an independent Greek state took part was the one fought at Actium in western Greece in 31 B.C. Cleopatra VII, last ruler of the Greek Ptolemaic dynasty, and her Roman ally, Mark Antony, were defeated by a Roman fleet commanded by Octavian (later Augustus, the first Roman emperor) and his admiral, Marcus Agrippa. After that, naval warfare played only an occasional and minor role in Mediterranean warfare until well after the fall of Rome.

SEE ALSO: Battle of Actium; Battle of Salamis; seafaring; weapons and warfare, land

weapons and warfare, siege

No one knows when the first sieges of towns, fortresses, or other fortified places occurred in the Greek sphere. But it is highly likely that sieges took place in the last few centuries of the Bronze Age because of the design and construction of the Mycenaean palace-citadels that rose at places like Mycenae, Tiryns, Thebes, and other sites on the Greek mainland. These citadels had high, thick walls made of huge

stones, some of them weighing more than 100 tons (91 metric tons). (The fortifications were so formidable that many Greeks of later ages assumed they had been erected by a race of giants.) The fact that these centers were so heavily fortified implies that attacks and sieges were fairly common. Exactly how the attackers and defenders in such sieges fought is unknown. But Homer's descriptions of the siege of Troy in the *Iliad* may contain a few echoes of siege methods in the eras before his own. (He lived in the early Archaic Age, well after the fall of Mycenaean civilization.) Descriptions by other ancient writers of the Trojan Horse (in which Greek warriors smuggled themselves inside the city) may well be based on garbled memories of large Bronze Age battering rams with carved horse heads on their ramming ends.

Sieges in Classical Times

In the centuries that followed, sieges remained an occasional feature of Greek warfare. But little is known about them before the late fifth century B.C. It appears that sieges may have become more common in the preceding century, because in the sixth century B.C. a number of Greek towns began adding large stone towers to their defensive walls. The towers provided bigger and more effective positions from which to rain down arrows, rocks, or other missiles on attackers. When the Athenians erected the famous Long Walls in the mid-fifth century B.C., they incorporated such towers at regular intervals. The first siege of the Classical Age about which any details are known was the Spartan siege of Athens's small neighbor, Plataea, in 429 B.C. at the beginning of the Peloponnesian War. In his chronicle of that conflict, Thucydides tells how the attackers erected a tall stockade around the town to keep the inhabitants from escaping. Then the Spartans constructed wooden retaining walls projecting outward at right angles to Plataea's stone defensive walls. They filled in the retaining walls with earth, building up a mound that eventually reached the top of the city's walls. As Thucydides writes, the defenders did their best to counter the attack: "The Plataeans . . . when they saw the mound growing higher and higher, constructed a wooden wall [on top of the battlements]. . . . It also had a defensive covering of [animal] skins and hides to preserve the woodwork from fire arrows. . . . The Plataeans also had the idea of demolishing part of their wall against which the mound was being built and carrying away the loose earth." (*The Peloponnesian War* 2.75) The Spartans also used battering rams and tried to dig tunnels under the walls. Their siege methods, which were copied directly from those of the Persians (who in turn borrowed theirs from an earlier Mesopotamian people, the Assyrians) eventually succeeded, and Plataea fell.

Important New Siege Weapons

Not long afterward some important new strides in siege warfare were made by Dionysius I, a ruler of the Greek city of Syracuse on the island of Sicily. His inventors created huge towers some six stories high that moved on wheels and carried large artillery pieces, including catapults and mechanical crossbows. Each bow was attached to a wooden framework equipped with a metal winch that slowly drew back the bowstring and fired a huge arrow. Dionysius used these and other effective new siege weapons to capture the Carthaginian island-fortress of Motya (off Sicily's coast) in 397 B.C. Most other Greeks were slow to incorporate these new methods, however. And not until Macedonia's King Philip II

showed their effectiveness in his sieges of the cities of Olynthus (349 B.C.) and Perinthus (340) did they become standard in warfare. The successful sieges of Halicarnassus (334) and Tyre (332) by his son, Alexander the Great, then became models followed by the Hellenistic generals in their own sieges.

Indeed, the Hellenistic realms spent enormous amounts of money, energy, and manpower prosecuting sieges, elevating such warfare to a veritable art. Greek inventors, engineers, and machinists produced a wide array of lethal devices, among them bigger siege towers, huge drills that could pierce stone walls, and larger and more lethal artillery. The latter included torsion-powered catapults. These worked by twisting bundles of animal tendons or human hair very tightly and then releasing them, thereby propelling large stones or spears up to a half mile (.8km) or more. Hellenistic Greek besiegers also mined (dug tunnels) under defensive walls, either to weaken them or to get soldiers into the city. To counter the mines, the defenders filled them with smoke or tried to dig their own mines under the attacker's mines.

The Siege of Rhodes

The largest and most famous siege of the age utilized all of these devices and methods. In 305 B.C. Demetrius, son of Alexander's general Antigonus, mounted a great siege of the main fortress of Rhodes, whose inhabitants had sided with his enemy, Ptolemy. Demetrius's soldiers built a small harbor for his ships (because the Rhodians had fortified and blocked off their own main harbor) and secured a beachhead on the mole at the front of the main harbor. The defenders countered by launching a devastating attack on the mole. Then Demetrius's men tried to tunnel under the walls, but the Rhodians stopped them by digging their own mines beneath them. The Rhodians also countered Demetrius's artillery with catapults of their own, which they mounted on platforms on the decks of ships. Finally, Demetrius brought up his great siege tower, the Helepolis, or "City-taker." It was nine stories tall and required thirty-four hundred men to move. From inside, Demetrius's soldiers fired catapults and other artillery, while eight penthouses, wooden galleries on wheels, protected the troops pushing the siege tower. This vast array of military technology and manpower was ultimately of no avail, however. The Rhodians damaged the great tower, forcing Demetrius to pull it back. And in the face of the defenders' phenomenal display of courage and ingenuity, he abandoned the siege. Meanwhile, the methods and siege devices he and other Greek siege masters employed were steadily adopted by the Romans, who made them part of the impressive military machine that went on to conquer the Greeks and other Mediterranean peoples.

SEE ALSO: Alexander III ("the Great"); Demetrius Poliorcetes; Dionysius I; Philip II; Rhodes; weapons and warfare, land

weights and measures

The Greeks had no universal standard of weights and measures recognized by all Greek cities and regions. Instead, local variants evolved, among the more prominent being those formulated in the Peloponnesus and Attica. The basic unit of measure in each locale was the foot. It measured 11.6 inches (29cm) in Attica, 12.6 inches (32cm) in the Peloponnesus, 13.1 inches (33cm) on the prosperous maritime island of Aegina, and there were many other versions. From their basic foot measure (*tompedos*), the Greeks calculated longer units of measure. One of the more important was the *stade* (or *stadion*), which measured six hundred Greek feet (183m). Although this unit varied slightly across the Greek sphere, on average a *stade* would be equivalent to about 625 modern feet (191m). Smaller units of length included the fathom (*orgyia*), equal to 6 feet (1.8m), or the distance covered by a person's outstretched arms; the pace (*bema*), equal to roughly 2.5 feet (.76m); and the cubit (*pekhys*), equal to about 1.5 feet (.46m), or the distance from a person's elbow to fingertip.

Greek units of area were originally calculated by how much land could be plowed by a team of oxen in a day; because this could vary from place to place and from farmer to farmer, such units were fairly imprecise. The basic unit was the *plethron*, roughly equivalent to 10,000 square feet (929 sq.m), in today's terms perhaps a quarter of an acre (.1ha).

Units of liquid and dry volume also varied widely in ancient Greece. One major liquid measure was that of a standard amphora, a large pottery vessel for transporting and storing wine and other commodities. The amphora measure, or *metretes* was roughly equivalent to a bit more than 8 modern gallons (about 39l). Common dry measures included the *khoinix*—in Attica the amount of grain rationed to one person for one day—and the larger *medimnos* (equaling 48 *khoinikes*)(52l).

Standards of weight, which were vital to trade among cities and nations, were as diverse as other units of measure. One of the most widely recognized systems was the one created in Attica in late Archaic times by the lawgiver Solon. Its units were the same as those of Athenian money—for

This colorful fresco from Knossos, in Crete, shows a trio of well-to-do and elegantly dressed Bronze Age women. © KEVIN SCHAFER/CORBIS

instance, one obol equaled twelve measures of barley; one drachma equaled six obols, or seventy-two measures of barley; and one mina equaled one hundred drachmae, or seventy-two hundred measures of barley.

SEE ALSO: money; trade

women

Throughout antiquity, Greek society was male-dominated, and women were, with occasional exceptions, second-class citizens, especially when compared to women in today's progressive, democratic nations. Yet it would be misleading to generalize too much about the lives and experiences of ancient Greek women. Though nearly all of them possessed fewer civic and legal rights than men, their status, treatment, and opportunities differed, sometimes significantly, from one city or kingdom to another and from era to era. Much of the difficulty in constructing a realistic picture of ancient Greek women's lives derives from the fact that the vast majority of the surviving evidence comes from Athens, and to a lesser degree from Sparta, in the Classical Age. Very little of a definite nature is known about women in other Greek states and eras. And it is possible that Athenian women led more restricted, regulated lives than women in some other Greek states, while treatment of women in Sparta may have been more liberal and equable than in most other places in Greece. A further complication is that the vast majority of the surviving written sources about Greek women were written by men. So a true female perspective is often lacking and scholars must be careful and critical in examining the ancient written sources available to them about Greek women.

Early Greek Women

Unfortunately, no written sources at all about women have survived from Greece's Bronze and Dark ages. However, some educated guesses can be made about Minoan women from archaeological evidence, including wall paintings and carved scenes on seals found in the Cretan palace-centers and at Akroteri on Thera, where the ruins of a Minoan town have been found. The Naval Festival Fresco from Akroteri and the Grandstand Fresco from Knossos, among others, show dominant female figures who were probably priestesses. Another painting from Knossos shows three young women who may be wives or daughters of palace-center officials. Their colorful attire and carefree demeanor suggest that at least some Minoan women were highly regarded and happy. They may well have enjoyed an unusual amount of status and freedom of movement and expression. However, no evidence has been found that these women had any political rights. Also, nothing is known about average Minoan women who lived outside the palace-centers, nor is anything of a definite nature known about the lives of everyday Mycenaean women. Perhaps some indirect information about these women can be found in Homer's epics, however. Most modern scholars think that Homer captured some dim memories of Bronze Age and Dark Age people that had survived through oral retellings over many generations. He then proceeded to place them in the social setting of his own time—the early Archaic Age. Homeric women (not counting the fanciful goddesses and sorceresses) are largely subservient to men. In general, men are seen as political leaders, warriors, hunters, and traders, while women tend to the home, raise the children, cook, and make clothes.

Most of the few surviving written descriptions of women in the generations following Homer tend to depict them as inferior in worth to men and not to be trusted. The Boeotian poet Hesiod calls the mythical first woman, Pandora, "the hopeless trap, deadly to men." From her, he says, "comes all the race of womankind, the deadly female race and tribe of wives who live with mortal men and bring them harm, no help to them in poverty but ready enough to share with them in wealth." (*Theogony* 587–592) A younger contemporary of Hesiod, the poet Semonides, agreed, writing that women constituted a plague inflicted on men by Zeus. It must not be inferred from these purely male tirades that Archaic Greek women either felt or acted inferior to their husbands. In fact, Hesiod's and Semonides' negative view of the opposite sex seems to have been based in large part on their dealings with women who were strong-willed, opinionated, and demanding. Nevertheless, Greek society in Archaic times remained patriarchal, with the male head of the household acting as the legal guardian (*kyrios*) of his wife, who was expected to attend to household duties. These duties included maintaining the household food storage, supervising the family slaves, cooking, spinning and weaving, bathing their husbands, and overseeing funeral preparations. In well-to-do households, female slaves performed most of the same duties, often working right alongside their mistresses. Evidence suggests that Archaic Greek women were not always confined in the home, however. Some poorer women and widows did work, usually as housekeepers, wool workers, or nursemaids.

Women in Classical Athens

In the late Archaic Age and early Classical Age, men in some, and perhaps many, Greek city-states passed laws that strictly controlled women's social and sexual behavior and limited what they could own or inherit. The laws enacted in Athens in the early sixth century B.C. by the social reformer Solon are the best-known example. His new law code included numerous restrictions on women, including one that limited the number of women who could participate in funerals and regulated their behavior at such gatherings. In Classical times, an Athenian woman's husband remained her *kyrios* in all legal matters. If he died and her sons were not yet eighteen, her father became her guardian until such time, if ever, that she remarried. Also, Athenian women normally did not own land, although they owned household properties such as furniture, clothes, jewelry, and slaves. (Usually they acquired such items as gifts, especially wedding gifts.) With few exceptions, Athenian women spent most of their time in the home. Here, the chief rationale and goal of fathers and husbands seems to have been to prevent respectable wives, mothers, and daughters from conversing with unrelated males. Husbands and fathers were highly preoccupied with their wives' and daughters' chastity and marital fidelity. And men outside the family unit were seen as potentially corruptive influences that threatened the stability of the family. Thus, on those infrequent occasions when a respectable woman did leave the house, a male relative or family slave customarily accompanied her. Similarly, when the man of the house was entertaining his male friends, his wife, daughters, mother, and sisters had to retire to the *gynaeceum*, or "women's quarters," located in the back of the house or upstairs. Evidently the rest of the time the family women had the run of the house and went about their various duties. These were largely the same domestic activities performed by most Greek women in the Archaic Age.

Spartan Women

If the lives of women in many other parts of Greece in the Classical Age were at least similar to those of Athenian women (which, because of the lack of proof, remains an assumption), the case of Spartan women was a marked exception. In Sparta a strict, regimented military system took young men away from their families for years at a time. This made a large percentage of Spartan men absentee husbands and fathers. It also meant that a Spartan man held much less authority and personal say in family life than an average Athenian man.

Indeed with the father and sons absent most of the time, a Spartan home was largely a female environment populated by mother, daughters, and other women. This made the typical Spartan woman more independent and assertive, and she enjoyed a number of rights and privileges that many other Greek women did not. Many Spartan women made and enforced the rules of their households, for example. And they were not confined in the home or denied contact and conversations with nonfamilial men. With minor exceptions, a female Spartan could appear in public whenever she pleased. Although men still held all the positions of real power in Sparta and their wives had no more political rights than Athenian women did, a Spartan woman could inherit land and other family property directly. And women in Sparta eventually gained control of large amounts of land. Aristotle, who felt that Spartan women enjoyed a great deal too much freedom, said that they owned two-fifths of Sparta's land by the mid-fourth century B.C.

Women Make Advances in the Hellenistic Age

In the Hellenistic Age Greek women in many places outside of Sparta experienced some improvements in their economic opportunities and legal and social status (although things did not change all that much for Athenian women). Documents written on papyrus, mostly found in Ptolemaic Egypt, indicate that women in that region (both Greek and native Egyptian) regularly gave and received loans; bought and sold land, slaves, and other property; inherited and bequeathed property and other legacies; and even made their own marriage contracts, perhaps without the consent of their male guardians. One surviving marriage contract from Greek-ruled Egypt, dated 311 B.C., reveals both the bride's considerable legal rights and her husband's obligation to respect them. He was forbidden by law to bring home a mistress or to have children by a mistress, whereas an Athenian man could still do both. Also, both the wife and husband named in the contract had equal recourse to seek legal and financial damages in case the other did not honor the document's contents. In addition, passages from Hellenistic poems, plays, and other writings suggest that Greek women were less segregated than before and in some areas could walk around the streets without a male escort. At the same time, Hellenistic literature began to depict romantic love and passion between men and women and emphasized them as sexual equals who were genuinely interested in each other's needs and pleasures. Finally, in the Hellenistic Age, more women became literate than ever before. And there is evidence that in some areas girls attended formal schools along with boys. This resulted in the emergence of several female poets and even a few women painters, sculptors, and philosophers. Granted, these accomplished women did not represent the norm, even in the more liberal Hellenistic period, yet a fair proportion of Greek women in that era enjoyed more freedom and opportunity than their grandmothers had known. At any rate, times were changing for women in others ways, in large part because of the absorption of the Greek lands by Rome in the last two centuries B.C. These lands became Roman provinces, and over time the lives of most Greek and Roman women in a sense merged in the larger melting pot of the vast Roman Empire.

SEE ALSO: children; citizenship; clothing; education; family; marriage and divorce

Women at the Assembly

A comedy by Aristophanes, produced circa 392 B.C. in Athens. As in his earlier comedy, *Lysistrata*, in *Women at the Assembly* (*Ekklesiazousai*) the playwright plays with what was then viewed as a radical, even ridiculous notion—women seizing political power from the city's men. To this end, an uppity woman named Praxagora leads a conspiracy. She and her cohorts disguise themselves as men, infiltrate a meeting of Athens's Assembly (*Ekklesia*), and vote to transfer most state authority from men to women. Praxagora, who has been chosen to rule the city, goes home and explains society's new rules to her husband. Among others, these include communal sharing of child-rearing responsibilities and the elimination of private property. Aristophanes proceeds to introduce various speeches and plot twists designed to show the absurdity of such a system.

SEE ALSO: Aristophanes, 1; *Lysistrata*

Works and Days

A long poem by Hesiod, dating from perhaps circa 700 B.C. The work combines several seemingly unrelated topics—a farmer's calendar, advice on sailing, a collection of wise adages, and some mythological stories—into a coherent whole by relating most of them to the overriding theme of the work ethic. As explained in the opening section of the poem, after their father's death, Hesiod and his brother, Perses, quarrel over how much of the family land each should get. And the poet urges Perses to end their ongoing feud. "Let us settle our dispute at once," Hesiod says, "and let our judge be Zeus, whose laws are just." (*Works and Days* 37–38). He then retells several myths that illustrate the importance of justice and hard work. Among the myths covered are those in which the Titan Prometheus steals fire from heaven and gives it to humans, and how Pandora, the first woman, brought a host of troubles into the world. Hesiod also says that Zeus is always on the lookout to punish humans for their crimes, so people should concentrate on working hard and dealing with one another fairly and justly. Continuing to explore the theme of work, Hesiod next offers Perses advice on how to be a successful farmer and a good citizen. Among the topics covered are fashioning a plow, selling goods at market, and determining which days are lucky or unlucky for planting and other activities. Like Hesiod's other long poem, the *Theogony*, and Homer's epic poems, *Works and Days* exerted a strong influence on Greeks in succeeding generations, helping them to understand what the gods were like and what these divine beings expected of humanity.

SEE ALSO: Hesiod; poetry; *Theogony*

wrestling

The most popular sport in ancient Greece, wrestling was practiced in both formal athletic games and in informal matches in gyms and fields.

SEE ALSO: athletics

writing

The Greeks had forms of writing in the Bronze Age but produced no known literature in that era. In the Dark Age they were illiterate, but in the Archaic Age they learned to write again, this time with an alphabet that allowed them to produce sophisticated literature. For more on the alphabet, writing, and literature, **see** biography; epigraphy; Greek language; libraries; panegyric; philosophy; poetry; theater and drama; writing materials; and the names of individual authors and their works.

writing materials

The chief writing material used by the Greeks and others in the Mediterranean world throughout most of ancient times was a kind of paper made from papyrus, a marsh plant native to Egypt. When writing began to become common across the Greek sphere in the 600s B.C., most of the papyrus came into that sphere through the Phoenician port of Byblos; hence, the Greek name for both papyrus and a book—*biblos*. Some surviving ancient paintings show people making papyrus. The plant's stem was split into thin strips, dampened with water, laid on a board, and then pressed to make sheets about 16 inches (40cm) wide and about half as long. Many of these sheets were pasted together to form a roll, usually about 33 feet (10m) long, wound around a wooden stick. Such a roll was generally referred to as a *book*. Thus, Thucydides' famous historical work, *The Peloponnesian War*, was said to be eight books long because it filled eight standard papyrus rolls. If a written work was longer than one roll, as Thucydides' was, its multiple rolls were kept in a bucket or wooden container. To write on such rolls, a person employed a reed or bronze pen dipped in ink made from carbon black (soot). When finished, the writer labeled the book with a little tag (*sillybos*) that hung from one of its ends.

Two other writing mediums were common in antiquity. One was the "leaf tablet," which dates from the seventh century B.C. or earlier in Greece. It consisted of a thin wooden board covered with a layer of wax, which the writer inscribed using a metal pen (stylus). He or she could later smooth out the wax (or add more wax) to create a fresh surface. The other ancient writing medium was vellum (from the Latin *vellus*), a kind of parchment made from the skin of cattle, goats, and sheep. At first it was used mainly in areas where papyrus was hard to come by. When bound books with individual pages, like those used today, began to appear in the first century however, vellum slowly began to replace papyrus. This was partly because vellum was tougher and lasted longer. The pages of an ancient bound book, called a codex, were sewn into a thin spine and placed between two thin wooden boards. These sorts of books had become much more common than papyrus rolls by the late fourth century A.D.

SEE ALSO: Greek language; libraries

Xanthippus
(ca. 525 B.C.–475 B.C.)

A noted Athenian general and the father of the popular Athenian politician Pericles. Xanthippus (zan-THIP-us) brought his fellow general Miltiades to trial (for deceiving the public) in 489 B.C., but a few years later Xanthippus was himself ostracized and had to go into exile. The Athenians recalled him in 480, however, to help fight the invading Persians, and he was elected general again and distinguished himself during the Greek victory over the Persians at Mycale in 479.

SEE ALSO: Battle of Mycale; Miltiades; Pericles

Xanthippus
(flourished mid-third century B.C.)

A skilled Spartan general whom the Carthaginians hired to reorganize and command their troops when a Roman army landed in North Africa during the First Punic War (264–241 B.C.). Xanthippus decisively defeated the Romans and captured their leader, Marcus Regulus.

SEE ALSO: Carthage; Rome

Xenophanes
(ca. 570 B.C.–ca. 470 B.C.)

An eccentric, though important, pre-Socratic Greek philosopher and poet. Born at Colophon in Ionia, Xenophanes (zen-OFF-uh-neez) traveled widely and ended up residing in Syracuse in Sicily and dying in the Greek city of Elea in southern Italy. None of his works, including his principal one, *On Nature*, has survived complete. But the existing fragments of his writings reveal a penetrating intellect concerned with the origins of humanity and human institutions, including religion. He rejected Homer's and Hesiod's descriptions of the gods as anthropomorphic (humanlike) beings and proposed the existence of a single, eternal deity of undetermined form, similar in many ways to the God of modern monotheistic faiths. "God is one," Xenophanes says,

> supreme among gods and men, and not like mortals in body or mind. . . . Without effort he sets in motion all things by mind and thought. . . . Mortals suppose that the gods are born . . . and that they wear man's clothing and have human voice and body. But if cattle or lions had hands . . . they would paint their gods and give them bodies in form like their own—horses like horses, cattle like cattle.(*On Nature* 1, 5–6).

Xenophanes also held that farming, the discovery of fire, and wine-making skills were developments of early human civilization, not gifts from the gods.

SEE ALSO: poetry; philosophy; science

Xenophon
(ca. 428 B.C.–ca. 354 B.C.)

One of the leading Greek historians and writers of the second half of the Classical Age. Born into a well-to-do Athenian family, Xenophon (pronounced ZEN-uh-phon) grew up during the Peloponnesian War. And like many young men of his generation, he became disillusioned with Athens's government, which made some rash and in some cases shameful moves in the war's last years, including unlawfully executing six of the city's generals for misconduct in 406 B.C. Xenophon was equally disillusioned when, in 399, an Athenian jury condemned to death his friend the philosopher Socrates. "Nobody ever saw Socrates do, or heard him say, anything" wrong, Xenophon points out, and

> he was never guilty of involving his country in an unsuccessful war, or in sedition or treason or any other calamity. And in his personal dealings he never deprived anyone of a benefit or got anyone into trouble. . . . So far from being an atheist [as the prosecutors charged at the trial], he was obviously the most devout of men. . . . He surely deserved high honor at the hands of his country [rather than a death sentence]. (*Memorabilia* 1.1.8, 1.2.57)

Xenophon did not attend Socrates' trial because at the time the young man was in faraway Asia, having become a mercenary soldier for a Persian prince named Cyrus, who wanted to dethrone his elder brother, King Artaxerxes II. In a huge battle fought at Cunaxa (in what is now Iraq), Cyrus was defeated and killed, but his ten thousand Greek followers, including Xenophon, survived. As Xenophon later described it in his *Anabasis*, the Greeks then endured incredible hardships as they fought their way across and out of the Persian heartland. The "Ten Thousand," as they became known, eventually made it to the Black Sea and from there most returned to Greece. However, Xenophon decided to continue his life as a soldier of fortune and signed on with the Spartans, who were fighting the Persians in Asia Minor. In 394 B.C. he fought alongside the Spartan king Agesilaus, whom he had come to know well, in the Battle of Coronea, in which Sparta faced a coalition of Greek states,

including Xenophon's native Athens. Afterward Xenophon could not go home because the Athenians had exiled him, so he retired to an estate near Olympia arranged for him by Agesilaus.

Thereafter Xenophon became a country gentleman, estate manager, and prolific writer. In addition to his widely read *Anabasis*, he penned the *Oeconomicus* (*Estate Manager*), which became a popular guide for well-to-do Greek landowners, and he wrote treatises on hunting and horsemanship and biographies of both Agesilaus and Cyrus II, founder of the Persian Empire. Xenophon's chief work, the *Hellenica* (*History of Greece*), made the ambitious attempt to chronicle the events of the Peloponnesian War from 411 B.C., where Thucydides had left off, and the events of the decades that followed the conflict. Regrettably, though it remains an important historical work, the *Hellenica* suffers from Xenophon's frequent omission of crucial events and his tendency to take sides rather than be objective, as Thucydides had been.

It became clear that Xenophon had taken the wrong side when Sparta was defeated by Thebes in 371 B.C., and he lost his estate. Sometime later the Athenians allowed him to return to his native city. But then, for reasons unknown, he moved to Corinth, where he died. In the centuries that followed, Xenophon's readable narratives made him the most popular Greek prose writer among the Romans and early modern Europeans.

SEE ALSO: *Anabasis*, 1; *Hellenica*; historical writing; *Memorabilia*; Socrates

xenos

In early Greek times, a "guest-friend," a person from a Greek city who was welcomed, protected, and sometimes lodged when visiting another Greek city. The visitor was expected to reciprocate by helping and protecting his benefactor when the latter visited his city. The custom of *xenia*—"guest-friendship" or "two-way hospitality"—began in Greece's Dark Age as a way to make it possible for travelers and diplomats to visit foreign towns without being abused or killed. Families of *xenoi* then perpetuated the custom down through the generations. Typically the host invited the guest to dinner on his first night in town, and as the guest was leaving town, he and the host exchanged gifts. In the Archaic and Classical eras, *xenia* mutated somewhat into *proxenia*, in which a citizen of a city was chosen to aid all visiting citizens from a second town. Thus, Athens had a *proxenos* for Plataean visitors, one for Milesian visitors, and so forth.

SEE ALSO: family; polis

Xerxes
(reigned 486–465 B.C.)

A Persian king who launched the largest single invasion force of antiquity—some two hundred thousand soldiers and up to a thousand ships—against Greece in 480 B.C. The son of King Darius I, Xerxes (ZERK-seez) inherited his father's vendetta against the Greeks for their defeat of a Persian army at Marathon in 490. After collecting troops from across his vast empire, Xerxes crossed the Hellespont on a bridge made of boats and marched around the northern rim of the Aegean. His army won a technical victory at Thermopylae by killing the handful of Greeks defending the pass, but at the price of some twenty thousand Persian casualties. Xerxes then occupied and burned

A modern painting shows the Persian king Xerxes watching the battle of Salamis. He was shocked when his fleet was defeated by the Greeks. AKG-IMAGES

Athens. His fleet was soundly defeated soon afterward, however, in a massive sea battle in the Salamis strait as he watched in horror from a nearby hilltop. Xerxes retired to Asia Minor, leaving behind a land army, which was also badly mauled the following year. Little is known about the rest of his reign, except that he constructed several large public buildings in his capital of Persepolis. He was ultimately assassinated and succeeded by his eighteen-year-old son, Artaxerxes I.

SEE ALSO: Battle of Marathon; Battle of Plataea; Battle of Salamis; Battle of Thermopylae, 1; Darius I; Greco-Persian Wars

a higher intelligence that manifests itself inside every person. Therefore, all people, no matter what their social station, are spiritual brothers and sisters.

SEE ALSO: philosophy

Zeno
(mid-fifth century B.C.)

A Greek philosopher and follower of the noted pre-Socratic thinker Parmenides, the founder of the Eleatic philosophical school. Zeno was famous for his paradoxes, which examined natural phenomena using a process that came to be known as *epicheirema* in Greek and *reductio ad absurdum* in Latin. Essentially, Zeno "proved" that something that seemed to be true could not really be true because if it was true, it would lead to absurd and impossible situations. According to Aristotle (who read Zeno's now lost works), for example, Zeno argued that the phenomenon of motion is only illusory. A body at rest is the same size as the space in which it rests, therefore, it lacks the space needed for movement, so an arrow that seems to be in flight is actually stationary. Aristotle labored to show that this was incorrect.

SEE ALSO: science

Zeno
(ca. 333 B.C.–262 B.C.)

A Hellenistic Greek thinker who established the Stoic school of philosophical thought, which became widely popular in the Greco-Roman world. Zeno (or Zenon), who hailed from the island of Cyprus, moved to Athens in 313 B.C. and studied at Plato's Academy. Around 300 Zeno began lecturing in the Athenian Agora in a building called the Stoa Poikile, from which his new school took its name. The Stoics believed that the universe is controlled by

Zenodotus
(early third century B.C.)

The first director of the famous Great Library at Alexandria and one of the leading early Hellenistic Greek scholars. Zenodotus is best known for editing Homer's epic poems, the *Iliad* and the *Odyssey*. His division of each of these works into twenty-four sections (called books) became standard and is still in use today.

SEE ALSO: Alexandria; Homer

Zeus

In Greek mythology, the leader of the Olympian gods and the chief champion of justice in the known universe. Zeus was definitely one of the oldest of the Greek gods, proven by versions of his name that appear in Mycenaean Linear B inscriptions dating from circa 1400 B.C. The consensus of modern scholarship is that his worship originated long before that time, however, perhaps in the third millennium B.C. or even earlier. The first Greek-speakers who entered the Greek mainland seem to have brought that worship with them from their Indo-European homeland in the north. Zeus was probably originally a storm god, a function he retained throughout antiquity, as demonstrated by his chief symbol, the thunderbolt, and his control of rain and thunder. Also, he is depicted as using thunderstorms to batter his enemies in Homer's *Iliad*.

However, it appears that sometime in the late Bronze Age Zeus took on the more lofty and moralistic image of the ruler of the world and supreme judge of both gods and humans. His many sides, guises, or manifestations, all reflecting his great power, were reflected in various epithets used to describe him—Zeus Kosmetas ("Zeus the Bringer of Order"), Zeus Polieos ("Zeus of the City," the protector of human city-states), Zeus Eleutherios ("Zeus Who Grants Political Freedom"), Zeus Xenios ("Zeus the Protector of Strangers," who punished those who broke the laws of hospitality), Zeus Hikesios ("Zeus the Protector of Religious Suppliants"), Zeus Ktesios ("Zeus the Guardian of Property"), and Zeus Soter ("Zeus the Savior"). Zeus's high moral authority and ultimate power of life and death, both often veiled in a mysterious aura, were put into glorious words by the great fifth-century B.C. Athenian playwrights. In his *Suppliant Women*, for example, Aeschylus has the chorus chant:

> For Zeus all things shine clear, though he hide them in black darkness from the eyes of men that perish. When by the nod of Zeus it is decreed that a thing be accomplished, the event falls firm on its feet. For the paths of his purposing heart stretch dark and tangled, baffling sight and thought. From their high-towering hopes he hurls mortals to their destruction; and there is no immortal who unsheathes against him the effortless power of the godhead. (*The Suppliant Women* 86–100)

A god of this versatility, stature, and power naturally inspired widespread respect, and the Greeks held many religious festivals and erected numerous temples and shrines in Zeus's honor. Chief among his temples was the Temple of Olympian Zeus at Olympia, where the famous athletic games were part of the local festival dedicated to him. Inside this temple rested an enormous statue of the god seated on a golden throne. Carved by the gifted Athenian sculptor Phidias, the monumental image was later listed as one of the Seven Wonders of the Ancient World. Another important shrine honoring Zeus was at Dodona in northwestern Greece. There, religious pilgrims came from far and wide to ask questions of the temple's oracle, second in prestige only to Apollo's oracle at Delphi. Dodona also featured a sacred oak tree, another of Zeus's symbols.

Because of his importance to the Greeks from the very beginnings of their civilization, Zeus appears in hundreds of myths, many of which have survived because they were committed to writing at one time or another. In his *Theogony*, for instance, Hesiod tells how Zeus was born the youngest of the six children of the Titans Cronos and Rhea. Worried that one of his offspring would challenge his power, Cronos swallowed them after they were born. But Rhea substituted a stone for Zeus, who was secreted away to be raised by nymphs. Later Zeus returned and, aided by his brothers and sisters, the Olympians, whom Zeus had forced Cronos to vomit out, launched an insurrection against Cronos and the Titans and defeated them. In another renowned myth about Zeus, he punished the Titan Prometheus for stealing fire from heaven and giving it to humanity. Fulfilling his dual role as divine judge and executioner, Zeus also flooded the region of Phrygia in Asia Minor because its inhabitants had refused to extend hospitality to a stranger in their midst, who was actually Zeus in disguise. When not judging and punishing people and gods, Zeus busied himself in other pursuits, including having affairs with both goddesses and mortals. Among the offspring of these liaisons were the goddess Athena (who sprang from his head clad in her armor!), three groups of minor deities (the Hours, Fates, and Graces), Persephone (who became queen of the Underworld), the nine Muses (goddesses of the fine arts), and the twin divinities Apollo and Artemis. Zeus's wife, Hera, was naturally jealous over her husband's infidelities and frequently tried to punish his lovers.

SEE ALSO: Dodona; Hera; Olympians; *Prometheus Bound*; religion

Chronology

ca. 3000–ca. 1100

Greece's Bronze Age, in which people use tools and weapons made of bronze.

ca. 2200–ca. 1700

A non-Greek-speaking people now called the Minoans establish Europe's first high civilization on the Greek island of Crete.

ca. 2000 (or possibly somewhat later)

Tribal peoples speaking an early form of Greek begin entering the Greek peninsula from the east or northeast; their descendants, whom scholars refer to as Mycenaeans, spread across mainland Greece.

ca. 1400

The Mycenaeans invade and take control of Minoan Crete.

ca. 1200–ca. 1100

For reasons still unclear, the Mycenaean kingdoms and fortresses suffer widespread destruction and rapidly decline.

ca. 1100–ca. 800

Greece's Dark Age, in which poverty and illiteracy are at first widespread and iron comes into use in the area.

ca. 800–ca. 500

Greece's Archaic Age, characterized by the rise of city-states, the return of prosperity and literacy, rapid population growth, and intensive colonization of the areas around the Mediterranean and Black seas.

776

The traditional date of the first Olympic Games held at Olympia in the northwestern Peloponnesus.

ca. 730–ca. 710

Sparta conquers the region of Messenia in the southwestern Peloponnesus and enslaves the inhabitants.

ca. 700

The Boeotian poet Hesiod composes the *Theogony*, about the creation of the world and the gods.

ca. 620

An Athenian named Draco creates a law code for his city, but most citizens soon view it as too harsh.

ca. 600

The Ionian city of Phocaea establishes a colony at Massalia, in what is now southern France.

594

An Athenian statesman named Solon reorganizes Athens's social and political system, making it more democratic.

ca. 575

Thales, a resident of the Greek city of Miletus, establishes the Ionian philosophical-scientific school.

ca. 558

Cyrus II establishes the Persian Empire (centered in what is now Iran), whose rulers and conquests will profoundly affect Greek affairs for centuries to come.

534

Athens establishes the City Dionysia, a religious festival that features the Western world's first plays, actors, and dramatic competitions.

ca. 530

The philosopher-scientist Pythagoras and his followers establish a school of learning at Crotona in southern Italy.

ca. 508

Building on Solon's reforms, a leader named Cleisthenes and his supporters transform Athens's government into the world's first democracy.

ca. 500–323

Greece's Classical Age, in which Greek arts, architecture, literature, and democratic reforms reach their height.

499

The Ionian Greek cities in western Asia Minor rebel against Persia. Five years later the Persians defeat the Ionians in a large sea battle and the revolt collapses.

490

Persia's King Darius I sends an expedition to sack Athens and a neighboring city, Eretria; the Athenians decisively defeat the invaders at Marathon (northeast of Athens).

480–479

Darius's son, Xerxes, launches a massive invasion of Greece; in a series of epic battles, the Greeks defeat the intruders, ending the Greco-Persian Wars.

478

The Athenians organize the Delian League, an alliance of more than a hundred city-states, intended to protect Greece from further Persian incursions.

472

The Athenian playwright Aeschylus produces his play the *Persians*, which describes the recent Greek naval victory at Salamis.

465–463

The island of Thasos attempts but fails to break away from the Delian League.

464

Sparta suffers heavy damage in an earthquake, and its slaves, the helots, rebel.

461

In Athens the conservative leader Cimon is ostracized (banished); his chief democratic opponent, Ephialtes, is assassinated, and another democrat, Pericles, becomes the city's most influential leader.

457

Pericles finishes construction of the Long Walls, a fortified corridor leading from Athens's port, Piraeus, to its urban center.

447

Construction begins on a major new temple complex atop Athens's Acropolis.

440–439

The island of Samos rebels against Athens, and Pericles besieges and subjugates the Samians.

438

In Athens the magnificent Parthenon temple is dedicated to the city's patron goddess, Athena.

432

Athens imposes a trade embargo on the nearby state of Megara, seen by many Greeks as a provocative act.

431

Sparta declares war on Athens, initiating the disastrous Peloponnesian War.

430–429

A deadly plague strikes Athens, killing many people, including Pericles.

423

The Athenian comic playwright Aristophanes writes *Clouds*, in which he lampoons the philosopher Socrates.

421

Athens and Sparta conclude the Peloponnesian War with the Peace of Nicias.

418

The war resumes and Sparta defeats Athens and Argos at Mantinea in the central Peloponnesus.

415–413

The Athenians send a large military expedition to Sicily in hopes of conquering the Greek city of Syracuse; the venture ends in total disaster.

405

The Spartan naval commander Lysander decisively defeats an Athenian fleet at Aegospotami, in the Hellespont, and the Spartans blockade Piraeus and besiege Athens.

404

Athens surrenders, ending the great war and initiating a Spartan hegemony (domination) of Greece.

399

In Athens the philosopher Socrates is tried and executed.

394

Sparta's King Agesilaus defeats a coalition of Greek cities at Coronea in western Boeotia.

382

The Spartans occupy the Cadmea (the Theban acropolis), an aggressive move most Greeks condemn.

380

The Greek orator Isocrates advocates a united Greek crusade against Persia.

371

The Theban general Epaminondas defeats the Spartans at Leuctra (near Thebes), initiating a period of Theban hegemony.

362

Epaminondas dies in battle at Mantinea.

359

King Philip II ascends the throne of Macedonia and begins forging Europe's first national standing army.

357

Philip seizes the northern Aegean port of Amphipolis, an Athenian colony.

351

Athens's great orator Demosthenes warns of the danger Philip's aggressions pose.

346

Philip seizes the sacred sanctuary at Delphi.

338

Philip and his son, Alexander (later called "the Great"), defeat a coalition of Greek states at Chaeronea in western Boeotia.

336

Philip is assassinated and Alexander becomes master of Greece.

334

Alexander crosses the Hellespont and launches an invasion of Persia.

333

Alexander defeats Persia's King Darius III at Issus in northern Syria.

331

After liberating Egypt from Persian control, Alexander founds the city of Alexandria in the Nile Delta.

326

Having overrun Persia, Alexander

invades western India.

323

Alexander dies in the Persian capital of Babylon.

323–30

Greece's Hellenistic Age, in which Alexander's generals, the "Successors," carve up his empire into several new kingdoms; during the second half of this period, Rome gains control of the Greek world.

305

One of the leading Successors, Demetrius, besieges but fails to capture the capital city of Rhodes.

301

Demetrius and his father, Antigonus, are decisively defeated by a coalition of the other Successors at Ipsus in central Asia Minor.

ca. 280

Three large Greek monarchies (the Macedonian, Seleucid, and Ptolemaic kingdoms) have by now emerged from the chaos of the long wars of the Successors.

218

The Second Punic War erupts between Rome, master of the Italian peninsula, and the empire of Carthage, centered in North Africa.

200–197

Having recently defeated Carthage, Rome invades Greece and defeats Macedonia's King Philip V at Cynoscephalae.

189

The Romans defeat the Seleucid ruler Antiochus III at Magnesia in western Asia Minor.

168

Rome defeats Philip's son, Perseus, at Pydna and dismantles the Macedonian kingdom.

146

A Roman general destroys the once-great Greek city of Corinth as an object lesson to any Greeks contemplating rebellion against Rome.

133

Attalus III, ruler of the Greek kingdom of Pergamum, dies and bequeaths his kingdom to Rome.

31

The Roman politician Octavian defeats Cleopatra VII, last of the autonomous Greek rulers of antiquity, at Actium in western Greece.

30 B.C.–A.D. 476

Greece's Roman Period, in which Rome rules the Greek lands.

A.D.

ca. 46

The influential Greek biographer and moralist Plutarch is born at Chaeronea.

168

The noted Greek medical researcher Galen becomes personal physician to the family of the Roman emperor Marcus Aurelius.

476

The last western Roman emperor is deposed. (Modern historians see this as the end of ancient times, including ancient Greek civilization.) However, the Greek-speaking eastern portion of Rome survives and mutates into the Byzantine Empire, which lasts until it is defeated by the Turks in 1453.

For Further Research

Selected Translations of Ancient Sources

A Note on Primary Sources

All classical quotations in this book not cited individually are taken from one of the following anthologies, cited below: Atchity (1996), Austin (1981), Knox (1993), Lefkowitz and Fant (1992), Pollitt (1990), Warner (1986), Wheelwright (1966).

Aeschylus, *Oresteia*, published as *The Orestes Plays of Aeschylus*. Trans. Paul Roche. New York: New American Library, 1962.

———, *"Prometheus Bound"; "The Suppliants"; "Seven Against Thebes"; "The Persians."* Trans. Philip Vellacott. Baltimore: Penguin, 1961.

Archimedes, *Works*. Trans. Thomas L. Heath. Chicago: Encyclopaedia Britannica, 1952.

Aristophanes, *The Complete Plays of Aristophanes*. Trans. Moses Hadas. New York: Bantam, 1962.

Aristotle, *Aristotle: Complete Works*. 2 vols. Ed. Jonathan Barnes. Princeton, NJ: Princeton University Press, 1988.

Arrian, *Anabasis Alexandri*, published as *The Campaigns of Alexander*. Trans. Aubrey de Sélincourt. New York: Penguin, 1971.

Kenneth J. Atchity, ed., *The Classical Greek Reader*. New York: Oxford University Press, 1996.

A collection of translations of ancient Greek writings, including those of Homer, Solon, Herodotus, Lysias, Xeno-phon, Aristotle, Sophocles, Demosthenes, and many others.

M.M. Austin, ed., *The Hellenistic World from Alexander to the Roman Conquest: A Selection of Ancient Sources in Translation*. Cambridge: Cambridge University Press, 1981.

Josephine Balmer, trans., *Sappho: Poems and Fragments*. Secaucus, NJ: Meadowland, 1984.

Morris R. Cohen and I.E. Drabkin, *A Source Book in Greek Science*. Cambridge, MA: Harvard University Press, 1973.

A collection of writings by ancient Greek scientists, with useful commentary.

Demosthenes, *"Olynthiacs," "Philippics," Minor Speeches*. Trans. J.H. Vince. Cambridge, MA: Harvard University Press, 1962.

Diodorus Siculus, *Library of History*. 12 vols. Cambridge, MA: Harvard University Press, 1962–1967.

Euripides, *"Medea" and Other Plays*. Trans. Philip Vellacott. New York: Penguin, 1963.

———, *Three Great Plays of Euripides*. Trans. Rex Warner. New York: New American Library, 1958.

Galen, "The Best Doctor Is Also a Philosopher," in *Selected Works*. Trans. Peter.N. Singer. New York: Oxford University Press, 1997.

Rhoda A. Hendricks, ed. and trans., *Classical Gods and Heroes: Myths as Told by the Ancient Authors*. New York: Morrow Quill, 1974.

Herodotus, *Histories*. Trans. Aubrey de Sélincourt. New York: Penguin, 1972.

Herodotus, *Histories*. Trans. Robin Waterfield. New York: Oxford University Press, 1998.

Hesiod, *Theogony*, and *Works and Days*, in *Hesiod and Theognis*. Trans. Dorothea Wender. New York: Penguin, 1973.

Homer, *Iliad*. Trans. E.V. Rieu. Baltimore: Penguin, 1950.

Homer, *Iliad*. Trans. Robert Fagles. New York: Penguin, 1990.

———, *Odyssey*. Trans. E.V. Rieu. Baltimore: Penguin, 1961

———, *Odyssey*. Trans. Robert Fagles. New York: Penguin, 1996.

Homeric Hymns in *Hesiod, Homeric Hymns, and Homerica*. Trans. H.G. Evelyn-White. Cambridge, MA: Harvard University Press, 1964.

Isocrates, *Isocrates*. Trans. George Norlin. Cambridge MA: Harvard University Press, 1928.

Bernard M.W. Knox, ed., *The Norton Book of Classical Literature*. New York: W.W. Norton, 1993.
A huge collection of excerpts from Greek and Roman poetry, drama, and historical writing.

Richmond Lattimore, trans., *Greek Lyrics*. Chicago: University of Chicago Press, 1960.

Mary R. Lefkowitz and Maureen B. Fant, eds., *Women's Life in Greece and Rome: A Source Book in Translation*. Baltimore: Johns Hopkins University Press, 1992.

Pausanias, *Guide to Greece*. 2 vols. Trans. Peter Levi. New York: Penguin, 1971.

Pindar, *Odes*. Trans. C.M. Bowra. New York: Penguin, 1969.

Plato, *Complete Works*. Ed. John M. Cooper. Indianapolis: Hackett, 1997.

Plutarch, *Moralia*, excerpted in *Plutarch: Essays*. Trans. Robin Waterfield. New York: Penguin, 1992.

———, *Parallel Lives*, excerpted in *The Age of Alexander: Nine Greek Lives by Plutarch*. Trans. Ian Scott-Kilvert. New York: Penguin, 1973.

———, *Parallel Lives*, excerpted in *The Rise and Fall of Athens: Nine Greek Lives by Plutarch*. Trans. Ian Scott-Kilvert. New York: Penguin, 1960.

J.J. Pollitt, ed. and trans. *The Art of Ancient Greece: Sources and Documents*. New York: Cambridge University Press, 1990. A compilation of translations of ancient sources dealing with painting, sculpture, architecture, and other arts.

Polybius, *Histories*, published as *Polybius: The Rise of the Roman Empire*. Trans. Ian Scott-Kilvert. New York: Penguin, 1979.

Sophocles, *The Complete Plays of Sophocles*. Trans. Richard C. Jebb. New York: Bantam, 1967.

Waldo E. Sweet, ed., *Sport and Recreation in Ancient Greece: A Sourcebook with Translations*. New York: Oxford University Press, 1987.
A collection of translations of ancient sources describing sports, games, music, dance, theater, and related leisure activities, accompanied by detailed, expert commentary.

Thucydides, *The Peloponnesian War*. Trans. Rex Warner. New York: Penguin, 1972.

Philip Wheelwright, ed., *The Presocratics.* New York: Macmillan, 1966.

A valuable collection of fragments from and ancient commentaries on the works of Thales, Anaximander, Parmenides, Empedocles, Democritus, Pythagoras, and other early Greek philosopher-scientists.

Thomas Wiedemann, ed., *Greek and Roman Slavery.* Baltimore: Johns Hopkins University Press, 1981.

A compilation of translations of ancient sources dealing with slavery.

Xenophon, *Anabasis.* Trans. W.H.D. Rouse. New York: New American Library, 1959.

————, *Hellenica*, published as *A History of My Times.* Trans. Rex Warner. New York: Penguin, 1979.

————, *"Memorabilia" and "Oeconomicus."* Trans. E.C. Marchant. Cambridge, MA: Harvard University Press, 1965.

Selected Modern Sources

The Acropolis Complex and the Parthenon

Manolis Andronicos, *The Acropolis.* Athens: Ekdotike Athenon, 1994.

John Boardman, *The Parthenon and Its Sculptures.* Austin: University of Texas, 1985.

Vincent J. Bruno, ed., *The Parthenon.* New York: Norton, 1996.

Ian Jenkins, *The Parthenon Frieze.* Austin: University of Texas, 1994.

Panayotis Tournikiotis, ed., *The Parthenon and Its Impact in Modern Times.* New York: Harry N. Abrams, 1996.

Alexander the Great: His Conquests and Impact

Paul Cartledge, *Alexander the Great: A New Life.* New York: Overlook, 2004.

Robin Lane Fox, *Alexander the Great.* New York: Penguin, 2004.

J.F.C. Fuller, *The Generalship of Alexander the Great.* Cambridge, MA: Da Capo, 2004.

Peter Green, *Alexander of Macedon, 356–323 B.C.: A Historical Biography.* Berkeley and Los Angeles: University of California Press, 1992.

N.G.L. Hammond, *The Genius of Alexander the Great.* Chapel Hill: University of North Carolina Press, 1997.

Guy M. Rogers, *Alexander: The Ambiguity of Greatness.* New York: Random House, 2005.

Nick Sekunda and John Warry, *Alexander the Great: His Armies and Campaigns, 334–323 B.C.* London: Osprey, 1998.

Archaeological Rediscovery of Greece

William R. Biers, *The Archaeology of Greece.* Ithaca, NY: Cornell University Press, 1996.

Lord Byron, *Childe Harold's Pilgrimage.* Whitefish, MT: Kessinger, 2004.

Michael Grant, *The Visible Past: Recent Archaeological Discoveries of Greek and Roman History.* New York: Scribner's, 1990.

Paul MacKendrick, *The Greek Stones Speak: The Story of Archaeology in Greek Lands.* New York: W.W. Norton, 1983.

Michael Shanks, *The Classical Archaeology of Greece.* London: Routledge, 1995.

Fani-Maria Tsigakou, *The Rediscovery of Greece: Travelers and Painters of the*

Romantic Era. London: Thames and Hudson, 1981.

Architecture and Engineering

L. Sprague de Camp, *The Ancient Engineers.* New York: Ballantine, 1995.

Peter Clayton and Martin Price, eds., *The Seven Wonders of the Ancient World.* New York: Barnes and Noble, 1993.

J.J. Coulton, *Ancient Greek Architects at Work*: Ithaca, NY: Cornell University Press, 1982.

A.W. Lawrence, *Greek Architecture.* Revised by R.A. Tomlinson. New Haven, CT: Yale University Press, 1996.

R.E. Wycherley, *How the Greeks Built Cities.* New York: W.W. Norton, 1976.

Art and Sculpture

John Boardman, *Greek Art.* London: Thames and Hudson, 1996.

———, *Greek Sculpture: The Archaic Age.* London: Thames and Hudson, 1985.

———, *Greek Sculpture: The Classical Age.* London: Thames and Hudson, 1985.

———, ed., *The Oxford History of Classical Art.* Oxford: Oxford University Press, 1993.

Robert M. Cook, *Greek Painted Pottery.* London: Routledge, 1997.

John G. Pedley, *Greek Art and Archaeology.* New York: Harry N. Abrams, 1993.

J.J. Pollitt, *Art in the Hellenistic Age.* Cambridge: Cambridge University Press, 1986.

Nigel Spivey, *Greek Art.* London: Phaidon, 1997.

Athens's Empire and Cultural Achievements

Donald Kagan, *Pericles of Athens and the Birth of Democracy.* New York: Free Press, 1991.

Malcolm F. McGregor, *The Athenians and Their Empire.* Vancouver: University of British Columbia Press, 1987.

Christian Meier, *Athens: Portrait of a City in Its Golden Age.* Trans. Robert and Rita Kimber. New York: Henry Holt, 1998.

Russell Meiggs, *The Athenian Empire.* Oxford: Oxford University Press, 1979.

C.A. Robinson, *Athens in the Age of Pericles.* Norman: University of Oklahoma Press, 1980.

George D. Wilcoxon, *Athens Ascendant.* Ames: Iowa State University Press, 1979.

The Bronze Age

Carl Blegen et al., *Troy: Excavations Conducted by the University of Cincinnati.* 4 vols. Princeton, NJ: Princeton University Press, 1950–1958.

Rodney Castleden, *Minoans: Life in Bronze Age Crete.* New York: Routledge, 1993.

Oliver Dickinson, *The Aegean Bronze Age.* New York: Cambridge University Press, 1994.

Robert Drews, *The Coming of the Greeks: Indo-European Conquests in the Aegean and the Near East.* Princeton, NJ: Princeton University Press, 1994.

———, *The End of the Bronze Age: Changes in Warfare and the Catastrophe ca. 1200 B.C.* Princeton, NJ: Princeton University Press, 1995.

Arthur Evans, *The Palace of Minos at Knossos*. 4 vols. London: Macmillan, 1921–1936.

J. Lesley Fitton, *Discovery of the Greek Bronze Age*. London: British Museum, 1995.

William Taylour, *The Mycenaeans*. London: Thames and Hudson, 1990.

Michael Wood, *In Search of the Trojan War*. Berkeley and Los Angeles: University of California Press, 1998.

The Dark Age and the Archaic Age

M.I. Finley, *The World of Odysseus*. New York: New York Review Books, 2002.

Kathleen Freeman, *The Work and Life of Solon, with a Translation of His Poems*. New York: Arno, 1976.

A.M. Snodgrass, *Archaic Greece*. Berkeley and Los Angeles: University of California Press, 1981.

———, *The Dark Age of Greece*. London: Routledge, 2000.

Chester G. Starr, *Individual and Community: The Rise of the Polis, 800–500 B.C.* New York: Oxford University Press, 1986.

———, *The Origins of Greek Civilization, 1100–650 B.C.* New York: W.W. Norton, 1991.

Carol G. Thomas and Craig Conant, *Citadel to City-State: The Transformation of Greece, 1200–700 B.C.E.* Indianapolis: Indiana University Press, 1999.

Family and Social Institutions and Customs

Sue Blundell, *Women in Ancient Greece*. Cambridge, MA: Harvard University Press, 1995.

James Davidson, *Courtesans and Fishcakes: The Consuming Passions of Classical Athens*. New York: St. Martin's, 1998.

N.R.E. Fisher, *Slavery in Classical Greece*. London: Bristol Classical, 1993.

———, *Social Values in Classical Athens*. London: Dent, 1976.

Frank J. Frost, *Greek Society*. Boston: Houghton Mifflin, 1996.

Robert Garland, *The Greek Way of Life*. Ithaca, NY: Cornell University Press, 1992.

Mark Golden, *Children and Childhood in Classical Athens*. Baltimore: Johns Hopkins University Press, 1993.

Sarah B. Pomeroy, *Families in Classical and Hellenistic Greece*. New York: Oxford University Press, 1999.

———, *Goddesses, Whores, Wives, and Slaves: Women in Classical Antiquity*. New York: Shocken, 1995.

Farming, Food, Commerce, and Trade

John Boardman, *The Greeks Overseas: Their Early Colonies and Trade*. New York: Thames and Hudson, 1999.

Alison Burford, *Land and Labor in the Greek World*. Baltimore: Johns Hopkins University Press, 1993.

Lionel Casson, *The Ancient Mariners*. Princeton, NJ: Princeton University Press, 1991.

———, *Ships and Seafaring in Ancient Times*. London: British Museum Press, 1994.

———, *Travel in the Ancient World*. Baltimore: Johns Hopkins University Press, 1994.

Andrew Dalby, *Siren Feasts: A History of Food and Gastronomy in Greece*. New York: Routledge, 1996.

M.I. Finley, *The Ancient Economy*. Berkeley and Los Angeles: University of California Press, 1999.

Victor D. Hanson, *The Other Greeks: The Family Farm and the Agrarian Roots of Western Civilization*. Berkeley and Los Angeles: University of California Press, 2000.

R.J. Hopper, *Trade and Industry in Classical Greece*. London: Thames and Hudson, 1979.

The Fourth Century B.C. and the Rise of Macedonia

J.K. Anderson, *Xenophon*. New York: Scribner's, 1974.

Eugene N. Borza, *In the Shadow of Olympus: The Emergence of Macedon*. Princeton, NJ: Princeton University Press, 1992.

John Buckler, *The Theban Hegemony*. Cambridge, MA: Harvard University Press, 1980.

N.G.L. Hammond, *Philip of Macedon*. Baltimore: Johns Hopkins University Press, 1994.

Miltiades B. Hatzopoulos and Louisa D. Loukopoulos, eds., *Philip of Macedon*. Athens: Ekdotike Athenon, 1980.

General Works on History, Geography, and Culture

Lesley Adkins and Roy A. Adkins, *Handbook to Life in Ancient Greece*. New York: Facts On File, 1998.

C.M. Bowra, *The Greek Experience*. New York: New American Library, 1959. Old and somewhat dated, but still a wonderful, insightful book.

Thomas Cahill, *Sailing the Wine-Dark Sea: Why the Greeks Matter*. New York: Doubleday, Anchor, 2004.

Paul Cartledge, *The Spartans: The World of the Warrior-Heroes of Ancient Greece, from Utopia to Crisis and Collapse*. New York: Overlook, 2003.

Robert Flaceliere, *Daily Life in Greece at the Time of Pericles*. Trans. Peter Green. London: Phoenix, 1996.

Charles Freeman, *The Greek Achievement: The Foundation of the Western World*. New York: Viking, 1999.

Michael Grant, *A Guide to the Ancient World*. New York: Barnes and Noble, 1996.

———, *The Rise of the Greeks*. New York: Macmillan, 1988.

N.G.L. Hammond, *A History of Greece to 322 B.C.* Oxford: Oxford University Press, Clarendon Press, 1986.

Robert B. Kebric, *Greek People*. New York: McGraw Hill, 2005.

Thomas R. Martin, *Ancient Greece: From Prehistoric to Hellenistic Times*. New Haven, CT: Yale University Press, 2000.

Sarah B. Pomeroy et al., *Ancient Greece: A Political, Social, and Cultural History*. New York: Oxford University Press, 1999.

Gods, Myths, and Religion

Manolis Andronicos, *Delphi*. Athens: Ekdotiki Athenon, 1993.

Walter Burkert, *Greek Religion, Archaic and Classical*. Oxford: Blackwell, 1987.

E.R. Dodds, *The Greeks and the Irrational*. Berkeley and Los Angeles: University of California Press, 2004.

Robert Garland, *The Greek Way of Death*. Ithaca, NY: Cornell University Press, 2001.

Donna C. Kurtz and John Boardman, *Greek Burial Customs*. Ithaca, NY: Cornell University Press, 1971.

Evi Melas, *Temples and Sanctuaries of Ancient Greece*. London: Thames and Hudson, 1982.

John D. Mikalson, *Athenian Popular Religion*. Chapel Hill: University of North Carolina Press, 1987.

Mark P.O. Morford and Robert J. Lenardon, *Classical Mythology*. New York: Oxford University Press, 2002.

Jennifer Neils, *Goddess and Polis: The Panathenaic Festival in Ancient Athens*. Princeton, NJ: Princeton University Press, 1992.

The Greco-Persian Wars

Ernle Bradford, *Thermopylae: The Battle for the West*. Cambridge, MA: Da Capo, 2004.

Peter Green, *The Greco-Persian Wars*. Berkeley and Los Angeles: University of California Press, 1998.

John Lazenby, *The Defense of Greece*. Bloomington, IL: David Brown, 1993.

Philip de Souza, *The Greek and Persian Wars, 499–386 B.C.* London: Osprey, 2003.

The Hellenistic Age and the Decline of Greece

John Boardman et al., *Greece and the Hellenistic World*. New York: Oxford University Press, 1988.

Walter M. Ellis, *Ptolemy of Egypt*. New York: Routledge, 1994.

Michael Grant, *From Alexander to Cleopatra: The Hellenistic World*. New York: Charles Scribner's Sons, 1982.

Peter Green, *Alexander to Actium: The Historical Evolution of the Hellenistic Age*. Berkeley and Los Angeles: University of California Press, 1990.

———, ed., *Hellenistic History and Culture*. Berkeley and Los Angeles: University of California Press, 1993.

Erich Gruen, *The Hellenistic World and the Coming of Rome*. Berkeley and Los Angeles: University of California Press, 1984.

Naphtali Lewis, *Greeks in Ptolemaic Egypt*. Oxford: Oxford University Press, Clarendon Press, 1986.

Don Nardo, *The Decline and Fall of Ancient Greece*. San Diego: Greenhaven, 2000.

Sarah B. Pomeroy, *Women in Hellenistic Egypt: From Alexander to Cleopatra*. New York: Schocken, 1990.

Graham Shipley, *The Greek World After Alexander, 323–30 B.C.* London: Routledge, 2000.

F.W. Walbank, *The Hellenistic World*. Cambridge, MA: Harvard University Press, 1993.

Homer, the *Iliad*, and the *Odyssey*

Kenneth Atchity et al., *Critical Essays on Homer*. Boston: G.K. Hall, 1987.

C.M. Bowra, *Homer*. New York: Charles Scribner's Sons, 1972.

Jasper Griffin, *Homer on Life and Death*. Oxford: Oxford University Press, Clarendon Press, 1983.

———, *Homer: The "Odyssey."* Cambridge: Cambridge University Press, 2003.

Joachim Latacz, *Troy and Homer: Towards a Solution of an Old Mystery*. New York: Oxford University Press, 2004.

M.S. Silk, *Homer: The "Iliad."* Cambridge: Cambridge University Press, 2004.

Literature, Philosophy, Science, and Ideas

Jonathon Barnes, ed., *The Cambridge Companion to Aristotle*. New York: Cambridge University Press, 1995.

Barry Cunliffe, *The Extraordinary Voyage of Pytheas the Greek*. New York: Walker, 2002.

Michael Grant, *Greek and Roman Historians: Information and Misinformation*. London: Routledge, 1995.

Simon Hornblower, *Thucydides*. Baltimore: Johns Hopkins University Press, 1987.

Peter Levi, *A History of Greek Literature*. New York: Viking, 1985.

David C. Lindberg, *The Beginnings of Western Science*. Chicago: University of Chicago Press, 1992.

A.A. Long, *Hellenistic Philosophy: Stoics, Epicureans, Skeptics*. Berkeley and Los Angeles: University of California Press, 1986.

Jacqueline de Romilly, *A Short History of Greek Literature*. Trans. Lillian Doherty. Chicago: University of Chicago Press, 1996.

George Sarton, *Ancient Science Through the Golden Age of Greece*. New York: Dover, 1993.

———, *Hellenistic Science and Culture in the Last Three Centuries B.C.* New York: Dover, 1993.

A.E. Taylor, *Socrates: The Man and His Thought*. Westport, CT: Greenwood, 1975.

C.C.W. Taylor et al., *Greek Philosophers: Socrates, Plato, Aristotle*. New York: Oxford University Press, 2001.

Rex Warner, *The Greek Philosophers*. New York: New American Library, 1986.

The Peloponnesian War

Victor D. Hanson, *A War Like No Other*. New York: Random House, 2005.

Donald Kagan, *The Archidamian War*. Ithaca, NY: Cornell University Press, 1991.

———, *The Fall of the Athenian Empire*. Ithaca, NY: Cornell University Press, 1991.

———, *The Outbreak of the Peloponnesian War*. Ithaca, NY: Cornell University Press, 1991.

———, *The Peace of Nicias and the Sicilian Expedition*. Ithaca, NY: Cornell University Press, 1991.

Politics, Democracy, Citizenship, and Justice

R.A. Bauman, *Political Trials in Ancient Greece*. New York: Routledge, 1990.

David Cohen, *Law, Violence, and Community in Classical Athens*. New York: Cambridge University Press, 1995.

J.K. Davies, *Democracy and Classical Greece*. Cambridge, MA: Harvard University Press, 1993.

Kathleen Freeman, *The Murder of Herodes and Other Trials from the Athenian Law Courts*. Cambridge, MA: Hackett, 1994.

Philip Brook Manville, *The Origins of Citizenship in Ancient Athens*. Princeton, NJ: Princeton University Press, 1990.

Don Nardo, *The Trial of Socrates*. San Diego: Lucent, 1997.

Eli Sagan, *The Honey and the Hemlock: Democracy and Paranoia in Ancient Athens and Modern America*. New York: HarperCollins, 1991.

Sports and Games

John G. Landels, *Music in Ancient Greece and Rome*. London: Routledge, 1998.

Stephen G. Miller, *Ancient Greek Athletics*. New Haven, CT: Yale University Press, 2004.

Don Nardo, *Greek and Roman Sport*. San Diego: Lucent, 1999.

———, *Leisure Life of the Ancient Greeks*. San Diego: Lucent, 2005.

Michael B. Poliakoff, *Combat Sports in the Ancient World*. New Haven, CT: Yale University Press, 1987.

David Sansone, *Greek Athletics and the Genesis of Sport*. Berkeley and Los Angeles: University of California Press, 1988.

Nigel Spivey, *The Ancient Olympics*. New York: Oxford University Press, 2004.

Judith Swaddling, *The Ancient Olympic Games*. Austin: University of Texas Press, 1996.

David C. Young, *The Olympic Myth of Greek Amateur Athletics*. Chicago: Ares, 1984.

Theater and Drama

C.M. Bowra, *Sophoclean Tragedy*. Oxford: Oxford University Press, 1965.

James H. Butler, *The Theater and Drama of Greece and Rome*. San Francisco: Chandler, 1972.

John Ferguson, *A Companion to Greek Tragedy*. Austin: University of Texas Press, 1972.

Don Nardo, ed., *Ancient Greek Drama*. San Diego: Greenhaven, 2000.

———, ed., *Readings on "Antigone"*. San Diego: Greenhaven, 2000.

———, ed., *Readings on Sophocles*. San Diego: Greenhaven, 1997.

Arthur Pickard-Cambridge et al., *The Dramatic Festivals of Athens*. Oxford: Oxford University Press, 1989.

Alan H. Sommerstein, *Greek Drama and Dramatists*. London: Routledge, 2002.

T.B.L. Webster, *Greek Theater Production*. London: Methuen, 1970.

Weapons and Warfare

J.K. Anderson, *Military Theory and Practice in the Age of Xenophon*. Berkeley and Los Angeles: University of California Press, 1970.

Peter Connolly, *Greece and Rome at War*. London: Greenhill, 1998.

Arthur Cotterell, *Chariot: The Astounding Rise and Fall of the World's First War Machine*. New York: Overlook, 2005.

P.A.L. Greenhalgh, *Early Greek Warfare: Horsemen and Chariots in the Homeric and Archaic Ages*. Cambridge: Cambridge University Press, 1973.

Victor D. Hanson, *The Wars of the Ancient Greeks and Their Invention of Western Military Culture*. London: Cassell, 1999.

———, *The Western Way of War: Infantry Battle in Classical Greece*. Berkeley and

Los Angeles: University of California Press, 2000.

J.F. Lazenby, *The Spartan Army*. Warminster, UK: Aris and Phillips, 1985.

Adrienne Mayor, *Greek Fire, Poison Arrows, and Scorpion Bombs: Biological and Chemical Warfare in the Ancient World*. New York: Overlook Duckworth, 2003.

Nicholas Sekunda, *Warriors of Ancient Greece*. Oxford, UK: Osprey, 1999.

A.M. Snodgrass, *Arms and Armour of the Greeks*. Baltimore: Johns Hopkins University Press, 1998.

John Warry, *Warfare in the Classical World*. Norman: University of Oklahoma Press, 1995.

L.J. Worley, *Hippeis: The Cavalry of Ancient Greece*. Boulder, CO: Westview, 1994.

Internet Sources

Aristotle, University of St. Andrews, Scotland (*www-history.mcs.st-andrews.ac.uk/history/Mathematicians/Aristotle.html*).

A useful, brief overview of Aristotle's life and teachings, with links to related topics and information.

Burial Rituals and the Afterlife of Ancient Greece, Kristina Bagwell, University of North Carolina (*http://people.uncw.edu/deagona/ancientnovel/Kristina.htm*.

An attractive, worthwhile general overview of two aspects of ancient Greek life related to religion.

A Day in the Life of an Ancient Greek, Hellenic Museum and Cultural Center (*www.hellenicmuseum.org/exhibits/dayinlife.html*).

A useful, easy-to-read general source for information on ancient Greek life, including on clothes, food, sports, art, and more.

The Greeks: Crucible of Civilization, PBS (*www.pbs.org/empires/thegreeks*).

Excellent online resource based on the acclaimed PBS show. Has numerous links to sites containing information about ancient Greek history and culture.

Perseus Project, Tufts University Department of the Classics (*www.perseus.tufts.edu*).

The most comprehensive online source about ancient Greece, with hundreds of links to all aspects of Greek history, life, and culture, supported by numerous photos of artifacts.

Index

About the Author

Historian and award-winning writer Don Nardo has published many books about the ancient world, including *Life in Ancient Athens*; *The Etruscans*; *Life of a Roman Gladiator*; *Religion in Ancient Egypt*; literary companions to the works of Homer, Sophocles, and Euripides; histories of the Assyrian and Persian empires; and Greenhaven Press's encyclopedias of ancient Mesopotamia, ancient Rome, and Greek and Roman mythology. He lives with his wife, Christine, in Massachusetts.

About the Consulting Editor

Robert B. Kebric is senior professor of ancient history at the University of Louisville in Kentucky. He is the author of four books (including the critically acclaimed *Greek People*) and numerous articles and essays, and has been a consultant for Time-Life Books and other presses and international news agencies.